DICTIONARY OF
MASS
Communication
& Media Research

A GUIDE FOR STUDENTS,
SCHOLARS AND PROFESSIONALS

DAVID DEMERS

MB **MARQUETTE**
BOOKS SPOKANE, WA

Printed in the United States of America

Library of Congress Cataloging-in-Publication Data

Demers, David P.
  Dictionary of mass communication & media research : a guide for students, scholars, and professionals / David Demers.
      p. cm.
  Includes bibliographical references and index.
  ISBN 0-922993-25-4 (pbk. : alk. paper)
  1. Mass media--Dictionaries. I. Title: Dictionary of mass communication and media research. II. Title.
  P87.5.D449 2005
  302.23'03--dc22

                                        2005009744

MARQUETTE BOOKS
3107 E. 62nd Avenue
Spokane, WA 99223
509-443-7057 (voice) / 409-448-2191 (fax)
books@marquettebooks.org
www.MarquetteBooks.org

DICTIONARY OF

MASS

Communication
& Media Research

A GUIDE FOR STUDENTS,
SCHOLARS AND PROFESSIONALS

OTHER BOOKS OF INTEREST FROM MARQUETTE BOOKS

Ralph D. Berenger (ed.), *Cybermedia Go to War: Role of the Internet and New Media During the 2003 Iraq War* (forthcoming 2006). ISBN: 0-922993-24-6

Ray Edwards, *Justice Never Sleeps: A Novel of Murder and Revenge in Spokane* (2005). ISBN: 0-922993-26-2

Dan Robison, *Wind Seer: The Story of One Native American Boy's Contribution to the Anasazi Culture* (2005). ISBN: 0-922993-27-0

John Burke, *From Prairie to Palace: The Lost Biography of Buffalo Bill* (2005). Introduction by Jason Berger; edited by Tim Connor. ISBN: 0-922993-21-1

Tonya Holmes Shook, *The Drifters: A Christian Historical Novel about the Melungeon Shanty Boat People* (2005). ISBN: 0-922993-19-X

Goetz, Ronald E., *The Kid: A Novel About Billy the Kid's Early Years* (2005). ISBN: 0-922993-20-3

John C. Merrill, Ralph D. Berenger and Charles J. Merrill, *Media Musings: Interviews with Great Thinkers* (2004). ISBN: 0-922993-15-7

Ralph D. Berenger (ed.), *Global Media Go to War: Role of Entertainment and News During the 2003 Iraq War* (2004). ISBN: 0-922993-10-6

C. W. Burbank, *Beyond Zenke's Gate* (2004). ISBN: 0-922993-14-9

David Demers, *China Girl: One Man's Adoption Story* (2004). ISBN: 0-922993-08-4

Larry Whitesitt, *Northern Flight of Dreams: Flying Adventures in British Columbia, Yukon, NW Territories and Alaska* (2004). ISBN: 0-922993-09-2

Melvin L. DeFleur and Margaret H. DeFleur, *Learning to Hate Americans: How U.S. Media Shape Negative Attitudes Among Teenagers in Twelve Countries* (2003). ISBN: 0-922993-05-X

David Demers (ed.), *Terrorism, Globalization and Mass Communication: Papers Presented at the 2002 Center for Global Media Studies Conference* (2003). ISBN: 0-922993-04-1

Table of Contents

Note to Reader

Italicized words are defined in this dictionary,
with the exception of bibliographic entries,
where italics is used to identify books,
journals, newspapers, and magazines.

The Index contains a complete
listing of the concepts and terms
defined in this dictionary.

Preface

During a conversation I had with a colleague in late 2004, I mentioned that I was writing this dictionary.

"How can you do that?" he asked. "Scholars in our field don't agree much on anything."

He had a good point. In the field of mass communication and the social sciences in general, scholars and professionals often disagree about how to define basic terms and concepts. The concept of *mass communication* itself is a good example.

One introductory textbook defines it as "the process through which messages reach the audience via the mass media." Another says mass communication is "the process of designing and delivering cultural messages and stories to diverse audiences through media channels as old as the book and as new as the Internet." A third textbook defines it as "the process by which a complex organization, with the aid of one or more machines, produces and transmits public messages that are directed at large, heterogeneous, and scattered audiences." And the dictionary you are now reading defines it as "the process of delivering messages to a large number of geographically separated people through a technologically based medium."

To be sure, these definitions share some common ground. All assume, for example, that mass communication is transmitted through some kind of technology, as opposed to face-to-face communication. Without some common agreement about concepts (or *intersubjectivity*, as social scientists call it), knowledge itself would not be possible.

But there are some significant differences in the definitions offered above. The first three limit the process of mass communication to mass media organizations, while the last one does not exclude individuals as mass communicators (via the Internet). The second and third definitions assume that audiences are diverse (or what some scholars call "mass" audiences), whereas the first and fourth make no assumptions about the character of the audience. The first and fourth imply that mass communication can take place in developing and homogeneous societies or nations, which often depend heavily on mass media such as radio.

To some scholars and professionals, differences like these are a source of frustration. They believe social science needs consensus. Others are even more critical. They see the differences as a sign of *postmodernism*—or the notion that science and knowledge are impossible.

But to me and others, the differences are a source of inspiration, because they stimulate new ideas and theories about mass communication and human behavior in general. For example, if individuals—not just institutions—have the power to mass communicate through the Internet, then what impact could this new form of *power* have on the distribution of ideas and knowledge in society? Could the *Internet* help decentralize political and economic power much like the *printing press* did after the 15th century? (See *information revolution* for details.) More specifically, could the Internet rob mass media of their power to mediate much of the information and knowledge generated in society?

To me, the most frustrating aspect of the social sciences isn't the fact that scholars disagree on definitions. It's the fact that many of them fail to define their concepts at all or do not spend enough time defining and refining their concepts (see *corporate media* as an example). Concepts are the building blocks of science, so they must not be taken for granted.

The key to defining good concepts is not to begin with the idea that one definition fits all. No single *conceptual definition* or *operational definition* is always right for every occasion, for definitions often depend upon context, time and place. Instead, the key is to define a concept that provides the greatest utility in explaining or interpreting the social problem under study. Thus, any of the four definitions of mass communication provided earlier in this preface may be useful in solving research problems, depending upon the context.

My goal in writing this dictionary, then, was not to compose the definitive dictionary on mass communication. I do not think that can be done, nor do I expect readers to agree with all of the definitions I've provided herein. Instead, my primary goal was to write a dictionary that would stimulate new ideas and theories about mass communication processes and effects—something other social science dictionaries and encyclopedias have been doing for me for many years.

I am grateful to a number of people who directly or indirectly helped in the production of this book. In particular, they include Ms. Carrie Lipe, Mr. Tim Connor and Dr. Paul J. Lindholdt for critiquing and copyediting the text. I thank Ms. Purba Das, Dr. Melvin DeFleur, Mr. Jethro Delisle, Ms. Linda Delisle, Dr. Douglas Blanks Hindman, Professor John Irby, Dr. Igor E. Klyukanov, Dr. Alex Tan, Mr. Ming Wang, and Mr. Lu Wei for reading portions of the book, correcting errors, and providing feedback about what terms to include or exclude.

I am especially grateful to Dr. Phillip J. Tichenor, my Ph.D. adviser, who stressed the importance of defining concepts and who played a significant role in defining my own research program. I also thank my wife, Theresa, and our daughter, Lee Ann, for putting up with my busy work schedule.

David Demers
Spokane, Washington
Summer 2005

A

ABC (American Broadcasting Company) a *television network* company owned by The Walt Disney Company.

absolutism the philosophical doctrine that truth is absolute and objective; opposite of *relativism.*

absolutist ethics the notion that there is a right or wrong response to any ethical situation.

Proponents of this perspective believe in hard and fast rules to guide decision-making, regardless of the circumstances or the situation.

See *absolutism* and *situational ethics.*

access law an area of media law that deals with the government's or public's "right" to access (i.e., obtain space or air time from) the mass media and the information they generate.

The U.S. Supreme Court has basically ruled that the First Amendment does not give the public a right of access to print media, such as newspapers and magazines. But there is a very limited right to access if the media are broadcast, and at the federal level journalists have no right to keep confidential their sources, notes, and film.

In the court case Miami Herald Publishing Co. v. Tornillo (1974), the U.S. Supreme Court ruled that a newspaper is not required to publish the comments of a politician who was attacked in a newspaper editorial. The court basically said that compelling the newspaper to print the reply would mean the newspaper would have to devote space and money to printing the reply, and this could have a chilling effect on the press.

This ruling does not apply to broadcast media, however. Unlike the print media, there are a limited number of airwaves. Although the FCC eliminated the *Fairness Doctrine* in 1987, the FCC still requires broadcasters to treat political candidates fairly.

At the federal level, the *First Amendment* provides relatively little protection to journalists who wish to keep confidential their sources, notes, and film. But many states provide protection through *shield laws.*

If a federal crime has been committed and journalists have evidence that could help solve that crime, journalists can be forced to turn over that information. This principle was established in Branzburg v. Hayes (1972).

The U.S. Supreme Court ruled that three reporters had to turn over information about confidential sources to grand juries investigating criminal activity. One of the grand juries was investigating drug use and sales. The other two were investigating the Black Panthers, a militant organization, according to the government.

In all three cases, reporters refused to give confidential information to the grand juries. They promised their sources confidentiality and argued it was necessary to obtain their cooperation. If reporters were required to turn over the names of confidential sources, the sources would be reluctant to talk to them, and the public would be deprived of valuable information about key social issues.

The court disagreed. It could not accept the argument "that it is better to write about crime than to do something about it."

Although journalists can be compelled to testify before grand juries, the high court did allowed Congress or state legislatures to pass laws to protect them. These are called shield laws. Twenty-eight states have them. But there is no federal shield law because journalists couldn't agree on what such a law should protect.

Shield laws basically state that no journalist engaged in a news-gathering capacity shall be compelled to testify in a legal proceeding or before a court about the information he or she has gathered. Oddly, the protection in some states extends only to reporters and to print journalists, not to photographers or broadcasters. Historically, journalists, and news organizations have not been very effective at lobbying for these and other protections. In fact, many journalists and news organizations believe politics should be left to legislators and citizens.

Sources: *Miami Herald Publishing Co. v. Tornillo*, 418 U.S. 241 (1974) and *Branzburg v. Hayes*, 408 U.S. 665 (1972).

access provider a company or institution that provides users with access to the Internet.

Access providers include for-profit companies that are usually called *Internet Service Providers* (ISPs), and not-for-profit providers, such as universities, which offer free access to students and staff.

account executive (AE) a public relations, advertising or marketing research practitioner who essentially is a sales person with a good working knowledge of the business.

The account executive sells a product or service (e.g., consulting services, advertising or research) to a client and then oversees the production or management of that product or service. Although other employees in the organization normally do not work for the AE, the AE usually oversees their work and has control over what gets presented to the client. The AE usually earns more money than the other specialists because the AE position is directly responsible for generating revenues.

acquisitions editor the person who plays a key role in acquiring manuscripts for a *publishing house.*

The acquisition editor often solicits book manuscripts from authors and helps make decisions about whether to publish the manuscript.

action *behavior* that is goal-directed, intentional or purposeful.

action research research motivated by a desire to solve social problems or improve social conditions.

action standard a criterion for determining whether to market or to continue research on a product, service or idea.

active audience the idea that mass media have limited effects on people because people consciously use media to achieve their own goals.

See *free will, determinism,* and *uses and gratifications.*

Adams, Samuel (1722-1803) the best example of an editor from the Revolutionary War period in American history.

Adams edited the "Boston Gazette," which became a center for radicals (or Patriots). Adams also helped organize the Sons of Liberty, the group that staged the Boston Tea Party and other political actions designed to call attention to the Patriot cause and weaken British power.

Adams signed the Declaration of Independence and held a number of appointed and elected political posts, including governor of Massachusetts. Public relations practitioners admire Adams for employing public relations principles to generate support for the anti-British political movement.

administrative research research that helps mainstream political, social, and economic institutions achieve their goals.

The term often has a negative connotation, suggesting that researchers who practice administrative research are blind to the abuses of power inherent in the *status quo.* In the 1970s, sociologist Todd Gitlin criticized sociologist *Paul Lazarsfeld* for conducting research that helped *mainstream media* to maintain power and control over consumers.

See *critical theory.*

Source: Todd Gitlin, "Media Sociology: The Dominant Paradigm," *Theory and Society,* 6:205-53 (1978).

advertising a form of persuasion in which one social actor purchases space or time from a media organization in an effort to influence the opinions or buying decisions of consumers or an audience.

Generally speaking, advertising and other forms of persuasion differ in that advertisers must pay a media organization for placing or airing content. Although some media organizations offer free advertising to nonprofit organizations (e.g., public service advertising), that advertising technically is not free because the media organization must absorb the costs of lost revenues.

Advertising is the main source of revenue for most magazines, newspapers, *television networks*, and radio stations.

Advertising content can be divided into two major categories: commercial and political. Commercial advertising includes all advertising that attempts to persuade consumers or businesses to purchase various kinds of products or services, such as automobiles or grocery items. Most ads fall into this category.

The second category, political advertising, also attempts to influence people, but the goal here is to persuade citizens to vote in a particular way or to support a particular issue or idea. Political parties and candidates purchase the bulk of political ads, especially just before an election. However, citizens and special-interest groups may also purchase ads to influence the political process.

The effectiveness of advertising depends heavily upon four major factors:

1. Consumer needs. The best advertising campaign in the world will be ineffective if there is limited demand for a product or service. During the early 2000s, many of the Internet companies discovered this. They offered services that on paper seemed great and their ads were very well done, but there was no consumer demand.

2. Quality of message. Does the advertisement attract and hold the attention of the consumer, and is it memorable? Many devices and methods are used to attract and hold attention, including humor, fancy graphics, attractive actors, catchy phrases, and songs.

3. Message repetition. How often does a consumer see an advertisement? As a rule of thumb, the greater the repetition, the stronger the persuasive effect. But this rule will not hold true if the product or service in the advertisement does not satisfy a consumer need or if the quality of the message is low.

4. Reaching the right consumers. Does the advertisement reach potential consumers of a product or service? If not, then the advertisement will not be effective. That's why placement is such an important part of the advertising process.

Advertising campaigns are often ineffective. However, effectiveness isn't always known because in many cases no post-evaluation is conducted.

The field of advertising also has developed several *codes of ethics*. The best known is the *Advertising Code of American Business*, which was developed in 1965 by the *Advertising Federation of America*, the Advertising Association of the West, and the Association of Better Business Bureaus, Inc., and endorsed by the International Newspaper Advertising Executives.

The code is concise, consisting of nine major points: (a) truth—advertisers should tell the truth; (b) responsibility—advertisers should substantiate their claims; (c) taste and decency—advertising should not be offensive; (d) disparagement—advertisers should not unfairly attack competitors or their products; (e) bait advertising—advertisers should offer products and services at the advertised price; (f) guarantees and warranties—advertising of guarantees and warranties shall be explicit; (g) price claims—advertising shall avoid price or savings claims that are false; (h) unprovable claims—advertising shall avoid the use of exaggerated claims; (i) testimonials—advertising containing testimonials should be real and honest.

See *Internet advertising, N. W. Ayer & Son,* and *subliminal advertising.*

Sources: E. Lincoln James, Corenealium B. Pratt and Tommy V. Smith, "Advertising Ethics: Practitioner and Student Perspectives," *Journal of Mass Media Ethics*, 9(2):69-83 (1994).

advertising agency an individual or private company that creates and/or places advertisements in *mass media.*

The first agency was founded by Volney Palmer in Philadelphia in 1843. He solicited ads, gave them to the newspapers, and billed the advertisers.

Currently about 15,000 independent advertising agencies do business in the United States. This number more than doubles to about 35,000 if media buying services, media representatives, display advertising, direct-mail advertising, and advertising material distribution services are added to the list. But in terms of public exposure, the advertising agencies get most of the attention (or glory or blame).

Advertising agencies are often classified into four different types.

1. Full-service advertising agencies offer a full array of services, including research, creative, placement, and public relations services.

2. Creative boutiques are "idea factories" and typically focus on creating the advertisement or campaign. They offer concept development, copywriting, and artistic services.

3. Media-buying services are independent agencies that specialize in buying space and time. These services typically can purchase space or time at a lower rate because they buy in volume.

4. Interactive agencies, relative newcomers to the field, focus on preparing advertising messages for new media, including the Internet, CD-ROMs, and interactive television. They are sometimes called cyberagencies.

Sources: U.S. Census Bureau, *1997 Economic Census, Professional, Scientific, and Technical Services, Series EC97554A-US* (December 1999).

advertising awareness a concept for measuring consumer awareness of advertisements.

See *aided advertising awareness, aided awareness, unaided advertising awareness,* and *total advertising awareness.*

advertising campaign an organized effort that uses advertising to promote a candidate, idea, product, company or service.

Advertising Council a nonprofit organization that focuses on producing and distributing public service advertisements.

The history of the Advertising Council goes back to World War II, when the advertising industry lent aid to the U.S. government and the war effort. The War Advertising Council, consisting of volunteers from advertising agencies and media organizations, created advertisements to support the war effort.

The WAC produced a total of 150 war-related campaigns, including campaigns to help raise bonds to pay for the war and to recruit women for civilian and military jobs. After the war, the organization dropped "War" from its name.

Sources: The Advertising Council Web site, <www.adcouncil.org>.

advertising tracking study a study designed to track *awareness* and effects of advertising.

See *aided awareness, unaided awareness,* and *total advertising awareness.*

affiliate a radio or television station that associates itself with a network.

See *television network.*

agenda-building the process through which an organization or society prioritizes its social, political or economic problems.

See *agenda-setting hypothesis.*

agenda-setting hypothesis the notion that the more news media emphasize an issue or event, the more importance readers or viewers place on that issue or event.

The agenda-setting hypothesis was developed by Max McCombs and Donald Shaw at the University of North Carolina, who argued that the power of mass media lies less in telling people what to think (persuasion) than in telling them what to think about (the agenda). In other words, top stories in the mass media set the agenda for public discussion, and this public agenda, in turn, sets the legislative agenda. Their ideas were built in part upon those of media professor Bernard Cohen, who argued that the media may not always be successful in telling people what to think but in what to think about.

McCombs and Shaw tested their theory in the 1968 presidential election. To maximize possible effects, they surveyed 100 undecided voters and asked them what they thought were the key issues in the campaign. McCombs and Shaw also content-analyzed newspapers, magazines, and television news broadcasts to determine how much emphasis the media placed on various issues. They found a strong correlation between the voters' agenda and the media's agenda. The top-ranked items on the media's agenda were also highly ranked on the voters' agenda.

Since the 1970s, hundreds of studies have found support for this hypothesis. Although many questions linger, agenda-setting played a big role in reviving the notion of powerful media effects. Mass communication researcher James Tankard writes that agenda-setting helped revive "the effects question in research. Much communication research up until the early 1960s had minimized the effects of mass communication. Through agenda-setting, it appeared that mass communication might have some significant effects after all."

See *Guard Dog Theory*.

Sources: Maxwell E. McCombs and Donald L. Shaw, "The Agenda-Setting Function of Mass Media," *Public Opinion Quarterly*, 36:176-187 (1972); Bernard Cohen, *The Press and Foreign Policy* (Princeton: Princeton University Press, 1963); James W. Dearing and Everett M. Rogers, *Agenda-Setting* (Thousand Oaks, CA: Sage, 1996); Werner J. Severin and James W. Tankard Jr., *Communication Theories: Origins, Methods, and Uses in the Mass Media*, 5th ed. (New York : Longman, 2001); and Maxwell McCombs, Donald L. Shaw and David Weaver (eds.), *Communication and Democracy: Exploring the Intellectual Frontiers in Agenda-Setting Theory* (Mahwah, NJ: Lawrence Erlbaum Associates, 1997); David Pearce Demers, Dennis Craff, Yang-Ho Choi, and Beth M. Pessin, "Issue Obtrusiveness and the Agenda-Setting Effects of National Network News," *Communication Research*, 16(6):793-812 (December 1989); James W. Tankard Jr., "Maxwell McCombs, Donald Shaw, and Agenda-Setting," pp. 278-286 in Wm. David Sloan (ed.), *Makers of the Media Mind: Journalism Educators and Their Ideas* (Hillsdale, NJ: Lawrence Erlbaum Associates, 1990), p. 284.

aggregation see *level of analysis*.

aided advertising awareness the percentage of *respondents* aware of advertising for a product, service or company after being prompted with questions or materials.

Measures of aided advertising awareness are used frequently in *advertising tracking studies*.

See *unaided advertising awareness* and *total advertising awareness*.

aided awareness the percentage of *respondents* aware of a product, service or company after being prompted with questions or materials.

See *unaided awareness* and *total awareness*.

aided recall the percentage of *respondents* who recall various characteristics or features of a product, service or company after being prompted with questions or materials.

Also see *aided awareness*.

Alien and Sedition Acts a law passed in 1798 by the Federalist-controlled Congress designed to muzzle anti-Federalist editors.

Editors who wrote stories containing "false, scandalous or malicious" comments about the Federalists could be fined $2,000 and imprisoned for two years. The law only punished those who wrote false statements, not truthful ones. But this act was a step back for freedom of the press.

Ten editors and publishers were convicted, and the laws created such a furor that the Federalists were unable to renew it. After *Thomas Jefferson* became president in 1800, he pardoned all those in jail and canceled remaining trials.

See *freedom of speech*, *freedom of the press*, and *Jefferson, Thomas*.

alienation a condition or state in which people feel estranged from a group or culture.

In *critical theory* and neo-Marxist media research in general, alienation is usually viewed as an outcome or effect of capitalist productive processes, and mass media are seen as producing content that helps mask these consequences from those who are alienated. *Karl Marx* argued that capitalism and the division of labor created jobs that alienated workers from the products of their labors. Workers are alienated partly because they work not for themselves but for a ruling class that oppresses them.

The de-skilling of labor is often cited as one of the reasons workers become alienated. However, alienation theorists point out that ordinary people typically do not blame capitalism for the problem, partly because mass media produce an ideology that justifies economic inequality and fails to link alienation to the structure of productive processes.

See *critical theory*, *ideology*, *Marx, Karl*, and *Neo-Marxism*.

Al-Jazeera a television station in Qatar that gained notoriety during the 2003 Iraq War when it broadcast videotaped messages from al Qaeda and its leader, Osama bin Laden.

The network, funded in its early years by the emir of Qatar, is often criticized by governments in the Middle East and the West. However, the station is popular with many ordinary people in the Middle East and was by far the most popular source of news there during the 2003 Iraq War.

The Al-Jazeera staff recognizes that its coverage offends a lot of governments and the West. But they say they are just trying to report the news objectively. In fact, most of the journalists who work for Al-Jazeera were trained at and once worked for Western news organizations like the *British Broadcasting Corporation* and *Cable News Network*.

Media scholars point out that Al-Jazeera's coverage of the 2003 Iraq War tended to be more favorable toward the Arab point of view. For example, the channel clearly showed more scenes of civilian casualties of the war than did Western *television networks*.

But scholars point out that Western news media coverage was also biased because it downplayed civilian casualties and relied more heavily on Western news sources than on non-Western sources.

Sources: Muhammad I. Ayish, "News Credibility During the 2003 Iraq War: A Survey of UAE Students," pp. 323-334 in Ralph D. Berenger (ed.), *Global Media Go to War: Role and News and Entertainment Media during the 2003 Iraq War* (Spokane, WA: Marquette Books, 2004); John Clark, "War Through Al Jazeera's Eyes," *The Los Angeles Times* (June 6, 2004), p. E10; and Stephen Quinn and Tim Walters, "Al-Jazeera: A Broadcaster Creating Ripples in a Stagnant Pool," pp. 57-72 in Ralph D. Berenger (ed.), *Global Media Go to War: Role and News and Entertainment Media during the 2003 Iraq War* (Spokane, WA: Marquette Books, 2004).

alternative hypothesis see *hypothesis*.

alternative media mass media that present news, information, and entertainment content that challenges dominant values or political and economic elites as well as *mainstream media*.

In the 1960s, alternative newspapers were often called "underground newspapers." They published content that opposed the war in Vietnam; supported women's, environmental, and civil rights; and criticized powerful multinational corporations. Today, the remnants of those newspapers have abandoned most of their radical ways and are money-making enterprises that tend to emphasize arts and entertainment more than politics.

The Independent Media Center, or Indymedia, is perhaps the best known radical media. The loosely knit organization maintains a Web site (www.indymedia.org) that allows virtually anyone to contribute news and information. Although some large cities have given rise to anti-capitalist, anti-globalization publications and Web sites, alternative media have limited influence because of lack of resources and more conservative political times.

See *mainstream bias*.

American Association of Advertising Agencies, The (AAAA) a trade association representing the advertising agency business in the United States.

Founded in 1917, AAAA's membership now accounts for about 75 percent of the total advertising volume placed by agencies nationwide. The main goal of AAAA, according to its Web site <www.aaaa.org>, is to offer its members services, expertise and information regarding the advertising agency business.

American Advertising Federation (AAF) a trade association that represents 50,000 professionals in the advertising industry.

AAF has a national network of 210 advertising clubs and college chapters. Its Web site <www.aaf.org> contains information about internships, scholarships, and jobs.

American Booksellers Association, The a nonprofit association representing independent bookstores (i.e., bookstores not owned by or affiliated with major chains or corporations).

The organization's Web site contains information about conferences and trends in the book industry <www.bookweb.org>.

American Society of Magazine Editors (ASME) a professional organization consisting of *editors* of consumer magazines and business publications.

This organization's Web site <www.magazine.org> contains information about editorial trends and issues, internships, jobs, and issues facing the magazine industry.

American Society of Newspaper Editors a nonprofit association composed of daily newspaper editors and people who serve the editorial needs of daily newspapers.

The organization's Web site <www.asne.org> points out that the organization promotes the interests of journalism and vigorously defends the First Amendment.

American Women in Radio and Television, Inc. a nonprofit organization devoted to advancing the interests of women in broadcasting.

The organization's Web site <www.awrt.org> contains information about the organization, the issues on which it focuses, and membership.

amplitude modulation (AM) see radio technology.

AM stereo a technology that allows transmission of stereophonic radio signals to consumers via AM (Amplitude Modulation) radio.

The concept of AM stereo goes back to the 1920s, and more than 300 AM radio stations are broadcasting in stereo in the United States today.

However, consumers never really embraced the technology, because of four major problems: (1) Radios capable of receiving AM stereo broadcasts cost about twice as much as conventional radios; (2) AM radio has over time become oriented more toward talk and news than music, which is the primary format for stereo; (3) There is a lack of stereo programming for AM stations; and (4) FM radio reception still has higher quality and remains the format of choice for music-oriented stations.

Most consumers are unaware of the AM stereo technology. Also, the concept of AM stereo radio, and even FM stereo radio, has become even less relevant with the advent of wireless Web radio and satellite radio.

See *radio technology*.

analog a method of analyzing or storing data that uses signals or pulses of varying degrees of intensity (as opposed to digital, which uses numbers).

See *recording format*.

analog computer a computer that uses analog to perform calculations or accomplish tasks, in contrast to a *digital computer*, which uses numbers (usually a binary system).
  See *recording format.*

analog recording see *recording format.*

analysis of variance an *inferential statistic* used when the *dependent variable* is a *continuous measure* and when the *independent variable* is a *nominal measure* that contains three or more *values.*
  A *t-test* is used if the independent variable is a *binomial.*

animated film a movie whose primary characters are animated; that is, created from drawings or computer graphics.
  The early animated films were made by hand, with artists drawing and coloring frame by frame. Increasingly, though, computers and advanced graphic technology have been used to produce animated films. "Toy Story," a 1995 box office hit, was the first film made completely with computer animation.

anonymous source a news source whose name is not revealed.

appellant the party to a lawsuit that loses and appeals the case to a higher court.
  See *appellee.*

appellee (or respondent) the party to a lawsuit that has won a case and becomes a defendant when the case is appealed to a higher court.
  See *appellant.*

a posteriori knowledge knowledge acquired after experience (i.e., from sensory perception).
  See *a priori knowledge, empiricism, epistemology,* and *rationalism.*

a priori knowledge knowledge acquired through means other than sense perception (before experience).
  Mathematical truths are an example.
  See *a posteriori knowledge, empiricism, epistemology,* and *rationalism.*

Arbitron the best known commercial media research service that estimates the number of people listening to various radio stations in a market.
  Radio stations pay Arbitron and other companies to provide such data, which is then used to set advertising rates. As a rule, the greater the number of listeners, the higher the advertising rates can be set.

Research companies issue periodic reports assigning ratings points to time slots or programs. One rating point is equivalent to one percent of the listening audience.

area probability sample a type of *cluster sample* in which geographic areas, such as census blocks, are sampled at the first stage of analysis; and units within those areas, such as households, are enumerated and sampled at the second stage of analysis.

Areopagitica a document written in 1644 by Englishman *John Milton*, probably the most widely cited work in defense of a free press.

Its most famous phrase is: "[T]hough all the winds of doctrine were let loose to play upon the earth, so truth be in the field, we do injuriously by licensing and prohibiting to misdoubt her strength. Let her [truth] and falsehood grapple; who ever knew truth put to the worse, in a free and open encounter?"

In short, Milton argued that truth will win out when it confronts falsehood. In principle, this idea is widely accepted, but in practice, media scholars point out that social actors with power can often manipulate information and ideas.

See *public relations* and *social control.*

Armstrong, Edwin Howard (1890-1954) inventor of FM radio and other broadcasting technologies.

At the age of 14, Armstrong became fascinated with the technology of wireless radio and one of its inventors, *Guglielmo Marconi.* Armstrong built his own wireless apparatus and later attended Columbia University's School of Engineering. In his junior year, he invented regeneration. Basically, he took Lee De Forest's Audion tube and substantially improved its ability to send and receive radio signals.

After hearing about Armstrong's work, De Forest, who is sometimes called the "father of radio," quickly filed a number of patents on variants of the regeneration technique. With the help of AT&T, De Forest then filed a patent lawsuit against Armstrong. The battle lasted 14 years and went before the U.S. Supreme Court several times. Although there was little evidence to support De Forest's claims, AT&T lawyers were able to get a sympathetic ruling from a lower court judge, which effectively broke Armstrong's patent.

Armstrong also invented the superheterodyne, a technique for improving reception and tuning. Superheterodyne is still used in radios today. Westinghouse paid him hundreds of thousands of dollars for the rights. Armstrong also invented a super-regenerative receiver, and RCA paid him millions for that one.

By the late 1920s, Armstrong was a multi-millionaire and on the faculty at Columbia University, where he worked full time on his inventions. The loss of the patent to De Forest was humiliating, but

Armstrong was determined to prove his worth. In the early 1930s, he invented the first workable FM radio system.

Researchers had tried FM radio in the 1920s, but they rejected it because the sound was worse than AM radio. Armstrong's wisdom was to vary the frequency of transmission, which eliminated interference and produced a much higher quality sound than AM radio. The sound was so good, in fact, that it was better than phonographs at that time.

He took his FM invention to RCA, but the company rejected it, because RCA had invested heavily in AM radio. So Armstrong sold the idea to smaller companies. In the late 1930s, RCA retaliated, asking the Federal Communications Commission to give away FM's frequency assignments (44 to 50 megahertz) to television, an emerging new technology. But the FCC saw through the ploy and gave the whole band to FM.

In response, RCA offered Armstrong a million dollars for his patents. Armstrong rejected the offer because RCA wouldn't give him royalties.

When World War II broke out, Armstrong allowed the military to use his patents without charge. FM radio was a tremendous aid to the Allied war effort.

Meanwhile, in 1945 RCA convinced the FCC to move the FM band to 88-108 megahertz, where it is today. (By the way, 44-50 megahertz would have been Channel 1 on television. That's why there is no Channel 1 today.) This effectively made Armstrong's system obsolete. FCC also voted to limit FM's broadcasting power and required them to send their programming over AT&T's expensive coaxial cables. This move effectively retarded the growth of FM radio.

In 1949, Armstrong brought a patent infringement lawsuit against RCA, which was now building FM receivers using his patents. RCA kept Armstrong on the witness stand for a year and even claimed that it had invented FM radio.

By 1953, Armstrong's patents had expired and he was near bankruptcy. His wife left him after an argument on Thanksgiving Day. About two months later, he jumped to his death.

His wife, Marion, eventually settled with RCA for $1 million and then filed lawsuits against Sylvania, Motorola, and CBS. She won all the cases and collected millions.

The scientific community has never accepted the court decision that gave patent rights to De Forest. The International Telecommunications Union elected Armstrong to the pantheon of electrical greats, which includes Alexander Graham Bell and Marconi.

See *radio* and *radio technology*.

Sources: Don V. Erickson, *Armstrong's Fight for FM Broadcasting: One Man vs. Big Business and Bureaucracy* (Tuscaloosa, AL: University of Alabama Press, 1973) and Lawrence Lessing, *Man of High Fidelity: Edwin Howard Armstrong, a Biography* (Philadephia: Lippincott, 1956).

ARPANET (Advanced Research Project Agency Network) a technology, introduced in 1969, that connected computers at government-supported research sites, mainly universities; the predecessor to the *Internet*.

Within a few years, ARPANET joined with networks developed by U.S. allies overseas and with networks at the Department of Energy, the National Aeronautical and Space Agency, and the National Science Foundation. In 1974, Vinton Cerf of Stanford University and Robert Kahn of the Defense Advanced Research Projects Agency (formerly ARPA), coined the term "Internet," short for "between networks."

See *Internet*.

art director (also called production designer) a person in the film-making industry who is responsible for designing the set, costumes, and background scenes for the film.

The art director also works directly with lighting and makeup personnel.

See *motion picture*.

aspect ratio the ratio of the width of a movie theater screen to its height.

During the 1950s, movie attendance dropped partly due to competition from television. In response, Hollywood studios began using cameras with a wider aspect ratio, meaning the width of the screen was proportionately much wider than the height. The rationale was that wider screens provided a more realistic image.

CinemaScope, SuperScope, WarnerScope, and Panavision were some of the names the studios gave to the process.

Associated Press (AP) a cooperative news service that supplies news stories, features, and other content to nearly 7,000 newspapers and broadcast media in the United States.

AP is the largest and most powerful news service in the world.

See *news service*.

association (a) a group of *social actors* that organize to pursue a particular cause or interest; **(b)** the statistical condition that occurs when some *variable* depends in whole or in part on another variable.

With respect to the second definition, a *state of independence* exists when no association between variables is present. A perfect *relationship* or association exists when changes in one variable depend wholly upon changes in another.

Association of American Publishers (AAP) a nonprofit organization that represents the interests of major book publishers.

Its Web site <www.publishers.org> contains information about the book publishing industry, as well as information about jobs and links to other sites.

Association for Education in Journalism and Mass Communication (AEJMC) a nonprofit education association representing 4,000 mass communication scholars, administrators, students, and mass media professionals.

The organization's Web site <www.aejmc.org> includes information about the organization, its goals, conferences, jobs, and research.

attitude a positive or negative feeling toward some object, person or issue.

attributes (a) categories of a *variable* (i.e., male and female are attributes for gender), **(b)** characteristics of a product, service or company, such as dependability, cost, quality and value (i.e., as used here, attribute is synonymous with a variable).

See *variable*.

audience people who are watching or listening to mass mediated content or who are the intended recipient of such messages.

This term is usually reserved for people who consume electronically transmitted content (e.g., from radio, television and/or the Internet). People who read mass mediated content from newspapers or magazines are usually called "readers."

audience flow see *programming*.

audio recording a disc, tape or other electronic device on which sound has been preserved.

Music is the most popular form of audio recording. But audio recordings are also made from comedy programs, dramas, and talk shows. In the United States and most Western countries, the recording industry produces audio recordings, especially musical recordings, for profit.

See *audio recording technology*.

audio recording technology the technology of converting audio sounds into a recording for later playback.

Early recording devices, such as Thomas A. Edison's phonograph, converted sound vibrations into grooves on a tinfoil cylinder or a disk. Electronic recordings were first produced during the 1920s.

During the 1940s, companies began manufacturing records from vinyl, a plastic resin made from petroleum. This resin was more durable and produced a better sound than shellac. Vinyl also enabled production of larger, long-playing (LP) records that could record the contents of an entire symphony on one side (up to 30 minutes). LPs ran at a speed of 33 revolutions per minute, which was much slower than 45s and 78s. In the late 1940s, the 45 rpm became the standard for singles and the 33 rpm for albums. The 78 eventually became extinct.

Sound quality was also improved by the advent of multiple-track recording and stereo technology. Multiple-track recording involved recording instruments and voices through separate microphones and tracks. The tracks were then mixed to produced the final music.

Stereophonic sound was produced by sending the sounds of some instruments or vocals to one channel, or speaker, and the sounds of the others to the other channel or speaker. Taken together, the industry called these technical improvements high-fidelity (hi-fi) sound, which meant the recorded sound approached original.

Audit Bureau of Circulation a nonprofit organization that verifies circulation claims of magazines and other print publications.

In the 1930s, magazine publishers were exaggerating the circulations of their magazines in order to secure advertising contracts. Advertisers, advertising agencies, and publishers created an independent "watchdog," the Audit Bureau of Circulation, often referred to as ABC (not to be confused with the broadcast *television network*), to audit and verify circulation claims. Participation was and still is voluntary, and publishers pay a fee for services. Today about 900 of the 25,000 magazines in the United States are ABC participants. Most major magazines participate.

authoritarian theory see *normative theory*.

autonomy the capacity to act in an independent manner.

The concept of autonomy is employed in many studies of job satisfaction of media workers and is one of the best predictors of workplace satisfaction.

Sources: David Pearce Demers, "Autonomy, Satisfaction High Among Corporate News Staffs," *Newspaper Research Journal*, 16:2 (Spring 1995), pp. 91-111.

average the average is often thought of as the *mean*, but the *median* and *mode* are also averages.

Also see *central tendency*.

awareness see *aided awareness* and *unaided awareness*.

awareness, attitude and usage study (AAU) a type of *tracking study* that monitors changes in *awareness, attitude,* and *usage* toward a product, service or company.

Ayer, Francis Wayland see *N. W. Ayer & Son*.

B

Baird, John Logie (1888-1946) a Scottish inventor credited with building the first television.

In 1926, Baird and a number of large companies were competing to be the first to invent television. Baird didn't have a lot of resources. His assistants worked without pay, and some of his materials included hat boxes and a coffin lid. But Baird beat the competition.

In London on January 26, 1926, Baird became the first person to televise moving objects publicly. His technology was crude, but it worked. And the achievement brought him great recognition.

But being first did not guarantee success. In 1937, the British Broadcasting Corporation selected a system developed by Marconi Electric and Musical Industries. Baird went on to develop color and three-dimensional television and worked on radar technology before and during World War II.

Source: Adrian R. Hills, "Eye of the World: John Logie Baird and Television (Part 1)," *Kinema* (Spring 1996), available online at <www.arts.uwaterloo.ca/FINE/juhde/hills961.htm>.

bandwagon effect see *spiral of silence.*

bandwidth a range of frequencies (expressed in cycles per second) within a radiation band required to transmit a radio signal.

banner (or banner tabulation or banner tabs) a type of computer-generated *cross tabulation* data table in which the *values* for a number of *variables,* such as *demographics,* run horizontally across the top of the table and the values for a single variable (usually a dependent variable) are contained in the rows.

banner ad an advertisement on the Internet shaped like a box, often extending across the top of a page.

See *Internet advertising.*

Barnum, Phineas Taylor (1810-1891) 19th-century showman who employed advertising and public relations campaigns to promote his circus and museum.

"PT" Barnum, as he is popularly called, was a master of promotion and advertising during the mid- to late 1800s. He promoted his museum of oddities and his circus show through newspaper advertising, handbills, and posters. When that didn't work, he'd come up with a gimmick to draw attention.

Barnum is credited with introducing a number of important techniques in advertising, including (1) keeping a brand or business name before the public; (2) originating methods of drawing attention; (3) providing more value than a competitor; and (4) using every advantage to get news media coverage of an event.

    Source: Irving Wallace, *The Fabulous Showman: Life and Times of P. T. Barnum* (New York: Alfred A. Knopf, 1959).

barriers to entry factors that impede the creation or founding of new mass media businesses, such as expensive equipment.

base in data analysis, the number of *cases* or *respondents* used in the denominator when calculating *percentages*, especially in a table.

BBC acronym for *British Broadcasting Corporation*.

behavior overt action of individuals.

    Behavior may or may not be intentional and, unlike *attitudes*, can be observed.

    See *action*.

behavioral intention a predisposition to perform a particular *behavior*.

    Purchase intent is one example of behavioral intention.

behavioral repertoire in *social cognitive theory*, the total number of learned responses available to a *social actor* in a given situation.

behaviorism a school of psychological thought based on the idea that human activity is best understood through observing behavior as opposed to studying the mind and consciousness.

behavior modification a method of changing behavior through the use of positive and negative reinforcement.

belief information a person has about other persons, objects or issues, whether accurate or inaccurate.

Berle, Milton (1908-2002) the first television superstar.

On June 8, 1948, Berle first appeared as host of "The Texaco Star Theater," a comedy-variety program that aired on NBC Tuesday nights at 8 p.m.

Berle was already a star of stage, film, and radio. But because his comedy partially relied on visuals, radio was not his best medium. He had a toothy grin and wore wacky costumes. He was the first man to dress as a woman on television. People loved it. They called him "Mr. Television" and "Uncle Miltie."

The ratings for his television program were as high as 80 percent, which meant that four out of five households watching television were watching his show. Needless to say, NBC loved him, too. They gave him a contract in 1951 that paid him $200,000 a year for life (later reduced to $120,000 in exchange for allowing him to appear on other *television networks*).

Ironically, though, Berle's success on television didn't last long. "The Texaco Star Theater" was dropped in 1953. Berle hosted several other television programs, his last in the 1960s. After that he appeared as a guest performer in films and on many television programs, and also in night clubs.

Sources: J. Y. Smith, "Milton Berle, 'Mr. Television,' Dies at 93," *The Washington Post* (March 28, 2002), p. A1.

Bernays, Edward L. (1891-1995) an early public relations practitioner who competes with *Ivy Lee* for the title of "father of public relations" and was later pejoratively called the "father of spin."

Bernays was born in Vienna in 1891 and immigrated to New York with his parents before turning 1. His father was a prosperous grain exporter. Bernays was the double nephew of Sigmund Freud; his father was Freud's wife's brother and his mother was Freud's sister.

Bernays's father wanted his son to work in agronomy, and Bernays earned a degree in agriculture from Cornell University. But Bernays found work editing a medical manual and eventually helped promote a play by enlisting endorsements from civic leaders. He became a Broadway press agent and, in that role, learned how to get newspaper write-ups for his clients.

During World War I he worked for the Committee on Public Information, headed by *George Creel*, and became convinced that public relations techniques could be applied to corporations as well.

In 1922, Bernays married Doris E. Fleischman, who helped him run their public relations firm. They consulted for major corporations, the U.S. government, and many U.S. presidents. Fleischman, an early feminist, was very talented but always lived in the shadow of her husband's reputation.

Bernays and Fleischman launched some very successful *public relations campaigns*, including one for Ivory Soap. But the Lucky Strike campaign was the most notable PR campaign.

In the 1930s, women refused to buy the brand because it came in a forest-green pack, which didn't match their wardrobes. American Tobacco didn't want to change the color of the pack because it had already spent millions of dollars in advertising. The solution, Bernays said, was to promote green as a new fashion color.

Enlisting the assistance of a local charity, Bernays planned a "Green Ball." He got fashion designers to provide green gowns, invited an art historian and psychologist to expound on the significance of green, organized a "Color Fashion Bureau" that sent press releases to the news media extolling the virtues of green, convinced a clothing manufacturer to sponsor a luncheon promoting green to fashion editors, and initiated a letter-writing campaign (on green paper, of course) to interior designers, department stores, and others hailing green as the new, dominant color of fashion.

It worked. Sales of Lucky Strike cigarettes among women soared.

Bernays generated a large number of critics who pointed out that the public didn't usually know which events had been staged and which were "real." This led one historian, Daniel Boorstin, to call them "*pseudo events.*" "By the time the P.R. men were done," wrote Neal Gabler of *The New York Times*, "it was often impossible to tell the real from the bogus, information from misinformation, and an actual event from a sponsored one. In short, Bernays helped erect a hall of mirrors that changed the nature of reality itself."

Several biographies argue that Bernays had a condescending attitude toward the public. Indeed, in his book "Propaganda," Bernays wrote that "the conscious and intelligent manipulation of the organized habits and opinions of the masses is an important element in democratic society. Those who manipulate this unseen mechanism of society constitute an invisible government which is the true ruling power of our country."

Yes, despite the controversy, Bernays continues to serve as a role model for some people in the field of public relations, because he was very skilled at influencing (or "manipulating") public opinion. He also became very wealthy from his work.

Fleischman died in 1980. Bernays wrote several other major books, including "Public Relations" and "The Engineering of Consent." He also taught at several universities and continued giving lectures up to 1995, when he died at the age of 103.

See *Lee, Ivy, pseudo event,* and *public relations.*

Sources: Edward L. Bernays, *Crystallizing Public Opinion* (New York: Liveright, 1923); Edward L. Bernays, *Propaganda* (New York: Liveright, 1928) ; Edward L. Bernays, *Public Relations* (Norman: University of Oklahoma Press, 1952); Edward L. Bernays, *The Engineering of Consent* (Norman: University of Oklahoma Press, 1955); Stuart Ewen, *PR! A Social History of Spin* (New York: Basic Books, 1996), quoted material obtained from <www.bway.net/~drstu/chapter.html>; Neal Gabler, "The Lives They Lived: Edward L. Bernays and Henry C. Rogers; The Fathers of P.R.," *The New York Times* (December 31, 1995), quoted material obtained from <http://partners.nytimes.com/books/98/08/16/specials/bernays-father.html>; and

Larry Tye, *The Father of Spin: Edward L. Bernays and the Birth of Public Relations* (New York: Henry Holt, 2001).

Berners-Lee, Tim (1955-) inventor of the *World Wide Web.*

Berners-Lee majored in physics at Queen's College at Oxford University, England, and graduated with top honors in 1976. In 1984, he accepted a fellowship at CERN, where he worked on systems for scientific data acquisition and system control.

In 1989, he proposed the World Wide Web, a software system that would allow *Internet* users to transfer and view information over the Internet easily. Before the creation of the Web, about 600,000 people, mostly scientists and government officials, used the Internet, which was not very user-friendly. But Berners-Lee's software was relatively easy to use and gave Internet users the power to create their own Internet sites and link to other sites. In fact, anyone with a computer and modem (a device for connecting a computer to a phone line) could easily enter *cyberspace.*

Berners-Lee made the software available to the public free of charge in summer 1991. For the next two years, he continued to refine the software. Within five years there were 40 million users. Today, about 600 million people around the world are connected to the Internet, primarily through the Web.

Berners-Lee could have gotten rich off his invention. In fact, several major computer companies offered him millions of dollars for exclusive right to develop and sell the software.

But he turned them down. He didn't want any company controlling the software that could link the world into one global system. He wanted it to be free. So in 1994 he founded the nonprofit World Wide Web Consortium (W3C) at the Massachusetts Institute of Technology in Cambridge, Massachusetts. The Consortium governs and improves Web technology. Berners-Lee is the director.

"I have profited so much from seeing the system take off and become so remarkable because I chose not to commercialize it," he told the "San Francisco Chronicle." "If I had tried to commercialize it, it would have prompted people to make separate and incompatible versions of it and it wouldn't have become this marvelous global system."

In July 2004, Queen Elizabeth II Knighted Berners-Lee. He also has won numerous awards and received several honorary doctorate degrees from institutions around the world. These awards include the Finnish Millenium Technology Prize, which included a $1.2 million award. This award pleased many people, who believe Berners-Lee deserves some financial compensation for his work.

Sources: Laura Evenson, "From the Creator of a Universe; Web Inventor's Book Shares His Goal," *San Francisco Chronicle* (October 21, 1999), p. B1.

Bernstein, Carl see *Woodward and Bernstein.*

Betamax see *video cassette recorder.*

B-film a low-budget *motion picture.*
    See *block booking.*

bias of communication the notion that newer forms of communication technology contribute toward centralization of political power.
    The idea was advanced by Harold Innis, a neo-Marxist Canadian economist.
    Source: Harold Adams Innis, *The Bias of Communication* (Toronto: University of Toronto Press, 1951).

Bill of Rights the first 10 amendments to the U.S. Constitution.
    See *First Amendment.*

binomial a variable with two values; often used synonymously with *dichotomy.*

bipolar scale a scale with opposing end points, such as good/bad, small/large, important/not important, moist/dry.

bivariate analysis research analysis that involves two variables.
    Correlation coefficients are often used in bivariate analysis.
    See *univariate* and *multivariate analysis.*

Blair, Jayson (1976-) a former "New York Times" reporter who fabricated news stories that embarrassed the "Times" and discredited the profession.
    In the late 1990s, Blair was a rising star in University of Maryland's journalism program. He left the university in May 1999 when the "Times" offered him a second internship. In 2001, at the age of 24, the "Times" hired him full-time. A year later the newspaper promoted him to the national desk.
    But in 2003, the newspaper fired him after it learned he had plagiarized and fabricated information for at least 36 stories written during his two years at the "Times." One story included a front-page exclusive about the Washington-area sniper shootings. The story reported that the U.S. attorney forced investigators to terminate their interrogation of suspect John Muhammad just before he was ready to confess. The claim was attributed to five unnamed law enforcement officials. But the story was fabricated.
    The "Times" conducted an extensive investigation of Blair, concluding he had committed "frequent acts of journalistic fraud." The newspaper, which was severely criticized for the incident, published a front-page apology to readers and corrected most of the errors. The paper's top two editors resigned.

In 2004, Blair wrote a book about his fall from grace, placing part of the blame on heavy substance abuse and on a bipolar disorder (manic-depressive mental illness). He also blamed the high-pressure newsroom.

Blair received a $150,000 advance from the publisher for writing a book titled, *Burning Down My Master's House: My Life at The New York Times.* See *ethics* and *Cooke, Janet.*

Sources: David Folkenflik, "The Making of Jayson Blair," *Baltimore Sun* (February 29, 2004); Jack Shafer, "The Jayson Blair Project: How Did He Bamboozle *The New York Times?*" *Slate* (May 8, 2003), <www.slate.com>; Rose Arce, "Jayson Blair Sells Tell-All Book," CNN.com (September 10, 2003); Marcia Purse, "Jayson Blair has Bipolar Disorder," Bipolar.com (2004); "*New York Times:* Reporter Routinely Faked Articles," CNN.com (May 11, 2003).

block booking a practice that, prior to the 1950s, forced independent theaters to show lower quality films, or *B-films*, before having the privilege of showing A-films (expensive productions with top stars).

The U.S. government ended this practice in the late 1940s and also forced the studios to sell their theater chains and monopolistic controls over film distribution.

See *vertical integration.*

block printing a method of printing that involved carving images on wood and dipping the image into ink and pressing it onto paper or some other surface.

The Chinese invented and refined the process of block printing during the 6th century A.D. Block printing greatly facilitated the distribution of Confucian texts, which extolled the values of devotion to parents, family and friends, ancestor worship, justice and peace. By the year A.D. 1000, the Chinese were publishing weekly reports called "Tching-pao." Crude forms of newspapers made from wood blocks also began to appear in Europe about the same time.

blog see *Weblog.*

Bly, Nellie (1865-1922) a newspaper reporter who gained international fame for traveling around the world in 72 days.

Born Elizabeth Cochrane, Nellie Bly landed her first job as a reporter after writing a letter to the editor that criticized the "Pittsburgh Dispatch" for failing to support women's right. The editor hired her in 1888 and she chose Nellie Bly as her pen name.

She wrote about tragic living conditions and political corruption in Mexico, went undercover to expose abuse in a mental institution, and was the first woman to cover the Eastern Front during World War I.

But she became most famous after taking up a challenge to beat the Jules Verne character Phineas Fogg's fictional record of circumnavigating the globe in 80 days. She did it in 72 days and sent back stories of her exploits from around the world.

book sheets of paper, parchment, or other materials with writing or printing on them, fastened together along one edge, usually between protective covers.

As simple as that definition may seem, it fails to resolve other questions, such as: How many pages must a book have? What constitutes a cover? And what about the so-called "electronic books?"

UNESCO (United Nations Educational, Scientific and Cultural Organization) defines a book as having 49 pages or more, but this number is arbitrary. Many children's "books" have fewer than 49 pages.

Other people try to distinguish books from other forms of media by declaring that books are only published infrequently, unlike newspapers and magazines, which usually appear at least once a month or more often. But even this doesn't always work, because some books, like reference manuals, can be published as frequently as magazines.

And how protective does the cover have to be? Some books have soft covers, others have hard or cloth covers, and some have no covers at all.

Some scholars argue that the single most distinctive character of a book is not the length, the cover, or frequency of publication, but the fact that books often provide more in-depth analysis of a specific idea or set of ideas than other forms of mass media. A book, in other words, is expected to treat a subject in-depth, or at least in more depth than other forms of media.

That's one of the reasons books often have had a greater capacity than other forms of media to change people and societies. They can better explore the boundaries of issues and problems. The Bible, Rachel Carson's "Silent Spring," and Karl Marx' "Capital" have all been cited as examples of books that have mobilized people and changed the world.

See *Carson, Rachel Louise*, and *Marx, Karl*.

book club an organization that encourages people to buy or read books.

There are two major types of book clubs. The first is a type of business created specifically by publishers or wholesalers for the purpose of selling books directly to consumers. Book-of-the-Month Club and Literary Guild are examples. They offer titles in specialized topics (mystery, classics, history, etc.), usually at a discount, depending on how many books a consumer purchases.

The second type of book club is best defined as a social activity, wherein a person or group of people get together and select books to read. *Oprah Winfrey*'s Book Club is an example. This type of book club doesn't sell books; it merely recommends titles to readers, who go elsewhere to purchase them.

book prospectus a short document that summarizes a proposed book project to potential publishers or literary agents.

The prospectus normally includes background information about the author, the proposed title for the book, an abstract of the book, a brief statement about the market potential for the book, a tentative deadline, and an outline of the book's contents. Some authors also will send a sample chapter or two.

bookseller a person or organization, such as a book store, that sells books.

In the 18th century, book publishers generally marketed and sold their own books. Many owned bookshops or hired salespeople, who traveled the countryside. Book publishers frequently placed ads in newspapers.

In the 19th century, book publishers increasingly began to specialize in publishing, leaving the book marketing and selling to independent booksellers. The publisher would sell the books to the book store owner at a discount, who would then mark the price of the books up to make a profit.

See *Carey, Mathew.*

boomerang response a media effect that is opposite of what was intended.

Bourke-White, Margaret (1904-1971) a photojournalist who gained a reputation for never letting manners get in the way of a good photo story.

For example, when Mahatma Gandhi was assassinated in 1948, she rushed to his Indian home, where family and friends warmly welcomed her, but asked her to take no pictures. She smuggled a camera in anyway, and took a shot before being thrown out. She even tried to get back in.

Bourke-White has been described as arrogant, demanding, and manipulative. But media critics point out that timidity and good photojournalism rarely mix well. The best photojournalists are tenacious, and Bourke-White is the quintessential example.

Bourke-White was one of the first female photojournalists in the United States, the first person in the United States to publish a photo story, and the first woman photographer attached to the U.S. armed forces during World War II. She didn't shy away from danger. She covered the infantry in the Italian campaign, and then covered the siege of Moscow. Her pictures of emaciated inmates in concentration camps and corpses in gas chambers stunned the world. Later, she covered the Korean War.

Bourke-White published six books in her lifetime. She came down contracted Parkinson's disease in 1952 and died in 1971.

Source: Elsa Dorfman, "A Review of Margaret Bourke-White: A Biography, by Vici Goldberg," *The Women's Review of Books* (March 1997).

B-picture see *B-rated film.*

Bradford, William (1663-1752) a printer who gained notoriety in the American colonies for publishing a copy of the colony's charter without first obtaining permission from local authorities.

Bradford, who had operated a printing press in Pennsylvania since 1685, published the colony's charter in 1689. He was ordered not to do any more printing without a license.

He then helped set up a paper mill. Bradford got into trouble again in 1692 and the authorities seized his press, but he was not punished. Eventually, though, Bradford was appointed to the position of Royal Printer to New York, a post he held for nearly a half century.

See *Franklin, Benjamin; Franklin, James; Harris, Benjamin;* and *prior restraint.*

Brady, Mathew B. (1822-1896) a 19th-century photographer best known for his pictures of the American Civil War.

Brady learned to take *daguerreotypes* in the 1840s. He opened studios and began taking portraits of presidents, politicians and famous people, including Daniel Webster, Edgar Allan Poe, and James Fenimore Cooper.

When the Civil War broke out, Brady decided to make a complete record of that conflict. He hired two dozen photographers and stationed them throughout the war zones. He invested $100,000 in the project, but after the war the government showed no interest in his project. He went bankrupt.

The War Department eventually purchased his pictures at auction for $2,840. The government paid him $25,000, but Brady never recovered and died an alcoholic in a hospital charity ward.

Source: Roy Meredith, *Mathew Brady's Portrait of an Era* (New York: W. W. Norton & Company, 1982).

brainwashing the act of changing a person's attitude, belief and/or value system through the use of psychological or physically coercive methods, such as through the use of *propaganda.*

brand a name and/or symbol used to identify a product or service.

brand awareness the percentage of *respondents* aware of a product, service or company after being prompted with questions or materials.

Measures of brand awareness are used frequently in *advertising tracking studies.*

See *advertising awareness.*

branding the process of assigning a name and/or symbol to identify a product or service.

More specifically, there are several ways to brand a product for sale:

1. Create your own brand. This involves using a company name or creating a separate brand name for the product line(s) or specific product.

2. Private Label. This involves packaging a product as a "store brand" or for another product company that can market the product as their own. Many food service products are privately labeled.

3. <u>Control Brand.</u> This involves packaging a product for exclusive distribution in a given geographical area or for specific markets. Typically, arrangements are made with one distributor for a given "control brand."
4. <u>Co-Branding.</u> This can be various combinations of the above options.

brand loyalty the degree to which consumers prefer one brand name product over another.

breach of confidentiality an area of media law which holds that a confidential source can sue a news organization if the news agency violates a confidentiality agreement.
This principle was articulated in Cohen v. Cowles Media (1991). Dan Cohen was a public relations consultant working for a candidate in the Minnesota governor's race. Cohen obtained copies of documents which showed that the opponent's running mate had admitted to shoplifting 12 years earlier. Reporters at local daily newspapers agreed to keep Cohen's name confidential. However, editors of the two newspapers overruled the reporters and stories identified Cohen as the source.
Cohen sued for breach of contract. The high court ruled that newspapers have no special immunity from general laws. Cohen was eventually awarded $200,000 in damages. Many journalists sided with Cohen in this case, because they believed the editors' decision to violate the confidentiality agreement was unethical.
Source: *Cohen v. Cowles Media,* 501 U.S. 663 (1991).

breaking news a journalist term referring to news that is unfolding in the present moment.
Also called *spot news.*

Brinkley, David (1920-2003) co-anchor for the "NBC Evening News" with Chet Huntley from 1956-1970.

British Broadcasting Corporation (BBC) a British broadcasting company that is chartered and funded by the government and operates as an independent company accountable to the people of Great Britain.

British cultural studies see *cultural studies.*

B-rated film a low-budget movie.

broadband a technology that allows high-speed transmission of multiple channels of digital data (voice, video, and text) over a single communications medium, often used to access the Internet.
The term broadband usually refers to high-speed service provided via a coaxial television cable. Wireless broadband technologies are now

becoming available, and may eventually surpass cable because there are no cables to string and maintain.

See *digital subscriber line.*

Broadcast Data Systems a weekly service that tracks 300 radio stations.

broadside (or broadsheet) a larger version of a *flysheet* that appeared after Gutenberg's movable-type printing press around 1450.

In England, broadsides were often published prior to public executions and were sold to spectators.

Most daily newspapers today are broadsheet, which is about 14 by 22 inches. Some newspapers are tabloid-sized, which is half the size of a broadsheet, or about 11 by 14 inches.

See *flysheet* and *Gutenberg, Johannes.*

Brown, Charles Brocken (1771-1810) early novelist and magazine publisher.

Brown has been called the "Stephen King of the late 18th and early 19th centuries." His first novel, "Wieland" (1798), is the story of Theodore Wieland, a religious enthusiast seeking direct communication with divinity. Wieland's father violates a vow to God and dies by spontaneous combustion. Wieland mistakenly assumes a ventriloquist's utterances are supernatural. Wieland goes insane and, acting upon the prompting of an "inner voice," murders his wife and children. When he learns about his deeds, he kills himself.

Brown called himself a "story-telling moralist." Many literary scholars today call him the founder of the American novel. In the magazine field, he is known as the first publisher to clearly articulate a philosophy for the field. In 1803, he founded "Literary Magazine" and "American Register."

The purpose of a magazine, he said, was to enlighten and amuse. In fact, in the first issue of "Literary Magazine and American Register," he said he had called upon his literary friends to contribute articles that "warm and enlighten." He added that many magazines fail financially because of lack of commitment to a set of principles, but the "public is always eager to encourage one who devotes himself to their rational amusement." He also noted that magazines, because they publish less frequently than daily newspapers, have more time to reflect and comment on the news.

Unfortunately, his own magazine only lasted four years. But his philosophy helped justify the role and function of magazines in society—a perspective that survives even today.

Source: James Playsted Wood, *Magazines in the United States: Their Social and Economic Influence* (New York: The Ronald Press Company, 1949), p. 37.

Brown, Helen Gurley (1922-) magazine editor who turned "Cosmopolitan" into a the leading magazine for young, professional women.

In 1965, Brown took over the editorship of "Cosmopolitan" magazine, a literary publication that was rapidly losing readers. The author of the best-selling book "Sex and the Single Girl," Brown turned "Cosmopolitan" into a magazine for young, career-minded women. Circulation climbed, and today "Cosmopolitan" has a circulation of about 3 million.

browser software that enables a computer user to link to the Internet and the *World Wide Web* and see or hear the images and text.

Netscape Navigator and Microsoft Internet Explorer are two examples of browser software.

bulletin board see *newsgroup*.

bureaucracy see *corporate media*.

business manager the person in a media organization who is responsible for the financial affairs of the company.

Accountants and bookkeepers report to this person and keep an eye on the bottom line.

buying intent see *purchase intent*.

C

Cable News Network (CNN) a cable television news network founded by Ted Turner, headquartered in Atlanta, and now owned by Time Warner, Inc.

See *Turner, Ted.*

cable television see *Community Antenna Television* and *television.*

callback another attempt to interview a potential *respondent* over the telephone, usually made because that person was not available on a previous attempt.

camcorder a television camera and videotape recorder combined into a portable unit.

camera a device for capturing and reproducing still or moving pictures.

The first camera was offered for sale in 1839 in London. In 1888, George Eastman produced the first camera that used roll-film.

See *daguerreotype* and *cinematographer.*

cameras in the courtroom a judicial rule or law that allows journalists to photograph and/or broadcast video from a *court of law.*

Before 1935, cameras and newsreels were widely permitted in trial courts in the United States. That changed after the trial of Bruno Richard Hauptmann, who was executed for kidnapping and murdering Charles Lindbergh's child. The coverage of the Hauptmann trial was likened to a "Roman holiday." In response, almost every state enacted laws or rules that banned in-court photography.

But in the mid-1970s, cameras began making a comeback in the courtroom. Proponents argue that the cameras promote openness and greater understanding of courts and, if properly controlled, do not interfere with the conduct of a trial. Today, 48 states (all but Mississippi and South Dakota) and the federal courts allow cameras in the courtroom under some conditions. The U.S. Supreme Court still maintains a ban on cameras, but the court has released audio recordings of its hearings.

Source: John Caher, "Decision Expected Shortly in Latest Challenge Over Ban on Cameras in Courts," *New York Law Journal* (May 14, 2001), p. 1.

campaign an organized effort to promote a candidate, idea, product, company or service, often used by politicians and advertising and public relations practitioners.

Campbell, John (1653-1728) publisher of the first continuously circulated machine-printed newspaper in the American colonies.

Although *Benjamin Harris* published the first machine-printed newspaper in the colonies in 1690, the authorities shut it down after one issue. Fourteen years later, on April 24, 1704, Campbell published the "Boston News-Letter." Campbell was a local postmaster who previously had been issuing handwritten newsletters to colonial authorities. Unlike Harris, Campbell made a special effort to please authorities, which helped the weekly survive for nearly two decades.

See *Harris, Benjamin.*

Cambridge Press the first print shop in the American colonies, established in 1630 in Cambridge, Mass.

From 1630 to 1670, Cambridge Press published 157 books and pamphlets. Of those, 63 were religious, four were poetry, eight were historical or biographical, and the rest were schoolbooks, official publications, Harvard (College) theses, and almanacs.

The first document printed was the "Freeman's Oath," to which every householder in the colonies had to subscribe before becoming a citizen of the colony. The oath, of course, was a mechanism of *social control*—a way of ensuring obedience to the Crown. The first book, entitled the "Bay Psalm Book," was published in 1640.

Cambridge Press was the only print shop in the colonies for 37 years. It closed in 1692, after which printing presses were set up in Boston, Philadelphia, and New York.

Sources: John Tebbel, *A History of Book Publishing in the United States: Volume I, The Creation of an Industry, 1630-1865* (New York: R. R. Bowker, 1972).

Carey, Mathew (1760-1839) an author and publisher who established the first successful general publishing house in the United States.

Carey fled Ireland in 1784 for the American colonies to avoid being imprisoned for publishing a newspaper whose purpose was, in his own words, "to defend the commerce, the manufacturers and the political rights of Ireland against the oppression and encroachment of Great Britain."

With a $400 loan from the famous Frenchman Lafayette, who'd helped the colonists win the Revolutionary War, Mathew established the "Pennsylvania Herald." The paper aligned itself with colonists who supported a strong central or federal government (Constitutionalists). The paper was very successful, but he sold it in 1788.

A year later he published his first book—the Douay (Catholic) Bible. The book was very successful. He published Protestant bibles, nature books, science books, literature, fiction, autobiographies, and children's books. He earned $300,000 in nine years, an amount that in today's dollars would be worth tens of millions.

Carey was also a book seller, establishing a statewide network of *booksellers*. He drew up a constitution for the American Company of Booksellers, the first professional book association. He also wrote several books himself, including "The Olive Branch."

Carey also gets credit for being one of the first publishers to create within his organization a *division of labor*—that is, specialized roles for employees. He had so much business that some employees only set type, while others set up and ran the printing presses or spent their time proofreading. The proofreader role became a recognized trade after the turn of the century.

Source: J. E. Hagerty, "Mathew Carey," in *The Catholic Encyclopedia, Vol. III* (New York: Robert Appleton Co., 1908; Online Edition, 1999, Kevin Knight).

carrier a person who delivers newspapers to homes and businesses.

Carson, Rachel Louise (1907-1964) an author whose book "Silent Spring" helped mobilize the environmental movement in the United States.

In 1957, a biologist sent Carson a copy of a letter to the editor which documented how the pesticide DDT had killed birds near her home. At the time, the public knew little about the dangers of DDT and other pesticides. Although many biologists and environmental scientists were aware of the dangers, the mainstream mass media had ignored many pleas to look into the problem.

Carson, who had worked for the U.S. Fish and Wildlife Service, contacted "The New Yorker" magazine, which suggested that she write the article herself. Carson ended up writing a book in 1962 and called it "Silent Spring"—a title originally intended for the book's chapter on birds.

Carson's argument was that indiscriminate use of pesticides and other chemicals could destroy life on earth. Chemicals were getting into the food chain and threatening all forms of biological life. She also criticized the government for spraying without first informing citizens, so they could take precautions, and for not conducting more research into the impact of chemicals on wildlife and ecosystems.

The U.S. chemical industry tried to discredit Carson, but the negative publicity backfired and created even more interest in her book. President John F. Kennedy asked the Science Advisory Committee to examine the effects of pesticides, and the Committee issued a formal report that backed up most of Carson's claims.

By the end of 1962, more than 40 bills had been introduced in various states to regulate the use of pesticides. In 1970, the U.S. government created the Environmental Protection Agency. In 1973, DDT was banned in the United States. And most importantly, "Silent Spring" helped mobilize environmental groups and movements around the world.

Unfortunately, Carson did not live long enough to see most of these social changes. She died of cancer in 1964.

See *book*, *social control* and *social change*.

Sources: Rachel Carson, *Silent Spring* (Greenwich, CN: Fawcett Publications, 1962).

cartoon a drawing or series of drawings or a short, animated moving picture that is usually intended to be humorous.

See *animated film* and *comics*.

cases the *unit of analysis* in a survey.

Usually, the cases are people (i.e., *respondents*). But cases may be a market (e.g., county or city) or an organization.

casting director the person who selects and hires the actors and helps negotiate contracts.

The *director* and *producer* are usually involved in selecting stars for lead roles.

Cataloging-in-Publication (CIP) data information created by the Library of Congress for the purpose of classifying books for storage in libraries and for retrieval through the Library of Congress subject headings cataloging system.

The CIP data is usually published on the copyright page of a book. The CIP data for this book, for example, is on page 4 of this book. The first of three sets of numbers at the bottom applies to libraries that classify books under the Library of Congress system; the second set is for those that use the Dewey Decimal system; and the third is a Library of Congress Control Number that is used to identify the book. The first four digits identify the year and the last six are a serial number.

In addition to providing basic information such as author name and title of the book, the CIP also includes information to help readers find books on various topics. This book is a reference book and thus is classified with other dictionaries of mass media. Thus, if one does a Library of Congress search and types in either of these three headings, this book along with others like it will pop up. The CIP also usually indicates whether the book has an index, bibliography, and illustrations.

To get CIP cataloging, a rough draft of the book is sent to librarians at the Library of Congress before publication. Self-published books are not eligible.

Cato's Letters a series of commentaries published between 1720 and 1723 in the "London Journal" that discussed the theories of liberty, representative government, and freedom of expression.

The commentaries, written by John Trenchard and Thomas Gordon, who used the pen name "Cato," had a strong influence in the colonies prior to the Revolutionary War.

causal analysis research that focuses on *cause and effect.*

category see *attributes* and *values (statistical).*

cathartic effect (or sublimation) the notion that viewing violent media content makes people less, not more, aggressive.
See *media violence.*

cause and effect the notion that all phenomena in the physical world, including behavior, is not random but has specific causes that can be isolated and studied through research.

To establish a cause and effect relationship, researchers usually say three criteria are needed: (1) The cause must precede the effect, (2) The cause and effect must be associated or related (see *association* and *relationship*), and (3) Other causes cannot be producing the effect of the cause under consideration (i.e., no *spuriousness*).

The first two are relatively easy to establish. The third is, strictly speaking, impossible to establish. Researchers can never rule out all of the possible variables or factors that may be producing an observed effect. However, through the application of sound logic and/or good *theory*, most researchers believe that one can draw conclusions about *data* that will produce useful results for marketing products and services or understanding mass media.

CBS (Columbia Broadcasting System) a *television network* owned by Viacom.

cell **(a)** in a *crosstabulation*, the *frequency* obtained for the joint distribution of one category, or *attribute*, from two *variables*; **(b)** in *sampling*, different groups of people who will be surveyed.

censor an official with the power to remove or prohibit the publication of material or the distribution of content.
See *First Amendment* and *prior restraint.*

censorship the act of removing or prohibiting publication or distribution of content.
See *First Amendment* and *prior restraint.*

census a *survey* of an entire *population.*

Center for Media and Democracy a nonprofit group that serves as a watchdog on mass media and public relations organizations.

The Center publishes "PR Watch," a quarterly journal that investigates public relations agencies that distort the truth. In addition to news and information, the organization's Web site <www.prwatch.org> includes forums that discuss PR issues and agencies.

central limit theorem a *theory* which states that *mean* and *variance* of a *sample* will equal the *population* mean and variance as the size of the sample increases.

See *sampling error*.

central location test a study in which *respondents* are brought to a facility and are asked to test a product before rating it.

Central location tests are frequently used for testing food and consumer products.

central tendency the average *value* in a *distribution*.

See *mean, median,* and *mode*.

centralization of ownership see *concentration of ownership*.

chain newspaper (or news organization) two or more newspapers (or organizations), in separate cities, owned by the same individual or company.

A newspaper not owned by a chain is often called an *independent newspaper* organization. During the 1970s and 1980s, many researchers studied the differences between chain and independent newspapers. Contrary to expectations, the findings generally showed that chain newspapers produced a more professional news product.

However, the research was criticized for employing crude measurement methods—i.e., a small chain of two newspapers was considered no different from a large chain with 100 newspapers. Since then, research has focused on using more complex variables, such as *corporate media* structure. In other words, chain ownership is just one measure or indicator of a organizational complexity.

See *corporate media*.

Source: David Pearce Demers, *The Menace of the Corporate Newspaper: Fact or Fiction?* (Ames: Iowa State University Press, 1996).

challenge programming see *programming*.

Chancellor, John (1927-1996) anchored the "NBC Evening News" from 1970-1982.

change agent an individual or organization that produces *social change*.

channel a frequency assigned to a radio or television station.

channel capacity the number of television or radio channels available through a cable or satellite system.

Children's Television Act of 1990, The a federal law that gave the Federal Communications Commission the authority to regulate the number of advertisements and the amount of entertainment content on broadcast television programs targeted to children.

The law requires over-the-air television stations seeking a license renewal to serve "the educational and informational needs of children." Basically, this means that some Saturday morning programming must be geared toward education, not just to entertainment. The Commission, from time to time, has delayed a license renewal when a station has not been able to meet this standard.

The Children's Television Act also limits commercial time during children's programming to 10½ minutes an hour on weekends and 12 minutes on weekdays. The limits apply to programming directed at children 12 and younger, since some in this age group cannot distinguish between commercial and noncommercial content.

chi-square an *inferential statistic* used with nominal or ordinal measures (i.e., qualitative or rank-order data).

See *levels of measurement.*

Chomsky, Noam (1928-) a world-renowned linguist who is best known in mass communication for his theory of propaganda, which argues that "the mass media of the United States are effective and powerful ideological institutions that carry out a system-supportive *propaganda* function by reliance on market forces, internalized assumptions, and self-*censorship*, and without significant overt coercion."

Chomsky built his worldwide academic reputation as a linguist. But during the Vietnam War he gained fame as America's best-known and most beloved critic of the war and U.S. foreign policy. Much of his writing since then has focused on misuse of power, mass media, and ideology.

In "Manufacturing Consent," Chomsky and Edward S. Herman, a professor emeritus of finance, present a theory of propaganda that "sees the media as serving a 'societal purpose,' but not that of enabling the public to assert meaningful control over the political process by providing them with the information needed for the intelligent discharge of political responsibilities. On the contrary, a propaganda model suggests that the 'societal purpose' of the media is to inculcate and defend the economic, social, and political agenda of privileged groups that dominate the domestic society and the state."

Chomsky also has argued that the propaganda system in the United States is far more insidious than propaganda systems in communist countries, because most people here think their news media are free and independent and, thus, are more likely to believe what they read and hear. But most people in communist countries know their news media are biased and often discount news reports.

Empirical research supports the main propositions of the propaganda theory. Research overwhelming shows that mass media, like other social institutions (e.g., schools, police, churches), produce content that supports dominant societal values and elite groups, often to the detriment of groups that represent the interests of minorities, workers, women, environmentalists, and homosexuals.

However, the theory has been criticized for failing to explain social change in the 20th century. If the mass media are simply tools of propaganda, then how can one explain the legislative and judicial changes that have on occasion provided some assistance to groups outside the power structure?

The theory of propaganda implies that mainstream news media are incapable of legitimizing or facilitating such changes, especially as news media grow and acquire the characteristics of the corporate form of organization. "[T]he dominant media firms are quite large businesses; they are controlled by very wealthy people or by managers who are subject to sharp constraints by owners and other market-profit-oriented forces; and they are closely interlocked, and have important common interests, with other major corporations, banks, and government."

See *ideology* and *corporate media*.

Sources: Edward S. Herman and Noam Chomsky, *Manufacturing Consent: The Political Economy of the Mass Media* (New York: Pantheon Books, 1988) and David Demers, "Questioning Chomsky 17 Years Later," *Global Media News*, 7(1/2):1, 4-6.

cinema a movie theater

CinemaScope see *aspect ratio*.

Cinématographe a device that functioned both as a camera and as a projector.

The Cinématographe was invented by French brothers Auguste and Louis Lumiére. It was much more economical than the *Kinetograph*,, because it ran at a speed of 16 frames per second rather than 40, using much less film. The Cinématographe also was lightweight (less than 20 pounds) and portable, which meant that film making could leave the studio. In fact, most of the early Lumiére films were shot outdoors. They were called documentaries, or "actualities."

See *Edison, Thomas Alva*.

cinematographer (also called director of photography or first cameraperson) the person responsible for operating or directing the cameras and implementing the *director*'s intentions in terms of mood and atmosphere of each scene.

cinematography the art of photography in film making.
See *cinematographer*.

circulation the total number of magazines, newspapers, newsletters or other printed materials distributed to a population or an area.

circulation manager the person responsible for enlisting new subscribers and for coordinating the delivery of magazines, newspapers or other printed materials to subscribers and/or to newsstands.

Citizen Kane see *Welles, George Orson*.

civic journalism (also called public journalism) a method of collecting news from ordinary people instead of from bureaucrats or powerful elites, such as state legislators, city hall officials, and corporate executives.

The civic journalism movement emerged in the early 1990s partly in response to concerns that news media were relying too heavily on powerful people and institutions for news. Critics argued that news media often failed to give a voice to the poor and working and middle-class people.

Civic journalism often begins with a social problem and seeks to understand that problem through forums and interviews that include ordinary citizens and the public. *Focus groups* are sometimes used as forums for gathering such information.

Although thousands of different projects have been conducted, the impact of this movement on journalism and social policy has been limited. Newspapers in smaller communities typically could not afford to conduct civic journalism projects. And, ironically, the movement has also been criticized for engaging in too much "advocacy journalism." In particular, traditional journalists, conservative critics, and bureaucrats often viewed civic journalism as an effort to challenge or change the status quo.

Nevertheless, the movement has drawn attention to the fact that traditional "objective" journalism, with its heavy dependence on powerful elites for news, is far from "objective" and reinforces mass communication research, which shows that traditional journalism contains a *mainstream bias*.
See *Pew Center for Civic Journalism*.
Source: Theodore L. Glasser (ed.), *The Idea of Public Journalism* (New York: The Guilford Press, 1999).

classical Marxism the theories and ideas of Karl Marx, unaltered.
See *neo-Marxism*.

classified advertising (or want ad) an inexpensive form of print advertising in which text is usually set in a small typeface and the advertisements are arranged according to product or service offered. See *display advertising.*

clear and present danger a legal principle which says that the government can prohibit speech only when it produces or is likely to produce violent actions or illegal behavior.

The clear and present danger principle was first introduced into American law during World War I, but the principle was not fully embraced until the 1960s. At issue in a series of U.S. Supreme Court opinions over a 50-year period was whether the United States government could punish Americans who published and distributed materials that were highly critical of the U.S. government, especially during wartime.

The first case (Schenck v. United States, 1919) involved Charles Schenck, the general secretary of the Socialist party in the United States during World War I. He and an associate were convicted on a charge of conspiracy to violate the Espionage Act of June 15, 1917. They had published and distributed to draftees a flier that urged them to refuse to serve.

The case reached the U.S. Supreme Court in 1919. The high court noted that in many places and at many times the defendant would have been within his constitutional rights to call for such action. But the court upheld the conviction, saying "the most stringent protection of free speech would not protect a man in falsely shouting fire in a theater and causing a panic. ... The question in every case is whether the words used are used in such circumstances and are of such a nature as to create a clear and present danger that they will bring about the substantive evils that Congress has a right to prevent."

In the same year, the court also ruled against five other socialists (Abrams v. United States, 1919) who were accused of publishing and disseminating pamphlets attacking the American expeditionary force sent to Russia by President Woodrow Wilson to defeat the Bolsheviks. The pamphlets also called for a general strike of munitions workers.

Again, the majority of the Supreme Court ruled that the publishing and distribution of the pamphlets during the war were not protected expression. However, in terms of impact on subsequent law, it was not the majority opinion but Justice Oliver Wendell Holmes' opinion that had the most impact. Holmes basically argued that the pamphlets distributed by Abrams did not attack the form of government of the United States. "It is only the present danger of immediate evil or an intent to bring it about that warrants Congress in setting a limit to the expression of opinion where private rights are not concerned."

In 1925, the high court once again ruled against a socialist who had been indicted for publishing a radical "manifesto" that urged people to go on strike (Gitlow v. People of the State of New York, 1925). But the court, for the first time, applied the *First Amendment* to the states. In other words, state governments were now prohibited from passing laws abridging freedom of speech and the press. That was not true before Gitlow.

However, the high court was still reluctant to protect socialists' expression. In two more cases after Gitlow, the court ruled against the socialist expression. In one of those cases (Dennis v. United States, 1951), the court ruled that teaching people to overthrow the U.S. government, even in cases where no action to do so was taken, is not protected speech.

In 1957, the high court began to reverse itself. It ruled that people can talk all they want about overthrowing the government (Yates v. United States, 1957). They can even express hope that a revolution will succeed. But they cannot actually attempt to carry such plans out or to commit illegal acts. In other words, they could not take action.

This ruling effectively brought an end to sedition trials. But an even more important decision was handed down in 1969. The case involved a Ku Klux Klan leader who was convicted of violating an Ohio law that prohibited unlawful methods of terrorism and crime as a means of accomplishing industrial and political reform (Brandenburg v. Ohio, 1969).

The high court voided his conviction because the Ohio law failed to distinguish between advocacy of ideas and incitement to unlawful conduct. "The constitutional guarantees of free speech and free press do not permit a State to forbid or proscribe advocacy of the use of force or of law violation except where such advocacy is directed to inciting or producing imminent lawless action or is likely to incite or produce such actions."

See *fighting words doctrine, hate speech,* and *hostile audience problem.*
Sources: *Schenck v. United States,* 249 U.S. 47 (1919); *Schenck v. United States,* 249 U.S. 47 (1919); *Gitlow v. People of the State of New York,* 268 U.S. 652 (1925); *Whitney v. California,* 274 U.S. 357 (1927); *Dennis v. United States,* 341 U.S. 494 (1951); *Yates v. United States,* 354 U.S. 298 (1957); and *Brandenburg v. Ohio,* 395 U.S. 444 (1969).

client (a) a person or organization that hires a mass communication firm or business (e.g., *advertising, public relations,* and *market research* firms) to solve a communication and/or marketing problem; **(b)** a computer connected to the Internet (see *host*).

close-ended measure a *question* in a survey that includes a list of answers from which *respondents* are asked to choose.
Here's an example: "How likely will you be to buy this product in the next six months? Very likely, somewhat likely, somewhat unlikely, or very unlikely?"

cluster analysis a *descriptive statistic* and also a *multivariate statistic* that groups *respondents* or *cases* on the basis of similar characteristics.
Cluster analysis is often used to create market segments that then can be targeted through advertising or marketing campaigns.
See *market segmentation, target marketing,* and *public relations campaign.*

cluster sampling a method of *sampling* which involves dividing the *population* into two or more subgroups and sampling from some, not all, of the subgroups.

For example, a *survey* might be administered to a sample of adults in 10 of 20 regions of the United States. Cluster sampling generally is less costly and time consuming than *stratified sampling*, but it contains more sampling error because not all subgroups, or clusters, are sampled. In fact, cluster sampling is subject to two sampling errors—one at the point where clusters are sampled and the other at the point where *cases* are selected in each cluster.

If the total number of actual clusters is small, cluster sampling should be used only if there is a high level of homogeneity between the clusters.

See *probability sampling*.

codebook a document used in data processing that contains information about *variables*, *values* of variables, and column locations in the dataset spreadsheet or file.

codes of ethics see *ethics*.

codex a format in which pages of a document or book are bound instead of being rolled up, like a scroll.

By the 6th century, about 90 percent of all books or long manuscripts were codex. Almost all books today are codex, but the term is antiquated and now is generally reserved to historical discussions about books.

coding the process of transforming responses in a survey into numbers for computer analysis.

coercion a type of social interaction in which an individual or group is compelled to behave in certain ways either by force or threat of force.

Although punishment or the threat of punishment often is effective in controlling individuals and organizations, non-coercive means of control, such as *socialization*, are often more effective and less expensive.

cognition the process of thinking, which includes memory, perception, judgment, and other factors that contribute to learning and knowing.

cognitive dissonance a state of mental discomfort created when information received is inconsistent with a person's previous *behaviors*, *attitudes* or *beliefs*.

An interesting finding in market research is that people's ratings of goods and services often increase after they buy them. Any reservations about the product or service diminish after the purchase, since such reservations would create dissonance.

cohort study a *longitudinal study* in which data is collected and analyzed over time from people sharing similar characteristics.

Generally, a cohort is defined as an age group. Thus, a *population* might be defined as everyone born in the 1960s, and samples from that group are drawn every five years to study how the cohort changes.

collateral materials service or products—such as research, published materials, photography, presentations—provided above and beyond the terms of a standard consulting contract.

Public relations firms and advertising firms usually charge additional fees for collateral materials.

colonization (of the mind) a pejorative term referring to media content or other cultural phenomena that subvert or distort genuine *attitudes*, *beliefs* or *values*.

Advertising messages, for example, are often accused of colonizing people's minds, drawing them into the dominant culture and encouraging unnecessary consumption of goods and services.

comics a cartoon or series of cartoons printed in newspapers or in paper booklets that usually tell a humorous or adventurous story.

The *Yellow Kid* is generally accepted as the first comic strip. It appeared in the "New York Sunday World" on Feb. 16, 1896. Most daily newspapers were publishing comics in the early 1900s.

In 1911, a collection of "Mutt and Jeff" comic strips from the "Chicago American" newspaper was published in book form. The first true comic book was published in 1929. "The Funnies" was a four-color book the size of a tabloid newspaper. The adventure genre in comic book publishing came in 1929 with the publication of "Tarzan" and "Buck Rogers."

In 1938, the comic book publishing industry received a further boost with the appearance of Action Comics' "Superman," which became a bestseller. "Superman" was followed by "Batman," "Wonder Woman," the "Green Lantern," "Fantastic Four" and "Spider Man."

The content of comic books became increasingly violent after World War II. Sales soared during the 1950s, but so did criticism. Psychiatrist Fredric Wertham became the leading anti-comic book moralist. His book, "Seduction of the Innocent," rocked the nation with claims that comic books were leading children into a life of crime and homosexual behavior. Although the industry placated the public with some self-censorship reforms, Wertham's claims were vastly exaggerated and unscientific, and he was discredited by other social scientists.

Like other forms of media, the comic book has followed a course of increasing specialization. Current genres include humor, action and adventure, mystery, politics, horror, and science fiction. The comic book also adopted the 32-page format, which was easy to print, carry and store.

In recent years, comic books have fallen on hard times. Sales have dropped from $850 million in 1993 to $200 million in 2003.

See *Yellow Kid.*

Sources: Michael Emery, Edwin Emery and Nancy L. Roberts, *The Press and America: An Interpretive History of the Mass Media,* 9th ed. (Boston: Allyn and Bacon, 2000); Teena Massingill, "Video Games Are Zapping Comic Books," Spokane *Spokesman-Review* (October 29, 2000), pp. D1, D4; James M. Pethokoukis, "Help, Spidey, Help! Comics Are Dying!" *U.S. News & World Report* (September 25, 2000), Vol. 129, No. 12; and Fredric Wertham, *Seduction of the Innocent* (New York, Rinehart, 1954).

comic book *see comics.*

commercial advertising see *advertising.*

commercial radio radio programming supported primarily by advertising revenues.

See *radio.*

commercial speech speech created for purposes of selling or promoting a product or service.

The U.S. Supreme Court has provided some legal protection to commercial speech but not as much as that for political speech.

The most definitive ruling on commercial speech comes from Central Hudson Gas & Electric Corporation v. Public Service Commission (1980). In an effort to conserve electricity, the New York Public Service Commission tried to ban utility company advertising that promoted the use of electricity.

The high court held that the ban violated the *First Amendment* rights of the utility company. The court ruled the government could restrict commercial expression if such expression were unlawful or misleading. But if that were not the case, then the government would need to demonstrate a substantial gain to be made in regulating the speech, and the proposed regulation would not be more extensive than necessary to advance the government interest.

See *corporate speech* and *symbolic speech.*

Sources: *Central Hudson Gas & Electric Corp. v. Public Service Commission,* 447 U.S. 557 (1980).

commercial television see *television* and *public television.*

commercialization the process of converting a not-for-profit organization or activity into a for-profit enterprise, or a commercial organization or activity.

This term, like *commodification,* is usually used pejoratively.

commodification the act or process of turning not-for-profit goods or services into commodities for sale.

The term "commodification"—and its close companion commercialization—most often appears in critiques of capitalism and advertising, and it almost always carries a negative connotation. Many scholars and media critics believe commodification is destroying indigenous culture and meaningful relations between people and groups. They often place the blame on corporations and *corporate media*.

commonality language, beliefs, culture or ideas that are shared among people.

communication the act of imparting, conferring or delivering messages, such as words or ideas, within or between groups of people.

The most popular statement about the process of communication comes from political scientist Harold Lasswell, who said the best way to study communication was to answer these five questions: (1) Who? (2) Says what? (3) In which channel? (4) To whom? (5) With what effect? More formally, these five questions correspond to five elements: a sender, a message, a medium, a recipient, and an effect. The illustration above shows the relationship between these elements. A sender creates or distributes a message through some medium to a recipient with some effect. More specifically:

1. The sender is the individual or organization that creates the message. Examples include newspapers, television stations or public relations companies, which are specifically organized to create messages for distribution to people.

In mass communication, the sender usually does not personally know the recipient. The sender also may not be able to control who receives a message, although a great deal of effort is often made to target specific kinds of people or audiences (see *market segmentation* and *target* marketing).

2. The message may be in the form of symbols, words or sentences, ideas, concepts, pictures, or any combination thereof. The message may be simple, complex or incomprehensible. The process of creating the message is referred to as *encoding*.

Understanding is not necessary for communication to take place, but shared understanding is usually necessary in order for people and organizations to achieve goals.

3. The medium (plural form is media) or "channel," as Lasswell calls it, is the mechanism through which the message is transmitted to the recipient. The medium may be verbal (spoken words), written (newspaper story), electronic (television program), nonverbal (hand gesture), or a combination of these (telephone conversation, for example, involves a combination of the verbal and electronic elements).

4. The recipient may be an individual or an organization, such as a newspaper reader or television viewer. The act of interpreting the message is called *decoding*.

If the recipient decodes or interprets the message in a manner identical to or close to the meaning intended by the sender, then *congruence* is said to exist. In other words, there is shared understanding.

When something interferes with the delivery of a message, this is called *noise*.

5. An effect occurs when some communication has taken place, even if the message is distorted. If the recipient did not receive the message, then no communication has taken place. But other effects are possible.

The recipient may use the information or contents of the message to make decisions or to take action. The recipient may also ignore or forget the message. In general, as time passes, the level of congruence between the original message and the recipient's recall of that message diminishes. Memories fade.

6. Feedback occurs when the recipient sends a message to the sender. The recipient then becomes the sender, and the communication process begins anew. Letters to the editor are an obvious example.

Also see *intrapersonal communication, interpersonal communication, group communication,* and *mass communication.*

Source: Harold D. Lasswell, "The Structure and Function of Communication in Society," in L. Bryson (ed.), *The Communication of Ideas* (New York: Harper, 1948).

Communications Act of 1934 a law passed by Congress that converted the Federal Radio Commission into the *Federal Communications Commission* (FCC), an agency that continues to regulate broadcast media and other telecommunications services.

The law, which superseded the Radio Act of 1927, gave the FCC control over wireless as well as wired communications, such as the telephone. The law also gave the FCC power to place limits on how many radio (and eventually television) stations one individual or company could own. Eventually, one individual or company was not allowed to own more than seven AM radio stations and seven FM stations, and no more than one AM and one FM in the same market. The seven-station limit also was imposed on the television industry in the 1950s, but since then *media ownership rules* have relaxed.

See *media ownership rules, Radio Act of 1912, Radio Act of 1927,* and *Telecommunications Act of 1996.*

Community Antenna Television (CATV) a wire-based television transmission system originally designed for remote areas in Arkansas, Oregon, and Pennsylvania where receiving over-the-air television signals was difficult.

But cable television companies eventually expanded to metropolitan areas, where cable was less costly to install per household and, thus, much more profitable. By 1970, about 4 million homes nationwide had cable television. Nearly 6 of 10 homes today subscribe to cable television.

community relations a department in many public relations firms with the responsibility of maintaining good relations with external publics, including citizens, customers, government officials, elected officials, and other corporations.

Community relations specialists often produce newsletters, fliers and brochures, and often help coordinate or sponsor community events to enhance the organization's image in the community. At many organizations, the community relations and media relations functions are handled by one department or individual.

See *corporate communications, media relations, public* and *public relations.*

compact disc (CD) a small optical disk with digital audio recorded on it.

composer in filmmaking, the person who creates the musical score that accompanies the filmed action. Some composers work with full orchestra, while others work alone, using synthesizers and other sophisticated electronic musical instruments.

computer an electronic device for performing mathematical or logical operations faster than the human mind.

The first mechanically operated computer is credited to *Herman Hollerith.* His machine sorted cards punched with holes. The first electronic computers appeared around World War II.

They were called mainframes, which basically meant they were large, sometimes taking up whole rooms, and were operated by specialized technicians. The minicomputer was smaller and less expensive, but still required a lot of specialized training to operate.

In contrast, the personal computer (PC), which was introduced in the 1980s, could be operated by virtually anyone. The PC, which was much less expensive and much easier to use, now dominates the computer market.

computer-assisted journalism a broad term that refers to a variety of different reporting methods that use computers to create news stories.

See *precision journalism.*

computer-to-plate production (CTP) a pre-printing process in which plates used in printing are created directly from computer images.

CTP eliminates the need for hard-copy layout and negative film-to-plate production. Using digital technology, the plates are produced directly from the computer.

computer virus software programs that attempt to erase information on a computer hard drive or disable a computer.

Viruses often are created by people who wish ill will on users or companies or who get a thrill out of being "cybervandals." Some viruses

are created by political organizations opposed to capitalism and
globalization.
    Most viruses spread through e-mail, when users open attached files.
Opening the files triggers the virus, which then writes or erases information
on a hard drive and sometimes copies itself and automatically e-mails itself
to other e-mail accounts.

concept an idea or a mental image for an abstraction.
    Watching television, age, *concentration of ownership*, income, and
education are examples of concepts. Concepts are the basic elements of
study in *mass communication research*.

concentration of ownership a term to describe the loss of small-scale
media organizations through bankruptcy, media mergers or acquisitions.
    Concentration of ownership is one of the most controversial trends in
mass media today. Many citizens, scholars and professionals believe
concentration of ownership is reducing diversity in the so-called
"marketplace of ideas" and thus threatens democracy. However, the
empirical evidence does not yet provide strong support for such arguments.
    The concept of concentration of ownership can be traced to the
writings of *Karl Marx*, who argued that competition in capitalism would
produce concentration of capital and ownership on a grand scale. More
specifically, he argued that competition drives capitalists incessantly to
search for ways to increase productivity. Capitalists innovate in two ways.
    The first is by increasing the *division of labor*. The second is through the
use of machinery. In either case, the end result is that innovation allows
capitalists to produce more units at a lower per-unit cost and thus reap
increased profits—at least until other competitors adopt the innovation.
When that happens, the supply of the product increases, prices fall, and
"surplus profits" vanish. The price remains relatively stable until another
innovation comes along, and then the cycle starts all over again.
    Marx argued that the major consequences of innovation were
concentration and centralization of capital. He defined concentration as
growth in capital or an increase in the size of companies. Capitalists must
continually reinvest profits in order to remain competitive. Most of the
reinvestment goes to production and development of new machines and
methods for reducing labor costs. This reinvestment increases the size and
scope of mass production and the ratio of capital to the labor process.
However, Marx argued that concentration of capital leads to an increase,
not a decrease, in the number of owners. This increase occurs because,
over time, capital is divided among family members, often through
inheritance, and earmarked for new ventures.
    Although ownership tends to become decentralized as a firm grows,
this process is slow and is more than offset by centralization of capital.
Marx defined centralization as the combining of capitals already formed,

i.e., a reduction in the number of competitive firms in a particular sector of an industry. Centralization occurs in two ways.

The first occurs when larger, more successful companies purchase the assets of weaker, less competitive and innovative firms. Economies of scale are primarily responsible for this centralization.

The second method of centralization occurs through the formation of joint-stock companies, which, Marx argued, often pool large amounts of capital together for the purpose of gaining greater control over a particular market. The credit and banking system plays an important role in funding such ventures.

In the broader context, Marx argued that concentration and centralization of economic power leads to increasing polarization of the classes and, eventually, revolution. Declining rates of profit will force many companies out of business. To remain competitive, others will need to lay off workers and replace them with machinery or lengthen the working day and cut wages. Over time, private enterprise as a whole becomes increasingly oligopolized and monopolized. Class consciousness will emerge as the ranks of the working and unemployed classes increase and will fuel revolutions that overthrow the bourgeoisie.

Scholars widely agree that history generally has failed to support Marx's predictions about the declining rate of profit, polarization of the classes, and revolution. There also is conflicting evidence about whether ownership of capital is becoming increasingly centralized. Some researchers claim that, despite variations across industries, the trend toward centralization has progressed since the 19th century. Others contend that the degree of centralization has changed little since the 19th century—maybe even declined since World War II—and that even in highly concentrated industries there is a great deal of competition.

The debate continues, but few scholars dispute the general observation that concentration of capital exists in many industries, including mass media industries. The top ten global media corporations account for more than half of worldwide advertising revenues. However, critics of concentration of ownership have failed to produce systematic empirical research showing that the diversity of ideas is adversely affected. In fact, scholars and professionals point out that the explosive growth in the Internet (e.g., Weblogs or "blogs") strongly suggests that there is more content critical of dominant groups and mainstream values than at any other time in history.

Sources: Karl Marx, *Capital: A Critique of Political Economy, Vol. 1*, trans. by Samuel Moore and Edward Aveling (New York: International Publishers, 1987 [1867]); S. Aaronovitch and M. Sawyer, *Big Business: Theoretical and Empirical Aspects of Concentration and Mergers in the United Kingdom* (London: Macmillan, 1975), p. 157; J. M. Blair, *Economic Concentration, Structure, Behaviour and Public Policy* (London: Harcourt-Brace, 1972); L. Hannah, *The Rise of the Corporate Economy* (London: Methuen, 1975); Paul M. Sweezy, *The Theory of Capitalist Development* (New York: Modern Reader, 1970); and Paul M. Sweezy and H. Magdoff, *The Dynamics of U.S. Capitalism* (New York: Modern Reader, 1972).

confidence interval a *range*, constructed around a survey finding, where there is a high probability of finding the true *population parameter*.

A confidence interval is one component of *sampling error*. The other is *confidence level*. Usually the confidence interval is calculated using two *standard errors*. The size of the confidence interval is determined by the *confidence level* selected.

See *sampling error*.

confidence level (level of confidence) one component of *sampling error*, more specifically probability theory, states that there is a 68 percent chance that a true *population parameter* lies within the range of one *standard error*. The confidence level, in other words, is 68 percent.

Under most circumstances, market researchers need to be more accurate than this. The most common confidence level used is 95 percent, which is about two standard errors (1.96 to be more accurate). Increasing the level of confidence increases the accuracy of the sampling error estimate, but it also increases the *confidence interval*, which has the effect of lowering the precision of the sampling error estimate.

See *sampling error*.

confidential source a person who gives information to news reporters but is granted anonymity and not cited in a news story.

See *access law*.

confounding variable a *variable* that produces *spuriousness*, which means that a *correlation* or *relationship* between two or more other variables vanishes when the confounding variable is controlled or taken into account.

conglomerate a group of diverse businesses or companies operated as a single organization.

Many advertising agencies are conglomerates, meaning they are composed of a dozen or so advertising, public relations, and marketing research companies, some of which specialize in certain products and services.

congruence the degree of shared understanding between how a message is interpreted and the original intent of sender.

If the recipient decodes or interprets the message in a manner identical to or close to the meaning intended by the sender, then congruence is said to exist.

See *communication*.

conjoint analysis a *descriptive* and *multivariate statistic* that separates consumer judgments into their components.

Conjoint is used primarily to identify the best combination of *attributes* for a particular product or service. For example, consumers might like the colors red and blue and they might like two different sizes of DVD players. But will they like players in both colors? Conjoint analysis helps discover the combination of colors, sizes or other features that appeals most to consumers.

Conrad, Frank (1874-1941) architect of the first commercial venture in radio.

Conrad, an engineer at Westinghouse in Pittsburgh during the 1920s, constructed a small transmitting station in his garage and began broadcasting phonograph records. Soon, people began asking him to play specific songs. He began broadcasting twice a week for two hours in the evening. A local department store then took out advertisements in local newspapers, telling readers they could buy a receiver to listen to Conrad's programs.

Recognizing the market potential of broadcasting, the Westinghouse Corporation, which was already manufacturing radio equipment, asked Conrad to build a 100-watt broadcast station on top of the company's factory. The first commercial radio station, KDKA, went on the air in Pittsburgh on November 2, 1920. The station broadcast the news that Warren Harding had defeated James Cox for president of the United States. By the end of 1921, eight radio stations were operating in the United States.

AT&T corporation launched its first radio station, WEAF, in New York City in 1922. The station broadcast the first paid commercial, which cost $50 and promoted a real estate company. By the end of 1922, the government had granted licenses to more than 550 radio stations. By 1925, more than two million radio sets were being sold per year, and the nationwide radio audience numbered 30 million.

Source: Eric Barnouw, *A History of Broadcasting in the United States*, Vols. 1-3 (New York: Oxford University Press, 1966, 1968, 1970).

constant a *concept* that has only one category, or *value*.

A *constant* is the opposite of a *variable*. If you ask people if they eat food, everyone would say "yes" because everyone eats. This is a constant; people do not differ in terms of this behavior. But if you ask them what they eat, their answers would vary. What they eat is a variable.

See *variable*.

construct a *concept* that is *operationalized* using two or more indices (plural of *index*) that are conceptually distinct but related to each other.

For example, socioeconomic status can be operationalized as the summation of three separate indices: education, income, and occupational prestige. Each of these indices, in turn, can be composed of more than one measure or indicator (e.g., education can be measured as consisting of years of formal public schooling and years of informal training on the job).

See *index*.

consumer a person who buys goods and services.

contagion effect the power of mass media reports to create a popular craze or, alternatively, an epidemic.
See *copycat effect*.

content analysis a methodology that involves collecting data from documents, newspapers or programming rather than from respondents.
The approach may use *quantitative analysis* or *qualitative analysis*.

contingency question a survey *question* that is asked only when a certain response is given to a previous question.

contingency table a table that displays the joint frequency *distribution* of two *variables*.
Same as *crosstabulation*.

continuous measure a *variable* whose *values* can, theoretically, take on any numerical value in a *range* of values.

control group in experimental research design, the group of subjects that resembles the experimental group in all respects except that no experimental stimulus is administered to the control group.

convenience sample a *nonprobability sample* in which *respondents* are selected without regard to the representativeness of the *sample*.
Convenience sampling is useful in the early stages of the study of a particular product or service. *Probability sampling* methods, which are generally more costly, may be employed later.

convergence the idea that traditional media formats (like print versus broadcast) are dying out and converging together (text with audio/video), particularly on the *Internet*.
During the late 1990s, many media scholars and professionals argued that advancing technology, especially the Internet, would kill off traditional media in a relatively short time. Instead of reading a newspaper to get the news of the day, people would go online, where they could also see audio/video news clips.
Of course, that hasn't happened, at least not yet. In fact, daily newspapers (the paper versions) continue to be very profitable. The Internet or some other technology may someday eliminate the paper newspaper, but there's still no concrete evidence it will happen any time soon.
Many reasons can be cited to explain why convergence did not occur as quickly as the pundits predicted. Three stand out: (1) low demand; (2) technological problems; (3) and lack of profits.

1. <u>Low Demand.</u> In 2003, only about 57 percent of the 109 million U.S. households, or 62 million, were online. Demand is relatively low for three major reasons.

The first is cost. Many low-income families cannot afford a computer. Although the price of computers has dropped dramatically through the years, even the least expensive desktop computer is still more than $500, and costs do not stop there. Consumers must also pay another $10 to $50 a month for Internet access.

The second major reason many households are not online is that some people are uncomfortable using computer technology, or they simply have no interest. This is particularly true among the elderly, who are less likely to go online.

The third reason is that the Internet, although offering many conveniences and services, still cannot satisfy consumers' needs better than some traditional media. For example, many people still prefer a hard copy newspaper or magazine, because they can find and read what they want very quickly and they can easily transport the printed version from place to place. In contrast, to read a story online, most consumers must sit down in front of their computer and then spend several minutes logging on and waiting for the Web site to load. The seemingly small inconveniences of online media become a major problem for people who are racing to get their families and themselves ready for school or work.

2. <u>Technological Problems.</u> The fastest way to replace an existing technology or mass medium is to provide a new technology or medium that does everything the old one does, plus more. In other words, a new technology generally will eliminate an old one only when it becomes a *functional substitute.*

The telegraph is the best example. Telephones and telecommunication technologies killed off the telegraph, because they could do everything the telegraph could do and do it better.

Online technology certainly has come a long way in a short time. However, in 2004 most consumers still cannot get high-quality video from cyberspace. High-speed Internet access is a great improvement over modem technology. However, it typically still cannot produce streaming or real-time audiovisual images that match broadcast television images. Moving images are often still crude and jerky.

In addition, accessing audio-visual content on the Internet can also be frustrating, even with high-speed access service. Users spend a lot of time clicking and waiting before viewing audio-visual content.

3. <u>Lack of Profits.</u> Online mass media have yet to generate substantial revenue and profits for their organizations. In fact, online advertising declined in the early 2000s and registered an increase in 2003. This is perhaps the most important factor inhibiting convergence.

Many advertisers are more comfortable with traditional media. They know anyone can turn on a television and receive their message. The medium is easy to use.

Although online advertising increased in 2003, many advertisers still remain skeptical because the effects of online advertising are not yet well understood. Many consumers dislike online advertising, especially pop-up ads (special boxes that automatically pop up when a Web site or hyperlink is clicked).

The fact that convergence has not, to date, occurred does not mean it won't happen sometime in the future. Many of the technological problems associated with online media will be solved in the years ahead. Voice-activation technology also may eliminate the need for a keyboard, so typing skills will be less necessary. As more people use the Internet, advertisers will no doubt follow.

In the meantime, most scholars view the Internet not as a replacement for traditional media but rather as a supplement. Online media offer advantages not available from traditional media. Many online newspapers, for example, offer subscribers a service that will automatically notify them via e-mail of stories of interest. Consumers also can easily search for information and stories at online media sites that archive their issues online. And e-mail is an expensive way to communicate with people.

conversational analysis a *qualitative research* methodology that analyzes person-to-person communication.

Cooke, Janet (1954-) a former "Washington Post" reporter who fabricated a story about an 8-year-old heroin addict and embarrassed the newspaper and the journalism profession.

On September 28, 1980, the "Washington Post" published a story about an alleged 8-year-old heroin addict named "Jimmy." He was a "precocious little boy with sandy hair, velvety brown eyes and needle marks freckling the baby-smooth skin of his thin brown arms," wrote Cooke, a 26-year-old reporter for the newspaper. The boy's mother and her boyfriend had turned the fourth-grader into a junkie.

Needless to say, the story created a sensation. The mayor, school officials, and Washington Police pleaded with the newspaper to identify the child. But the newspaper refused, citing confidentiality agreements. Cooke told editors her sources threatened to kill her if the boy's name was made public. "Washington Post" editors themselves didn't know the child's last name. They trusted Cooke.

The story was good—so good it won a *Pulitzer Prize* in April 1981. But Jimmy wasn't real. Cooke made up the story. She'd also fabricated parts of her resume to get the job at the newspaper. Two days after receiving the Pulitzer, the "Washington Post" forfeited the prize and fired Cooke.

As a result of this incident, a "Washington Post" *ombudsman* interviewed 47 reporters and editors and identified numerous problems in the editing process. Perhaps the most interesting finding was that, prior to publication, none of the journalists expressed concern or compassion for Jimmy. Another Post ombudsman argued that if editors had shown such concern, the story probably would never have been published in the first place.

See *ethics* and *Blair, Jayson.*

Sources: Janet Cooke, "Jimmy's World," *Washington Post* (September 28, 1980), p. 1A; David A. Maraniss, "Post Reporter's Pulitzer Prize Is Withdrawn; Pulitzer Board Withdraws Post Reporter's Prize," *Washington Post* (April 16, 1981); Charles B. Seib, "Could a Little Caring Have Prevented a Hoax?" *Presstime* (June 1981), p. 35; and Lloyd Grove with Beth Breselli, "The Reliable Source," *The Washington Post* (March 23, 2000), p. C3.

copycat effect a type of media effect in which the subject imitates what he or she hears, sees or reads in the media.

From time to time, individuals charged with murder or other crimes claim they committed the acts after seeing a similar crime in a movie or on television. However, the courts have consistently failed to recognize such defenses.

copyright the exclusive right to publish, produce or sell a literary, dramatic, musical or artistic work.

The purpose of copyright law is to encourage individuals to create works of literature and art. The law does this by protecting the commercial rights of the creator.

Basically, the creator has a monopoly over the profits that a work generates for a certain amount of time. After that, the work enters the public domain, which means anyone can copy or distribute the work for a profit. The logic here is that copyright should not last forever, because it impedes the distribution of important ideas and thoughts.

The United States first enacted copyright legislation in 1790. Initially, it protected books, maps and charts. During the 19th century, protection was extended to prints, musical composition, paintings and photographs. The law worked fairly well in this country.

However, there were no international copyright agreements. As a consequence, there was a great deal of piracy. American Harriet Beecher Stowe's anti-slavery novel "Uncle Tom's Cabin," for example, sold 1.5 million pirated copies in England, for which she received no royalties. But most of the piracy occurred the other way around, with American publishers reprinting the works of famous English and European authors. Many countries around the world signed an international copyright agreement in 1886, but the United States did not sign on until 1954.

The U.S. copyright law was modified three times during the 20th century, in 1909, 1976 and 1998. Protection was extended to film, radio, television, computer programs, and other electronic and communication technologies. The most recent revision came largely in response to a request from The Walt Disney Company, whose "Mickey Mouse" character was about to lose its copyright. The 1998 revision extended copyright protection by 20 years. For works created by an author, the copyright now runs for the life of the author plus 70 years. For works created by employees or certain contracted workers, the copyright last 95 years from the date of first publication or 120 years from the date of creation, whichever ends first.

For works created before Jan. 1, 1978, and after 1922, determining the copyright can be very complicated. It depends on whether the copyright was renewed (no longer an option) and when the work was created. Works created earlier than 1923 are now in the public domain.

To qualify for a copyright, a work must be "original," which means it must be created with some intellectual effort. The work is protected starting from the instant it is produced. However, to win damages in a copyright infringement lawsuit, the work normally must be formally copyrighted with the Library of Congress.

Copyright law protects expression and the way it is produced (e.g., the arrangement of words and sentences). However, the law does not protect ideas. No one can copyright an idea or a thought. They can only copyright the unique way in which such is expressed (i.e., wording in sentences or lyrics). Procedures, processes, concepts or discoveries also cannot be copyrighted.

Copyright law allows communicators to use small portions of copyrighted works without penalty. Journalists and scholars, for example, can cite short passages of copyrighted works in the stories or articles they produce.

But copying too much can get them into trouble. The ability to win a copyright lawsuit depends on a number of factors, including the amount of copyrighted material used, the purpose for which the material was used (educational use receives more protection, for example), and the effect on the originator's profits. The latter is particularly important.

All original works of literature and art are automatically copyrighted as they are produced. They are protected under common law copyright. However, if someone pirates a work, the author or publisher can only recover damages if the book has a Certificate of Registration on file with the Library of Congress.

To protect their works, publishers and authors complete a short form, pay a small fee, and send two copies of the work to the Library of Congress, which issues a "Certificate of Registration." Publishers and authors should also prominently display the copyright symbol—Copyright © 2005—near the front of the book or manuscript. This is usually placed on the second or fourth page in a book, which is appropriately called the "copyright page."

See *pirating*.

corantos primitive news sheets introduced in London in 1621. They lacked regularity but contained political and economic news or interest to politicians and merchants.

corporate communications a department in many public relations firms responsible for maintaining good relations with internal publics, which include employees, executives and stockholders.

Corporate communications personnel often produce and distribute newsletters, whose function is to create a sense of community and belonging within the organization. They also produce annual reports for investors and stockholders and provide feedback to executives about the concerns and needs of employees, investors and stockholders.

See *community relations*, *media relations* and *public*.

corporate newspaper see *corporate media*.

corporate media a mass media organization characterized by a large, complex organizational structure and rationality in decision-making.

The corporate media organization is one of the most misunderstood concepts in mass communication research. Part of this stems from the fact that many scholars, especially critics, have failed to define this term.

The corporate media organization can trace its roots to the Middle Ages and the joint-stock company, which was created in the 16th and 17th centuries to fund large public works projects. The typical newspaper organization in the United States during the 17th and 18th centuries was an individually owned and managed enterprise. The organization was small, and role specialization was limited.

Today, however, the typical daily is owned by a chain or group and exhibits the characteristics of big business—a professional style of management, a highly developed *division of labor* and role specialization, emphasis on rules and procedures, a hierarchy of authority, and rationality in decision-making. More formally, German sociologist Max Weber defines a corporate organization as a group controlled by an administrative staff engaged in a continuous purposeful activity. Weber defined a bureaucracy as a corporate organization in which behavior is goal-directed and decision-making is rational. This meant that bureaucratic organizations try to reduce the production and distribution of goods or services into routines so as to find the most efficient and effective way to reach a goal.

In addition to (1) rationality, Weber argued that bureaucracies are characterized by (2) a hierarchy of authority, (3) employment and promotion based on technical qualifications, (4) a set of rules and procedures that define job responsibilities and how tasks are accomplished, (5) formalistic impersonality, and (6) a highly developed division of labor and role specialization.

Weber pointed out that authority in a bureaucracy is vested in the position rather than in the individual, which minimizes the disruption that occurs when an individual leaves the organization. Selection for employment or promotion is based on technical competence or expertise rather than patronage or social position, and loyalties are given to the organization and its set of rules and procedures, not to individuals. In exchange, employees are compensated and promoted.

Interpersonal relations in bureaucracies are more impersonal than those in non-bureaucratic organizations, but Weber argued this was necessary to efficiently accomplish the goals of the organization. Tasks in a bureaucracy are highly specialized and delegated to individuals who ultimately are accountable for their performance. Rules control and standardize behavior, enabling managers to control a large number of workers. And the division of labor and role specialization generate economies of scale and increase the productive capacity of the organization.

Although Weber believed bureaucratic organizations are very efficient, he did not regard them as a panacea. He believed they tend to monopolize information, resist change, and threaten individual freedom and democratic principles. Many critics of media corporations, especially *global media*, strongly agree. A number of empirical studies have questioned the extent to which bureaucracies are rational or efficient. Others even argue that bureaucracies are self-destructive.

All these criticisms have had some merit. But time has shown that corporate organizations are often capable of adapting to changes in the environment, and they still remain the most effective and efficient way to coordinate the work of large numbers of people. In fact, no other organizational form has displaced the corporate form.

For comparison purposes, the opposite of the corporate media organization is the entrepreneurial media organization, which scores low on the six Weberian characteristics mentioned above.

Although professionals and scholars often talk in terms of these dichotomies (corporate vs. entrepreneurial, global vs. nonglobal), these ideal types are better conceptualized on a continuum, in which all media organizations may be rank-ordered. *Global media* represent one extreme end of the continuum—they are the largest, most complex corporations. The small, locally owned and managed country weekly is at the other end.

Anecdotal and case study research suggests that corporate media are concerned more about profits than with product quality or public service. However, national probability surveys fail to support these findings. In fact, several surveys show that corporate newspapers actually place less emphasis on profits as an organization, more emphasis on product quality, and produce content that is more critical of dominant elites and value systems.

See *critical theory*.

Sources: David Pearce Demers, *The Menace of the Corporate Newspaper: Fact or Fiction?* (Ames: Iowa State University Press, 1996); H. H. Gerth and C. Wright Mills (eds.), *From Max Weber: Essays in Sociology* (New York: Oxford University Press, 1946); and Max Weber, *The Theory of Social and Economic Organization*, trans. A. M. Henderson and Talcott Parsons (New York: The Free Press, 1964 [1947]).

corporate speech speech that comes from a business, a corporation or a representative thereof (as opposed to speech coming from an individual).

The U.S. Supreme Court has given some protection to corporate speech rights, but not as much as it has given to political speech. In one case (Consolidated Edison Co. v. Public Service Commission, 1980), the court ruled that the commission could not prohibit the utility company from inserting a flier in its billing statements that promoted nuclear power as a form of energy. In the second case (Pacific Gas & Electric Co., v. Public Utilities Commission of California, 1986), the court ruled that the commission could not force a utility company to insert a flier from a third party opposed to the views of the utility company.

See *commercial speech* and *symbolic speech*.

Sources: *Consolidated Edison Co. of New York Inc. v. Public Service Commission of New York, Inc.*, 477 U.S. 530 (1980); and *Pacific Gas & Electric Co. v. Public Utilities Commission of California*, 475 U.S. 1 (1986).

corporation (a) a legal entity (or group or organization) that enjoys a number of rights similar to those of an individual, including the right to sue, purchase property, and sell goods and services, and **(b)** a form of organization that has a complex organizational structure and emphasizes rationality in decision-making (see *corporate media*).

Corporation for Public Broadcasting see *Public Broadcasting Service*.

correlation see *correlation coefficient*.

correlation coefficient a statistic that measures the strength and direction of a *relationship* between two *variables*.

Pearson's product-moment correlation coefficient is probably the best known correlation coefficient. Gamma, Phi, Somer's D, and the Contingency Coefficient are some others.

couch potato a pejorative term for a person who spends a lot of time watching television instead of doing things that involve physical activity or exercise.

counter programming see *programming*.

court of law a judicial forum that hears evidence and renders a verdict about the guilt or innocence of a criminal defendant or, in civil cases, rules in favor of one side to a dispute over another.

The U.S. Supreme Court is the only court specifically empowered in the U.S. Constitution. But that document allows the government to establish other courts as needed. Consequently, the United States has two major court systems: one for the federal government and one for the 50 states and its territories (e.g., Puerto Rico).

1. <u>Federal Courts.</u> Cases originate in federal court when the issues revolve around the U.S. Constitution or a federal law, or when one of the

parties to a lawsuit is the U.S. government or is a resident of a different state or country. Cases originate in state courts when they involve disputes over state constitutions, state statutes or when both of the parties are from the same state.

The federal court system has three levels: district court, appeals court, and the U.S. Supreme Court. The federal court system also contains courts that deal with taxes, customs, patents, military matters, and claims against the government. But these courts normally do not adjudicate matters that affect mass media.

At the "bottom" of the federal court system are 94 U.S. District Court systems. These are trial courts, meaning most federal civil and criminal cases originate there and involve presentation of evidence and arguments. Juries are used to determine issues of fact. Judges decide issues that involve the law.

If the case goes to trial, the party that loses may appeal to the U.S. Court of Appeals, the second or middle level. More formally, there are 13 federal judicial circuits—12 of which are geographical and one for special appeals. Each circuit has one court of appeals and between three to fifteen appeals court judges. Usually cases are heard by three-judge panels, though in special cases all judges in a circuit may hear a case. Only attorneys appear before the appeals court. Witness testimony is only taken in the trial courts. The party making the appeal usually argues that the trial court erred in deciding the case. The decision of the appeals court may then be appealed to the U.S. Supreme Court.

The U.S. Supreme Court has nine members. Its decisions are always final and binding on all courts in the land. But the court may (and often has) overturn its own rulings. The high court has final say on questions involving the constitutionality of laws and actions. Interestingly, this power is not vested in the Supreme Court by the Constitution itself. The court simply ruled in 1803 (Marbury v. Madison) that it had the power to determine the constitutionality of laws.

The Supreme Court is very selective. It hears and makes judgment on only about 150 of the 6,000 cases that come before it every year. When it turns a case down, the judgment of the last court (usually the federal court of appeals or a state supreme court) is binding on the parties. Those decisions also become precedent, but only for the circuit or state in which the decision is made.

All federal judges are nominated by the president and confirmed by a majority of the U.S. Senate. They are appointed for life. The logic here is that life appointments insulate judges from political pressures.

2. <u>State Courts.</u> Each of the 50 states has its own system of courts, usually consisting of four levels: (1) municipal courts, which deal with minor crimes, such as parking tickets or small claims (disputes that involve small amounts of money); (2) trial courts, which are usually called circuit courts or superior courts and focus on more serious (felony) crimes and civil lawsuits that involve larger amounts of money; (3) courts of appeal; and (4) one state supreme court.

Like the federal system, a party that loses in one court usually has the ability to appeal to a higher level. If the dispute involves only state statutes, the highest court of appeal will be the state supreme court. However, if the dispute involves constitutional or federal issues, the decision of the state supreme court can normally be appealed directly to the U.S. Supreme Court.

The appointment of state court judges varies. In some states or jurisdictions, judges are elected. In others, they are appointed. Most state supreme court judges are appointed by the governor with confirmation from one or both houses of the state legislature.

See *lawsuit.*

Sources: *Marbury v. Madison*, 1 Cranch 137, 2 L.Ed. 60 (1803).

covariation an *association* or *correlation* between two variables.

covering law see *scientific law.*

creative specialists people who work for advertising or public relations companies or departments and whose function is to create an advertisement, advertising campaign, and/or a public relations campaign.

The list of creative specialists includes writers, artists, graphic designers, photographers, and video and audio producers. They are primarily responsible for producing the content of an advertising or a *public relations campaign.* They usually work directly with the *account executive* and the client's representatives.

Creel, George (1876-1953) a former newspaper editor who headed The Committee on Public Information during World War I.

Creel, appointed by President Woodrow Wilson, hired a talented group of journalists, scholars, and press agents to drum up support for the United States and hatred of the Germans. The committee mailed thousands of news releases, which in turn generated about 20,000 columns of newsprint every week. In addition, the "Creel Committee" helped raise war bonds, called "Liberty Loans." These campaigns were very successful, and much of the credit was given to Creel.

criterion variable the *variable* to be explained or predicted. Same as *dependent variable.*

critical theory a term that refers to a collection of theories which hold that mass media disseminate an *ideology* that justifies capitalism as an economic system (particularly vast inequalities in wealth) and helps economic and political elites maintain their dominance over ordinary people.

Critical theory draws its intellectual strength from political theorist *Karl Marx*, from Antonio Gramsci, and from the Frankfurt School, a group of neo-Marxist scholars who fled Germany just before World War II. Marx argued that capitalism was a repressive economic system because a small group of elites (capitalists or bourgeoisie) maintained wealth by exploiting the labor of the working masses (the proletariat). Marx predicted that the working and unemployed classes would eventually revolt when they realized they were being exploited. However, the much-anticipated revolutions never came in capitalist countries. The first one happened in Russia, which had a feudal economic system.

By the 1920s, Marx's followers had come up with an explanation for the lack of revolutions: Mass media and other cultural institutions such as schools were disseminating propaganda, or ideology, that prevented workers from realizing they were being exploited. The workers were suffering from "false consciousness," and they could not revolt without achieving "class consciousness."

Also central to critical theory is the concept of *hegemony*. This is usually defined as the ability of the ruling classes to dominate or control private groups (e.g., churches, mass media), which in turn manipulate knowledge, values and norms to serve the interests of the ruling classes.

Like *guard dog theory*, critical theory contends mass media are agents of *social control*. Mass media produce news and entertainment programming that reinforce dominant values and institutions, especially those connected with capitalism. However, critical theory holds that such control is extremely repressive, whereas guard dog theory makes no formal value judgments about the good or bad aspects of such control.

Critical theorists view capitalism as "evil" partly because it exploits people's labor. In fact, the profits from labor usually go to a small group of elites (stockholders or executives). Indeed, the wealth structure of virtually all capitalist countries has a small number of rich elites and a large number of middle-class people, working-class people, and poor people. The mainstream mass media in such countries are seen as repressive because they produce content (business news, advertising) that helps capitalists achieve their goals. In contrast, the concerns of working classes and the poor receive little attention, critical theorists argue. Critical theorists also are extremely critical of mainstream social science research, which they often pejoratively call "administrative research," because it helps elites maintain control over the masses.

Traditionally, critical theorists have relied more heavily on logic or formal theory than on empirical research (see *empiricism*) to back up their arguments. Some do not conduct empirical research. Nevertheless, many case studies of media content and some quantitative studies support their theories. There is, for example, research showing that mass media tend to give more favorable coverage to corporations than to labor unions or groups that represent poor people and the disadvantaged.

Some of the early critical theorists hoped for a revolution, one that would emancipate people from the alleged horrors of capitalism. However, emancipation seems far off in this post-communist era. As a consequence, many contemporary critical theorists have trimmed revolutionary rhetoric from their writings. In fact, few today advocate socialism or communism as an alternative to capitalism. Many reluctantly accept capitalism and the free market and are content to call for reform (e.g., more democratic media) rather than revolution.

The major strength of critical theory is that it draws attention to corporate power. Large media corporations are, indeed, often guilty of abusing their power. But critical theory's major weakness is that it fails to account for *social change*. Research shows, for example, that corporate media often produce content critical of the *status quo*, which in turn has promoted social change benefitting many disadvantaged groups. One consequence of these critiques is that in recent years critical theory has lost some of its critical edge—few scholars now talk about emancipation through the elimination of capitalism.

See *Frankfurt School*, *hegemony*, *ideology*, and *Marx, Karl*.

Sources: Theodore Adorno and Max Horkheimer, *Dialectic of the Enlightenment* (London: Verso, 1979) and Herbert Marcuse, *One-Dimensional Man* (Boston: Beacon Press, 1964); Karl Marx, *Capital: A Critique of Political Economy*, vol. 1, trans. by Samuel Moore and Edward Aveling (New York: International Publishers, 1987 [1867]); Antonio Gramsci, *Prison Notebooks* (New York: International Publishers, 1971); Robert W. McChesney, "The Political Economy of Global Communication," pp. 1-26 in Robert W. McChesney, Ellen Meiksins Wood and John Bellamy Foster (eds.), *Capitalism and the Information Age: The Political Economy of the Global Communication Revolution* (New York: Monthly Review Press, 1998); David Demers, *Global Media: Menace or Messiah?* revised ed. (Cresskill, NJ: Hampton Press, 2002); David Demers, "Has Critical Theory Lost It's Critical Edge?" *Global Media News*, 3(4):4 (Fall 2001).

Cronkite, Walter (1916-) CBS News anchor from 1962 to 1981.

He acquired the title of "most trusted journalist" in America, according to polls. He continues to give commentaries and host documentary specials.

cross-media ownership a condition in which a company or an individual owns two or more mass media organizations in different media segments or industries (e.g., newspapers, magazines, television stations, radio stations, etc.).

For example, a company that owns a newspaper and a television station has cross-media ownership; one that owns two television stations does not. Many scholars and citizens are critical of cross-media ownership, because they argue this can reduce *diversity* in the *marketplace of ideas*.

cross-sectional study a study at one point in time.

crosstabulation a table that displays the joint frequency *distribution* of two *variables*.

Same as *contingency table*.

Cullers, Vince (1924-2003) founder, in 1956, of the first Black-owned advertising agency.

In 1971, Cullers and Ed McBain created a new advertising agency in Chicago (Burrell Communications) that specialized in targeting African

American consumers. Their clients included McDonald's, Coca-Cola, Procter & Gamble and Stroh Brewery.

cultivation theory the notion that the more television people watch, the more they acquire the beliefs, values, and attitudes portrayed on television, and the more they support authoritarian police measures.

Cultivation theory was developed by George Gerbner and his colleagues, who argued that television had adverse consequences for individuals and for society. More specifically, they argued that television, especially violent programming, "cultivates" a "consciousness" that generates support for tough policing and authoritarian controls.

"Gerbner and (his colleague Larry) Gross tried to demonstrate that television and its effects should not be considered on their own, outside of their social context," write media scholars James Shanahan and Victoria Jones. " ... In particular, they argued that the violence issue might be seen as problematic by elite classes because it suggested the possibility that lower classes might rise up and present a disruption to established order. In their view, however, violence on television was not a dysfunctional outcome of mass communication but an attempt to portray the boundaries of legitimate power and authority. In short, violence was seen as a symbolic 'demonstration of power' that serves the function of social control."

Using survey research as their primary methodology, Gerbner and his colleagues found that heavy viewers of television were more likely than lighter viewers to overestimate their chances of becoming a victim of a crime, to overestimate the number of people employed in law enforcement, and to see the world as a "meaner" place. "In short, heavy viewers apparently had 'absorbed' the message that the world is dangerous ... and violent messages performed the function of promoting the perception of a need for dominant authority and established social order. Thus, cultivation was established as a theory of *social control.*"

Interestingly, many scholars at the time failed to get the point. They saw cultivation theory as psychological theory. Of course, heavy viewing did lead to cultivation of a "mean world syndrome." Heavy viewers saw the world as a "meaner" place than light viewers. This was a psychological effect. But cultivation was not simply another "hypodermic needle theory." Gerbner and his colleagues argued that the effects of television accumulate over long periods of time, rather than being immediate or instantaneous. And these effects had implications for controlling people—they provided more support for an authoritarian police state.

One of the strengths of cultivation analysis is that it combined a *quantitative research* approach with a critical view of mass media. However, the survey research methodology often yielded weak correlations, and this methodology has been heavily criticized. In response, cultivation theorists argue that small effects accumulate over long periods of time. In addition, they point out that the logic of the theory is extremely strong and is supported by other research.

Sources: George Gerbner, Larry Gross, Michael Morgan and Nancy Signorielli, "Growing up with Television: The Cultivation Perspective," pp. 17-41 in Jennings Bryant and Dolf Zillmann (eds.), *Media Effects: Advances in Theory and Research* (Hillsdale, NJ: Lawrence Erlbaum Associates, 1994).; James Shanahan and Victoria Jones, "Cultivation and Social Control," pp. 31-50 in David Demers and K. Viswanath (eds.), *Mass Media, Social Control and Social Change: A Macrosocial Perspective* (Ames: Iowa State University Press, 1999), p. 35.; George Gerbner, Lawrence Gross, Michal Morgan, Nancy Signorielli and Marilyn Jackson-Beek, "The Demonstration of Power: Violence Profile No. 10," *Journal of Communication*, 29(3):177-196 and Michael Morgan and Nancy Signorielli, *Cultivation Analysis* (Newbury Park: CA: Sage Publications, 1990).; Paul Hirsch, "The 'Scary World' of the Nonviewer and Other Anomalies: A Reanalysis of Gerbner et al.'s Findings on Cultivation Analysis," *Communication Research* 7:403-456 (1980).

cultural studies a theoretical perspective that sees mass media as producing symbolic content that supports discriminatory or oppressive practices toward women, minorities, homosexuals, labor unions and/or environmental activists.

Cultural studies gained momentum during the 1960s and 1970s and had its strongest following in Great Britain under the leadership of scholars like Stuart Hall and Raymond Williams, but it was also promoted by James Carey, an American scholar.

Cultural studies shares a lot with *critical theory*, except the emphasis is less on media economics or capitalism and more on other aspects of culture, such as gender, race, ethnicity, sexual orientation and subcultural groups (e.g., environmental and anti-globalization groups). Following a more humanistic approach, cultural theorists believe their role is to expose the discriminatory aspects of mass media and popular culture. They hope such expositions will encourage oppressed groups to "resist" the "dominant hegemonic order."

Like the critical studies perspective, cultural studies focuses heavily on *ideology* and almost always involves a critical assessment of mass media. However, cultural theorists focus more on audiences and the meaning they derive from media "consumption" than on the content of media messages themselves.

Moreover, cultural theorists don't assume that audiences always interpret media content from the perspective of the message creator. Meaning depends upon the context, or situation, in which the mass communication occurs.

Thus, cultural theorists are sensitive to the idea that different people may interpret media content differently. A good example was the 1970s television comedy "All in the Family." Archie Bunker, the lead character, was a bigot and sexist who held archaic beliefs about minorities and women. The liberal producers of the show believed audiences would readily see through the parody. Liberal audiences did, but Archie's outrageous conduct and views also reinforced the attitudes and opinions of many conservatives.

In general, cultural theorists are more likely than critical theorists to concede that popular culture, such as television and movies, can produce content that challenges dominant values and elite groups. In other words, their theory of ideology tends to be less rigid and more open to the idea of "resistence." However, as a rule, popular culture is not empowering, and the goal of cultural theorists is to expose the discriminatory aspects of television programming and other media forms.

Like *guard dog theory* and *media systems theory*, cultural studies argues that one must look at society as a whole in order to understand mass communication. The focus, however, is less on the effects of specific mass media content (i.e., what do media do to people?) than on the ritual of communication itself and on the meaning that people ascribe to it. As Carey puts it: "Cultural studies attempts to think about the mass media not in relation to this or that isolated problem (violence, *pornography*, children) or institution (politics, economy, family) or practice (film production, conversation, advertising), but as elements, in Raymond Williams' phrase, 'in a whole way of life.' Societies, in this view, are complex, differentiated, contradictory, interacting wholes. They are threaded throughout, held in this complex unity, by culture: by the production and reproduction of systems of symbols and messages."

Carey and some cultural theorists argue that the growth of mass media has taken away "meaningful" rituals of communication. They seek to restore a "lost public"— one in which real debate, social participation in politics, and social intellectualism might once again occur. Others argue this view romanticizes the past. Historically, ordinary citizens have never had much say in governance. However, most cultural theorists share a common goal: to work for a better world, one in which communication is more democratic and equitable to people of all walks of life.

The cultural studies perspective has been criticized for placing values over knowledge. Like the *critical theory* perspective, it also has had limited impact on public policy partly because of a complex lexicon. The approach appeals to intellectuals, however, and thus is popular in academic institutions worldwide.

Sources: Stuart Hall, "Culture, the Media and the Ideological Effect," pp. 315-48 in James Curran, Michael Gurevitch and Janet Woollacott (eds.), *Mass Communication and Society* (London: Edward Arnold, 1977); Stuart Hall, "The Rediscovery of Ideology: The Return of the Repressed," pp. 15-47 in Stuart Hall et al. (eds), *Culture, media, language: Working papers in cultural studies, 1972-1979* (London: Hutchinson, 1982); James Carey, "The Origins of the Radical Discourse on Cultural Studies in the United States," *Journal of Communication*, 33:313 (Summer 1983); Neil Vidmar and Milton Rokeach, "Archie Bunkier's Bigotry: A Study in Selective Perception and Exposure," *Journal of Communication*, 24(1):34 (Winter 1974); Raymond Williams, *The Long Revolution* (London, 1961).

culture the symbolic and learned aspects of human society, which includes language, custom, beliefs, skills, art, norms and values.

This definition needs to be distinguished from the one which refers to "culture" as "refined ways of thinking, talking, and acting"— popularly expressed in the comment, "she's got culture." In other words, the concern for most social scientists is not with the aesthetics of culture, per se; rather, the focus is on values, beliefs, customs or cultural content (e.g., media content) and how they serve as instruments of control or change.

cuneiform a sophisticated symbolic (or pictographic-ideographic) system invented by the Chinese that uses small wedge-shaped marks to represent objects and ideas.
See *hieroglyphics*.

custom magazine publishing a type of magazine publishing in which one media company publishes a custom designed magazine for another company.
Custom magazines may be distributed and/or sold to internal *publics*, such as employees or members of an organization, or to the general public. The Meredith Corporation, for example, publishes "Family Money" for Metropolitan Life Insurance Co. and "Weekend" for Home Depot. Airline magazines, which are available free of charge to people who fly one of the major airlines, are other examples.

cyberagency an advertising agency that specializes on promoting goods and services through the Internet.
See *advertising agency*.

cybernetics the study of communication, control, and regulation of complex biological, electronic, and mechanical systems.
General systems theory draws on many principles of cybernetics, but the field of study has not had much effect on mass communication, primarily because it doesn't grant enough *free will* to mass communicators and consumers of media.

cyberporn *pornography* available on the *Internet*.
Cyberporn is the one of the most controversial types of content on the Internet. There are about 100,000 pornography Web sites in the United States. Altogether they generate about $7 billion in revenues. Surfers who want access to pornography usually pay a monthly fee. In exchange, they get access to pictures and videos (or even live performances). Internet pornography is one of the few businesses that has been consistently profitable on the Internet.
Although many groups and people dislike pornography and want to ban it, the U.S. Supreme Court has ruled that pornography is not by its nature obscene. Only extremely offensive and lewd pictures and acts, including child pornography, generally fail to get First Amendment protection.
Nevertheless, anti-pornography groups on the left (especially feminists) and on the right (conservative and religious) continue to lobby against cyberporn. Much of the concern is focused on protecting children who use the Internet.
A number of software programs that attempt to filter pornography Web sites are available. AOL and other ISPs and browsers also offer filter options.
However, a study by the Australian Broadcasting Authority has concluded that most Internet filtering programs are ineffective when it comes to protecting children from harmful material on the Internet. About

50 percent of the programs failed to block access to pornographic and racist material. Other programs were more effective, but they also inadvertently blocked access to many useful sites, including health care Web pages.

cyberspace the imaginary space or world created when computers link together and exchange information or data.

Cyberspace is most often applied to and sometimes used as a synonym for the Internet. The origins of the term "cyberspace" are usually traced to the science fiction novel "Neuromancer" (New York: Ace Books, 1984) by William Gibson, who used the term to refer to the imagined world created by people who communicated with each other via computers.

cylinder press see *rotary press.*

D

daguerreotype an early photographic process in which pictures were produced on chemically treated metal or glass.

The daguerreotype was invented in France in the late 1820s. Although daguerrotypes were popular in Europe and the United States, they could not be easily reproduced for publication in newspapers or magazines. A woodcut or lithograph was needed to reproduce pictures for this venue. In contrast, the *halftone*, which could be produced from paper negatives and positives, was easily and cheaply produced.

dailies short film clips that allow the director to see how the film is progressing.

data facts or figures from which conclusions are inferred.

Day, Benjamin see *penny press*.

decoding the act of interpreting a message.
See *communication* and *oppositional decoding*.

deconstructionism a method of criticism that involves probing for hidden meanings or contradictions within messages or media content.
See *discourse analysis*.

deduction a method of reasoning in which *hypotheses* are developed from a more general set of principles.
See *induction*.

Deep Throat a confidential source used by Bob Woodward of the Washington Post during the Watergate scandal investigation.

In 2005, former FBI official W. Mark Felt and his family announced that he was "Deep Throat"—a name coined by Washington Post editor Benjamin Bradlee and derived from a well-known pornographic movie playing at the time.

Felt, who was second in command at the FBI, met occasionally with Woodward in a parking garage, providing tips that helped him find additional information tying the scandal directly to President Richard Nixon.

See *Woodward and Bernstein.*

defamation a communication that injures the good name or reputation of a person or corporation, or which tends to bring a person or corporation into disrepute.

See *libel.*

defendant the party in a lawsuit who is accused of committing a wrong or illegal action.

de Forest, Lee see *Armstrong, Edwin Howard,* and *motion picture technology.*

demo a recording or video that musicians or job-seekers use to sell themselves to recording companies or prospective employers.

"Demo" is short for "demonstration."

democratic participant theory see *normative theory.*

demographic research research that focuses on the impact or nature of *demographics,* such as gender, race, age, income, education.

demographics social characteristics of a *population.*

Demographics include characteristics such as gender, race, age, income, education, occupation, marital status and place of residence. Demographics are used to help market products and services to consumers and audiences.

See *psychographics.*

deontological ethics an action or behavior is ethical if it follows a pre-established set of rules or principles without reference to the consequences of that action.

See *ethical decision-making.*

dependent variable in *causal analysis,* the dependent variable is the effect and usually the variable that researchers seek to explain.

descriptive analysis research in which the goal is to describe a group in terms of its *beliefs, attitudes, behaviors* or other characteristics (e.g., *demographics*). Contrast with *explanatory analysis.*

descriptive statistics *statistics* used to summarize and characterize *data.* Examples are *percentages, frequencies, means,* and *correlation coefficients.* See *inferential statistics.*

designated market area (DMA) a geographical area divided into two or more smaller areas for purposes of marketing a good or service.

For example, when it comes to the television market, the United States is divided into 210 DMAs, which consist of all counties whose largest viewing share is given to stations in that same market area. As a rule, the bigger the market, the greater the number of advertisers and, consequently, the greater the advertising revenues.

determinism the doctrine that the human will is not free but determined by physical, organic, psychological, social or cultural factors or phenomena.

Thus, to say that a human act or decision is determined is to argue that, given the antecedent conditions of the actions, people could act or think in no other way. The doctrine of determinism usually is interpreted as implying that people are not responsible for their actions, because actions are thought to be causally determined by forces out of their control. Therefore, if a person watched a violent television program and then imitated that behavior a short time later, he or she would not be responsible for the violent behavior.

The concept of determinism can be refined further in the distinction between supernatural and natural determinism. Supernatural determinism is the belief that human action, as well as all natural phenomenon (such as earthquakes, floods), is caused or determined by gods, devils or some other supernatural deity. Historically, virtually every civilization or social system has subscribed to a body of supernatural beliefs. Many modern religious groups continue to hold such beliefs, even if they concomitantly subscribe to the belief that humans were created with a "free will." However, with the decline of religion and the rise of secular forms of social organization (i.e., state, corporation, professions), supernatural determinism is no longer as powerful a force as it once was.

Natural determinism is the belief that actions are determined by the impersonal workings of nature. Economic laws of supply and demand fit into this category, as well as sociobiological models, and genetic laws of behavior, such as the ideas that intelligence and criminological behavior are determined mainly at birth. The emergence of natural determinism as an ontological doctrine was tied closely to the growth of the physical sciences during the 17th and 18th centuries. Some scientists who subscribe to natural determinism reduce action or mental processes to materialistic forms (i.e., chemical or physiological forces). In its strongest form, this view holds that people are like puppets or robots, whose actions are controlled by materialistic forces in nature. Most contemporary social scientists deride this view, but many phenomena—such as the unconscious patient on the operating table who will verbally respond with talk or singing after his or her brain is physically stimulated by a needle—defy simple explanation.

The idea that psychological, social or cultural factors can shape human behavior is often portrayed as being incompatible with free will, but a probabilistic theory of social action suggests that both can exist without subscribing to a deterministic model.

See *free will* and *probabilistic theory of social action*.

development media theory see *normative theory*.

dichotomy a *variable* having two categories.

Gender, with the categories "male" and "female," is an example of a dichotomous variable.

differentiation see *product differentiation* and *structural differentiation*.

diffusion the process through which an innovation is adopted and spreads through an organization or society.

Diffusion research suggests that the process for many innovations follows the shape of an s-curve: slow at first, followed by rapid growth, and then leveling off. Diffusion research suggests that mass media influence early adopters (people who adopt an innovation first), but later adopters are more influenced by *change agents* (i.e., the early adopters or people specifically hired to promote an innovation).

digital using numbers that are digits (usually binary, on/off, true/false, etc.) to represent all of the variables in an equation.

digital computer a computer that uses numbers instead of continuous or wavelike signals to perform calculations.

See *analog computer*, *computer*, and *recording format*.

digital divide see *digital gap hypothesis*.

digital format see *recording format*.

digital gap hypothesis the *knowledge gap hypothesis* applied to digital technology, especially computers (i.e., people and countries rich in resources acquire digital technology at a faster rate than those poor in resources).

See *knowledge gap hypothesis*.

Digital Millennium Copyright Act of 1998 a law that makes it a crime to electronically duplicate and distribute copyrighted materials or to create software that allows others to duplicate and distribute copyrighted works.

See *copyright*.

digital subscriber line (DSL) a technology that allows high-speed transmission of digital (voice, video, and text) data over conventional copper telephone lines, often used to access the Internet.
  See *broadband.*

digitization see *recording format.*

Direct Broadcast Satellite (DBS) a television satellite system introduced in 1994 that uses a small dish that can be installed almost anywhere.
  Today more than 20 million homes, or about one in six homes in America, are hooked up to satellite television. The two biggest companies are DirecTV, which has 12 million subscribers, and the DISH Network, which has 9 million.

direct marketing the process of marketing, advertising or selling a good or service directly to consumers, instead of using traditional mass media such as newspapers, magazines, television or radio.
  Direct mail and the Internet are the two most popular forms of direct marketing.
  See *market segmentation* and *target marketing.*

director in filmmaking, the person who helps hire the actors and production team and has control over the entire film-making process.
  The director, who may also be a screenwriter and a producer, visualizes the movie and guides the production crew and actors to carry out that vision. The director is heavily involved in every step of production, including editing.

director of photography see *cinematographer.*

disc jockey a person who hosts a radio show whose primary *format* is music.

discourse analysis a methodology that seeks to uncover the hidden motivations or ideology embedded within text or mass media content.
  Discourse analysis may employ quantitative or qualitative approaches, but the latter is far more popular. Some scholars argue that discourse analysis is basically *deconstructionism*, or the attempt to expose the hidden meaning of messages and symbols. Discourse analysis generally assumes that reality is socially constructed through the use of language and symbols.
  Although many discourse researchers employ an inductive approach, some discourse analysis is tied to *postmodernism*, which means that it views scientific methods and most aspects of Western culture with disdain. As such, discourse analysis usually involves a negative critique of the message and its creator. Discourse analysis also has been criticized for failing to provide a set of rules for guiding analysis.

Nevertheless, discourse analysis is useful in that it draws attention to the motives of those who create the messages and the power they wield.
See *postmodernism*.

discriminant analysis a *multivariate statistic* and *descriptive statistic* in which the *dependent variable* is a nominal measure and the *independent variables* are *continuous* (see *continuous measure*).
Discriminant analysis is often used to explain buying behavior (a nominal measure). The results are often presented in the form of a *perceptual map* showing which variables have the most influence on buying a product or service.
See *levels of measurement*.

disinformation false information spread to discredit an idea or *social actor*.

display advertising print advertisements generally larger than classified advertisements and often containing pictures or graphic elements.
Display advertising can cover one or more pages of a newspaper or magazine. Display advertising (mostly containing text) first began appearing in some newspapers in the 1830s. In the late 1840s, advertisers who placed small ads complained because big ads dominated attention. "The New York Herald" temporarily banned display ads, but this solution was short-lived because display ads were very profitable.
See *classified advertising*.

distribution an array of *cases* for a particular *variable*.

distributor an individual or organization that stocks publisher's books and promotes them for sale to book retailers and libraries.
Contrast with *wholesaler*.

diversity of ideas the number and variety of ideas, particularly political ideas, in a society or in an organization.
One of the assumptions underlying Western notions of political democracy is that voters have access to a broad range of ideas and opinions. Without such access, they presumably cannot make good decisions and democracy cannot function. The assumption is that truth will win out over falsehood when both compete in the so-called *marketplace of ideas*.
Although not all scholars find the marketplace of ideas metaphor appealing, critical scholars generally agree that no political system is fair or just if it suppresses ideas critical of those in power. As such, many scholars have focused on the issue of whether the growth of *corporate media* leads to the suppression of ideas and, thus, also to the suppression of democratic processes.
Mainstream critics like Ben H. Bagdikian cite two major reasons or factors to explain why global and corporate media contribute to the loss of

diversity. The first one is *concentration of ownership*, or the idea that fewer media owners means fewer ideas.

The second reason cited to explain the loss of diversity is greed. More specifically, large, corporate media are believed to place more emphasis on profits than on product quality and information diversity than will small, entrepreneurial media.

Critics use anecdotes and examples to back up their arguments, but other scholars have pointed out that these case studies may not be representative of the population of mass media. In fact, some national probability surveys have supported the opposite conclusion—that corporate media enhance, rather than inhibit, the diversity of ideas.

See *corporate media* and *marketplace of ideas*.

Sources: Ben H. Bagdikian, *The Media Monopoly*, 2nd ed. (Boston: Beacon Press, 1987), p. x; Dennis W. Mazzocco, *Networks of Power: Corporate TV's Threat to Democracy* (Boston: South End Press, 1994); Edward S. Herman and Robert W. McChesney, *The Global Media: The New Missionaries of Corporate Capitalism* (London: Cassell, 1997); David Pearce Demers, *The Menace of the Corporate Newspaper: Fact or Fiction?* (Ames, IA: Iowa State University Press, 1996); David Demers, "Who Controls the Editorial Content at Corporate News Organizations? An Empirical Test of the Managerial Revolution Hypothesis," *World Futures: The Journal of General Evolution*, 57:103-123 (2001); Douglas Kellner, *Television and the Crisis of Democracy* (Boulder: Westview Press, 1990); and Herbert I. Schiller, *Culture Inc.: The Corporate Takeover of Public Expression* (New York: Oxford University Press, 1989).

division of labor a process in which productive tasks or social organizations become separated and more specialized.

Adam Smith applied the concept to workshops and factories. In his 1776 book, "An Inquiry Into the Causes of the Wealth of Nations," Smith argued that a nation's wealth was not to be found in gold or agriculture, but rather in the productive capacity of labor. Create a division of labor and production will increase. Such an increase, in turn, produces wealth.

Emile Durkheim, a sociologist, also applied the concept to social life. In his 1893 book, "The Division of Labor," Dirkheim argued that modern societies are characterized by a complex social division of labor. People belong to different churches, have different hobbies, and work different jobs. He argued that the division of labor in a society creates interdependence, helping people bond.

Karl Marx, in contrast, argued that division of labor de-skilled labor and alienated workers. Many contemporary Neo-Marxists continue to argue that most jobs in the economy are boring and deprive people of meaning in life.

The impact of the division of labor on modern life is extensive. In fact, the economies of scale derived from the division of labor are primarily responsible for the growth of large-scale media organizations, or what we now call *global media* corporations.

See *corporate media*.

DMA see *designated market area*.

documentary film a film or television program that analyzes news events or social conditions with little or no fictionalization; its primary purpose is usually to educate.
See *feature film* and *animated film*.

domain name a unique name that identifies an Internet address (or *Uniform Resource Locator*).
The domain name has two or more parts, separated by dots. The part on the right is most general; the parts on the left are more specific. For example, www.us.gov is the domain name for the U.S. government. The suffix ".gov" is called a *zone* and indicates that the owner of the domain name is a governmental agency. The ".us" part refers specifically to the United States.
Getting a domain name is easy. A user simply goes online to any of the dozens of companies that offer the service and pays a small fee (under $30) to register a name for one year or longer. These domain name companies usually also offer server space to post information for a Web site.
About 50 million domain names are currently in use. This number is expected to continue to grow in the coming years.
See *Internet, Internet Protocol, Uniform Resource Locator,* and *zone.*

domestic theatrical films distributed in the United States.

dominant value see *values (social).*

Douglass, Frederick (1817-1895) a journalist who founded one of the first successful black newspapers in the United States.
Douglas, the son of a black slave woman and a white man, escaped from slavery in 1838. He paid for his freedom in 1845 and in 1847 founded "The North Star," a newspaper that fought for racial and sexual equality. In the 1970s, Douglass emerged as a symbol of black achievement and inspiration.
See *Du Bois, W. E. B.*

Du Bois, W. E. B. (1868-1963) a journalist and sociologist who became the most important black protest leader in the first half of the 20th century.
William Edward Burghardt Du Bois was born in 1868 in Massachusetts. He endured many racial insults as a child. At age 15, he became the local correspondent for the "New York Globe," a position he used to urge Blacks to politicize themselves.
Two years later he attended college in Nashville, and it was there that he witnessed discrimination and racism in its most extreme forms. After graduation, he entered Harvard graduate school, attended school in Germany, and became the first black man to earn a Ph.D. at Harvard. His dissertation, "The Suppression of the African Slave Trade in America," remains the authoritative work on that subject.

He took a teaching job and conducted empirical research on African American life in America, writing numerous papers and books, including "The Souls of Black Folks," which criticized Booker T. Washington's more conservative, or accommodating, approach to securing equal rights. Du Bois became more radical as time passed, but he never joined the communist party.

He founded and edited for 25 years "Crisis" magazine, which was published by the National Association for the Advancement of Colored People (NAACP), a group he helped create in 1909. Du Bois was a superb writer. His mission was to make people aware of the problems that faced African Americans. He wanted racial equality and fought tirelessly all his life to achieve that goal. But he became disillusioned at the end of his life, renounced his U.S. citizenship, and moved to Ghana, where he died in 1963.

Historians today widely agree that Du Bois is the most important black protest leader in the first half of the 20th century, and he continues to influence many contemporary civil rights leaders.

See *Douglass, Frederick*.

Sources: Gerald C. Hynes, "A Biographical Sketch of W. E. B. Du Bois," available at <www. Duboislc.org>; Manning Marable, W. E. B. Du Bois, *Black Radical Democrat* (Boston: Twayne, 1986); David Levening Lewis, *W. E. B. Du Bois: Biography of a Race, 1868-1919* (New York: Owl Books, 1993).

duopoly a market in which two companies compete with each other; an *oligopoly* with only two competitors.

DVD digital versatile disc or digital video disc, a CD ROM disc that offers much more storage capacity than a conventional CD and records much higher quality video images than video cassette tapes.

See *video cassette recorder*.

dyad two persons or *social actors* interacting.

A dyad is the most elemental unit of *interpersonal communication*.

E

e-book (or digital book) a book in which the text is stored and presented electronically.

The e-book eliminates the conventional printing process, which involves ink and paper and binding. The idea of e-books was initially very attractive to publishers because digital books are less expensive to produce—there are no printing or shipping costs. They can also be downloaded directly from Web sites, either into a computer's software or into a handheld laptop specially designed for book reading.

There are advantages for readers as well. They don't have to lug around heavy books. E-book users may also work online and make direct links to other Web sites.

But e-books have not sold well. Many people say they prefer the feel of paper. Although the technology for e-books is improving, and they are becoming more user-friendly, their future is still in question.

ecology see *media ecology*.

e-commerce the term used to describe business transacted on the Internet.

Internet users spent an estimated $70 billion online in 2004, purchasing a wide array of products and services, including books, cars, vacations, insurance, toys, CDs, magazine subscriptions, and loans. Convenience is a major reason for using the Internet. Internet spending was expected to grow by 20 percent a year through 2007.

Young people are more inclined to use the Internet for entertainment purposes. They download music, play games, and visit media entertainment sites. By contrast, business people are more inclined to use the Internet to access news and information. A Pew Internet & American Life survey found that 22 percent of Internet users sought election news online in 2002, compared with 15 percent in 1998.

Source: Jupiter Research, "Online Retail Spending to Soar in the U.S.," summary available from <www.nua.ie>.

ecoporn stylized nature photography or films that objectify nature for human aesthetic pleasure.

Edison, Thomas Alva (1847-1931) an inventor who gained fame in the field of mass communication for inventing the phonograph and for helping invent early film cameras and film projectors.

Edison invented the phonograph in 1877. His tinfoil phonograph consisted of a cylinder, a horn, and a hand crank. A decade later it was one of the most popular devices of the 19th century. In 1888, Edison made the first "celebrity" recording of a 12-year-old pianist virtuoso.

In the 1880s, he commissioned one of his laboratory assistants, W. L. D. Dickson, to build a *Kinetograph*, a film camera, and a *Kinetoscope*, a film projector. In 1894, the Kinetoscopes were commercially produced and marketed, becoming very popular. Kinetoscope parlors charged 25 cents for admission to about five machines, each of which showed short clips of circus or vaudeville acts. Although both machines worked well, Edison and his assistant were never able to create a practical machine that could synchronize sound with pictures. They gave up on that project.

Although Edison's motion picture inventions eventually lost favor, his role in the motion picture industry did not end there. In the mid-1890s, he purchased the rights to another state-of-the-art projector, which was called the Vitascope, and began mass producing it. Soon many vaudeville houses were showing Edison and Lumiére "films," although the modern concept of the motion picture as a story or narrative had not yet taken shape. The public saw these experiments as animated photographs or living pictures.

Sources: Michael Chanan, *Repeated Takes: A Short History of Recording and Its Effects on Music* (New York: Verso, 1995); Michael Campbell, *And the Beat Goes On: An Introduction to Popular Music in America, 1840 to Today* (New York: Schirmer Books, 1996); Raymond Fielding, *A Technological History of Motion Pictures and Television: An Anthology from the Pages of the Journal of the Society of Motion Picture and Television Engineers* (Berkeley: University of California Press, 1983).

editor a person who assigns stories, edits them, or manages reporters or other workers in a mass media organization.

At larger news organizations, the city or metropolitan editor, for example, manages reporters and assigns story ideas. An editorial page editor oversees the production of content for the opinion/commentary and the letters-to-the-editors pages. The wire editor edits copy from wire services.

These editors, in turn, report to a managing editor, who is responsible for the entire editorial production process on a day-to-day basis. The managing editor then reports to a top editor, sometimes called an *editor-in-chief*, who deals with more long-term issues and financial matters. Smaller news organizations usually combine the roles of managing editor and editor-in-chief.

editor-in-chief the top editor in a news organization.
This title is usually used only in large organizations that have many other editors performing specialized tasks and need to distinguish the top-ranking editor from all others.

educational television (or public television) *television* whose primary goal is to educate rather than entertain.
See *Public Broadcasting Service*.

effect see *cause and effect*.

elaboration likelihood model a theory of attitude change that sees attitude formation as a product of the directness of information processing.

elements see *cases*.

elite an individual or a group who, as a function of either being born into or acquiring dominant social characteristics (such as high social status, majority race, upper social class, high levels of education, and dominant gender), enjoys more access to resources, more control over life choices, and more economic, political, and religious *power* than other individuals or groups.
Journalists depend heavily on elites for the news, and research shows they have a disproportionate influence on the shaping of news content and what people think about.
See *social control*.

e-mail a technology for sending small files, which usually contain interpersonal messages, from one computer to another.
E-mail also is called *simple mail transfer protocol* (SMTP). Larger files are sent *file transfer protocol* (FTP).

embedded journalists journalists who accompany military forces during armed conflict for the purpose of reporting on that conflict.
The notion of embedding journalists is not new, but it received a great deal of notoriety during the 2003 Iraq War, when the U.S. military allowed 600 journalists from the United States and other friendly countries to accompany the troops. Subsequent studies showed that embedded reporters produced news stories more favorable to the position of the U.S. military than stories produced by other journalists covering the war.
Sources: Stephen D. Cooper and Jim A. Kuypers, "Embedded Versus Behind-the-Lines Reporting on the 2003 Iraq War, pp. 161- 172 in Ralph D. Berenger (ed.), *Global Media Go to War: Role of News and Entertainment Media During the 2003 Iraq War* (Spokane, WA: Marquette Books, 2004).

emotional distress a concept in media law that allows people to sue media organizations when news stories cause them emotional distress.

A plaintiff can sue for emotional distress when a story or defendant's actions are outrageous and go beyond the bounds of decency. But winning such lawsuits is difficult.

For example, the evangelist Jerry Falwell sued "Hustler Magazine," a pornographic publication, for libel and emotional distress after it published a parody advertisement which stated that Falwell had sex for the first time in an outhouse with his mother. The high court ruled in Hustler Magazine v. Falwell (1988) that public figures can collect damages for emotional distress inflicted by a cartoon or caricature if the plaintiff can prove malice. Falwell was unable to win because he could not prove that the ad was published with malice. The high court also rejected Falwell's libel claim because no reasonable person could have believed the statements about Falwell were factual.

In rare instances, plaintiffs may also win lawsuits against the media for negligent infliction of emotional distress. For example, one lower court ruled in favor of rape victims who agreed to be interviewed on camera on the condition they not be identified. However, the faces and voices of the women were not masked well enough and one woman was identified by her family.

See *libel*.

Source: *Hustler Magazine, Inc. v. Falwell*, 485 U.S. 46 (1988).

empirical research research that subscribes to the philosophical doctrine of *empiricism*.

empiricism the idea or philosophical doctrine that knowledge is obtained through experience, experiment or observation (i.e., sensory experience), as opposed to being acquired through the application of reason.

See *rationalism* and *positivism*.

encoding the process of creating a mass media message.

See *communication*.

Enlightenment, Age of (or Age of Reason) an 18th-century European movement characterized by *rationalism*, learning, and *empiricism*.

Enlightenment thinkers like Jeremy Bentham in England, Jean-Jacques Rousseau in France, and *Thomas Jefferson, Benjamin Franklin* and Thomas Paine in America wrote books and articles that embraced reason and scientific knowledge and disputed ideas based upon traditional authority, dogma, and religious speculation. One of the most influential Enlightenment writers was France's *Voltaire*, who wrote "Candide," a powerful attack on organized religion.

entrepreneurial media a mass media organization that has a simple organizational structure.

See *corporate media* and *global media*.

epistemology the theory of knowledge, or how we, as humans, come to know what we know.

Epistemology is a branch of philosophy that examines the role of sense perception in the acquisition of knowledge, as well as the possibility of attaining objective knowledge (i.e., knowledge beyond appearances or what our senses can detect). Epistemology also focuses on developing criteria that justify one theory over another.

Two of the most common ways of acquiring knowledge include sense perception and hypothesis testing.

See *ontology, paradigm,* and *positivism.*

ethical decision-making the process through which mass media practitioners make ethical decisions.

Codes of ethics often provide clear guidelines to mass media practitioners when they confront *ethical dilemmas.* But not always. In those cases, some scholars argue that a media professional needs at least two things to make a good decision: (1) a general understanding of ethics and ethical decision-making concepts or processes, and (2) a set of rules, such as the *Potter Box* (discussed below), for making a decision.

The notion that there is a right or wrong response to any ethical situation is called *absolutist ethics.* Proponents of this perspective believe in hard and fast rules that should be applied regardless of the circumstances or the situation.

In contrast, *situational ethics* holds that decisions should be made without rigid adherence to a set of rules. The facts of the situation must be weighed before making a decision, and two similar events may be treated differently.

These two approaches have their advantages and disadvantages. The absolutist position can be criticized for being inflexible. Moreover, no set of rules can take into account every situation or event. The situational ethics position is often criticized for being a contradiction in terms. If every situation is treated differently, then how can one talk about ethical conduct, which implies a set of rules to guide behavior?

In practice, media workers employ a mix of both perspectives. General rules guide behavior, but each situation is also unique and must be evaluated before making a decision. Beyond this, Ethics Professor John C. Merrill divides the world of ethics into two major camps.

The first is pragmatic ethics, which holds that journalists and other media workers should do whatever they can to get the job done. An action is moral if it succeeds in reaching the goal, such as telling the truth. The ends are more important than the means. The key motivation is the desire for success. An extreme form of pragmatic ethics is Machiavellism, which would even justify illegal actions to achieve a goal.

Merrill points out that pragmatic ethics doesn't play much of a role in contemporary discussions of ethics, because most journalists want to focus more on what is the right or best thing to do. For this, they turn to humanistic ethics. The focus may be altruistic (concern for others) or egoistic (self-development or self-improvement), but in either case humanistic ethics makes the assumption that social integration or stability is good. In other words, ethical decisions should benefit the group, community or society and contribute to social order.

Merrill divides humanistic ethics into three more categories:

1. *Deontological ethics*, which says an action or behavior is ethical if it follows a pre-established set of rules or principles without reference to the consequences of that action. Workers who follow the rules are ethical, and those who do not are unethical. Moreover, a media worker has a duty to follow the rules, irrespective of the consequences of those rules.

The rules may come from reason, religious authorities, political leaders, employers or categorical imperative. The latter term was coined by Immanuel Kant, who is often cited as the most prominent proponent of deontological ethics. He argued only actions that come out of a duty to a set of rules or principles were ethical. His categorical imperative states that an action is ethical for a person if that is what that person would have everybody else do. For example, no one would want everyone else to lie, so lying is unethical.

2. *Teleological ethics*, which states that a rule or action is moral if it produces good results, especially for society. In practical terms, this involves asking the question: What are the consequences of publishing this story or picture? This is an "ends" approach. The teleological approach is often called "relative" because it involves assessing the outcomes of an action (e.g., a news story) on a case-by-case basis.

John Stuart Mill is the most often cited proponent of the altruistic version of the teleological approach. He said a rule or action is moral when it produces the greatest good for the greatest number.

Russian immigrant and writer Ayn Rand is a proponent of the egotistical version. She argued that an action is moral when it produces the greatest good for the individual. However, consistent with the "invisible hand" theory of free-market economics, she argued that individual egoism would generate benefits for society as a whole.

3. *Personalist ethics*, which holds that an action or rule is ethical if the individual makes decisions based on mystical insights, "god," intuition, emotion, conscience or instinct. This approach is called nonrational, because it does not involve the use of reason to guide action. Rather, action is based on subjective feelings or emotions. Existentialism, which holds the universe is purposeless and people must oppose this hostile environment with their free will, is often classified as a personalist ethical approach.

Merrill argues that in practice journalists use all three approaches. In addition, one can argue that all three often can be used to reach opposing conclusions.

The upshot of all this is that ethics involves many subjective decisions. In the final analysis, it boils down to what social scientists call *intersubjectivity*. This is the notion that truth or the rightness of an action is determined largely by agreement among people. In this case, the truth is determined by the rules that media professionals themselves generate.

But such rules do not always provide clear guidelines. So how does one reach an ethical decision when no clear guidelines exist?

Many scholars and professionals turn to former Harvard Divinity School ethicist Ralph Potter, who developed a decision-making process called the *Potter Box*. Quite simply, this involves four steps to reach an ethical decision.

The first step is to define the situation. This often involves asking a simple question: Should journalists engage in the behavior? Beyond this, a prudent journalist also would want to know whether there are laws prohibiting the behavior.

The second step is to identify important values and weigh the importance of competing values.

The third step is to identify formal ethical principles that might apply, such as the Society of Professional Journalists' Code of Ethics.

The fourth step, according to Potter, is to choose loyalties. The journalists could be loyal to themselves, to the newspaper, to the sources, to the university, and/or to the community.

See *ethics, ethical dilemmas, Society of Professional Journalists.*

Sources: John C. Merrill, *Journalism Ethics: Philosophical Foundations for News Media* (New York: St. Martin's Press, 1997). See especially Chapter 3; Niccolo Machiavelli, *The Prince* (New York: Bantam Books, 1966), originally published in 1513; John Stuart Mill, *Utilitarianism* (Indianapolis: Hackett Publishing Company, 1979), originally published in 1861; Ayn Rand, *The Virtue of Selfishness* (New York: New American Library, 1964); Ralph B. Potter, "The Logic of Moral Argument," pp. 93-114 in Paul Deats (ed.), *Toward a Discipline of Social Ethics* (Boston: Boston University Press, 1972).

ethical dilemmas a situation in which an individual or an organization must choose between two or more courses of action, each of which presents conflicts in values, and/or when there is not widespread agreement regarding whether process or intended outcomes are ethical.

In the media setting, *codes of ethics* often reduce ambiguity for media professionals when confronting a situation that involves ethical conduct. Lying (e.g., the *Janet Cooke* incident), for example, is clearly a violation of all journalism codes of ethics. However, there are many areas of disagreement, and codes of ethics do not always provide easy answers. These are called ethical dilemmas, and they include, among other things:

1. Censorship. Almost everyone agrees that the government shouldn't censor mass media, except perhaps in cases of national security. But the issue of censorship also applies to the mass media themselves, because they continually make decisions about what should and what should not be published or broadcast.

For example, should news media always publish or broadcast letters to the editor and commentaries that criticize people, especially the news organizations and its staff? Many journalists believe they should. But not all news organizations follow this policy.

2. Hate Speech. Should news media publish or broadcast letters that contain "false information" or so-called "hate speech?" Many newspapers

refuse to publish "hate speech" letters, for fear of offending community groups, or inciting violence or a public backlash.

However, *First Amendment* advocates argue that the corrective for "bad speech" isn't censorship, but more speech. They also argue that editing to exclude so-called "false information" puts the journalist in the elitist position of judging the truth. Even false ideas, First Amendment advocates point out, can contribute to a healthy public debate.

3. Coverage of Terrorism. Should news media publish transcripts from or broadcast videotapes made by terrorists?

In October 2001, a month after the 9/11 attack, the White House asked the six major U.S. television news organizations to censor videotaped statements made by Osama bin Laden and other terrorists. These organizations agreed with the White House that propagandistic statements could incite hatred and potentially endanger more American lives.

However, many journalists disagreed with this decision. They argue that the public has a right to know what terrorists are saying, and withholding such information may make it more difficult for people to protect themselves and to understand the issues.

4. Anonymous Sources. Should news media publish information from anonymous sources?

Some journalists argue that anonymous sources should never be used because those sources can give false information without being accountable. However, others argue some news could never be reported without anonymous sources, who often have legitimate reasons for protecting their identity.

5. Full Disclosure. Should public relations officials exclude information that casts an individual or organization in a bad light?

Some public relations professionals argue their goal is to promote the positive, not the negative, aspects of an individual or an organization. Unless a journalist or a citizen asks, negative information need not be offered. Others argue that public relations professionals have an obligation to provide full disclosure if that information affects the public.

6. Profane Language. In June 2004, Vice President Dick Cheney, a Republican, told Sen. Patrick Leahy, a Democrat, to "fuck off" or "go fuck yourself" during a heated exchange on the Senate floor (aides who overheard the discussion had different versions). Should mass media publish or broadcast profane or so-called obscene language?

Some media did and some did not. Opponents argue that mass media should not publish content offensive to large numbers of people in the community, irrespective of whether it is legal. However, others argue that deleting or editing words can often change the meaning of a message and lead to inaccurate perceptions. Another, a middle-of-the-road perspective, is that exceptions to the profane rule can be made when, for example, a controversy specifically erupts over lewd language itself (e.g., lyrics of a song).

7. <u>False Identities and Hidden Cameras.</u> Should journalists use false identities or hidden cameras in order to uncover wrongdoing or illegal activities?

Some journalists argue false identities or hidden cameras should never be used, because they can reduce public confidence in journalism as an institution. Others argue that false identities can be used (e.g., going "undercover") when there is no other way to uncover a wrongdoing or illegal activity (e.g., false military reports, drug smuggling). During the 1970s, the "Chicago Sun Times" operated a "fake" bar and restaurant to expose bribes made to city officials.

8. <u>Exaggerated Advertising Claims.</u> Should advertising contain exaggerated claims?

Some advertising professionals argue that advertising should never exaggerate the effectiveness or performance of a product or service. Others point out, however, that most advertising contains exaggerated claims, which is OK because the public has come to accept such claims as part of the advertising industry.

9. <u>Rape Victims' Names.</u> Should a news organization publish the name of a rape victim?

Some journalists argue that a woman's name should not be used because it could subject her to public ridicule or shame. Others argue that rape victims must be accountable to the public, because their accusations can send a person to prison for a long time. A third perspective, not often used, is to ask the defendants and rape victims themselves what they prefer.

10. <u>Journalists' Conflict of Interest.</u> Should journalists accept favors, gifts or services from news sources in order to get a story?

Some journalists argue they should never accept anything of value from a source, even if it would not affect the way they report a story. These professionals believe accepting gifts from sources leads to a public perception of conflict of interest, which damages public trust in the profession. Others argue that if there is no other way to report a story, or if a news organization does not have the resources to cover an important story, it's acceptable to receive a favor or gift as long as the news organization makes that information public.

11. <u>Owners' Conflicts of Interest.</u> Should owners of news media also own or have major investments in other non-media businesses in a community? Should owners use their news media holdings to advance their own personal interests?

Some journalists argue that news media owners should not have other business investments in a community, because such investments make it difficult for the organization to report with objectivity on those holdings. Most journalists also argue that media owners should not use their media holdings to advance their own personal interests, because it would be self-serving, violating public trust and the journalistic tradition of impartiality.

Other journalists argue that owners of news media should be allowed to invest in anything in a community, irrespective of how those investments may affect news coverage. Newspapers, they argue, are part of their communities and therefore have an interest in promoting the economic health of their community.

12. Sensitive Pictures. Should a news organization publish or broadcast a picture of a naked woman running from a burning building or a child who has been killed or injured?

Some journalists argue that publishing or broadcasting these kinds of pictures violates personal privacy of individuals or the families. Others contend these kinds of pictures are powerful statements about fragility and preciousness of human life.

13. Participant Tape Recording. Should news media voice record sources without their knowledge to protect themselves against libel lawsuits?

Some journalists argue that *participant monitoring* (or second-party tape recording), which means only one of the parties knows the recording is being made, violates the privacy of a source. Others point out, however, that since the information is given on the record, it is no different from taking copious notes, except there is recorded (objective) evidence.

(By the way, third-party tape recording, in which the party doing the taping is not part of the conversation, is always illegal without a court-ordered wiretap.)

14. Over-Dependence on Elites. Should news media get most of their news and information from elite sources, or should they reach out more to disadvantaged or non-mainstream groups?

Some scholars and professionals argue it is unethical for the news media to depend so heavily on powerful groups. They urge journalists to collect more news from disadvantaged groups, such as minorities and the poor. Other scholars and professionals argue that *civic journalism* or public journalism is one method for overcoming this problem and that journalism today is more sensitive to the needs of these groups than ever before.

ethics a set of rules or principles to guide behavior.

In higher education, ethics (or moral philosophy) is also a discipline concerned with what is morally good and bad, right and wrong. Morality is the rightness or wrongness of an action. But the use of the term in the field of mass communication is primarily concerned with ethics as a set of principles, not as a discipline of study.

A *code of ethics* is a collection of principles or rules spelling out how a group of professionals, in this case media workers, should act. A code is a mechanism for controlling mass media workers, although journalists often do not face formal punishment or jail time for violating a code.

For example, the American Society of Newspaper Editors' "Canons of Journalism," which was enacted in 1922, stated that journalists should be truthful, and those who use their power for selfish reasons violate a public trust. When *Janet Cooke* and *Jayson Blair* fabricated some facts for their stories, their actions violated codes of ethics but not the law.

The study of ethics is as old as the study of philosophy. Media ethics has a much shorter history. The first formal, or written, set of rules guiding the profession emerged in the 1860s at a newspaper in Philadelphia. Less formal notions existed before that.

Although formal, written rules of conduct did not appear until the 1860s, informal, unwritten rules existed much earlier. For example, during the 1700s, many newspapers refused to publish crime stories because of concerns such news may contribute to juvenile delinquency.

In 1864, the Philadelphia Public Ledger listed 24 rules of journalistic conduct. Among other things, the rules stressed accuracy and fairness when covering the Civil War. The first formal critique of journalism ethics appeared in 1889 in "The Forum." The first code of conduct for journalists was spelled out in a speech in 1890. By this time, according to Dicken-Garcia, there was a great deal of discussion about journalism education and ethical training. Journalists clearly had come to the conclusion that personal opinion and news should be separated.

The first formal, written code of ethics appeared in 1910. The Kansas Editorial Association adopted a code written by William E. Miller. More importantly, in 1911 Will Irwin, a famous newspaper reporter and book author, wrote a 15-part series, "The American Newspaper," for "Collier's Magazine." The article provided a history of the medium and exposed unethical practices.

In the early 1900s, the advertising industry also became increasingly concerned about the impact of unethical practices on its industry. Many manufacturers of so-called "patent medicines" often made unsubstantiated claims. In 1911, the Associated Advertising Clubs of America debated the problem of fraudulent advertising at its annual conference. By the 1920s more than 20 states had enacted statutes making deceptive and fraudulent advertising illegal.

Before he died in 1911, newspaper magnate Joseph Pulitzer gave $2 million to establish the School of Journalism at Columbia University and emphasize ethics in the curriculum. During the 1920s, many state journalism associations and individual news organizations initiated their own codes of ethics. The most significant of these codes was the "Canons of Journalism," created in 1922 by the *American Society of Newspaper Editors (ASNE)*. Among other things, the code stated that (1) journalists who use their power for selfish reasons violate a public trust; (2) freedom of the press is a vital right of "mankind"; (3) journalists should not accept bribes or money from news sources; and (4) journalists should be sincere, truthful, accurate, impartial and fair.

The first textbook on the ethics of journalism was published in 1924. In 1926, Sigma Delta Chi (now known as *The Society of Professional Journalists*) patterned its code after the ASNE code. During the 1920s, many large newspapers also began creating their own codes of ethics. Larger papers had a greater need for such formal rules because their staffs were larger and more difficult to control through informal rules.

During the 1930s, Congress established the *Federal Communications Commission (FCC)* to regulate radio stations, which must operate "in the public interest, convenience, and necessity." Essentially, the FCC said radio station owners have a moral obligation to provide audiences with content benefitting the community and/or promoting social integration. In 1949, the FCC strengthened the notion that the airwaves are public property, requiring broadcasters to report all sides in a controversy.

But the most significant statement on ethics and the media in the 1940s came from the Commission on Freedom of the Press, which was funded in part by "Time" magazine publisher *Henry R. Luce* and "Encyclopedia Britannica."

The Commission, led by University of Chicago educator Robert Maynard Hutchins, questioned whether freedom and democracy could survive in a social system where the communication channels are concentrated in the hands of a few. "Have the units of the press, by becoming big business, lost their representative character and developed a common bias—the bias of the large investor and employer?" Later, the commission added: "Our society needs an accurate, truthful account of the day's events. ... These needs are not being met. The news is twisted by the emphasis on firstness, on the novel and sensational; by the personal interests of the owners; and by pressure groups."

The Commission coined what later came to be called the *Social Responsibility Theory* of the press. Basically, this was the notion that a free press must be accountable to society—it must be responsible and must contribute to the social good (see "Normative Theories of the Press" below for elaboration).

By 1950, the so-called *ethic of objectivity* had become a firmly established practice in journalism. The assumption was that truth would emerge if journalists kept their personal opinions out of stories, quoted all sides to a story, and gave roughly equal coverage to those sides.

However, objectivity itself became a target of attack during the so-called "McCarthy era," which began in February 1950 when Sen. Joseph R. McCarthy, a Republican from Wisconsin, charged that 205 communists had infiltrated the U.S. State Department. Although he was never able to substantiate these and many other charges, McCarthy held many press conferences and the news media quoted him extensively and covered his senatorial hearings. McCarthy was eventually exposed as a fraud and censured by the Senate, but not before he had ruined many careers and lives.

During the 1960s, the mass media were criticized for publishing and broadcasting false information about the Vietnam War (information that supported the U.S. military) and for failing to cover civil rights. The Kerner Commission issued a report indicting the U.S. media for failing to cover black communities and issues relevant to this community.

These criticisms fueled a "new journalism" movement that was highly critical of objectivity and traditional reporting methods. Instead of objectivity, the "new journalists" advocated various forms of subjectivity, which they said was more effective at revealing the truth. Truman Capote's "In Cold Blood" is the good example of the genre, which reported on real-life events but included people's motivations and feelings.

The Watergate scandal in the early 1970s also gave alternative journalism a shot in the arm. Investigative reporting, in particular, was seen as a method that could overcome some of the problems associated with the ethic of objectivity and routine news reporting. What distinguished investigative reporting from routine news reporting was that the burden of proof lay on the journalist, not the sources, per se.

The new journalism movement began to wane in the late 1970s, as the Vietnam War ended and new laws and court decisions provided more rights and protections to women and minorities. The ethic of objectivity survived and remains the primary guiding principle in U.S. journalism.

Press councils, which first emerged in the early 1970s, were also another mechanism for defining ethical behavior and controlling journalists. The first one was created in Minnesota in 1971. A National News Council was created in 1974, but it disbanded for lack of support and only three states currently have press councils (Minnesota, Washington, Oregon, and Hawaii).

Janet Cooke's fabricated story about an 8-year-old heroin addict helped fuel public distrust of news media organizations in the early 1980s. A national poll showed that during the 1970s about 25 percent of the public had "a great deal" of confidence in the press. That figure dropped to about 14 percent in 1983.

The nonprofit *Poynter Institute for Media Studies* offered its first ethics course for journalists in 1984. The *Freedom Forum*, another foundation that focuses on ethics and First Amendment issues, was established in 1991. The Society of Professional Journalists revised its code of ethics in 1996.

Responding in part to concerns that news media depended too heavily on powerful bureaucratic elites for news, many newspapers in the 1990s began conducting *civic journalism* or public journalism projects. The Pew Charitable Trusts in 1993 created *The Pew Center for Civic Journalism*. The Center bills itself as "an incubator for civic journalism experiments that enable news organizations to create and refine better ways of reporting the news to re-engage people in public life."

The civic journalism movement is credited with playing a small role in decentralizing political power. However, civic journalism has not led to radical reforms in local communities.

See *Blair, Jayson; Cooke, Janet; ethic of objectivity*, and *Society of Professional Journalists*.

Sources: George Henry Payne, *History of Journalism in the United States* (New York: D. Appleton, 1925), pp. 251-253; W. S. Lilly, "The Ethics of Journalism," *The Forum*, 4:503-512 (July 1889); C. C. Bonney, "The Duties and Privileges of the Public Press," in W. W. Catlin (comp.), *Echoes of the Sunset Club* (Chicago: Sunset Club, 1891), p. 16; Will Irwin, "The American Newspaper: A Study of Journalism in its Relation to the Public," reprinted in Clifford F. Weigle and David G. Clark (eds.), *The American Newspaper by Will Irwin* (Ames: Iowa State University Press, 1969) [The original was published in Collier's Magazine; Nelson Antrim Crawford, *The Ethics of Journalism* (New York: A. A. Knopf,

1924)]; Commission on Freedom of the Press, *A Free and Responsible Press* (Chicago: University of Chicago Press, 1947).

ethic of objectivity a proscription that journalists, when covering news stories, should keep personal opinions out of news stories, cover all sides of the story, and give roughly equal weight to all sides; opinions are properly expressed only on the editorial and op-ed pages, or in "news analyses."

The history of the ethic of objectivity goes back almost to the origins of mass media themselves. However, it did not become a social institution until the late 19th and early 20th centuries, when journalists copied the methods of the social sciences (objectivity in observation).

By 1950, the so-called *ethic of objectivity* had become a firmly established practice in journalism. The amplification by the press of irresponsible and highly damaging charges made by Sen. Joseph McCarthy (beginning in February 1950) resulted in a backlash of criticism. The ethic of objectivity came under further assault during the 1960s, when the U.S. military disseminated false information to journalists in order to promote U.S. involvement in Vietnam and Southeast Asia. Some journalists were not easily misled, but editors at home were reluctant to publish content critical of U.S. policy.

Mainstream journalism and the ethic of objectivity also came under assault after race riots erupted in many U.S. cities in the late 1960s. The Kerner Commission issued a report indicting the U.S. media for failing to cover black communities and issues relevant to them. Heavy reliance on bureaucratic officials (most of whom were white) as sources of news was partly to blame.

The ethic of objectivity was further challenged by the "new journalism" movement of the 1960s and 1970s. The new journalists, who included Tom Wolfe, Jimmy Breslin, Gay Talese, Norman Mailer, Truman Capote, and Nicholas von Hoffman, wrote articles and books reporting on real-life events but using elements of fiction writing, such as people's motivations and feelings and extensive analysis of events and surroundings.

Despite these assaults, the ethic of objectivity survived and remains the primary guiding principle in U.S. journalism. Defenders of objectivity pointed out quite correctly that, despite its limitations, the "objective approach" is effective in providing readers with a greater number and variety of alternative points of view.

Most journalists are quick to acknowledge that objectivity is difficult to achieve in practice. But few either recognize or acknowledge that journalistic norms and practices actually generate their own bias—one that tends to support mainstream power groups and powerful elites and institutions over less powerful and unorthodox groups. That's part of the reason the mass media are often called the "*mainstream media.*"

See *ethics* and *mainstream bias*.

ethnography a qualitative method of inquiry that involves direct observation and documentation of social organization, customs, beliefs, etc., in a group, organization or small society.

Sometimes researchers "join" the group or society in order to better understand and document it.

ethnomethodology a qualitative method of inquiry that understands and/or explains the world and human events as a product of the rational accomplishment of individuals.

Ethnomethodology was devised by Harold Garfinkel, who sought to reveal methods people use to construct a sense of social reality. Ethnomethodologists are critical of social scientists, believing this approach treats people as "cultural dupes." Conversational analysis is one form of ethnomethodology.

expectancy-value theory a theory of persuasion that attempts to predict behavior as the product of *beliefs, attitudes,* and intentions.

explanatory analysis research in which the goal is to account for why something is as it is.

At the heart of explanatory analysis is the concept of *cause and effect.*

ex post facto hypothesizing hypothesizing that is undertaken after the *data* are analyzed to explain findings not anticipated by original *hypotheses.*

external public see *public.*

external validity the extent to which the results from an experiment may be generalized to people and situations outside the experimental setting.

See *internal validity.*

extras actors who work full or part time for a film studio or filmmaker but have minor roles in movies, often with no speaking part.

F

face validity a *measure* or *indicator* that logically appears to be a good *measure* of some *concept* (i.e., has "face value").

factor analysis a *descriptive statistic* used primarily to reduce three or more *continuous measures* to a smaller number of measures.

The primary function of factor analysis is to improve measurement. Factor analysis essentially correlates three or more variables and then creates new variables, or factors, that maximize the variance within and minimize the variance between (the other factors). The factors themselves can be used to create new variables.

For example, factor analysis has been used to create quality variables for news media. Journalists are asked to rate the importance their organization places on "increasing profits," "maximizing profits," "reducing costs," "responding to readers' needs," "doing the job well," "improving the news product," "being the best," and "hiring the best employees."

The factor analysis shows the first three items are strongly correlated with each other (profit index) and the last five items are strongly with each other (quality index), but the two indices are not strongly correlated. The two indices are then used in subsequent analysis, rather than the seven individual items, because the indices are more refined and contain less measurement error.

fairness doctrine a requirement, formally announced in 1949 by the Federal Communications Commission (FCC) but since rescinded, that broadcasters are obligated to air diverse views on public issues.

The FCC believed broadcasters should devote a reasonable amount of their programming to controversial issues of public importance and to provide contrasting points of view. There was not enough room on the radio spectrum for everyone to have their own radio station. Therefore, the FCC felt it was "fair" for those with a license to present a wide range of perspectives.

Although the theory was good, in practice the Fairness Doctrine created many problems for broadcasters. Many complaints and lawsuits were filed, and some broadcasters complained the doctrine actually stifled a robust debate, because broadcasters would be required to provide the other side of a perspective, or perhaps many other sides. In 1987, the FCC eliminated the Fairness Doctrine.

false light the public portrayal of someone in a distorted or fictionalized way.

See *privacy, invasion of.*

Farnsworth, Philo T. (1906-1971) inventor of the dissector tube, which became the basis for television.

Farnsworth obtained an early patent for the invention but lost other patent battles to RCA. Farnsworth invented more than 160 different electronic devices for television. He also was the first to broadcast a 60-line television image.

feature film a full-length movie, usually about 90 minutes, whose primary function is to entertain rather than to educate.

Compare with *documentary film* and *animated film.*

feature story a style of writing that usually involves the use of delayed leads and places importance on telling a good story.

Feature stories often focus on pleasant or happy events or interesting people (personality profile). Hard news, in contrast, often focuses on social and political problems. But sociologists point out that features and hard news both reinforce general norms and values in a society.

See *inverted pyramid.*

Federal Communications Commission (FCC) a federal government agency responsible to Congress that regulates over-the-air broadcast media and telecommunications.

The FCC was created with passage of the *Communications Act of 1934.* The FCC bills itself as an "independent United States government agency, directly responsible to Congress." However, the selection of commissioners is a highly political process, and their decisions have a major impact on the broadcasting industry.

The FCC regulates interstate and international communications that involve radio, television, wire (which includes telephone), satellite, and cable. The FCC has jurisdiction over the 50 states, the District of Columbia, and U.S. possessions.

The President of the United States appoints five commissioners, with confirmation from the Senate, to 5-year terms. The President also selects one commissioner to serve as chairperson. Only three commissioners may be members of the same political party, and none is allowed to have a financial interest in any commission-related business.

The FCC has seven bureaus and 10 staff offices, where responsibilities include processing applications for licenses and other filings, investigating complaints, conducting investigations, developing and implementing regulatory programs, and taking part in hearings.

The Mass Media Bureau regulates AM and FM radio and television broadcast stations, as well as Multipoint Distribution (i.e., cable and satellite) and Instructional Television Fixed Services. The Bureau issues broadcast licenses that specify the community of license and the channel and operating power of the station. This information ensures broadcasts will be picked up without static interference within a specified service area.

The single most important power of the FCC is to issue or revoke radio and television over-the-air broadcast licenses. The licenses are issued for a period of eight years, and when one expires the broadcaster must file for a renewal. The FCC grants renewals only if it finds that "the public interest, convenience, and necessity would be served." The Commission makes a decision after obtaining public feedback, but rarely does it revoke a license.

The FCC does not have the authority to select or dictate broadcast programming. However, it can restrict *indecent programming*, place limits on the number of commercials aired during children's programming, and set rules for access during elections. These rules apply only to broadcast radio and television stations; they do not apply to cable-only stations.

The *Children's Television Act of 1990* also gave the FCC the authority to regulate the number of advertisements and the amount of entertainment content on programs targeted to children.

In 1971, the FCC adopted the prime-time access rule, which limits to three hours an evening the amount of commercial *television network* programming in the 50 largest markets. The rule was intended to encourage local, not just national, programming during the four prime-time hours, and to provide a market for independent producers. However, most local stations have turned to syndicated programming, such as game shows and situation comedies. The problem is that local programming is expensive to produce and often cannot pay for itself.

See *Children's Television Act of 1990*, *indecent programming*, *media ownership rules*, *Radio Act of 1912*, *Radio Act of 1927*, *Communications Act of 1934*, *Stern, Howard*, and *Telecommunications Act of 1996*.

Source: Federal Communications Commission Web site <www.fcc.gov>.

Federal Trade Commission (FTC) a regulatory body established by Congress in 1914 with authority to prosecute advertisers who engage in false advertising.

More generally, the role of the commission is to enforce federal antitrust and consumer protection laws. It "seeks to ensure that the nation's markets function competitively, and are vigorous, efficient, and free of undue restrictions." The Commission also advances the policies underlying Congressional mandates through consumer education.

See *Wheeler-Lea Amendments*.

Source: The Federal Trade Commission Web site <www.ftc.gov>.

feedback an element of *communication* in which a receiver of a message responds to the sender.

See *communication*.

Fessenden, Reginald (1866-1932) a Canadian inventor who discovered amplitude modulation (AM radio) and who is often called the "father of radio."

On Dec. 24, 1906, Fessenden became the first inventor to transmit the human voice via wireless radio from Brant Rock, near Boston, to several ships at sea. He also invented 200 other electronic components.

However, the Canadian government had signed an exclusive wireless deal with *Guglielmo Marconi*, who had developed the wireless telegraph, and Fessenden also lost control of many of his patents to unscrupulous partners.

See *telegraph*.

fighting words doctrine a legal principle that, while it does not ban hate speech, says the government may prohibit speech that urges people to use violence.

The U.S. Supreme Court defines "fighting words" as words that "by their very utterance inflict injury or tend to incite an immediate breach of the peace." If violent or illegal actions are likely to take place, then such words or speech is not protected by the First Amendment, but hate speech that does not lead to violent action is protected.

These principles were established in two major decisions. The first was in 1971, when the Supreme Court overturned the conviction of an anti-Vietnam War protestor who wore a jacket with the words "Fuck the Draft" on the back (Cohen v. California, 1971). The message did not constitute fighting words, the court said, because it was not a direct personal insult and presented no danger of violent physical confrontation.

Similarly, hate speech targeted against individuals or ethnic groups is also protected so long as it does not involve actions that physically harm people.

This principle was established in a case that involved a 17-year-old boy who burned a cross in the fenced yard of an African American family. The City of St. Paul, Minn., convicted the man for violating an ordinance that made it a crime for anyone to place a symbol, object or graffiti on property if it was likely to arouse "anger, alarm or resentment in others on the basis of race, color, creed, religion or gender."

The U.S. Supreme Court overturned the ordinance in 1992. The court said the man could not be prosecuted for hating people. But he could be prosecuted if his actions violated other laws, such as trespassing or damage to property. The man was also indicted for conspiring to interfere with the family's right to housing.

See *clear and present danger, hostile audience problem.*

Sources: *Chaplinsky v. New Hampshire*, 315 U.S. 568 (1942) and *Cohen v. California*, 403 U.S. 15, 20 (1971).

file transfer protocols (FTP) a technology for transmitting larger files from computer to computer.

Smaller files can be sent through *simple mail transfer protocol*, more popularly known as *e-mail*.

film (a) a plastic-like material used to record photographs or motion pictures; **(b)** a *motion picture*.

See *motion picture.*

film editor in filmmaking, the person who edits and cuts the sound tracks and film negatives or videotapes to produce the final product.

This process involves adding or deleting sounds, dialogue, and special effects. The film editor works closely with the *director*.

film projector a device that projects an illuminated film image onto a screen, which allows many people to watch the image at the same time.

The film projector replaced the *Kinetograph*, which only allowed one person to view at a time.

See *Edison, Thomas A.*

filthy words see *indecent programming.*

First Amendment the first Bill of Rights, ratified in 1791, which states, in its entirety: "Congress shall make no law respecting an establishment of religion, or prohibiting the free exercise thereof; or abridging the freedom of speech, or of the press; or the right of the people peaceably to assemble, and to petition the Government for redress of grievances."

The First Amendment and the other nine Bill of Rights were not part of the original Constitution drafted by James Madison. He wanted a strong federal government. But some of the new U.S. states were leery of centralized power because they'd just finished fighting Great Britain partly over the lack of local control.

To ensure passage of the U.S. Constitution, Madison agreed to head a committee that wrote the 10 amendments in the Bill of Rights. Actually, there were 12 amendments, but the first two failed to get approval. By default, the third one became the First Amendment.

For more information on how the government and courts define freedom of speech and the press, see *law, prior restraint, fighting words doctrine, clear and present danger, hostile audience problem, corporate speech, commercial speech, symbolic speech.*

first cameraperson same as *cinematographer.*

fixed-fee arrangements in the field of public relations, a method of charging clients that involves a set fee for a specific service.

flak a derogatory term for a public relations practitioner, especially one who distorts the truth.
    In military terminology, flak is the shrapnel that comes from antiaircraft fire and its purpose is to prevent an aircraft from achieving its objective. In the field of mass communications, flak refers to people who insert themselves between their organizations and the news media.

Fleischman, Doris E. see *Bernays, Edward L.*

flysheet a small, one-sided untitled sheet of paper that contained news reports and other information.
    The flysheet was one of the predecessors to the modern newspaper. European wood-block printers published them during the early 1400s.

focus group a method of gathering *marketing research* data in which a small group of *respondents* talks informally about a product, service, company or issue.
    A moderator usually directs or guides the focus group, seeking answers to specific questions that will help a company improve product development, sales or marketing.

folio (a) a page number; in book publishing, the folio is usually placed in the upper left-hand corner on even-numbered pages (verso) and the upper right-hand corner on odd numbered pages (recto); **(b)** a sheet of 11 x 17" paper that, when printed and folded, results in two 8½ x 11" pages; **(c)** a large book, usually with a length of 15 inches or more.

format (a) the shape, binding, type face, size, paper, etc., of a book, newspaper or magazine; **(b)** general arrangement or plan of a radio station (e.g., music, talk radio), television program or an Internet Web site; **(c)** characteristics of recording media (e.g., disks, tapes, compact discs).
    See *recording format.*

format clock (or programming wheel) in radio programming, a pie chart that divides an hour's worth of programming into different segments.
    A format clock ensures continuity and predictability in programming.

Foster, Jodi (1962-) one of Hollywood's most prominent female directors and actors.
    Foster was only three years old when she starred in her first television commercial, promoting Coppertone suntan lotion. By the time she was 8,

she had starred in 40 commercials. Before she turned 14, she had performed in about a dozen television shows and a half-dozen movies.

Her biggest performance came at age 14, when she starred as a 12-year-old prostitute in Martin Scorsese's gritty drama, "Taxi Driver" (1976). She won her first Oscar nomination. Since then, she has won a Best Actress Oscar for her performance as a rape victim in "The Accused" (1988); a Best Actress Oscar for her performance as a federal agent in "The Silence of the Lambs" (1991); a Best Actress Oscar nomination for "Nell" (1994); and a Golden Globe nomination for her performance as an astronomer in "Contact" (1997).

In recent years, Foster has increasingly turned to working behind the camera. She made her directorial debut in 1991 with "Little Man Tate," in which she also starred. In 1995, she directed "Home for the Holidays." Her third directorial project is "Flora Plum," which focuses on a penniless girl who is taken in by a circus freak. And she has more than a half-dozen other projects in the works.

Foster attended Yale University and immersed herself in comparative literature studies. She was thrust into the limelight in 1981 when John Hinckley Jr. shot President Ronald Reagan and claimed he did it to impress Foster, his idol.

Sources: Louis Chunovic, *Jodie: A Biography* (Chicago: Contemporary Books, 1995); Philippa Kennedy, *Jodie Foster: A Life on Screen* (New York: Carol Publishing Group, 1996); and Buddy Foster, *Foster Child: A Biography of Jodie Foster* (New York: Dutton, 1997).

four-color process a method of printing in which color is reproduced by breaking down color photographs into four separate colors—magenta, cyan, yellow, and black.

In offset printing, plates are created for each of the colors and then inked to create the image. Color inkjet and laser printers also use cartridges representing each of the four colors, and some printers even divide the colors further into lighter and darker (e.g., light magenta, dark magenta).

fourth estate the notion that the news media are adversaries of government and serve to check its power.

In 1638, the term "Fourth Estate" was used to refer to the British Army. The other three were the three estates of Parliament: one representing the nobility, another the clergy, and the third the House of Commons. How the term came to be associated with the news media isn't entirely clear.

Nineteenth-century writer Thomas Carlyle gives credit for the term to Edmund Burke, an eighteenth century British statesman and political philosopher. Burke once commented that in addition to the three estates there was the Reporters' Gallery in Parliament, "a fourth estate more important than they all. It is not a figure of speech or witty saying; it is a literal fact, very momentous to us in these times."

Some historians, however, doubt this report. The first reliable citation is an essay by Thomas Bington Macaulay in 1828, who wrote that "the gallery in which the reporters sit has become a fourth estate of the realm."

Whatever the origins, the concept plays an important role in the ideology of contemporary journalism, and is closely allied with the *watchdog theory*—or the idea that the press should actively search for abuses of authority and power. More formally, the assumption behind the fourth estate concept is that the press acts as a checking mechanism, constantly reminding government groups about where ultimate sovereignty resides. Some scholars trace these ideas to *Thomas Jefferson*, the third U.S. president.

Jefferson argued the press was an essential source of information and guidance and should be free from governmental control. In addition to educating the individual, the press should serve as a check on the government, to prevent it from infringing on the rights of the individual.

Although the fourth estate and watchdog concepts are widely recognized in journalism, research suggests the news media in Western countries act more like a *guard dog* than a watchdog.

Sources: Thomas Carlyle, *Heroes: Hero-Worship and the Heroic in History* (New York: Cas. Scribner and Sons, 1841), p. 164; Dominic F. Manno, "The 'Fourth Estate': Who Used the Term First?" pp. 24-25 in Hiley H. Ward, *Mainstream of American Media History: A Narrative and Intellectual History* (Boston: Allyn and Bacon, 1997); George A. Donohue, Clarice N. Olien and Phillip J. Tichenor, "A Guard Dog Conception of Mass Media," paper presented at the annual meeting of the Association for Education in Journalism and Mass Communication, San Antonio, Texas (August 1987), pp. 2-3; and Andrew A. Lipscomb (ed.), *The Writings of Thomas Jefferson*, Volume 11 (Washington, D.C.: Thomas Jefferson Memorial Association, 1904), pp. 32-34.

four-walling a method of paying movie theaters in which a distributor pays the theater a fixed fee for renting the theater and then takes all the ticket proceeds.

framing the theory or process of how a mass media message obtains its perspective, point of view, or bias.

The idea of framing appears to have originated with sociologist Erving Goffman, who argued that frames are basic cognitive structures which guide perception. They generally are not consciously created but are unconsciously adopted in the course of communicative processes.

In the field of mass communication, some researchers think of framing as a theory, while others think of it as a process. But in either case, framing analysis begins with a simple question: How did the news media "frame" that event or story? In other words, what angle, perspective or point of view did the story have, and what angles, perspectives or views were excluded?

When these descriptive questions are answered and followed up with an analysis of why the media framed an event or story a certain way, then researchers are said to be engaging in theoretical analysis. The theory used to explain a particular frame may draw on a variety of perspectives in psychology, sociology or other disciplines.

Sources: Erving Goffman, *Frame Analysis: An Essay on the Organization of Experience* (New York: Harper & Row, 1974) and Diatram A. Scheufele, "Framing as a Theory of Media Effects," *Journal of Communication*, 49:103-119 (1999).

Frankfurt School a small group of scholars, loosely organized, who fled Germany before World War II and whose theoretical work draws heavily on *Karl Marx*'s theory of *ideology* and *Antonio Gramsci*'s concept of *hegemony*.

Founded in 1923, the Institute for Social Research in Frankfurt was a magnet for young Marxist intellectuals, including Theador Adorno, Herbert Marcuse, and Max Horkheimer. When Adolph Hitler came to power in 1933, the Institute moved to New York, where it was affiliated with the Sociology department of Columbia University. In 1949, Horkheimer took the Institute back to Germany, but Marcuse remained in the United States and in 1964 published an influential book titled, "One-Dimensional Man."

In it, Marcuse argued that technology has played a major role in the survival of modern capitalism. A highly technologized culture, he asserted, generates affluence, which removes dissent; promotes development of a bureaucratic welfare state that dominates people's lives; increases leisure time that creates the illusion of freedom; stimulates automation that shifts the labor force into white-collar positions and reduces the sense of work-place repression; and blurs the distinction between consumption patterns. More than Gramsci, Marcuse emphasizes the structural controls that contribute to maintenance of capitalism and represses the development of class consciousness.

The Frankfurt theorists and their followers shared a belief that ideology inhibited the development of class consciousness, a condition most presumed was necessary for social change. Some felt that mass media had the potential to make ordinary people aware of the exploitative aspects of capitalism. However, Adorno and Horkheimer were pessimistic about the potential for emancipation—the culture of neocapitalism is a mass culture, imposed from above, not by any indigenous culture; it promotes obedience, impedes critical judgment, and displaces dissent.

Descendants of the Frankfurt School, who are often called critical theorists (see *critical theory*), have developed more sophisticated theories of ideology, some of which empower the exploited classes or groups and incorporate resistance movements. But the movement has suffered from dogmatic perspectives and from the failure to advance a workable economic solution to the "problem" of capitalism. In fact, many contemporary critical theorists have abandoned the original goal of emancipation and now seek reform rather than revolution—an action that de-radicalizes the perspective and pushes it toward *mass media systems theory* and other more pluralistic perspectives.

See *ideology, hegemony, critical theory* and *mass media systems theory*.

Sources: Herbert Marcuse, *One-Dimensional Man* (Boston: Beacon Press, 1964); Theodore Adorno and Max Horkheimer, *Dialectic of the Enlightenment* (London: Verso, 1979); David Demers, "Has Critical Theory Lost It's Critical Edge?" pp. 263-270 in David Demers (ed.), *Global Media News Reader*, rev. ed. (Spokane, WA: Marquette Books, 2003).

Franklin, Benjamin (1706-1790) a renowned
statesman and scientist who helped make
American journalism respectable and profitable.

Franklin was born Jan. 17, 1706, in Boston,
Massachusetts, the 1ᵗʰ child and the 10th son of
17 children. His father was a soapmaker and
candlemaker.

Franklin learned to read early and
devoured every book he could get his hands on.
But his formal education ended at age 10. He
was apprenticed at age 12 to his older brother,
James, a printer. James was very strict with Ben.
He worked him 14 hours a day and boxed his
ears if he misbehaved.

Benjamin Franklin

In 1721, James founded a weekly
newspaper called the "New-England Courant" and asked readers to
contribute articles. Ben typeset these articles and knew he could write as well.
So in 1722 he wrote 14 essays that satirized the Boston authorities and
society. He anonymously signed them Silence Dogood, a fictitious Boston
widow. The articles were immensely popular. But when James found out Ben
was the author, he put an end to them.

In late 1722, James was imprisoned for publishing articles critical of the
authorities. He was released a short time later and forbidden to publish a
newspaper. To get around this rule, he made Ben the publisher.
Unbeknownst to the authorities, however, James had Ben sign papers that
allowed James to retain ownership and control of the newspaper. Several
months later, Ben had an argument with James and ran away from home.
Ben could not find work in New York City so he moved to Philadelphia,
which became his home for the rest of his life.

In 1729, Ben purchased the "Pennsylvania Gazette" and turned it into
the best newspaper in the colonies. The popularity of the newspaper brought
in advertising revenue, and Franklin excelled as a printer, writer, and
advertising copywriter. More than half of his income came from the
newspaper, the rest from his printing business.

From 1732 to 1757 he published "Poor Richard's Almanack," a rich
source of prudent and witty aphorisms on the value of thrift, hard work, and
the simple life, such as "God helps those who help themselves." In 1748, at
age 42, Franklin retired to live comfortably on his income. However, his life
was anything but leisurely.

He helped other printers set up newspapers in other colonies. He also
was deputy postmaster general of the colonies. He helped found an
insurance company, a hospital, and a college that later became the University
of Pennsylvania. When he invented the free-standing "Franklin stove" in
1740, he refused to take out a patent on it because he didn't feel it was right
to benefit personally from such inventions. He wanted everyone to benefit.

He invented lightning rods, which saved many buildings around the world. And he invented bifocal lenses.

Franklin was elected to the Pennsylvania Assembly in 1751 and spent the next 40 years as a public official in one capacity or another. He signed the Declaration of Independence in 1776 at the age of 70. But his most important political contribution was serving as the colonial diplomatic representative to France, where he secured money and resources to help the colonists fight the war against Britain.

Franklin returned home in 1785 and served as president of University of Pennsylvania for three years and attended the Constitutional Convention of 1787. He died April 17, 1790, at the age of 83.

Sources: Benjamin Franklin, *The Autobiography of Benjamin Franklin* (Boston: Bedord Books of St. Martin's Press, 1993); Benjamin Franklin, *The Papers of Benjamin Franklin*, edited by Leonard W. Labaree and Whitfield J. Bell, Jr. (New Haven: Yale University Press, 1959); Car Van Doren, *Benjamin Franklin* (New York: The Viking Press, 1938); and Michael Emery and Edwin Emery, *The Press in America: An Interpretive History of the Mass Media*, 6th ed. (Englewood Cliffs, NJ: Prentice Hall, 1988).

Franklin, James (1696-1735) the older brother of famous Benjamin Franklin and the first newspaper publisher to publish without formal permission of the authorities.

In 1721, James refused to publish his "New England Courant" "with authority." His newspaper, which was the third one founded in the colonies, frequently criticized religious and political leaders. James was jailed and forbidden to publish. But he got around this by naming his brother, Ben, the publisher. Ben eventually ran away and went on to became one of the most respected and admired journalists and Americans in history.

See *Franklin, Benjamin.*

Freedom Forum a private foundation established in 1991 by Allen Neuharth, former chairman of the Gannett Corporation, one of the nation's largest newspaper companies.

The Forum, which is the successor to a foundation started in 1935 by Frank E. Gannett, focuses on free speech and free press issues and has three major projects: the Newseum, First Amendment Issues, and newsroom diversity. The foundation is not associated with Gannett and is financially independent <www.freedomforum.org>.

Freedom of Information Act (FOIA) a federal law that took effect July 4, 1967, and has been modified several times since. It basically states that all federal government records are public except those specifically exempted by law.

There are nine categories of exemptions. They include: (1) matters of national security, (2) agency rules and practices (e.g., personnel rules and practices), (3) statutory exemptions (information deemed confidential in federal statutes), (4) confidential information on businesses collected by the government, (5) agency memoranda (to encourage frank discussion between bureaucrats on policy matters, (6) personnel, medical and other records that would invade the privacy of citizens or employees, (7) law enforcement investigative material, (8) banking reports and (9) information about oil, gas, and water wells and drilling. State laws on access to records are similar, and include many of the same exemptions.

Despite these laws, journalists often have difficulty obtaining information from government offices. The process can be long and frustrating. For example, one reporter has been waiting 30 years for records that courts have determined must be released. One reason these problems persist is because the federal law and many state versions don't provide strong penalties for violators.

freelance writer an independent writer who works by the job or on short-term contract, receiving an hourly wage, as opposed to an "in-house" writer working on salary.

freedom of the press (or free press) the notion that people should be able to publish or broadcast what they want without interference from the government or anyone else.

For more information on how the government and courts define freedom of speech and the press, see *First Amendment, law, prior restraint, fighting words doctrine, clear and present danger, hostile audience problem, corporate speech, commercial speech, symbolic speech.*

freedom of speech (or free speech) the notion that people should be able to say what they want without interference from the government or anyone else.

For more information on how the government and courts define freedom of speech and the press, see *First Amendment, law, prior restraint, fighting words doctrine, clear and present danger, hostile audience problem, corporate speech, commercial speech, symbolic speech.*

free will (or voluntarism) a doctrine that views human will as independent of antecedent physiological or psychological conditions, providing humans the ability to freely choose between alternative courses of action.

Although free will is the basis of responsibility and the justification for punishing people who commit crimes, this does not mean behavior is arbitrary. A decision to act has to be an expression of the person who makes it. This decision may take motivational factors into account, but the decision is not causally determined by these factors.

In the social sciences, the debate between *determinism* and free will is often framed in slightly different terms. For sociologists, the question is usually one of agency versus structure, or whether social actors (individuals or groups) can engage in volitional, purposive action as opposed to action determined or constrained by aspects of the social structure (e.g., roles). For *uses and gratifications* communication researchers, it is a question of active versus passive usage of the mass media. Although the terminology differs in sociology and uses and gratifications research, the basic question is the same: Is human action the product of deterministic forces or is it the product of free will?

Many qualitative researchers and humanist scholars lean heavily toward the former. Many quantitative researchers and social scientists lean heavily toward the latter. A third view is the *probabilistic theory of social action* that sees humans making choices constrained or enabled by physical, organic, psychological, social or cultural factors or phenomena.

See *determinism* and *probabilistic theory of social action*.

frequency (a) the number of times something occurs and **(b)** in the field of broadcasting, the number of periodic oscillations or waves per unit of time, most often expressed in cycles per second or hertz (e.g., the frequency of a radio or television station)

Friendly, Fred W. (1915-1998) former president of *CBS* who resigned in protest in 1966 when the network ran an episode of "I Love Lucy" instead of the first U.S. Senate hearings questioning America's involvement in Vietnam, which were broadcast on *ABC* and *NBC*.

Friendly was an award-winning broadcast journalist who helped produce *Edward R. Murrow's* "See It Now" program. After resigning from CBS, Friendly helped set up *Public Television* and taught at Columbia University.

f-test an *inferential statistic* produced by *analysis of variance*, *regression*, and other statistical procedures.

functionalism see *structural functionalism*.

functions of mass media see *structural functionalism*.

functional substitute an economic and sociological term referring to the capacity of one technology or social organization to perform all of the functions of another.

During the 1950s, for example, television became a functional substitute for radio in terms of dramatic and comedic programming. Within several years, almost every major radio drama and comedy program had been converted into a television program, and the radio versions of the programs were eliminated. Television was a functional substitute because it offered sound, like radio, and because it also offered something else: visuals in the form of moving pictures. Radio survived because it turned to music programming.

Despite improvements in technology, few new media are able to serve as substitutes for older media. That's because use of media involves not just technology but also culture. For example, electronic books (e-books) have not faired well partly because many people like the feel and look of a hard-

G

gag order a judicial order that prevents people and/or the news media from talking about a legal case or from publishing information about it.

The most noteworthy gag-order case was decided in 1966 (Sheppard v. Maxwell,1966). Sam Sheppard, a medical doctor, was accused of killing his wife on July 4, 1954, in their Cleveland suburban home. The news media gave extensive coverage to the case, partly because of rumors of extramarital affairs. Police often fed the news media with evidence pointing to Sheppard's guilt but not introduced at trial.

The coverage was highly sensational and prejudicial against Sheppard. Sheppard's attorney asked the court for a continuance (delay), a change of venue (location), and a mistrial, but the judge denied the requests. The jury was not sequestered (put into seclusion), and no attempt was made to limit their exposure to news stories. Sheppard was convicted.

But the U.S. Supreme Court ruled that Sheppard did not receive a fair trial and that the trial court should have taken more precautions.

Sheppard was acquitted after a new trial. But his life as a physician was ruined. He became a professional wrestler and died in 1970 of liver disease. Recent DNA evidence suggests that the window washer, who had a criminal history, was the killer. But an Ohio jury refused to rule in favor of Sheppard's son, and the case is still technically unsolved.

The Sheppard case, which served as the model for the 1960s hit television show, "The Fugitive" (and in 1993 a movie starring Harrison Ford), had both positive and adverse consequences for the news media. On the one hand, the court ruled that judges, not the press, must take the responsibility for ensuring that a defendant receives a fair trial. The court can do this by (1) changing the venue, (2) issuing a continuance, (3) sequestering the jury, (4) admonishing the jury, (5) ordering witnesses and others not to talk to the press, and (6) regulating the courtroom and courthouse. On the other hand, the high court ruled that trial court judges can, if necessary, issue gag orders on the press to ensure the defendant receives a fair trial.

Many courts did issue gag orders during the 1960s and 1970s. But in 1976, the U.S. Supreme Court curtailed the practice. The key case was Nebraska Press Association v. Stuart (1976). Erwin Simants was accused of raping and fatally shooting a 10-year-old girl and then murdering the witnesses, which included her grandparents, father, brother, and sister. At Simants' arraignment, a county judge issued a gag order prohibiting publication of anything from the public pretrial hearings. The judge also gagged the press.

The U.S. Supreme Court, in a unanimous decision, struck down the gag order. The Court ruled that other measures short of prior restraint should have been used first. This test proved to be relatively rigorous, and few gag orders have been issued against *news media* since then.

See *law.*

Sources: *Sheppard v. Maxwell,* 384 U.S. 333 (1966) and *Nebraska Press Association v. Stuart,* 427 U.S. 539 (1976)

galleys (or galley proofs) uncorrected pages or proofs of a manuscript, sent to authors for editing and sometimes to book reviewers just prior to publication.

Garrison, William Lloyd (1805-1879) a prominent abolitionist editor whose newspaper, "The Liberator," fueled the abolitionist movement and influenced many people.

gatekeeper a term that emphasizes the power of news organizations to select some news or events for publication or broadcast (i.e., "open the gate") and to reject others ("close the gate").

gazette to speak the news.

In ancient Rome, most people couldn't read but they could pay professional speakers a coin called a "gazet" to speak the news. That's why some modern newspapers still call themselves a "Gazette."

generalization in social science research, a statement or proposition that identifies a nonrandom pattern of behavior or activity but does not meet the invariability assumption of a scientific law.

In the hard sciences, a law is defined as a sequence of events that occur with unvarying uniformity under the same conditions. For example, the law of gravity states that every time a physical object is dropped, it will fall to the earth. That statement is a law because it always will happen as long as the earth rotates in space.

On the other hand the social sciences, such as mass communication research, deal with generalizations rather than laws because human behavior rarely if ever occurs with unvarying uniformity under the same conditions. For example, although thousand of studies have found that violent television programming increases aggressive behavior in some children, all children who see violent programming do not behave aggressively. Violent programming increases the probability of aggression, and this proposition is called a generalization.

See *law, probability theory of social action,* and *media violence.*

generalizability the extent to which the findings from a study can be extended to **(a)** other people or populations or **(b)** other *concepts* or conditions (e.g., Do the reasons for buying one type of product extend to another type of product?).

globalization increasing social, economic, and political *interdependence* around the world.

The term "globalization" is most often associated with economic growth and the exchange of goods and services between countries around the world. But the concept also entails social and political interdependence, meaning that social actors increasingly rely on people around the world to achieve social and political goals.

See *global media* and *corporate media.*

global media large-scale mass media organizations that generate print or electronic messages or programs for dissemination to large numbers of people around the world.

Some scholars and analysts prefer the term "transnational media corporation" when talking about global media companies. Total sales or revenues are often used to rank-order such organizations. However, other researchers use Max Weber's corporate/bureaucratic model to conceptualize global media. In other words, a global medium is a large-scale corporate organization (see *corporate media*).

See *corporate media.*

Sources: David Demers, *Global Media: Menace or Messiah?* (Cresskill, NJ: Hampton Press, 1999); H. H. Gerth and C. Wright Mills (eds.), *From Max Weber: Essays in Sociology* (New York: Oxford University Press, 1946); and Max Weber, *The Theory of Social and Economic Organization,* trans. A. M. Henderson and Talcott Parsons (New York: The Free Press, 1964 [1947]).

global public relations *public relations campaigns* that seek to maintain or improve the image of a company in more than one country.

The McDonald's Corporation, for example, discovered that its fast-food restaurants were not always as warmly greeted in some countries as in the United States. In some places McDonald's has become the open target of anti-capitalist, anti-American sentiment. In response, the company has developed PR campaigns designed to combat that image and cater to the needs of the host country.

Graham, Katherine (1917-2001) former publisher of the "Washington Post" who became one of the most influential women in American mass media.

Graham's mother was an educator and her father was a publisher. In 1933, Katherine's father purchased the "Washington Post," and Katherine began working at the paper five years later. In 1940 she married Philip Graham, and five years later she left the "Post" to raise her family. Philip Graham eventually became publisher of the newspaper, which under his control also acquired the "Times-Herald" and "Newsweek" magazine. In 1963, Philip Graham committed suicide, and Katharine Graham assumed control of the Washington Post Company. She was publisher from 1969 to 1979 and held other key positions in management until she died.

Under Graham's leadership, the "Post" became known for its investigative reporting, which included publication of the "Pentagon Papers" (see *New York Times v. United States*) and the *Woodward and Bernstein* Watergate investigation. Graham won a *Pulitzer Prize* in 1998 for her autobiography, "Personal History," which was praised for its honest portrayal of her husband's mental illness. She died after being injured in a fall.

Source: Susan Baer, "Journalism Giant Katharine Graham Dies in Idaho at 84," Spokane *Spokesman-Review* (July 18, 2001), p. A1, A7.

gramaphone a *phonograph* that used a disk rather than a cylinder.

In 1894 Emile Berliner in the United States filed the first patent on a Gramaphone. Disks were much easier and less expensive to produce than cylinders. He expanded operations in Europe and his company eventually became Victor.

The Gramaphone was extremely popular. During the 1890s, people could put a coin in a slot to hear a short song or a skit from the device, which used disks 10 or 12 inches in diameter and contained several minutes of recorded music. During the early 1900s, the *recording industry* began mass producing records, mostly classical recordings.

See *Edison, Thomas A.*

Gramsci, Anotonio see *hegemony*.

Greeley, Horace (1811-1872) an influential 19th-century newspaper editor who supported responsible capitalism, westward expansion and labor unions and opposed slavery, alcohol, gambling, prostitution, and capital punishment.

During his lifetime, Greeley was the most important editor in the United States. His daily and weekly versions of the "New York Tribune" were extremely influential. He ran for president but lost.

greenwashing a PR tactic whereby corporate stakeholders adopt visual or written rhetoric to make themselves seem more environmentally responsible.

Gross, Terry (1951-) the current host of National Public Radio's hour-long "Fresh Air" talk-interview program.

Gross began her radio career in 1973, hosting and producing arts, women's, and public affairs programs for a public radio station in Buffalo,

New York. Two years later she joined the staff of "Fresh Air," which was then a local interview and music program at WHYY-FM in Philadelphia. In 1985, the program was distributed nationally, and it now airs on more than 160 public radio stations. Her 5,000 guests have included Ice-T, Nancy Reagan, Tom Hanks, Monica Lewinsky, Jerry Seinfeld, Toni Morrison, and Studs Terkel.

Sources: National Public Radio's Web site <www.npr.org>; Eleanor Yang, "NPR's Terry Grosss: Asking the Smart Questions," *Los Angeles Times* (April 15, 2000), p. F20; and Anthony Violanti, "A Breath of Fresh Air," *The Buffalo News* (December 17, 2000), p. 4F.

grounded theory a *qualitative research* approach in which hypotheses or theories are derived through an inductive process, case by case.

Grounded theory usually involves collecting qualitative or quantitative data from people or documents until a point is reached where new observations no longer provide additional information or knowledge. At that point, the researcher typically generates a hypothesis or theory for further testing or a generalization that may stand on its own.

Source: Barney G. Glasser and Anselm L. Strauss, *The Discovery of Grounded Theory: Strategies for Qualitative Research* (Chicago: Aldine, 1967).

group communication see *organizational communication.*

guard dog theory the notion that mass media primarily serve the interests of powerful political and economic groups but can and do criticize those groups, especially when members of the *elite* class violate system values or when they criticize each other.

Guard dog theory was developed by University of Minnesota mass communication researchers Phillip J. Tichenor, George A. Donohue, and Clarice N. Olien, who pointed out that mass media are neither lap dogs of the powerful nor watchdogs of the weak and oppressed. Rather, media provide support for the power structure even while producing some content critical of it and elites.

The researchers do not reject the idea that media reports and public opinion may at times shape legislative actions. However, elites are the ones who primarily control the media agenda and, hence, public opinion. That's because reporters get most of their news and information from elites. Such dependency means news is shaped from the perspective of the rich and powerful. Information and knowledge flow from the top down, not from the bottom up.

Thus, guard dog theory holds that media are a guard dog not for the entire community but for political and special interest elite groups that hold political and economic power. The guard dog model is basically a *social control* model. The mass media are seen as one institution among many others (family, church, state, schools, courts, police) that play a role in supporting and maintaining a social system.

One implication of the guard dog model is that social change comes slowly. Elites usually resist changes that might affect their power and status.

And because they hold power, change usually comes only when elite groups have an interest in changing the system. If elites have no interest in change, there often is little media coverage. Lack of attention to a problem or issue is a powerful media effect. However, psychological or survey research approaches can't measure these kinds of effects, because these research tools focus mostly on the effects of persuasive messages.

The guard dog model can be applied to media in all social systems or communities. However, the Minnesota Team's research program found that the structure of a community or society affects the way news and information are controlled. For example, media in small communities, such as weekly newspapers, tend to downplay social conflict and publish a lot of positive or booster news. In contrast, the metropolitan daily often publishes a lot of news about social conflict, partly because those communities contain a larger number of groups competing for limited resources. One implication of these findings is that mass media in larger communities have a greater capacity to facilitate social change than those in small communities.

See *lap dog theory* and *watchdog model.*

Sources: George A. Donohue, Clarice N. Olien, and Phillip J. Tichenor, "A Guard Dog Conception of the Mass Media," paper presented to the Association for Education in Journalism and Mass Communication (San Antonio, Texas, August 1987); George A. Donohue, Phillip J. Tichenor and Clarice N. Olien, "A Guard Dog Perspective on the Role of Media," *Journal of Communication,* 45(2):115-132 (1995); and George A. Donohue, Phillip J. Tichenor and Clarice N. Olien, "Mass Media Functions, Knowledge and Social Control," *Journalism Quarterly,* 50:652-9 (1973).

Gutenberg, Johannes inventor of the movable type press.

Gutenberg is often remembered for having invented the first printing press. But this is not true. The Chinese invented wood block printing nearly a thousand years earlier, and the Koreans published a book using a press in about 700 AD.

What Gutenberg invented around 1450 was a new type of printing process, one that used movable type. He also invented more advanced forms of ink. A 42-line Bible was the first book printed on his press (now called the "Gutenberg Bible").

But his real legacy lies not in the inventions. It lies in the *information revolution* that his printing press started—a revolution that in many areas of the world weakened the power of political and religious rulers and set the stage for representative democratic government.

Tragically, Gutenberg did not live long enough to see this shift in power, nor did he fully enjoy the fruits of his labor. An investor sued him a few years after he set up the press, and he lost control of his printing shop. He died a decade later.

See *information revolution.*

Habermas, Jürgen (1929-) a German social theorist who is best known in mass communication for his Theory of Communicative Action.

Habermas is a critical theorist who argues that valid knowledge emerges through open and free dialogue between people. He rejects the idea of a neutral science, arguing that facts and values cannot be easily separated because they are bound up with the political problems stemming from the freedom to communicate and exchange ideas.

Habermas also rejects *positivism*, economic *determinism*, and technical rationality (i.e., the idea of equating humanity with economic efficiency; see *corporate media*). But he continues to defend the Enlightenment's goals of reason and logic and in recent years has been a major critic of *postmodernism*.

Habermas' Theory of Communicative Action is a normative theory that seeks to locate community (or emancipate people) through communicative rationality. True rationality can only occur in an "ideal speech situation," one in which all people are able to raise moral and political concerns without undue domination or ideological distortion.

See *critical theory, ideology,* and *postmodernism.*

Source: Jürgen Habermas, *The Theory of Communicative Action* (Boston: Beacon Press, 1981).

hackers sophisticated computer programmers who try to break into computer networks, servers, and computer systems with the goal of stealing information or destroying data.

halftone a continuous tone picture converted into small black and white dots that are large enough to be inked on printing presses but small enough to appear invisible to the naked eye.

The first halftone ("Shantytown") was published on March 4, 1880, in the "New York Daily Graphic." By the 1890s, magazines were widely using halftones, which were easily and inexpensively reproduced in publications. By 1915, newspapers also were publishing halftone pictures.

Hamilton, Andrew see *Zenger, John Peter (the trial of)*.

Havas see *news service*.

hardcover a book bound in boards, or a substance harder than paper. Also called hardback, case-bound, clothbound or hardbound. See *paperback* and *trade books*.

Harris, Benjamin (1673-1716) an early colonial printer who published the first machine-printed newspaper in the colonies.
    "Publick Occurrences, Both Forreign and Domestick" appeared in Boston on September 25, 1690. It was three pages long and contained stories about Indians who kidnaped several children, a smallpox epidemic, a fire in Boston a week before, the possible bribery of the friendly Mohawk Indians by someone who had caused them to turn against the colonists, and a scandal involving the French king and his daughter-in-law.
    The last two items angered colonial authorities, who imposed *prior restraint* and ended Harris' publishing career in the colonies. Harris went back to London, where he ran a coffee house and sold books.
    See *Campbell, John*.

hate speech see *fighting words doctrine*.

health communication (a) news or information about health-related issues and matters; **(b)** a genre of mass communication research that focuses on the effects of mass media in creating and/or solving social health problems.
    Health communication is a growing field of research in mass communication, partly because the U.S. government has made grants available to researchers. Much of the research focuses on the effects of *media violence* and alcohol and smoking advertisements, especially on children.

Hearst, William Randolph (1863-1951) a newspaper publisher who employed investigative reporting and sensationalistic news-gathering practices to build a nationwide network of newspapers and magazines.
    Hearst was the only child of George Hearst, a multimillionaire miner and rancher, and Phoebe Apperson Hearst, a school teacher. Hearst attended but dropped out of Harvard University. In 1887, at age 23, Hearst became "proprietor" of the "San Francisco Examiner," which his father accepted as payment for a gambling debt.
    In 1895, Hearst purchased the "New York Morning Journal" and entered into a circulation war with *Joseph Pulitzer*, his former mentor and owner of the "New York World." Both newspapers wrote stories that exaggerated facts to stimulate newspaper sales. This was particularly the case

before the Spanish-American War in 1898. The newspapers implied that the Spanish had blown up the battleship Maine in Cuba, but there was no evidence to support such claims. The competition between the newspapers was so intense that Hearst hired away many of Pultizer's top journalists.

Hearst was elected to the U.S. House of Representatives in 1903, but failed in his attempts to win the mayorship of New York City and the governorship of New York. He built a national chain of 28 newspapers and 18 magazines, some of which are still part of the Hearst Corporation (including "Cosmopolitan" magazine). The Great Depression weakened his empire and by 1940 he'd lost control of his company.

Hearst was widely criticized for using his media empire to advance his own personal interests. This abuse of power was adroitly illustrated after the production of Orson Welles' film "Citizen Kane," which was loosely based on Hearst's life. Hearst tried to discredit Welles and stop production and distribution of the film. These efforts were not successful, but the film on its initial release lost money.

See *Pulitzer, Joseph* and *yellow journalism.*

Hefner, Hugh (1926-) founder of "Playboy" magazine, which in the 1950s ushered in a new openness about sexuality in the United States.

Hefner founded "Playboy" in 1953. "Playboy" featured partially nude photos of women and articles written by leading writers. The first issue featured Marilyn Monroe on the cover and sold more than 51,000 copies.

"Playboy's" circulation reached 7 million in 1972, but afterward began to decline because of competition from "Penthouse" and "Hustler" magazines, which offered more explicitly erotic photography. But Hefner, who'd built a financial empire that included Playboy Clubs around the world, stuck with his soft-core approach.

In the 1980s, all of the "Playboy Clubs" were closed and many other operations were curtailed. Ironically, Hefner, once perceived as a liberator of sexual repression, was now being cast by feminist groups as the repressor.

In 1982, his daughter, Christie, was named president of Playboy Enterprises. A Playboy Channel was launched and closed down. The company now operates a successful pay-per-view cable television venture called "Playboy at Night." The circulation of "Playboy" has remained steady at about 3 million, which means it continues to be one of the largest magazines targeted to men in the world.

hegemony control of intellectual life by cultural means.

The concept of hegemony is usually traced to the writings of the Italian thinker *Antonio Gramsci,* who elevated the role of *ideology* in Marxist scholarship during the early part of this century.

Gramsci attacks the structural, materialist strain of Marxist thought and advocates a return to the Hegelian or humanistic side of Marx in his earlier years. Gramsci wants to increase attention on politics and the state because he sees this as the source of power. He defines the state as including not only traditional governmental institutions (army, political leaders, and groups) but also "civil society," which includes churches, schools, unions and mass media.

State domination, he argues, is accomplished through two means: coercion and persuasion. Central to his analysis of the latter is his concept of hegemony, which is the ability of the ruling classes to dominate or control private groups (churches, media), which in turn manipulate knowledge, values, and norms to serve the interests of the ruling classes.

Although Gramsci sees capitalist societies as founded on the ideological subordination of the working class, he does not subscribe to a full-fledged incorporation model. The working class has a dual consciousness: "One which is implicit in his activity and which in reality unites him with all his fellow-workers in the practical transformation of the real world; and one, superficially explicit or verbal, which he has inherited from the past and uncritically absorbed."

See *ideology* and *Marx, Karl.*

Source: Antonio Gramsci, *Prison notebooks* (New York: International Publishers, 1971, p. 333).

Heinrichs, Ernest H. (1862-1926) the first person to head a press agent (or public relations) department.

In 1888, George Westinghouse hired Heinrichs, a journalist, to help him promote his alternating current (AC) system of electricity. Westinghouse readily admitted that he wasn't very skilled at handling the news media. Heinrichs worked for Westinghouse until he died in March 1914.

Hennock, Frieda (1904-1960) the first woman appointed to the *Federal Communications Commission (FCC)* and a tireless advocate of educational television.

Hennock was born in Kovel, Poland, in 1904. She was the youngest of eight children. In 1910, she immigrated with her family to New York City. Her father was a real estate broker and banker.

Hennock entered Brooklyn Law School after high school. She graduated in 1924 but had to wait a year before being admitted to the bar because she was only 21.

Hennock became one of New York's most successful female lawyers. She began her practice in 1926 with $56. A year later she formed a partnership with a man partly because of discrimination against women lawyers. The two dissolved the firm about seven years later because of disagreements.

Hennock then took a job as assistant counsel to the New York Mortgage Commission from 1935-1939. She also lectured on law and economics at the Brooklyn Law School. In 1941, Hennock became the first woman and the first Democrat to associate with Choate, Mitchell and Ely, one of New York City's most prestigious law firms.

Hennock was appointed to the FCC in 1948, partly because of her support for the Democratic Party. Hennock relinquished a substantial income from her law practice to take the FCC position.

Hennock worked long hours and devoted much of her effort to reserving channels for educational use. She wanted 500 channels reserved for noncommercial purposes. The commission eventually settled on 242 channels.

Hennock also encouraged educators to apply for the channels even if they didn't have the funds to operate them. She spent many weekends traveling to cities and promoting educational television in speeches and magazine articles. Hennock also sought stricter controls on children's programming, because she was concerned about the effects of violence, crime and horror.

In 1951, Hennock was nominated for a federal judgeship, but the American and New York City bar associations refused to endorse her because she was a woman. She also came under intense scrutiny for a friendship she had with a married federal judge. Although no evidence of an affair was ever presented, she withdrew her name.

Hennock left the FCC in 1955 and married a real estate broker. She went back into corporate law and then started her own firm. She died in 1960 of a brain tumor.

Sources: Maryann Yodelis Smith, "Frieda Barkin Hennock" in Barbara Sicherman and Carol Hurd Green (eds.), *Notable American Women: The Modern Period—A Biographical Dictionary* (Cambridge, MA: Belknap Press of Harvard University Press, 1980).

hermeneutics a humanistic method and theory of interpreting human activity or behavior.

The origins of hermeneutics can be traced to the problems associated with errors that occurred when monks hand-copied Bibles prior to the invention of the *printing press*. Hermeneutics involves recovering the "authentic" version, which also includes an analysis of the experiences of the author. The assumption is that an artistic or scientific work cannot be understood without an analysis of the author's experiences and/or social conditions in which the work is produced.

More specifically, a scientific article or book is to be interpreted by reference to the outlook or world-view of an author and/or a society , and in turn the work itself can be understood as representative of that outlook or world-view. This is called the hermeneutic circle.

Hermeneutics is critical of positivism, but hermeneutics itself has been criticized in turn for failing to resolve the problem of interscholar agreement, i.e., the problem of how to validate interpretations.

See *humanism, positivism*, and *phenomenology*.

Source: Z. Bauman, *Hermeneutics and Social Science* (London: Hutchison, 1978).

hieroglyphics a picture or symbol (pictographic-ideographic system) that the ancient Egyptians and other cultures used to represent a word or sound.

Hieroglyphics are similar to *cuneiform* except the letter uses wedge-shaped marks rather than pictures.

Hollerith, Herman (1860-1929) inventor of a machine, an early computer, that could tabulate census data from punch cards.

For much of the 1800s, the U.S. census was conducted by hand, which took a long time and produced many errors. In 1890, the government turned to Hollerith, an engineer, for assistance. He had devised a machine that could tabulate the results. The process involved punching holes in a card that represented a person's age, sex, and ethnicity. The cards were then run through a machine that sorted them into piles.

For nearly three years, 80 clerks operated 100 machines that processed about 1,000 cards an hour. Three years may seem like a long time, but it was the shortest census analysis on record, shaving four years off the previous record.

The Hollerith Electric Tabulating System was also used in the 1900 census. Hollerith's company was very prosperous, but ill health forced him to sell it in 1911. The new company was called Computing-Tabulating-Recording Company. In 1924, the company renamed itself International Business Machines (IBM) which, of course, would later go on to play a key role in the development of computers and operating systems.

See *computer* and *King, Augusta Ada*

Sources: Martin Carmpbell-Kelly and William Aspray, *Computer: A History of the Information Machine* (New York: Basic Books, 1996); Christos J. P. Moschovitis, Hilary Poole, Tami Schuyler, and Theresa M. Senft, *History of the Internet* (The Moschovitis Group, 1999); Peter H. Lewis, "A Glimpse into the Future as Seen by Chairman Gates," *The New York Times* (December 12, 1993), Sec. 3, p. 7; Cynthia Flash, "Microsoft, NBC Launch News Venture," *News Tribune* (July 14, 1996), p. 1.

Hollywood Ten see *House Un-American Activities Committee.*

Home Box Office the first premium cable movie channel. It began broadcasting in 1972.

host (or server) a computer linked to the Internet.

Hosts are the technological backbone of the Internet. They are computers that are "wired" together. The servers, in turn, are usually connected to other personal computers which are used to "surf" the Internet. They are called clients.

hostile audience problem an area of media law which focuses on whether speech can be banned if it makes audiences become violent.

If an audience menaces a speaker to the point where the physical safety of the speaker is at risk or a general melee is possible, can the police arrest the speaker even if she or he is not intentionally inciting to violence? If a speaker has generated threats from passers-by, can he or she be denied a permit to speak?

These questions invoke the hostile audience problem. The U.S. Supreme court has basically ruled that if the speech leads to or is likely to lead to violence, the speech can be banned.

In 1951, the Supreme Court ruled that police were within their authority to arrest a man because his audience was getting restless. However, the high court ruled in the same year that New York City could not deny a speaking permit to a man who had aroused complaints in the past. The latter was considered *prior restraint.*

See *clear and present danger, fighting words doctrine,* and *prior restraint.*

Sources: *Feiner v. New York,* 340 U.S. 315 (1951) and *Kunz v. New York,* 340 U.S. 290 (1951).

household penetration a term used by media researchers indicating the number of newspapers (or other media) sold divided by the number of total households.

House Un-American Activities Committee (HUAC) a Congressional committee that investigated alleged communist infiltration of government and Hollywood film studios in the early 1950s.

HUAC called more than 100 Hollywood witnesses from 1950-52, some of whom testified against their colleagues. However, eight screen writers and two directors, later known as the Hollywood Ten, refused to testify and were sentenced to serve up to a year in prison.

Fearing repercussions, producers fired the Hollywood Ten and expressed their support for the HUAC. The studios then blacklisted many producers, writers, directors, and stars who were suspected of communist associations. This move destroyed the careers of many innocent people.

The "red scare" didn't subside until 1954, when broadcaster Edward R. Murrow, host of the national television news program "See It Now," criticized Sen. Joseph McCarthy of Wisconsin. McCarthy had orchestrated many of the allegations, and Murrow showed that many of his accusations were false. McCarthy was eventually censured by Congress.

See *Murrow, Edward R.*

Hovland, Carl a psychologist who gained notoriety for his experiments on media effects during World War II.

In 1942, the U.S. War Department hired Hovland, a Yale University professor, and other scholars to study the effects of training films and information programs on soldiers. The government wanted to find better ways to teach soldiers how to hate the enemy, love their country, and increase loyalty to their military unit.

This was no small task. Many of the 15 million men and women who entered the service had limited knowledge of public affairs and the enemy. They didn't read a newspaper or follow political news.

To expedite the process, the government turned to Hollywood director Frank Capra. He produced seven 50-minute documentary films. The Army began making them part of the training for new recruits. The films, collectively called the "Why We Fight" series, traced the history of World War II, presenting it (needless to say) from a very pro-American perspective.

The War Department assumed the films would convey factual knowledge as well as boost morale and support for American policies. To assess whether these objectives were achieved, the researchers designed a number of experimental studies. Some recruits were exposed to the films and some were not, and the results were compared. More than 4,000 recruits participated.

As expected, the recruits who saw the films learned a lot from them. The films also had some impact on opinions. However, the films had little effect on improving attitudes toward British allies and were very ineffective in strengthening overall motivation among the recruits to fight. More specifically, the films had no effect on increasing willingness to serve, resentment toward the enemy, and attitudes toward demanding unconditional surrender.

Source: Carl Hovland, Irving Janis and Harold H. Kelley, *Communication and Persuasion* (New Haven: Yale University Press, 1953).

human agency another term for *free will.*

humanism a broad philosophical doctrine that rejects the search for scientific laws of human behavior (e.g., positivism) and seeks to understand human behavior, events, and activities by focusing on human reason, actions, values, motives, and thoughts.

Humanism also rejects supernatural explanations of the world and focuses on the humans as the agents of history and social change. As such, it places primacy on human agency or free will and sees the world as fluid and changeable. In fact, many humanist scholars believe researchers have an obligation to speak up and to change the world. Facts cannot and should not be separated from values.

As might be expected, humanism is most prominent in the humanities (e.g., art, music, literature, theater, philosophy) and in history. But the field of mass communication and the social sciences (sociology, political science, economics) also have a fair share of humanist scholars.

Humanism's greatest strength is that it recognizes the importance of human agency in understanding human action. Its greatest weakness is the failure to recognize that human action also is constrained or enabled by social, political, and economic conditions that often lie outside of the control of any individual social actor.

See *mass communication research, mass communication researcher, positivism* and *probability theory of social action.*

humanist see *humanism, mass communication researcher* and *positivism.*

humanistic ethics see *ethical decision-making.*

Huntley, Chet (1911-1974) co-anchored the "NBC Evening News" with David Brinkley from 1956-1970.

hyperlink an element in an electronic document that, when clicked, links the user to another document or another place in the same document.

Hypertext Markup Language (HTML) see *World Wide Web*.

HyperText Transfer Protocol (HTTP) see *World Wide Web*.

hypodermic needle theory see *magic bullet theory*.

hypothesis an untested statement intended about a *relationship* between two or more *variables*.

A hypothesis contains three elements: an *independent variable*, a *dependent variable*, and a statement about the relationship between the two.

The research hypothesis, sometimes called the alternative hypothesis, reflects a researcher's expectation about the relationship between two or more variables. A null hypothesis is a statement that two variables are unrelated. When analyzing relationships, the null hypothesis is tested rather than the research hypothesis, because most social scientists believe a relationship between two variables cannot be proved; it can only be disproved or falsified.

I

iconoscope the first electronic camera suitable for a television studio.
The device was invented by Vladimir K. Zworykin, a Russian immigrant
hired by David Sarnoff at Radio Corporation of America. The iconoscope
was publicly unveiled at the 1939 New York World Fair. The demonstration
was a big success. Two years later the *Federal Communications Commission*
adopted what amounted to RCA's standard for black-and-white television.
See *Sarnoff, David.*

idealism an ontological doctrine which asserts that only minds and their
thoughts exist; matter does not exist; everything is an idea in some mind.
See *materialism.*

ideological state apparatuses social institutions, which includes the mass
media, that produce content or ideas (*ideology*) that support elites who control
the state.
The term was coined by Louis Althusser, a Marxist scholar.

ideology (a) a set of ideas or beliefs; **(b)** a set of ideas or beliefs that
promote, explain or justify a system of class relations and conceal social
contradictions in the interests of the dominant or ruling class.
The first definition of ideology is employed by many public opinion
pollsters and mainstream researchers. It does not make reference to the
"truth value" of ideology. The ideas or beliefs may be true or false; the
researcher is typically interested in understanding how values influence
behavior, such as voting patterns.
In contrast, the second definition, which is offered by *Karl Marx* and
classical Marxist scholars, frames ideology as a set of false ideas that support
capitalism as an economic institution. More specifically, Marx and Friedrich
Engels wrote in the "Germany Ideology" that "the ideas of the ruling class
are in every epoch the ruling ideas: i.e., the class which is the ruling material

137

force of society is at the same time its ruling intellectual force. The class that has the means of material production at its disposal has control at the same time over the means of mental production, so that, thereby, generally speaking, the ideas of those who lack the means of mental production are subject to it."

Marx and Engels define ideology as a set of ideas or beliefs that promote, explain or justify a system of class relations. More specifically, ideology conceals social contradictions in the interests of the dominant class.

There are debates about whether Marx believed dominant ideology left room for a non-dominant culture, but it is clear that contemporary Marxist scholars place much greater emphasis on ideology and other elements of the superstructure (other cultural industries, such as mass media, and the state) to explain the stability of capitalism. The shift in emphasis began shortly after World War I, when it became evident to many Marxist scholars that, contrary to Marx's laws of motion, capitalism was not collapsing under the weight of its own internal contradictions (see *concentration of ownership*) and the working classes were not developing a revolutionary consciousness.

Antonio Gramsci and the *Frankfurt School* theorists surmised that revolutionary consciousness did not rise in part because of the influence of mass media, which produce hegemonic content helping to legitimate social inequalities and privileges of the dominant groups. Gramsci defined *hegemony* as control of intellectual life through cultural means.

Ideology justifies ownership and rights of property and the profits of ownership and the mechanisms (e.g., market forces) that preserve the wealth of property. Inequalities are also explained by economic laws of supply and demand and the functional importance of different occupations. The social value placed on individual mobility, technical competence and achievement—i.e., meritocratic beliefs—makes inequality and income differentials appear to be fair, just, and the result of natural law. Inequalities also are legitimated by beliefs that the state represents the interests of the masses, not elites, and that the state enacts welfare policies to counter inequalities that occur during recessions and depressions.

Historically, one of the major criticisms leveled against the ideology thesis is that it fails to account adequately for social change. Indeed, capitalism has proved itself to be a highly adaptable system, one which eventually recognized the rights of workers to organize and collectively bargain and one which, in the United States, created a large middle class.

Another major criticism of the ideology thesis is that there is very little evidence to support the notion that working classes are incorporated into a dominant ideology. Some scholars point out that the ideologies of subordinate and dominant classes in feudalism, early capitalism, and late capitalism were never in agreement. The ruling classes subscribed to the ideas which supported the prevailing economic and political institutions, but the subordinate classes did not.

These and other problems have led some scholars to abandon theories of ideology altogether. But ideology continues to be an important line of research in mass communication, because it helps explain the relative lack of revolutionary movements in modern capitalism.

See *critical theory, concentration of ownership, hegemony* and *Marx, Karl.*

Sources: Karl Marx and Friedrich Engels, *The German Ideology* (London: Lawrence & Wishart, 1938; original work published in 1845) and Nicholas Abercrombie, Stephen Hill and Brian S. Turner, *The Dominant Ideology Thesis* (London: Allen & Unwin, 1980).

image-building the notion that successful advertising focuses less on defining a product or service and more on creating an association in the consumer's mind between the product and an idealized image of freedom, sexual attractiveness, happiness, youth, power, and the like.

Image-building has been used to sell automobiles, luxury items, and cigarettes, products that people often use as outward symbols of a social status or image they want to portray to others.

immediacy the swiftness with which a mass medium reports the news.

Historically, radio's big advantage over television and newspapers was immediacy—it provided the fastest up-to-the-minute newscasts, sometimes reporting live. In recent decades, television has erased some of this advantage because of 24-hour news programs like CNN. But radio continues to have an edge because it is more widely available and allows a listener to engage in other activities, such as driving a car, at the same time. Television demands more attention from a viewer.

imitation behavior that copies, imitates or reproduces previously observed behavior in others.

See *media violence.*

imperialism see *media imperialism.*

incidence the *percentage* of people or *cases* engaging in some activity or *behavior,* such as buying a particular product.

incunabula books published during the first 50 years of modern printing (before 1500).

Incunabula is Latin for "cradles." Scholars estimate that 35,000 editions were published during this time period in Europe (excluding single sheets and pamphlets).

indecent programming words or images aired on over-the-air broadcast media that violate decency standards set by the *Federal Communication Commission (FCC).*

The most famous case of indecent language took place in 1975, when comedian George Carlin delivered a 12-minute "Filthy Words" monologue on a New York City radio station. He told listeners that he would talk about the words "you couldn't say on the public airwaves," including "shit, piss, fuck, cunt, cocksucker, motherfucker and tits." A New York father who heard the dialogue while driving with his son complained to the FCC.

The FCC declared that Carlin's words were indecent and warned Pacifica Foundation, the radio station licensee, that it could be fined up to $10,000 and jailed for up to two years under the federal criminal code. The FCC decision was reversed by a U.S. Court of Appeals but later reinstated by the U.S. Supreme Court. The high court ruled that the FCC didn't censor the radio station. It censured the station after the program aired. The court said the restrictions on indecency did not violate the *First Amendment*, because the government has a right to regulate indecency when it is intrusive and accessible to children.

The most famous case of indecent exposure occurred during halftime at the 2004 Superbowl, when Justin Timberlake pulled on the front of Janet Jackson's outfit and exposed her breast briefly on national television. The FCC received thousands of complaints.

During the late 1980s and 1990s, the FCC began enforcing the indecency rules with more rigor. More than two dozen stations were reprimanded. The most prominent case involved "shock jock" Howard Stern, whose ribald talk radio program generated several complaints. Infinity Broadcasting Corporation eventually paid the U.S. government $1.7 million—the largest amount ever collected by the FCC—to settle the complaints. Although Infinity never admitted guilt, the settlement scared many broadcasters and strengthened the FCC's ability to regulate indecency during daytime hours.

See *Federal Communications Commission, First Ammendment* and *Stern, Howard*.

independent filmmakers people who produce films but do not work for one of the major corporate studios in Hollywood or other cities around the world.

The most notable independent film company is DreamWorks SKG, which was founded in 1994 by *Steven Spielberg*, Jeffrey Katzenberg, and David Geffen.

independent newspaper a newspaper not owned by a chain or group.
See *chain newspaper* and *corporate media*.

independent variable in *causal analysis*, the independent variable is the cause.
See *cause and effect*.

in-depth telephone survey a *qualitative* method of research in which a limited number of *respondents* are interviewed for an extended length of time.

index a *concept* or *measure* composed of two or more *indicators*.

Usually the index is created by simply adding the *values* of the measures together. Most often the goal is to improve measurement. The plural form is "indices."
See *concept, construct* and *measurement error.*

indicator often considered interchangeable with the term *measure*, but more restrictively refers to the measures used to create an *index.*

induction a method of reasoning in which *hypotheses* are developed from observing particular cases.
See *deduction.*

Indymedia (Independent Media Center) an *alternative media* that maintains Web sites around the world (www.indymedia.org).
See *alternative media.*

inferential statistics statistics used to make inferences to *populations* from *samples.*
Inferential statistics help researchers determine whether differences observed in *data* exist in the population or whether they occurred by chance because of *sampling error. Chi-square, analysis of variance,* and *t-tests* are some examples of inferential statistics.
See *sampling error.*

infomercials audio and/or visual programming, usually a half-hour in length, that seeks to sell or promote a product or service, often by promoting the usefulness of it.
Infomercials became popular on cable television during the 1990s. The term is derived from two other words: information and commercial. But critics charged that infomercials often deceive consumers, because they are staged to look like a talk show.

informants see *unit of observation.*

information gaps see *knowledge gap hypothesis.*

information superhighway the idea of transporting a lot of information via computers very quickly.
The information superhighway metaphor emerged after the Cuban missile crisis. Experts were concerned about the impact a nuclear or atomic bomb could have on cutting off communication between military commanders and units in America. So a U.S. scientific government agency called Advanced Research Projects Agency (ARPA) commissioned Paul Baron of the Rand Corporation to produce a system that would allow the U.S. military to maintain control over its nuclear arsenal and planes even if a nuclear attack wiped out conventional communication systems.

The information superhighway metaphor was derived partly from the interstate highway system, which President Dwight D. Eisenhower initiated in the 1950s (an idea, by the way, that he borrowed from the German Autobahn) in part to transport military troops and equipment around the country quickly. In the case of computers, however, the goods to be transported were information, and the idea was to transport information from one point to another even if part of the highway system were disabled.

See *Internet* and *World Wide Web*.

Information Technology Association of America, The (ITAA) a trade association representing the U.S. information technology industry.

It's Web site <www.itaa.org> provides information about the IT industry and the issues affecting it, as well as information about the association's programs.

information revolution rapid growth in information and knowledge associated with industrialization and urbanization.

Virtually everyone in industrialized nations has heard of this term. But many have little understanding of why the "information revolution" occurred or its consequences.

The history of humans in various places around the world is generally a history of the growth of information and knowledge. But the term "information revolution" is often associated with the invention of *Johannes Gutenberg's* movable type printing press, because that event triggered a rapid growth in the number of published books and knowledge. Even more important, the printing press helped decentralize political and religious power.

More specifically, during Gutenberg's time, ordinary people had few rights and little power. Emperors, kings, nobles, lords, religious leaders, and tribal chiefs ruled in most areas of the world—some with an iron fist. Most of them monopolized the production and dissemination of knowledge and ideas, which helped them maintain power.

But Gutenberg's printing press and the information revolution in general made it much more difficult for elites to control the production and distribution of knowledge and ideas. In fact, the printing press enabled people who were critical of those in power to easily and inexpensively produce and distribute their ideas. The press contributed to the development of representative democratic government, although the shift took several more centuries and was more evolutionary than revolutionary.

Today many different forms of mass media are encompassed under the rubric of the "information revolution." This includes books, newspapers, magazines, radio, motion pictures, television, records, and the Internet. Some scholars have even suggested that the Internet is now helping to decentralize power from traditional mass media.

infotainment information-based media content or programming that also includes entertainment content in an effort to enhance its popularity with audiences and consumers.

injunction see *law*.

inoculation effect a media effect obtained when audiences or readers are informed in advance that a particular message is designed to influence them; the forewarning generally inoculates the subject and, thus, decreases the power of the message.

insert advertisements advertising content that is published on a separate sheet or sheets of paper and inserted into a magazine or newspaper.
    Contrast with *run-of-press advertisements*.

instant messenger services a service allowing e-mail users to "converse" in real time. They can send and reply to messages instantly.

instrument fancy term for a *questionnaire*.

intercept study a survey method in which people are approached in stores or malls and are interviewed for the purpose of gathering opinions about a topic, a concept or a product.

interdependence a condition or process where one social actor depends upon another to achieve a goal.
    Most people who live in highly industrialized, urbanized societies have a high level of interdependence. They depend heavily on others for food, clothing, shelter, work, health care, entertainment, etc. In contrast, people who live in less developed, agricultural based societies tend to be more self-sufficient.

internal public see *public*.

internal validity the extent to which the findings from an experiment accurately reflect what happened in the experiment itself.
    See *external validity*.

International Association of Business Communicators (IABC) an association that represents business and marketing communication professionals around the world.
    IABC's Web site <www.iabc.com> contains news, information, and research data on business and marketing communication.

International Communication Association (ICA) a nonprofit education association representing 65 countries and 3,500 scholars and professionals interested in international communication.

Its Web site <www.icahdq.org> contains information about its conferences and other member resources..

International Standard Book Number (ISBN) a unique, 10- or 13-digit international identifier used for books and designed to supplement bibliographic descriptive records.

The ISBN is used to order, distribute, and inventory books. It reduces mistakes and saves time. In addition, the ISBN provides a lot of information about a book and its publisher. For example, the ISBN number for this book is 0-922993-25-4.

The first digit or set of digits is called a "group identifier." It identifies a country, area or language area participating in the ISBN system. The digit "0" includes the United States and 10 other countries where English is the dominant language.

The next set of digits is called the "publisher prefix." This identifies publishers within a group. In this case, "922993" represents Marquette Books. The publisher prefix may contain up to seven numbers. As a rule of thumb, the lower the number the larger the publisher.

The third set of digits—"25"—identifies the title (i.e., the book itself). The "title identifier" may consist of up to six digits, and most publishers use them up in chronological order, so it shows how many books the publisher has published. In this case, Marquette Books has published 24 books before this one.

The last digit is called a "checking digit," which is used to double-check the validity of the ISBN.

In 2007, the book publishing industry will be converting to a 13-digit ISBN number partly to avoid running out of numbers.

Internet a network of computers, which now spans much of the globe, that allows individuals and organizations to communicate and exchange information with each other.

Vinton Cerf of Stanford University and Robert Kahn of the Defense *Advanced Research Projects Agency* coined the term in 1974. "Internet" literally means "between networks."

See *ARPNET* and *USENET*.

Internet advertising advertisements that appear on the *Internet*.

There are three major types of Internet advertisements: banner, pop-up, and interstitials.

The most popular is the banner ad, which is simply a box that contains a message, sometimes stretching across the top of the page. The banner ad is the online version of the newspaper display ad. The skyscraper ad is the vertical version of the banner ad (taller than it is wide). Banner advertisements may contain audio and moving objects. These are called rich media ads.

The second type of advertisement is the pop-up, which appears when a user clicks a tab or logs on to a site. These are more intrusive, often forcing the user to shut them down before completing a task on a Web site. If a banner or pop-ad contains a link to another site, it is called a text-linked advertisement. Clicking on the ad takes the user to another site, where additional information is provided or where the user can order a product or service.

Interstitials are ads that come on or play between pages on a Web site. They are similar to television ad, which play between sections of a program. Some interstitials play in the main browser window, while others play in new, smaller windows. Regardless of format, most interstitial ads perform very well on the basis of both click-through recall and brand recall.

Businesses may create their own ads or hire advertising agencies to do that job. In either case, the advertisement almost always seeks to persuade consumers or businesses to buy products or services.

Internet Corporation for Assigned Names and Numbers, The (ICANN) a nonprofit organization that helps coordinate the Internet, issuing Internet domain names and IP addresses, among other things.

The organization's Web site <www.icann.org> contains news and information about the Internet and links to other sites involved in coordinating the Internet.

Internet Protocol a unique number that identifies servers on the *Internet.*

Each server and computer connected to the *Internet* is identified by a number, called an Internet Protocol, and by a name or names. For example, the number assigned to the Web server at Washington State University is 134.121.0.99. The server also has a *domain name*: http://www.wsu.edu. The name is easier to remember than the number, but typing http://134.121.0.99 into a browser's "address" or "location" search window also will take you to the home page Web site for the Washington State University.

The name system was devised to make it easier for users to access Web sites. A server or computer has one IP number but may have more than one name. The domain name is created by the owner of the host. Washington State University presumably selected the prefix "wsu" because it was short and easy to remember. The suffix, "edu," is called a *zone.*

Initially, IP numbers and domain name addresses were supplied free of charge by the National Science Foundation. However, the explosive growth of the Internet in the 1990s forced the agency to turn the task over to other non-governmental groups.

In 1998, the *Internet Corporation for Assigned Names and Numbers* was formed. This not-for-profit corporation oversees the addressing system, but private companies do most of the registering.

See *domain name, Internet, protocol, Uniform Resource Locator,* and *zone*

Internet Service Providers (ISP) organizations that give computer users access to the Internet, usually through a modem and telephone line or a cable connection, for a small monthly fee.

CompuServe was the first successful ISP. America Online was founded in 1989 as a dial-up information service, but didn't offer Internet access until 1994.

Internet Society, The an international organization that serves as a clearinghouse for Internet information and education as well as facilitates and coordinates Internet-related initiatives around the world.

The organization's Web site <www.isoc.org> contains information about access, censorship, copyright, digital divide, and a host of other topics. See *Internet*.

Internet survey a *survey* administered through the Internet.

An Internet survey is generally the least expensive way to gather survey *data* because *interviewers* will not have to be hired, there are no long-distance telephone bills, and there is no postage. However, the Internet survey does not work well with general populations, who distrust the Internet and are suspicious of survey sponsors. *Responses rates* can be very low. The Internet survey works best with targeted audiences who are familiar with the sponsor and who have a vested interest in the results.

Source: Donald A. Dillman, *Mail and Internet Surveys: The Tailored Design Method*, 2nd ed. (New York: Wiley, 2000).

interpersonal communication communication that occurs between a small number of individuals.

That communication may be face-to-face or mediated by some technology, such as the telephone or Internet (e-mail). Good examples are the conversations people have with friends or students have with professors. See *communication*.

interstitials see *Internet advertising*.

intersubjectivity a condition that exists when two or more scientists or media researchers studying the same phenomena come to the same conclusion.

interval measures see *levels of measurement*.

intervening variable a *variable* that mediates, or explains, at least part of the *relationship* between two other variables.

interviewers people who field a *survey research* study.

intrapersonal communication *communication* that takes place within a person—that "inner voice," so to speak.

In this case, the sender and recipient are the same person. Everyday life involves a great deal of inner monologue as people attempt to understand the world and make personal decisions.

See *communication*.

inverse relationship same as negative relationship.

See *relationship*.

inverted pyramid a style of writing often used in journalism that involves putting the most important facts first, with the lead, or first sentence, usually providing a summary of the main ideas.

There are two reasons for writing in the inverted pyramid form. First, most people don't spend a lot of time with the newspaper, so providing the most important information first gives them the gist of a story. Second, when filling the news hole, some stories have to be trimmed, and it is better to trim the least important than the most important information.

Feature stories usually employ delayed leads or use anecdotes to illustrate the main themes or ideas.

See *news*.

isomorphism in social science research, the idea that two presumably different concepts or constructs are actually measuring the same thing.

J

jacket the paper slip cover wrapped around hardbound books, used primarily to promote the book.

Jefferson, Thomas (1743-1826) the third president of the United States who was also a champion of the *First Amendment*.

After the Revolutionary War, Jefferson became the leader of the anti-Federalists (or "Republicans," which ironically became the Democratic Party in the 19th century) and argued for a responsive government—one that meets the needs of the people.

Jefferson believed that even though individuals make mistakes, the majority of the populace could make sound decisions if given access to accurate and truthful information. He advocated education and argued that the press was an essential source of information and

Thomas Jefferson

guidance and should be free from governmental control. In 1787, he wrote: "were it left to me to decide whether we should have a government without newspapers, or newspapers without a government, I should not hesitate a moment to prefer the latter."

In addition to educating the individual, the press should serve as a check on the government, to prevent it from infringing on the rights of the individual. "No experiment can be more interesting than that we are now trying, and which we trust will end in establishing the fact, that man may be governed by reason and truth. Our first object should therefore be, to leave open to him all the avenues to truth. The most effectual hitherto found, is the freedom of the press."

But Jefferson wasn't always upbeat about the role of the press. In 1813, after years of being criticized by Federalist newspapers, he wrote: "The newspapers of our country by their abandoned spirit of falsehood, have more effectually destroyed the utility of the press than all the shackles devised by Bonaparte."

See *Alien and Sedition Acts, seditious libel, fourth estate.*

Source: Saul K. Padover, *Thomas Jefferson on Democracy* (New York: Penguin, 1939).

Jennings, Peter (1938-) ABC World News Tonight anchor since 1983.

Johnson, John H. (1918-) one of the most successful black publishers in U.S. history.

Johnson was born in Arkansas City, Ark., in 1918. At the time, there were no high schools for blacks in Arkansas City. Johnson repeated eighth grade rather than end his education.

A short time later, his family moved to Chicago, where Johnson graduated from DuSable High School. He was an honor student and served as senior class president, yearbook editor, and editor of the newspaper. His classmates included Nat King Cole and Redd Foxx.

After a speech Johnson gave at a Chicago Urban League event, American businessman Harry Pace offered him a scholarship and a job at Pace's company, Supreme Life Insurance Company. One of his jobs was to select articles from magazines and other publications to keep Pace abreast of current events of interest to blacks.

Johnson started Johnson Publishing in 1942 with $500 he borrowed using his mother's furniture as collateral. His first magazine was "Negro Digest," the forerunner of "Ebony." The company now has a book division and also publishes "Jet" magazine, the top-ranked black news weekly with a readership of more than 8 million.

Johnson Publishing employs nearly 3,000 people and annually earns nearly $400 million. The company owns Fashion Fair Cosmetics, the world's leader in makeup and skin care for people of color, and Supreme Beauty products, which offers hair care products for men and women.

The company produces television shows and the Ebony Fashion Fair, the world's largest traveling fashion show, which has donated over $47 million to charity. The Johnson family gives to many charities, including the United Negro College Fund and the Boys and Girls Clubs of America.

Johnson has received many awards, including the Presidential Medal of Freedom. His autobiography, "Succeeding Against All Odds," was updated in 2004.

joint-operating agreement a contractual relationship in which two newspapers in the same city have separate editorial staffs but share staff devoted to production, circulation, and advertising.

Congress passed the Newspaper Preservation Act of 1970, allowing newspapers to create joint operating agreements. The purpose was to stem the decline of competing dailies in large cities, but the program has been only a partial success.

About a dozen joint-operating agreements still exist, but those numbers are expected to decline because it is still much more efficient economically to publish one newspaper than two. Only very large cities, like New York City and Chicago, can financially support more than one daily, and the newspapers that have survived in those cities reach different markets. "The New York Times" and "Chicago Tribune," for example, are preferred by a more white-collar reader and the "New York Daily News" and the "Chicago Sun-Times" are preferred by a more blue-collar reader.

joint-venture in filmmaking, a method of funding a project which involves two or more film studios or distributors pooling resources and sharing costs and profits. This approach reduces risk, especially for expensive productions.

jukebox a phonograph or compact disc player that plays back music when money is inserted into it.

K

Kinetograph an 18th-century film camera.

The Kinetograph used a clock to ensure intermittent but regular movement of a perforated film strip through the camera. The machine exposed 40 frames per second and used up to 50 feet of film. It was invented by W. L. D. Dickson, one of Thomas Edison's assistants.

See *Edison, Thomas Alva* and *Kinetoscope*.

Kinetoscope an 18th-century film projector.

The Kinetoscope was a large box weighing about a thousand pounds that projected a film for individual viewing. Invented by W. L. D. Dickson, one of Thomas Edison's assistants, the Kinetoscope was replaced by the *film projector*.

See *Edison, Thomas Alva,* and *Kinetograph*.

King, Augusta Ada (1815-1851) the world's first computer programmer.

King was the daughter of Anne Milbanke and poet Lord George Gordon Byron, who at the time was involved in a notorious sex scandal. Determined to suppress any wildness in her daughter, Milbanke separated from Byron and encouraged her daughter to study mathematics and science. Milbanke hired Augustus De Morgan, a famous mathematician and logician, to tutor her daughter.

Ada became fascinated with the Analytical Engine, a device proposed by Charles Babbage, a famous mathematician and inventor. (By the way, he was the guy who suggested that the weather of years past could be read from tree rings.) The Analytical Engine was designed to analyze punch cards and would have been the world's first mechanical digital computer, but it was never built.

Nevertheless, Ada came to understood the machine so well that she published a definitive paper on it in 1843. The Analytical Engine went beyond simple arithmetic, she pointed out, because it operated on general symbols rather than on numbers. She predicted that such a machine could be used to compose complex music and graphics, and have both practical and scientific uses. She was right.

Thus, in the 1840s Ada became the world's only expert on the process of sequencing instructions on the punch cards. She was, in other words, the world's first computer programmer. It would be another 100 years before anyone understood computing as well as she did.

Ada married and had three children. She enjoyed music, poetry, and horses, and associated with high society, including Charles Dickens. However, after publication of her paper, her health began to fail. She died at the age of 36, as did her father.

Source: Betty A. Toole (ed.), *Ada, the Enchantress of Numbers* (Mill Valley, CA: Strawberry Press, 1992).

knowledge *beliefs* that are verified or true.
See *a prior knowledge* and *a posteriori knowledge*.

knowledge-gap hypothesis the notion that the gap in knowledge between people, groups or nations high in social status and those low in social status increases as the amount of information or knowledge on an issue or topic increases.

When this proposition is applied to the Internet and global media systems, researchers usually call it the "digital divide" or "digital gap" hypothesis, but few of them recognize its origins.

The knowledge gap hypothesis was originally proposed in 1970 by University of Minnesota media sociologists Phillip J. Tichenor, George A. Donohue and Clarice N. Olien, who argued that "as the infusion of mass media information into a social system increases, segments of the population with higher socioeconomic status tend to acquire this information at a faster rate than the lower status segments, so that the gap in knowledge between these segments tends to increase rather than decrease" (see graphic next page.)

High status people gain knowledge faster than less because they (1) have better communication skills (e.g., can read more quickly), (2) have more "stored knowledge" that enables them to understand new information more quickly, (3) have more contact with other people who are highly knowledgeable, and (4) have more interest in consuming public affairs knowledge. The researchers also point out that (5) mass media organizations target more highly educated people because they have more disposable income, which is attractive to advertisers.

The knowledge-gap hypothesis can be applied to individuals, communities, groups or to nations. From a worldwide perspective, the argument is that the "information-rich" countries (e.g., France, Great Britain, Japan, United States) are gaining more knowledge and, thus, greater power and influence over the "information-poor" countries (e.g., African and Latin American countries).

Knowledge-Gap Hypothesis

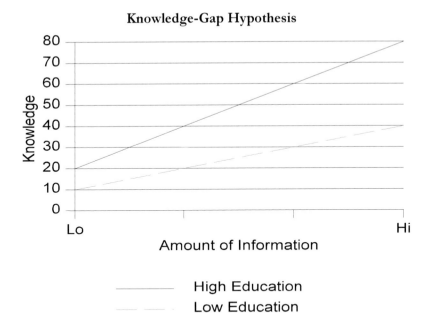

——————— High Education

— — — Low Education

The "Minnesota Team" tested its theory using longitudinal public opinion data on sending an astronaut to the moon and on cigarette smoking. Prior to World War II, for example, most people, regardless of status, didn't believe it was possible to send a spaceship to the moon. However, as technology advanced and media began publishing reports that space travel was possible, the gaps in knowledge between high-status and low-status individuals widened. That's because high-status people were reading more and were talking about science more than low-status people.

Mass communication scholars Cecilie Gaziano, Kasisomayajula Viswanath, and John R. Finnegan Jr., who have reviewed the literature on the knowledge gap hypothesis, generally find support for it. But there is little agreement on what can be done to reduce gaps.

Take, for instance, the popular children's television show "Sesame Street," which originated in the United States and is broadcast in many countries around the world. When this program was first proposed in the 1960s, the goal was to help disadvantaged children living in inner-city areas catch up intellectually to their peers from the higher-status suburbs (e.g., to correct a knowledge gap).

Studies showed that the program boosted the verbal and math test scores of children from disadvantaged backgrounds. However, the program also boosted scores for children from advantaged backgrounds—even more. In fact, the knowledge gaps got even bigger because parents of high-status children were giving their children more encouragement to watch the program, and were spending more time with them during the programming. The knowledge-gap hypothesis refutes the assumption that gaps in knowledge between individuals, groups, and nations can be equalized simply by pouring a lot of information into a social system. To the contrary, pumping more information into a system generally produces greater gaps in knowledge. But limiting information or access to it is clearly not the answer. Gaps can be lessened with education and more intensive media campaigns, but policy makers have done little to address the problem locally or globally.

Sources: Phillip J. Tichenor, George A. Donohue, and Clarice N. Olien, "Mass Media and Differential Growth in Knowledge," *Public Opinion Quarterly*, 34:158-170 (1970), and George A. Donohue, Phillip J. Tichenor, and Clarice N. Olien, "Mass Media and the Knowledge Gap," *Communication Research*, 2:3-23 (1975); K. Viswanath and J. R. Finnegan Jr., "The Knowledge Gap Hypothesis: Twenty-Five Years Later," pp. 187-227 in B. R. Burleson (ed.), *Communication Yearbook, Vol. 19* (Thousand Oaks, CA: Sage, 1996) and Cecilie Gaziano, "The Knowledge Gap: An Analytical Review of Media Effects," *Communication Research*, 10:447-486 (1983).

Kuhn, Thomas see *paradigm*.

L

label see *recording label.*

lap dog theory the notion that the news media produce content that serves the interests of political and economic elites to the exclusion of the public, the poor, and disadvantaged groups.

The lap dog metaphor is usually attributed to neo-Marxist scholars who study *ideology,* or the "production" of ideas that help support and maintain capitalism as an economic institution. The metaphor oversimplifies the position of most critics, however, who concede that modern news media can produce content critical of those in power. But this content has little impact on changing society partly because ordinary people have limited access to economic and political resources.

Lasker, Albert (1880-1952) advertising executive who promoted the *reason-why principle.*

Albert Lasker began his advertising career in Chicago in 1898 at Lord & Thomas, one of three major advertising companies in the United States. He quickly moved from office boy to copywriter, but he had an restless, inquisitive mind and questioned the role and function of advertising. "What is advertising?" he would ask many people in the business.

But he didn't get a satisfactory answer until he met John E. Kennedy, another copywriter visiting Chicago. Advertising is salesmanship in print, Kennedy told him. Readers need reasons to buy products.

Lasker employed the "reason-why principle" throughout his career, and it remains an important guiding force behind advertising copywriting today. It also became the foundation for more sophisticated approaches to developing ads, including the use of social science research methods to understand consumers' needs and wants.

See *reason-why principle.*

Lasswell, Harold (1902-1978) a political scientist who helped shape and define the field of mass communication.

Lasswell is most famous for two major contributions.

The first major contribution is his identification of three functions of mass media: (1) surveillance of the environment; (2) correlation of the parts of society in responding to the environment; and (3) transmission of the social heritage from one generation to the next.

The second major contribution was to define a five-step analytical model for studying media processes and effects: who, says what, in which channel, to whom, with what effect?

See *structural functionalism*.

Source: Harold Lasswell, *The Communication of Ideas* (New York: Harper & Row, 1948).

latent function an unintended consequence of mass media use.

See *manifest function*.

law (a) a rule of conduct (or formal norm) that has been approved, sanctioned or implemented by an authority (e.g., a legislature or head of state), and **(b)** in science, a sequence of events that occur with unvarying uniformity under the same conditions (see *mass communication research* for elaboration).

Laws (first definition above) enacted by governments can be divided into two major categories: criminal and civil. The key distinction is that people may go to jail when a criminal law has been violated. Civil law, in contrast, attempts to resolve private disputes between private parties. Monetary damages are the most popular remedies. Usually one party pays another to settle a dispute.

Most legal disputes that involve mass media are civil. Almost all cases of *libel*, for example, are civil offenses. However, *seditious libel* (i.e., criticism of the government) is a criminal offense. A legal wrong committed by one person against another also is called a tort, except when the wrong involves "breach of contract" (a separate category). Torts may also arise from criminal acts (assaults, rape, etc.). As such, victims or families of victims may sue offenders in civil court, usually for monetary compensation.

There are six major types of law: constitutional, statutory, administrative, executive, common, and equity.

1. Constitutional Law. The Constitution of the United States, which includes its amendments, is the highest law of the land. This document takes precedence over all other laws, rules, and regulations.

In terms of the mass media, the most important law in the Constitution is the *First Amendment*, which states, in its entirety: "Congress shall make no law respecting an establishment of religion, or prohibiting the free exercise thereof; or abridging the freedom of speech, or of the press; or the right of the people peaceably to assemble, and to petition the Government for redress of grievances." Each of the 50 states also have constitutions, many of which guarantee citizens "freedom of speech and the press."

Although the wording of the First Amendment seems simple and straightforward, in practice there are many disagreements about how to interpret it. The final arbiter, however, is the U.S. Supreme Court.

Several other amendments, including the Fourth, Sixth and Fourteenth, also can have an impact on mass media organizations.

2. Statutory Law. This is law that is enacted by legislators at the federal, state or local levels. At the federal and state levels, the laws are usually called statutes.

At the local level (city and county government), the laws are usually called ordinances. Statutes and ordinances govern many aspects of mass communication, including privacy, copyright, access to government records, obscenity, and operation of electronic media.

3. Administrative Law. This is law that is generated by government administrative agencies, such as the *Federal Communications Commission (FCC)*. The FCC, for example, assigns television and radio frequencies and regulates broadcast and telecommunication companies, which include television stations and telephone companies.

Congress empowered the FCC because it doesn't have the technical expertise to regulate these companies. The FCC and other agencies create many rules and regulations but ultimately are responsible to Congress.

4. Executive Law. This is law created by the President of the United States and other governmental executives.

Executive law doesn't affect mass communication processes or industries very often. Perhaps the greatest impact comes from the power the President has to nominate Supreme Court justices and other governmental officials (such as members of the Federal Communications Commission), who may be more or less sympathetic to the First Amendment and concerns of mass media industries and workers.

The President also has the authority to classify many government records "top secret," which affects the ability of news organizations to report on government activities.

5. Common Law. This is judge-made law.

Common law represents the accumulation of rulings made in state courts and often reflects traditional ideas and customs. Precedent is the guiding principle. In other words, if two essentially similar cases arise, the decision on the second case should be in accordance with the first. More formally, the judicial policy upon which common law is based on "stare decisis," which basically means "let past decisions stand."

The right to privacy, for example, emerged first in the courts. This right has been bolstered in recent decades by the passage of many federal and state statutes protecting an individual's records. Common law exists only in state courts. The Supreme Court ruled there is no common law at the federal level.

6. Law of Equity. The law of equity allows the courts to take action that is fair or just when other remedies are unavailable. The injunction, or

restraining order, that halted publication of the "Pentagon Papers" is an example. Only judges can use the law of equity. Juries are limited to deciding questions that revolve around facts (e.g., Is someone guilty?).

See *court of law* and *lawsuit.*

Lazarsfeld, Paul (1901-1976) an Austrian-born scholar who founded the Bureau of Applied Social Research at Columbia University.

Lazarsfeld pioneered the use of *quantitative research* statistics and data analysis on media, including radio. He and his colleagues were most interested in learning about why people vote the way they do and the impact of newspapers and radio on voter choice.

The Lazarsfeld team of researchers surveyed 3,000 voters in Erie County, Ohio, at six different points in time prior to and after the 1940 presidential election in which Democrat incumbent Franklin Roosevelt ran against Republican challenger Wendell L. Wilkie. They found that two-thirds of the respondents said both radio and newspapers were important sources of information about the election. During the last 12 days of the campaign, about half of the respondents listened to at least one political discussion on radio and read one front page newspaper story on the election. However, when asked to choose between the two news sources, radio was clearly the "most important" source of information.

Even more surprising, the study found that many people ignored mass media coverage of the election altogether. Many got their information from other people. This eventually spawned what came to be known as the *two-step flow of communication.* The basic idea was that opinion leaders, or those who followed the election more closely, played a role in influencing other voters. Opinion leaders were more educated and affluent than other citizens.

The most important contribution of this study is that it began challenging assumptions about the powerful effects model of mass media. Demographic and personal characteristics of voters limited, or moderated, the effects of mass media. This finding was validated by *Carl Hovland's* research.

Source: Paul F. Lazarsfeld, Benard Berelson, and Hazil Gaudet , *The People's Choice* (New York: Columbia University Press, 1948).

lawsuit a dispute in which one or more parties files a formal grievance in a civil *court of law.*

The party that files the lawsuit is called a plaintiff, or the one who is alleging that a wrong or illegal action occurred. The party who is being sued is called a defendant, or the one who is accused of committing the wrong or illegal action.

If one of the parties is displeased with the court's decision, it may appeal the case to state or federal courts of appeal. The party then becomes the appellant, or the party making the appeal. The other party becomes the respondent, or appellee.

See *court of law* and *law.*

Lee, Ivy (1877-1934) a journalist who helped define the field of public relations and who competes with *Edward L. Bernays* for the title of "father of public relations."

After graduating from Princeton University in 1898, Lee did post-graduate work at Harvard and Columbia Universities but dropped out due to lack of money. He worked as a newspaper reporter for the "New York American," "The New York Times," and the "New York World." He specialized in business news. His first public relations work came in 1903, when he served as publicity manager for the Citizens' Union.

Lee worked a press job with the Democratic National Committee before opening his public relations firm with George Parker in 1905. In 1906, a group of coal mine owners hired him to improve their public image, and Lee issued his "Declaration of Principles," which was mailed to city editors:

"This is not a secret press bureau. All our work is done in the open. We aim to supply news. This is not an advertising agency; if you think any of our matter ought properly to go to your business office, do not use it."

In 1908 he began working full time for the Pennsylvania Railroad, where he was in charge of its publicity bureau. He spent much of his time fighting lower freight rates. In 1914, he helped Rockefeller counter adverse press coverage of strikes at Colorado Fuel and Oil Company mines. Fifty-three workers and their family members, including 13 women and children, had been killed.

Lee's tactics were successful but they helped earn him the title of "Poison Ivy," partly because he discredited a union trying to organize the workers. Lee urged the Rockefellers to publicize their charity work and reportedly urged Rockefeller to hand out dimes to children wherever he went.

During World War I, Lee served as publicity director and assistant to the chairman of the American Red Cross. In 1919 he first used the term "public relations." Prior to that, he referred to what he did as "publicity."

During the 1920s, he urged the U.S. government to recognize the Soviet Union, arguing that commerce and the free flow of ideas would kill communism. In the late 1920s and early 1930s, he did consulting work for a German company, which led to charges he was working for the Nazis. But there was no proof of this.

He died of a brain tumor.

See *Bernays, Edward L.* and *public relations.*

Sources: Ray Eldon Hiebert, *Courtier to the Crowd: The Story of Ivy L. Lee and the Development of Public Relations* (Ames: Iowa State University Press, 1966). Quoted material is from Sherman Morse, "An Awakening on Wall Street," *American Magazine,* Vol. 62 (Sept. 1906), p. 460.

Lee, Spike (1957-) one of the leading African American directors and screenwriters in Hollywood.

The film "Do the Right Thing," released in 1989, catapulted Lee into international stardom. This movie explored racial tensions in the city,

Form of Explanation by Level of Analysis

Form of Explanation	Level of Analysis	Academic Discipline*	Examples of Phenomena Studieda*
Probabilistic Generalizations	Cultural	Communication, Law, Philosophy, History, Linguistics, Sociology, Literature	Values, Rituals, Language, Laws, Public Opinion, Norms, Technology
	Social	Communication, History, Sociology, Economics, Political Science, Social Anthropology,	Status, Roles, Power, Organizations, Institutions, Groups,
	Psychological	Communication, History, Psychology, Psychiatry Social Psychology, Cognitive Psychology	Attitudes, Beliefs, Individual Values Cognitions, Personality
	Organic	Biology, Medicine, Physical Anthropology, Psychobiology, Sociobiology	Cells, Organs, Tissues, Nerves, Diseases
Law-Like Propositions	Physiological	Physics, Chemistry, Mathematics	Forces, Motion, Atoms, Molecules

*Illustrative, not a comprehensive listing.

challenging conventional views and assumptions about race, class, and sex, and earning Lee a Best Screenplay Oscar nomination.

Since the late 1980s, nearly everything Lee has written and directed has been a success, either at the box office, with critics, or both. This includes "Mo' Better Blues," "Jungle Fever," "Malcolm X," "Crooklyn," "Girl 6," "Get on the Bus," "He Got Game," "4 Little Girls," and "Summer of Sam." The movie "4 Little Girls" was nominated for a Best Documentary Feature Oscar.

Sources: James Earl Hardy, *Spike Lee* (New York: Chelsea House, 1996); Jim Haskins, *Spike Lee: By Any Means Necessary* (New York: Walker & Co., 1997); and Mark A. Reid (ed.), *Spike Lee's Do the Right Thing* (New York: Cambridge University Press, 1997)

level of analysis an abstract system for conceptualizing phenomena for study.

If a researcher wanted to study the United States, she or he could study individuals, neighborhoods, communities, states, or regions of the country. Individuals are often thought of as the "lowest" level of analysis and regions the "highest." As one goes from the individual to the region, observations are often aggregated and the level of explanation tends to become less specific and more general.

Through the years, scholars have proposed a number of different level-of-analysis schemes. In terms of analyzing human behavior, one of the more useful is a five-level scheme shown in the table on the previous page. Each of the "levels" conceptually builds upon the one below it.

For example, the "psychological" presupposes the existence of physical matter (physiological level) and living matter (organic level). Culture is conceptualized at the "highest" level of analysis, because it can exist only when all four of the other levels exist.

The field of communication usually involves the study of the three "highest" levels of analysis (psychological, social and cultural). A study that focuses on media effects often focuses on the psychological level but may also involve elements of the social and cultural levels.

Although law-like propositions are often applied to explain phenomena at the physiological level, many researchers argue that explanations become less deterministic and more variant as one moves up the hierarchy. As such, these researchers tend to search for generalizations (general patterns) rather than laws of human behavior.

See *probabilistic theory of action* and *determinism*.

levels of measurement a four-level system (nominal, ordinal, interval, and ratio) for classifying *variables* that determines which statistics to use for analysis.

Nominal variables contain categories or values that differ qualitatively, but not quantitatively. Religion, race, gender, and marital status are examples.

Ordinal variables can be rank-ordered, but the distance between the values is not necessarily equivalent. *Attitudes, beliefs*, and *behavioral intentions* are ordinal measures. Responses are usually recorded on two to seven-point *scales* (e.g., strongly agree to strongly disagree). Ordinal measures can be partially ordered, where some responses have the same value, or fully ordered, which means that each case has a unique value and may be rank-ordered from highest to lowest.

Interval variables contain categories that also can be rank-ordered, but the distance between the *response categories* is equal. IQ scores are an example. The distance between 100 and 110 is the same as the distance between 120 and 130, but because there is no true zero as a starting point, the differences cannot be multiplied or divided. Someone with an IQ of 200 is not twice as smart as one with a score of 100.

Ratio variables have a true zero-point and, therefore, can be divided and multiplied. Age, years of formal education, and income are examples. A person who is 50 years old is twice as old as one who is 25.

Levels of measurement are crucial for determining what type of statistics to use in data analysis. For example, Pearson's R correlation coefficient is used when both variables are measured at the interval or ratio level of measurement.

LexisNexis an online service capable of searching millions of legal documents, court cases, and mass media news services.

LexisNexis is one of the most popular search tools in mass communication. LexisNexis is owned by Reed Elsevier, a Dutch company, and one of the largest media companies in the world.

libel a defamatory statement in writing.

Defamation is communication that injures the good name or reputation of a person or corporation, or which tends to bring a person or corporation into disrepute. *Slander* is oral, or spoken, defamation. Broadcast defamation is libel when there is a written script and is slander when there is no script.

Definitions of libel vary from state to state. But words that expose people to public hatred, shame, contempt, ridicule, or disgrace, or derogate people in their personal or professional lives are generally defamatory if they are false. In mass communication, news stories or press releases that deal with crime, immorality, financial unreliability, or incompetence generate the most problems.

Libel can be subdivided into three categories: civil libel, seditious libel and criminal libel. Civil libel is defamatory statements against citizens or groups. *Seditious libel* is defamation or criticism of the government or its officers. Sedition is an illegal act intended to disrupt or overthrow the government. Criminal libel is libel for which a person may go to jail. Some states still have criminal libel statutes on the books, but few cases of criminal libel have occurred in recent years.

Any living person can file a civil libel lawsuit. If a dead person is libeled, relatives cannot sue in the name of the deceased. However, if the libelous material defames the family, it may sue.

To prove libel, a person or organization must: (1) show that the libelous communication was published; (2) prove the plaintiff was identified in the communication; and (3) demonstrate that the communication is defamatory (i.e., show a reputation has been damaged).

If the libeled person is a public official or public figure, he or she must also prove malice (discussed subsequently).

Plaintiffs who bring libel lawsuits may sue for actual damages as well as punitive damages, which are designed to punish the offender and to serve as a general deterrent to the rest of the community. Punitive damage awards can be very large, so media organizations are especially concerned about libel lawsuits.

Until the 1960s, libel law was governed by a standard known as "strict liability." This meant that if a media organization defamed someone, it was responsible for that harm, regardless of how it came about.

But in the 1964 Supreme Court case New York Times v. Sullivan, the U.S. Supreme Court eliminated strict liability as it applied to government officials. The court ruled that government officials would have to prove malice in order to win a libel lawsuit.

The case involved an advertisement placed in *The New York Times* by a civil rights group called the Committee to Defend Martin Luther King and the Struggle for Freedom in the South.

The ad stated that Alabama State College student leaders were expelled from school after singing "My Country 'Tis of Thee" on the State Capitol steps, that police armed with shotguns and tear gas ringed the campus, and that the dining hall was padlocked in an attempt to starve them into submission. The ad also contained information about King.

While the ad was generally true, it did contain several errors. Student leaders were not expelled for singing. The dining hall had not been padlocked. Although deployed in large numbers, the police had not "ringed" the campus. "The New York Times" ad staff did not check the accuracy of the advertisement.

Five Alabama government officials, including L. B. Sullivan, one of three elected Montgomery police commissioners, retaliated by filing a lawsuit against the "Times" for $3 million. At trial, Sullivan argued that even though he was not personally named in the ad, the charges defamed him because he supervised the police department. Relying on the rule of strict liability, the Alabama trial court ruled in favor of Sullivan and the other plaintiffs, awarding them $500,000—the largest libel judgment in Alabama at the time. The Supreme Court of Alabama upheld judgment, but the U.S. Supreme Court reversed the decision.

The high court said Alabama's libel law was unconstitutional because it did not adequately safeguard freedom of speech and press. At issue was "a profound national commitment to the principle that debate on public issues should be uninhibited, robust, and wide-open, and that it may well include vehement, caustic, and sometimes unpleasantly sharp attacks on government and public officials." The court said *First Amendment* freedoms could not survive if a "pall of fear and timidity" was imposed upon the press and public.

The Court threw out strict liability as it applied to government officials and established a new constitutional rule: Public officials, such as elected politicians and government administrators, could recover damages for defamation only if they could prove the statement was made with actual malice. To prove malice, plaintiffs who were public officials would have to show that a defendant published the statement either (1) knowing it was false or (2) with reckless disregard for the truth. The court said the malice rule was reasonable because public officials have greater access to mass media and, thus, are better able to counter false statements made against them.

Although the Supreme Court ruled in favor of the "Times," the Sullivan opinion left two key questions unanswered: What actually is "malice?" And who is a "public official?" The first question was partially answered the same year, when the Supreme Court ruled in a separate case that the malice rule applied to criminal libel cases, not just civil (Garrison v. Louisiana, 1964).

In 1967, the court also expanded the definition of who must prove malice to include public figures, such as sports stars and celebrities (Curtis

Publishing Co. v. Butts and Associated Press v. Walker, 1967). Public figures, the court said, were persons who could command public interest and counter defamatory remarks through their access to the media. The court also ruled against the media in one case but did not adequately check the facts of a story (Curtis Publishing Co. v. Butts, 1967).

In 1974, the court refined the definition of a public figure even more, basically limiting this definition to people in the limelight or who voluntarily thrust themselves into the limelight (Gertz v. Welch, 1974). Those who are involuntarily drawn into a public dispute do not need to prove malice.

The court also said public figures, such as public officials, differ from private individuals because (1) they invite attention and comment and (2) they ordinarily have access to media so they can counteract false statements about them.

In 1979, the court ruled that plaintiffs could force journalists to testify about thought processes and editorial conversations in an effort to show malice (Herbert v. Lando (1979)).

In addition to the "malice rule," the three most important defenses for libel are the following:

1. Truth. Truth is almost always a defense, and the best defense, for libel.

2. Reporter's privilege. News stories that quote defamatory comments made in official proceedings are protected if the stories are fair and the quotes accurate.

3. Protection for fair comment and criticism (opinion). Editorials and commentaries often use harsh language when criticizing a person, group or idea. The Supreme Court has ruled the First Amendment protects any expression about matters of public concern that cannot be proven false. Moreover, editorials and commentaries that use "exaggerated language" are protected from libel suits, as long as it is obvious the statements are not true.

4. Statutes of limitations. Most libel actions cannot be initiated if they are not filed within a specified amount of time. The statute of limitations for most libel and slander cases is one to two years.

5. Consent. People who give their consent to publish a defamatory statement cannot win a libel suit. Consent can be inferred when the plaintiff encouraged or participated in the defamatory publication.

6. Privilege for broadcast by political candidates. Broadcast stations have an absolute privilege to air libelous comments during political broadcasts, such as live debates. The Supreme Court created this protection in 1959.

7. Self-interest or self-defense. The courts have allowed some people to defame others if they are responding to attacks on their own reputation. The courts have ruled that people can use reasonable means to defend their reputations, but the line between self-defense and libel is not very clear.

8. Proof of previous bad reputation. A plaintiff who has a "bad reputation" cannot win a libel lawsuit, so one defense is to attack the plaintiff's reputation. However, the courts usually have interpreted

"reputation" very narrowly. Thus, a drug dealer may still win damages if a news report incorrectly accuses him or her of murder.

Winning a libel suit in court is difficult. Mass media come out on top about four out of five times. However, losing one case can seriously impact the bottom line. The average award is $2.5 million. Although the best way to avoid lawsuits is to be accurate and truthful, there are at least six other ways to avoid or reduce liability: (1) libel insurance, (2) retraction, or printing a correction or apology, (3) relying on a credible source, (4) stopping the presses or retrieving copies, (5) and having lawyers review sensitive stories.

See *emotional distress, physical harm, privacy, prior restraint, symbolic speech, corporate speech, commercial speech*.

Sources: *New York Times v. Sullivan*, 376 U.S. 254 (1964); *Garrison v. Louisiana*, 379 U.S. 64 (1964); *Curtis Publishing Co. v. Butts* and *Associated Press v. Walker*, 388 U.S. 130, 1967; *Gertz v. Robert Welch, Inc.*, 418 U.S. 323, 1974); *Herbert v. Lando*, 441 U.S. 153 (1979); *Milkovich v. Lorain Journal Co.*, 497 U.S. 1 (1990); and *Farmers Education & Cooperative Union of America v. WDAY Inc.*, 360 U.S. 525 (1959).

libertarian theory see *normative theory*.

Library of Congress Cataloging Number (LCCN) a unique seven- or eight-digit number for cataloging books in library systems.

In a typical LCCN, such as 2001039953, the first four digits identify the year in which the application was filed (one year before the copyright date, which was 2002). The last set of digits is a unique number for the book.

Most nonfiction and scholarly books have LCCN because academic libraries are markets for them. Many fiction works do not have a LCCN number.

See *International Standard Book Number* and *Cataloging-in-Publication Data*.

Likert scale a type of ordinal scale that measures respondents' level of agreement with statements that express a favorable or unfavorable *attitude* toward a *concept* or idea.

The scale usually consists of categories such as "agree strongly," "agree somewhat," "disagree somewhat," and "disagree strongly."

See *levels of measurement*.

limited effects model a term applied to a broad set of empirical data which shows that mass media have limited persuasive power or influence.

During the 1940s and 1950s, a number of empirical studies showed that mass media have limited ability to change people's opinions or attitudes. This led media scholar Joseph Klapper to conclude in 1960 that people have more influence on each other than the mass media have on them. Other researchers argued that people's basic values and social ties to groups (family, church, friends) are major reason why the persuasive effects of mass media are limited. More specifically, the research showed that

- The more people value their membership in a group, the less affected they are by messages that advocate positions counter to group norms. In other words, strong ties to a group insulate people from counter-group messages.
- The more credible the source of the information, the greater the effect of a persuasive message. Low credibility sources are perceived as more biased and fair than high credibility sources.
- The more strongly people hold a particular belief or value, the less they will expose themselves to information that contradicts their views. Researchers dubbed this *selective exposure*, and they also found that people engage in *selective attention* and *selective retention* (i.e., they only pay attention to what they want to hear or see and only remember what they want to remember).
- The more threatening or fear-arousing a message, the greater its ability to change attitudes, beliefs, and behavior. Some studies showed, however, that too much fear can create intense anxiety and interfere with a person's ability to process the message.
- The more knowledgeable people believe they are about a topic or issue, the more difficult it is to change their attitudes and opinions.
- The lower a people's self-esteem, the more easily they are influenced by a persuasive message.

Source: Joseph T. Klapper, *The Effects of the Mass Media* (Glencoe, IL: The Free Press of Glencoe, 1960).

limited liability an investment concept which means that if a company or corporation goes bankrupt, stockholders only lose their investments—they do not have to pay other debts.

Linotype machine a trademarked name for a machine that set letterpress type from about the 1880s to the 1960s.

An operator, who sometimes would wear green caps or eyeshades, would strike a key that released a metal slug that fell into a form which, in turn, was used to create plates for printing presses. The Linotype machine was replaced by offset printing, which relied upon photographic images to make plates.

LISREL a statistical program for estimating direct and feedback relationships among variables.

LISREL is short for Linear Structural Relations. The software program is similar to *path analysis* but also has the advantage of measuring feedback, or nonrecursive, effects. LISREL also allows researchers to do confirmatory *factor analysis*.

literary agent an individual or organization that represents writers and attempts to secure publishing contracts with publishers.

The first literary agent set up shop in 1875. The idea was to free up writers to concentrate on their craft. Publishers sometimes resented the agents because they would negotiate for higher royalties as well as their own cut of the profits. However, respectable agents also saved publishers time.

Many agents, then as today, signed contracts only with writers who showed promise or were competent at their craft. Today, some publishers will not deal directly with writers. They only deal with agents.

literary journalism a genre of literature, sometimes called creative nonfiction, that uses literary skills when writing nonfiction.

Literary journalism often uses stories or narratives to capture and maintain reader interest. The goal is to combine facts with good writing. See *new journalism.*

logistic regression analysis a *regression analysis* in which the dependent variable is dichotomous with the values of "0" and "1."

log-linear analysis a multivariate statistical method that examines relations among categorical or nominal variables in contingency tables. See *levels of analysis.*

longitudinal study a study that is conducted at two or more points in time.

Luce, Henry (1898-1967) founder of ""Time magazine and Time Inc., which went on to become the world's largest media company.

Luce and Briton Hadden were only 23 years old when they proposed publishing a weekly news magazine. Both were living at home with their parents. Neither had experience running a magazine business. And both had only limited experience as journalists at their student newspaper at Yale University and for a brief time at daily newspapers.

They argued that Americans were poorly informed about political matters, not because the information was not already out there, but "because no publication has adapted itself to the time which busy men are able to spend on simply keeping informed." Their proposed weekly magazine would publish short, easy-to-read stories neatly organized by subjects. They would call their new magazine "Time."

They put together a prospectus and approached potential investors, most of whom were former classmates or their relatives. They scraped together $86,000 and published the first issue on March 3, 1923. It was 32 pages and sold for 15 cents. The news was organized into 22 departments, including aeronautics, art, books, cinema, crime, education, finance, law, medicine, music, the press, religion, science, sport, and theater.

But the first issue was less than impressive. Newsstand sales were disappointing—only half of the 5,000 sent out were sold. Some subscribers didn't receive the first issue and others received two or three copies. Some subscribers canceled. Advertising revenue was less than expected. They lost

$40,000 that first year. But the magazine survived. In fact, circulation climbed to 70,000 in less than two years. And two years after that "Time" turned a profit.

Today, Time magazine is part of Time Warner Inc., the world's largest media corporation. In fact, the revenues from Time, as well as other magazines and businesses started with the profits from Time magazine, enabled the corporation to expand and grow throughout the 20th century.

Unfortunately, Hadden wasn't there to see this happen. He died of a streptococcus infection in 1929.

But Luce went on to become one of the most influential and controversial publishers in the history of journalism. He was a conservative and often used his publication to advance conservative causes. He would often censor and edit journalists' reports if they ran contrary to his views. Even though his politics did not endear him to many journalists, few dispute the notion that he was one of the most influential publishers of the 20th century. In fact, in one book on the history of magazines, he is the only publisher or journalist to have a chapter named after him (see Chapter 13 in Tebbel and Zuckerman).

After the success of "Time," Luce went on to found "Fortune" (1930), "Life" (1936) and "Sports Illustrated" (1954) magazines. Time Inc. also acquired book publishing companies, radio and television stations, television and film production companies, and a paper-making plant.

Luce had two sons from his first marriage. His second marriage was to Claire Boothe (Brokaw) Luce, an accomplished playwright, Congresswoman, and ambassador to Italy. Luce died of a heart ailment in 1967.

Sources: Sam Kuczun, "Henry Robinson Luce," pp. 435-437 in Joseph P. McKerns, *Biographical Dictionary of American Journalism* (New York: Greenwood Press, 1989); John Tebbel and Mary Ellen Zuckerman, *The Magazine in America: 1741-1990* (New York: Oxford University Press, 1991); James Playsted Wood, *Magazines in the United States: Their Social and Economic Influence* (New York: The Ronald Press Company, 1949), pp. 143-156.

Luther, Martin (1483-1546) a German priest who in 1517 allegedly affixed to the door of a church his "Ninety-five Theses," which questioned or challenged some of the practices of the Catholic church.

This event might have gone unnoticed, except that copies of the theses were printed and widely circulated. Eventually, the church excommunicated Luther, but his "Reformation Movement" led to the birth of many Protestant churches and denominations.

M

magazine a *periodical,* usually paperbacked, illustrated, and published four or more times a year, that contains content that appeals to readers with specialized needs.

The term "magazine" is derived from Arabic and Old French and literally means "a storehouse or granary." Magazines, along with *newsletters* and *scientific journals,* are also classified as *periodicals,* meaning they are published regularly.

Magazine Publishers of America (MPA) an association representing consumer magazines.

The organization's Web site <www.magazine.org/home> contains a great deal of knowledge about the magazine industry, including information about jobs, internships, conferences, and professional development. It also contains links to associations that represent magazine editors.

magic bullet theory (or *hypodermic needle theory*) a powerful "theory" of media effects, which contends that (as the metaphor implies) mass media have the power to shoot or inject audiences with various kinds of effects, most of which are seen as harmful.

This simplistic view, which dominated thinking in the 1920s and 1930s, has been replaced by many more complex theories of media effects.

See *mass communication research, limited effects model,* and *theory.*

mail survey a *survey* administered through the mail.

Next to the Internet survey, a mail survey is generally the least expensive way to gather survey *data* because *interviewers* will not have to be hired and there are no long-distance telephone bills. It is often assumed that mail surveys of the general public produce low response rates, but research shows that it is possible to obtain *response rates* that are equivalent to or even better than *telephone surveys.*

171

Source: Donald A. Dillman, *Mail and Telephone Surveys: The Total Design Method* (New York: Wiley, 1978).

mainstream bias the notion that mass media, especially news media, produce content that helps support dominant elites and value systems, despite the media's adherence to the *ethic of objectivity*.

Conservative activists often accuse journalists of producing news stories that contain a liberal bias. Conversely, liberals often accuse the media of producing stories that contain a conservative bias. In response, journalists often argue that they don't take sides during disputes and that the news they produce is neutral.

Many media sociologists point out that none of these perspectives is very accurate. The news media produce a bias, but when viewed from a broad perspective, it is neither liberal, conservative or neutral. It is mainstream, or a centrist, middle of the road perspective. In fact, that's part of the reason the mass media are often called the *"mainstream media."*

The mainstream bias is easy to illustrate during a presidential election. Presidential races include more candidates than just those in the Democratic and Republican parties. In 2000, for example, 16 people ran for president (not all names are on all state ballots).

Under the ethic of objectivity, news stories ideally should give each candidate in a presidential election equal coverage—that is, each should receive the same amount of space, same placement, and the same balance of views. But, of course, that is never the case. The candidates from the two major political parties generally receive more than 95 percent of the news coverage.

When candidates from alternative parties complain, journalists point out that they don't give much coverage to their campaigns because they don't have much money or much public support. The candidates then respond that they can't raise money or get public support without media coverage. Catch-22.

The mainstream bias stems from the structural dependence that journalists have on government and on established power groups for the news. *News beats* are anchored in the powerful institutions in a society and these institutions help legitimate the role of news media in society, just as the media help legitimate the institutions and the elites who run them.

The mainstream bias, sociologists point out, helps maintain *social order* (or the *status quo*) because it marginalizes extreme perspectives on both the left and right wings of the political spectrum.

See *alternative media, ethic of objectivity, social change, social control, social order.*

mainstream media mass media that contain a *mainstream bias.*
See *alternative media.*

mainstreaming a term in *cultivation theory* that refers to the power of television content to alter people's beliefs or ideas about the world in a direction that brings them more into the reality that is portrayed on television.

mall intercept study see *intercept study*.

managerial revolution hypothesis the notion that as organizations grow and acquire the characteristics of the corporate form of organization, power and control over day-to-day operations shifts from the owners to the professional managers.

The shift in power occurs in large part because increasing complexity in organizational structure forces the owners to rely more and more heavily on highly skilled experts and technocrats for key decisions.

In the field of mass communication, the managerial revolution hypothesis challenges the idea that large-scale corporate or global mass media are unable to facilitate *social change* that benefits disadvantaged groups and the poor. Research shows that U.S. daily newspaper owners and publishers play less and less of a role in day-to-day decisions about editorial matters as the newspaper exhibits the characteristics of the corporate form of organization. Editors play a more prominent role.

Proponents of the managerial revolution hypothesis point out that this shift in power does not mean that the owners or their representatives (board of directors) have no say in the operation. However, their authority over day-to-day decision-making is greatly weakened. Increasingly, the experts—i.e., the journalists and other managers—make the decisions, and the owners become increasingly dependent upon their knowledge and advice.

This shift in power also does not mean that managers or editors at *corporate media* are not concerned with profits. Profit-making is crucial for the survival of any business. But the research shows that corporate newspaper organizations place less importance on profit-making and more emphasis on product quality and on maximizing growth of the organization.

See *corporate media*.
Sources: David Demers, "Who Controls the Editorial Content at Corporate News Organizations? An Empirical Test of the Managerial Revolution Hypothesis," *World Futures: The Journal of General Evolution* 57:103-123 (2001) and David Pearce Demers, *The Menace of the Corporate Newspaper: Fact or Fiction?* (Ames: Iowa State University Press, 1996).

manifest function an intended consequence of mass media use.
See *latent function*.

Manutius, Aldus (1484-1530) a Venice publisher who became famous for printing and distributing Greek poetry and philosophy to much of the Western world during the late 1500s and early 1600s.

Marconi, Guglielmo (1874-1937) inventor of the wireless telegraph.
Marconi was the son of a wealthy Italian father and an Irish mother. He received a private education but also attended a university for a short time.

He began experimenting with electromagnetics in 1894. Within a year he was able to send and receive signals beyond the range of vision.

He took out a patent in 1896, but the Italian government wasn't interested. Instead, the British Admiralty installed Marconi's radio on some of its ships.

In 1901, he sent a signal across the Atlantic Ocean. In 1909, he and Karl Ferdinand Braun, who extended the range of the wireless signal, shared the Nobel Prize in Physics.

See *telegraph*.

marginals computer-generated *frequencies* of the number of *respondents* giving an answer to all of the *questions* in a survey.

market niche see *niche marketing*.

market research the scientific or scholarly study of consumer behavior.

Market researchers employ social science theories and quantitative or qualitative research methods to identify and to understand consumers' needs and behaviors. In the field of mass communication, this research most often involves (1) identifying groups of consumers that have similar needs for information or entertainment content (see *segmentation analysis* and *target marketing*) and studying (2) why consumers buy or consume media products or programs (see *media effects*) and (3) the effects of advertising and promotion campaigns (see *advertising*).

market segmentation the process of identifying groups of consumers, or segments, with similar wants and needs.

Demographics, psychographics or geographics may be used to identify the segments. Of the three, demographics is the most widely employed, because advertising agencies and public relations practitioners can target market segments through their usage of mass media.

Market segmentation is used primarily to reduce the costs of marketing and advertising. The goal is usually to identify only those consumers that represent the best prospects (or targets) for a product or service.

See *direct marketing* and *target marketing*.

marketing the act of producing, pricing, promoting, and distributing a good or service.

marketing manager the person in a media organization responsible for promoting the organization's products or services, including publicity, advertising placement, and sales distribution.

marketing research same as *market research*.

marketplace of ideas a metaphor which holds that ideas, like commodities, compete with each other for acceptance and that eventually "false" ideas will fall away, while "truthful" ideas will rise to the top.

The metaphor was coined by U.S. Supreme Court Justice Oliver Wendall Holmes, who wrote a dissenting opinion in Abrams v. United States (1919). Borrowing from John Milton's "Areopagitica" (1644) and John Stuart Mill's "On Liberty" (1859), Holmes wrote:

"But when men have realized that time has upset many fighting faiths, they may come to believe even more than they believe the very foundations of their own conduct that the ultimate good desired is better reached by free trade in ideas—that the best test of truth is the power of the thought to get itself accepted in the competition of the market ... That at any rate is the theory of our Constitution. It is an experiment, as all life is an experiment."

See *diversity of ideas.*

Marxism a general theoretical approach based on the ideas of *Karl Marx.*

Marx, Karl Heinrich (1818-1883) a 19th-century intellectual whose writings on *ideology* and *concentration of ownership* make him one of the most influential figures in the history of mass communication and the social sciences.

Marx was born into a comfortable middle-class Jewish family in Germany. His father was a lawyer. When he was 17, Marx enrolled in the Faculty of Law at the University of Bonn. There he became engaged to Jenny von Westphalen, whose father introduced Marx to romantic literature and Saint-Simonian politics. A year later Marx went to the University of Berlin, where he studied Hegelianism and other subjects for the next four years.

Marx joined the Young Hegelian movement which produced a radical critique of Christianity and, by implication, of Prussian autocracy. Marx couldn't get a job at a university, so he became editor in 1842 of the influential "Rheinische Zeitung," a liberal newspaper backed by industrialists. Marx's articles on economic questions led the Prussian government to close the paper. Marx then left for France.

He arrived in Paris late in 1843 and made contact with other German workers and French socialists. He also edited the short-lived "Deutsch-Französische Jahrbücher" which sought to connect French socialism with German Hegelians. Marx became a communist and began writing the "Economic and Philosophical Manuscripts" (1844), which remained unpublished until the 1930s. The Manuscripts outlined a humanist conception of communism. In Paris, Marx also developed his lifelong partnership with Friedrich Engels (1820-1895).

Marx was expelled from Paris at the end of 1844 and moved to Brussels, where Engels' family, who were well-to-do industrialists, made their home. Marx studied history and developed what came to be known as the materialist conception of history, which argued that "the nature of individuals depends on the material conditions determining their production." Marx traced the history of various modes of production and predicted the present one—industrial capitalism—would collapse and be replaced by communism.

At a conference in London at the end of 1847, Marx and Engels were commissioned to write a summary of their position, which became "The Communist Manifesto." Shortly thereafter, a wave of revolutions broke out in Europe. Marx moved back to Germany, where he founded another newspaper supporting a radical democratic position. But it was closed down by the Prussian authorities and Marx fled to London, where he lived out the rest of his life.

During the 1850s the Marx family, which now included four children (and two more would soon follow), lived in poverty (only three of the children survived to adulthood). The family's main source of income came from Engels. Marx also worked part time as a foreign correspondent for the "New York Daily Tribune," for which he wrote weekly articles.

The first volume of Marx's major work on political economy, "Capital" ("Das Kapital"), was published in 1867. In it, Marx argued that profits would fall, leading to the collapse of industrial capitalism (see *concentration of ownership*). Volumes II and III were finished during the 1860s but Marx continued to work on them and they were published posthumously by Engels.

Marx's health deteriorated in his later years and he died March 14, 1883, and was buried at Highgate Cemetery in North London. In an eulogy, Engels said: "On the 14th of March, at a quarter to three in the afternoon, the greatest living thinker ceased to think. ... Just as Darwin discovered the law of development of organic nature, so Marx discovered the law of development of human history: the simple fact, hitherto concealed by an overgrowth of ideology, that mankind must first of all eat, drink, have shelter and clothing, before it can pursue politics, science, art, religion, etc.; that therefore the production of the immediate material means, and consequently the degree of economic development attained by a given people or during a given epoch, form the foundation upon which the state institutions, the legal conceptions, art, and even the ideas on religion, of the people concerned have been evolved, and in the light of which they must, therefore, be explained, instead of vice versa, as had hitherto been the case."

Marx's ideas continue to have a strong influence on scholars in political science, sociology, economics, and mass communication. In particular, critical theory and contemporary theories of corporate structure draw heavily on the ideas of Marx.

See *ideology, critical theory* and *concentration of ownership*.

Sources: Karl Marx, "Economic and Philosophic Manuscripts of 1844," pp. 66-125 in Robert C. Tucker (ed.), *The Marx-Engels Reader*, 2nd ed. (New York: W. W. Norton & Company, 1978); Karl Marx and Friedrich Engels, *The Communist Manifesto*, trans. by Paul M. Sweezy (New York: Monthly Review Press, 1964); Karl Marx, *Capital: A Critique of Political Economy*, trans. by Samuel Moore and Edward Aveling (New York: International Publishers, 1987 [1867]); and Richard P. Applebaum, *Karl Marx* (Newbury Park, CA: Sage, 1988).

mass communication the process of delivering messages to a large number of geographically separated people through a technologically based medium. The term "mass" generally refers to a large number of people who do not personally know each and come from different walks of life. The term "mass communication" is almost always associated with mass media. But the Internet has now made it possible for one individual to communicate to large numbers of people. What makes a communication "mass" is the number of people or groups reached. In other words, the concept of "mass" communication itself should be conceptualized and measured on a continuum as opposed to an all-or-none condition (i.e., a dichotomy).

On one end of that continuum is the *dyad*, which involves communication between two individuals or groups. On the other end is mass communication, which involves communication from at least one individual or group to all other individuals and groups in a social system.

Mass media rarely have the ability to communicate to all people in a large society, so in the real world most instances of "mass communication" fall between the two extremes—in the center, or what scholars often call group or organizational communication. But all social communication can be classified somewhere along this continuum, and there is no precise number for defining mass.

In recent years, some scholars have argued that mass media are losing their "mass" character because readers and audiences for many traditional mass media are declining. Indeed, during the 1960s, 90 percent of Americans who turned on their television sets were tuned to one of the three major *television network*s (ABC, CBS or NBC). Today, those networks are reaching fewer than 30 percent of the people who watch during prime time, and this figure continues to decline.

Media economists attribute this decline primarily to increasing competition from cable television programming. However, despite these declines, new markets around the world have enabled some mass media, such as CNN (Cable News Network), to grow and capture the attention of hundreds of millions of readers, listeners or viewers. And there is no evidence to suggest mass audiences will disappear any time soon. In fact, research shows people continue to spend more and more time with mass media.

mass communication research the scientific or scholarly study of mass communication processes and effects.

The history of mass communication research as a formal discipline is usually traced to World War I and concern over the effects of propaganda. Before that time, political scientist Harold Laswell points out, the prevailing wisdom was that people were rational human beings who could not be easily manipulated by mass media. But the widespread use of propaganda during WWI on both sides of the conflict seemed to challenge the rationality assumption, and many people believed propaganda could easily manipulate the so-called "masses."

After the war, parents, politicians, and religious leaders in the United States became increasingly concerned about the effects of motion pictures on children. In the mid-1920s, tens of millions of children were attending silent movies every week. There they watched gangsters shoot each other and the police and saw sophisticated women and men making love (e.g., kissing and hugging) in glitzy New York apartments. In response, the Motion Picture Research Council invited scholars and educators to design studies to assess the effects of movies.

The result was *The Payne Fund Studies,* the first major scientific study of mass *media effects.* The studies found that movies could change attitudes toward racial groups (positive and negative), stimulate emotions (including terror, fright, sorrow), disturb sleep patterns, and generate norms contrary to contemporary values (e.g., promiscuousness).

These and other findings contributed to the idea that mass media had powerful effects. That belief was reinforced in 1938, when CBS radio broadcast *Orson Welles'* adaptation of H. G. Wells' classic book, "War of the Worlds." The broadcast was so believable more than a million people panicked.

The Payne Fund Studies and the War of the Worlds incident gave rise to what researchers later would refer to as the *magic bullet* or hypodermic needle theory of media effects. As the metaphors imply, the mass media were viewed as having the power to shoot or inject audiences with various kinds of effects, most of which were viewed as harmful. But this powerful effects model was relatively short-lived.

As World War II approached, government and political elites were increasingly concerned about the effects of mass media, especially propaganda. The concern was greater during WWII than during WWI because there was a new medium for transmitting propaganda—radio. Radio provided almost instantaneous news and information reports, and that scared a lot of scholars and politicians. Adolph Hitler, for example, used radio to generate support for his invasion of Poland in 1939 and to stir up hate against Jewish people.

But research by *Paul Lazarsfeld* and *Carl Hovland* called into question the simple magic bullet model. They found that demographic and personal characteristics of voters and people limited, or moderated, the effects of mass media. This finding was further validated by Hovland's research.

During the 1940s and 1950s, scores of other studies supported what came to be called the *limited effects model.* People do not easily change their opinions or attitudes, partly because their values and social ties to groups (family, church, friends) insulate them from the persuasive effects of mass media. But those conclusions, which were based on psychological research, were not generalized to all research on mass media.

During the 1960s, Marshall McLuhan's concept of the "global village" helped swing the pendulum back toward the idea that media could have powerful effects. But the lasting impact came from scholars who studied media from a sociological perspective and were more empirically driven (McLuhan was primarily theoretical and speculative).

Two of those scholars were Max McCombs and Donald Shaw, who coined the *agenda-setting hypothesis*. They basically argued that the power of mass media lies less in telling people what to think (persuasion) than in telling them what to think about (the agenda), and their research and others provided strong support for their model.

Mass communication researchers Phillip J. Tichenor, George A. Donohue, and Clarice N. Olien also advanced what they later called *guard dog theory*, which basically held that media are a guard dog not for the entire community but for political and special interest elite groups that have power. The guard dog model is a *social control* or *mass media system* model. It sees mass media as one institution among many others (family, church, state, schools, courts, police) that play a role in supporting and maintaining a community or society.

Also working from a sociological perspective, Melvin DeFleur and Sandra Ball-Rokeach introduced *media dependency theory* in the 1970s. This theory posited that people who live in highly industrialized and urbanized societies depend very heavily on mass media to achieve their goals, and that people become more dependent on mass media as society becomes more complex (or structurally differentiated). This dependency, in turn, increases the power of media in people's lives.

Although many social scientists avoided making value judgments about whether social control was good or bad, George Gerbner and his colleagues weren't among them. In the late 1960s and 1970s, they developed *cultivation theory*, which held that the more television people watch, the more they acquire the beliefs, values, and attitudes that are portrayed on television. Gerbner and his colleagues argued that television, especially violent programming, "cultivates" a "consciousness" that generates support for tough policing and authoritarian controls.

Similarly, "critical theorists"—who drew their intellectual strength from the radical political theorist *Karl Marx* and from the *Frankfurt School*, a group of neo-Marxist scholars who fled Germany just before World War II—argued that the mass media and other cultural institutions, such as schools, were disseminating an *ideology* that prevented ordinary people from realizing they were being exploited in modern capitalism. The workers and people were suffering from "false consciousness," and they could not revolt without achieving "class consciousness."

Also building on the work of Marx was the *cultural studies* perspective, which initially had its strongest following in Great Britain under the leadership of people like Stuart Hall, but was also promoted by James Carey, an American scholar. Cultural studies shares a lot of common ground with *critical theory*, except that the emphasis is less on media economics or capitalism than on other aspects of culture, such as gender, race, ethnicity, sexual orientation, and sub-cultural groups (e.g., environmental and anti-globalization groups). Cultural theorists see mass media as producing

Social Science vs. Humanist Mass Communication Researchers

Criteria	Social Science Approach	Humanist Approach
What Influences Behavior?	Outside Forces	Internal Choices
Preferred Method of Study	Quantitative (Experiment, Survey)	Qualitative (Observation, Interview)
Key Strength	Can Generalize Findings	In-Depth Understanding
Key Weakness	Superficial Understanding	Not Generalizable

symbolic content that supports discriminatory or oppressive practices toward women, minorities, homosexuals, and environmental activists.

During the 1960s and 1970s, these major perspectives were supplemented with many more narrowly focused theories which suggested that the limited effects model was too narrowly drawn. They included: *spiral of silence hypothesis, knowledge-gap hypothesis, uses and gratifications*, and *social cognitive theory*.

Today, the field of mass communication research is extremely diverse, employing a wide range of biological, psychological, sociological, and cultural approaches. However, as with other social sciences, the field of mass communication research can be roughly divided into two major camps or approaches: social science and humanism. The differences between these two approaches are summarized in the table above.

As a rule, the social science approach tends to see human behavior as being affected or influenced by factors or forces outside of people's control. In fact, social scientists often argue that economic, social, political, psychological or, in some cases, biological forces affect the way people think or behave.

Some social scientists even search for universal laws of human behavior. A *scientific law* (or covering law) is a sequence of events that occur with unvarying uniformity under the same conditions. A law about television violence, for example, might state that aggressive behavior always arises after viewing violent programming. However, most social scientists are not this *deterministic*. They search instead for *generalizations* about human behavior, following in essence a *probabilistic theory of social action*.

Humanists, in contrast, tend to be less interested in generalizing to populations of people than in understanding why individual people do what they do. Many reject the idea of universal laws and believe humans are influenced less by "forces" than by their own free will. Humanists could point out, quite correctly, that not everyone who watches television violence commits murder or engages in violent behavior. People have power over their actions, despite the amount of television they watch. (Legal systems, by the way, are usually predicated more upon the humanist than the social science model—they assume people have control over and are responsible for their actions.)

Another criterion separating the social scientist from the humanist involves the question of whether research can or should be objective. The social scientist generally argues that a researcher can and should be objective, or detached from what he or she studies. Facts or observations can and should be separated from personal values about whether something is good or bad. Facts stand for themselves. The question of whether facts are good or bad is separate. In fact, many social scientists who study violence on television believe they should not personally get involved in political efforts to solve any alleged problem. They see that as matter for politicians and voters.

In contrast, most humanist scholars believe researchers have an obligation to speak up and to change the world. Facts cannot and should not be separated from values. Indeed, when a researcher selects a topic for study, that is itself a value judgment. The humanist argues that scholars should ask questions not only about "what is" but also about "what ought to be." As a rule, humanists tend to be more critical of mass media organizations and more socially and politically active. Many offer solutions to alleged problems and want to change the world.

Historically, the social science and humanist approaches have often been in conflict. The social scientist often accuses the humanist of failing to be rigorous in his or her research. The humanist, on the other hand, often accuses the social scientist of treating human beings like dupes or robots. But neither approach is superior to the other. Each has strengths and shortcomings.

One key advantage of the methods social scientists use—such as surveys and public opinion polls—is they often enable scientists to make generalizations about large populations of people. However, because such studies often involve interviews with hundreds or thousands of people, the depth of knowledge about individual cases tends to be superficial. These studies normally are not very useful in terms of providing detail about individual people or cases.

The methods of the humanist, in contrast, often yield a great deal of in-depth understanding about reasons individual people or groups do what they do. However, the findings from case studies cannot be generalized to larger populations. The findings are said to be more idiosyncratic.

There are, of course, many researchers who cannot be easily classified into the two general approaches. Sociologists may lean in either camp or have a foot in both camps. Media system theorists, for example, see people as having the ability to choose alternative courses of action, but those choices are "constrained" by the social structure. System theorists also employ a wide variety of research methodologies, giving rise to the title "scientific humanists."

Also see *Payne Fund Studies*, *mass communication researcher*, and *scientific inquiry*.

Sources: Melvin L. DeFleur and Sandra Ball-Rokeach, *Theories of Mass Communication*, 3rd ed. (New York: Longman, 1975); George Gerbner, Larry Gross, Michael Morgan and Nancy Signorielli, "Growing up with Television: The Cultivation Perspective," pp. 17-41 in Jennings Bryant and Dolf Zillmann (eds.), *Media Effects: Advances in Theory and Research* (Hillsdale, NJ: Lawrence Erlbaum Associates, 1994); Theodore Adorno and Max Horkheimer, *Dialectic of the Enlightenment* (London: Verso, 1979); Herbert Marcuse, *One-Dimensional Man* (Boston: Beacon Press, 1964); Stuart Hall, "Culture, the Media and the Ideological Effect," pp. 315-48 in James Curran, Michael Gurevitch and Janet Woollacott (eds.), *Mass Communication and Society* (London: Edward Arnold, 1977); Stuart Hall, "The Rediscovery of Ideology: The Return of the Repressed," pp. 15-47 in Stuart Hall et al. (eds), *Culture, media, language: Working papers in cultural studies, 1972-1979* (London: Hutchinson, 1982); and James Carey, "The Origins of the Radical Discourse on Cultural Studies in the United States," *Journal of Communication*, 33:313 (Summer 1983).

mass communication researcher a person who studies *mass communication* and/or *mass media*.

Although no precise figure is available, at least 25,000 scholars in the United States study mass media. Most of them teach in one of the 700 or so communication or journalism and mass communication programs at universities and colleges. Most call themselves mass communication researchers. However, several thousand psychologists, sociologists, economists, historians, and scholars from other disciplines also study the origins and effects of mass communication.

Much of the research produced by these scholars is presented at national conventions. The major mass media research associations in the United States include the *Association for Education in Journalism* and *Mass Communication*, *International Communication Association*, and *National Communication Association*. The field is also served by scores of journals that cater to mass communication researchers. This includes "Communication Research," "Critical Studies in Mass Communication," "Human Communication Research," "Journal of Broadcasting and Electronic Media," "Journal of Communication," "Journalism & Mass Communication Quarterly," and "Journal of Popular Culture."

In addition to teaching and research, mass communication scholars can also serve as watchdogs of mass media themselves. Scholars often criticize media, and this criticism may at times have an effect on public policy making.

Like other scholars in the social sciences, mass communication researchers can be divided into two major camps: the *social scientists* and the *humanists* (see *mass communication research* for details).

See *mass communication research*.

mass media organizations that produce news or entertainment content and distribute that content to a large number of geographically separated people through a technologically based medium.

Although mass communication is often associated with mass media, these two terms are not identical. The Internet has enabled individuals and nonmedia organizations to engage in mass communication, even though they may not fit the traditional definition of a mass media institution. What distinguishes mass media is that they are organized primarily for the purpose of producing mass communication. Many mass media companies are privately owned, which means they also seek to earn a profit.

Mass communication is a social process—it is the act of transmitting messages to a large number of people or groups. Mass media, on the other hand, are *social institutions* that produce messages (like news, information, and entertainment programming) for mass communication. As social institutions, mass media pursue goals and engage in repetitive activities (e.g., gathering the news) on a regular basis.

A *newspaper*, for example, is a mass medium (singular for mass media). The journalists who work for newspapers are engaged in repetitive news gathering practices every day, and their behavior is shaped by formalized rules and roles. Every day, journalists gather news and write up stories. This repetitive behavior gives the organization a sense of permanence or stability, and without repetition of some kind, there can be no organization.

Traditionally, the list of mass media has included organizations that produce *books, newspapers, magazines, motion pictures* and *records*, and programming for *radio* and *television*. The *Internet* is usually excluded from this list because it is not a mass medium per se—it is a technology and a method of delivering information to people.

Still, nearly all traditional mass media organizations have created their own Web sites. This, in turn, has blurred the lines separating these media forms, since a Web page can integrate text, still pictures, graphics, video and sound in one package. In fact, many researchers believe this *convergence* of technology will mean an end to traditional media like the printed newspaper and the over-the-air television.

However, new technology doesn't necessarily spell doom for traditional forms, at least not in the foreseeable future. More realistically it means that the information/entertainment environment will add yet another layer of complexity.

Mass media organizations vary considerably in size and form. But when it comes to their impact on individuals and society, all mass media perform a similar function—they produce content that generally helps maintain *social systems* (i.e., the *social control* function).

See *social control* and *mass communication*.

Source: K. Viswanath and David Demers, "Mass Media from a Macrosocial Perspective," pp. 3-28 in David Demers and K. Viswanath (eds.), *Mass Media, Social Control and Social Change: A Macrosocial Perspective* (Ames: Iowa State University Press, 1999).

mass media effects see *media effects*.

mass media processes see *media processes*.

mass media systems theory a sociological theory which posits that mass media are institutions contributing to the maintenance of a community or society, usually in a way that supports the status quo or serves the interests of powerful economic and political elites.

Media systems theory traces its origins to systems models in sociology. More formally, George A. Donohue, Phillip J. Tichenor and Clarice N. Olien point out that the mass media may be characterized as an institution, or subsystem, which, among other things, functions to process and disseminate information that helps maintain the social system as a whole, other subsystems, or the media subsystem itself. Mass media share facets of controlling, and being controlled by, other subsystems.

The researchers define a social system as "a series of interrelated subsystems with primary functions including the generation, dissemination, and assimilation of information to effect further control as a means to an end or as an end in itself." Social control is not the only function served by the media, but all communication processes have a control function within them, either latent or manifest.

The maintenance function, according to Donohue, Tichenor and Olien, may be fulfilled by two sets of processes: feedback-control and distribution control. Feedback control means that the media perform a feedback, or regulatory, function for other subsystems. The information provided is used to make decisions or take various actions that, in turn, perform a maintenance function.

Distribution control, on the other hand, can occur either independent of or in conjunction with feedback control. Distribution control serves a maintenance function through selective dissemination and withholding of information. Censorship is the most extreme form of distribution control. A more common example is the downplaying of conflict news that occurs in small community newspapers.

Media system theory does not assume that the content of the media is always functional for maintenance of the whole system, subsystems, organizations or individuals. News coverage is sometimes dysfunctional for many elite groups, particularly when those groups fight over fundamental questions of resource allocation. Empirical evidence also demonstrates that news reports sometimes are favorable toward alternative or challenging groups. Some studies also indicate that exposure to media reports may produce beliefs that run counter to the dominant values.

Nevertheless, the fact that mass media rely much more heavily on established power groups for news means that news content generally legitimizes those groups and the dominant values in the system. Under a systems model, the argument is that media content, when taken as a whole, contributes to social order—it serves the needs of various elite groups and helps them to achieve their goals, often to the disadvantage of less powerful groups.

Social change can occur and the ideas of challenging groups can make their way into the general value system (e.g., the changing role of women in society). But *mainstream media* do not normally challenge the basic institutions and values of the system, nor do they produce major shifts of power. Instead, they play an important role in regulating and controlling change. See *social change, social control.*

Sources: George A. Donohue, Phillip J. Tichenor and Clarice N. Olien, "Mass Media Functions, Knowledge and Social Control," *Journalism Quarterly,* 50:652-9 (1973) and David Pearce Demers, *The Menace of the Corporate Newspaper: Fact or Fiction?* (Ames: Iowa State University Press, 1996).

mass medium singular of *mass media.*

mass society theory a general theoretical orientation that sees modernization in general and *social differentiation* in particular as alienating people and fragmenting society.

People who live in a mass society are said to be more vulnerable to mass *media effects* because they suffer from anomie (i.e., a state of normlessness). Mass society theorists generally believe that mass media can easily manipulate people who live in mass societies.

materialism an ontological doctrine which asserts that only matter and the physical properties of matter exist. See *idealism.*

McLuhan, Marshall (1911-1980) a Canadian scholar who gained popular fame during the 1960s for his theories of mass media and the notion that electronic media were creating a global village.

McLuhan was born in Edmonton, Canada, and as a child was independent, stubborn, and bullying. He was not a good student.

But he did well at the University of Manitoba, where he studied English, geology, history, Latin, economics, and psychology. In 1934 he spent two years in England, studying at Cambridge University.

He completed his doctoral dissertation, regarding the rhetoric of Thomas Nashe, in 1942. McLuhan was a member of the department of English at St Michael's College of the University of Toronto from 1946-1977. He directed the Center for Culture and Technology from 1963.

McLuhan was not a conventional professor and many of his colleagues discouraged graduate students from taking his courses. He supervised only seven Ph.D. theses.

In 1959 McLuhan became the director of the Media Project of the National Association of Educational Broadcasters and the United States Office of Education. In 1962, he won the prestigious Governor General's Award for "The Gutenberg Galaxy," which was translated into several languages. He wrote "Understanding Media" in 1964 and "Medium is the Massage" in 1967, which are his three most popular works. (Note: The title of latter book should have been "Message" rather than "Massage," but when the typesetting error was shown to McLuhan, he told the publisher "to leave it alone—it's great, and right on target.")

McLuhan disagreed with *Karl Marx*'s notion that the economy or mode of production was the most important engine of social change in history. McLuhan argued that technological innovation was more important.

More specifically, he argued that the form of a mass medium was more important than its message when assessing media effects. Print media, such as newspapers, alienate people from each other, because reading is a solitary activity. Before the printed word, people learned about the world through personal experience and word of mouth. They experienced the world through their senses—sight, sound, smell, taste, and touch. Story-telling was a primary means of transmitting knowledge and ideas, and this face-to-face form of communication bonded people together socially.

Written documents and books make people less dependent upon personal experience and interpersonal communication, McLuhan argued. With books and newspapers, they can learn about the world in isolation from each other. There is less need to socialize. The written word engages the mind, not the senses. Reading is linear, rational, solitary, and individualistic. The written word "detribalizes" society.

Thus, according to McLuhan, much of the alienation people experience in modern society has its basis not in the content of ideas, but rather in the way they consume them. This is what he meant by the oft-cited phrase, "the medium is the message." In other words, the content of the messages is much less important for social integration than the medium itself.

The implication of McLuhan's argument is that alienation reached its peak during the early 1900s, before the appearance of movies, radio, and television. However, things allegedly were now changing. Electronic media are "retribalizing" modern society, he argued. People are increasingly experiencing the world through the senses again (sight and sound, at least). Music videos, in particular, would be considered particularly powerful in this regard, because they excite the senses. The world is becoming a global village.

McLuhan's theory has many shortcomings. Empirical research on reading the local newspaper, for example, shows that print media are very effective at making people feel connected to a community. Although reading is a solitary activity, people often discuss what they read with others. Book clubs are very effective at making people feel part of a group or community.

McLuhan also believed electronic media would annihilate the printed word. But there is no evidence to suggest that sales of books are waning; in fact, just the opposite is happening—sales have generally increased since the 1960s. In addition, the Internet complements rather than eliminates the printed word.

McLuhan's notion that an electronic global village can integrate people as strongly as a face-to-face one is also overdrawn. Television is a one-way medium (at least at the present). The Internet is a two-way medium, but this, too, is no substitute for personal interaction and human intimacy. And if people are supposed to be less alienated in today's electronic world than they were at the turn of the century (when print media were at their peak), then why haven't suicide rates decreased? The causes of alienation are not to be found simply in the particular form of mass communication society engages in—the causes are also tied to how meaningful people find their personal and professional lives.

Yet, despite these qualifications, there is some merit to the idea that global media help integrate people from different cultures and perspectives into one global system. Many examples can be cited, including the coverage of Princess Diana's funeral. Hundreds of millions of people around the world (30 million in the United States alone) viewed this event.

In 1967, doctors removed a large tumor from base of McLuhan's brain, an operation that changed his personality, making him hypersensitive. In 1979, he suffered a stroke and died a year later.

Sources: Marshall McLuhan, *Understanding the Media* (London: Routledge & Kegan Paul, 1964); Marshall McLuhan, *The Gutenberg Galaxy: The Making of Topographic Man* (London: Routledge & Kegan Paul, 1962); Marshall McLuhan and Quentin Fiore (coordinated by Jerome Angel), *Medium Is the Massage* (New York: Random House, 1967).

mean the sum of the individual *values* in a *distribution* divided by the total number of *cases*.

The mean age of three people age 40, 30, and 20 is 30 (40+30+20)/3=30). Although the *mean* is widely used as a measure of the *average*, it can provide a distorted picture of *central tendency* when there are extreme *outliers* in a distribution. In such cases, the *median* is often used.

measure a *concept* that has been *operationalized*.

measurement error the degree to which the observed or measured *values* deviate from the actual or true values.

Measurement errors fall into one of two categories, systematic or random. Systematic or nonrandom errors form patterns that bias the results. One example: During an interview, some people say they are younger than they actually are when asked to give their age.

On the other hand, random measurement error means there is no pattern to the errors—they are random. If husbands are asked to guess their wives' income, a few may underestimate and a few may overestimate. Mistakes made by interviewers when recording responses is another example of a random measurement error. In research, systematic errors are generally more serious, since they can bias the data.

measures of central tendency *descriptive statistics* that measure the central point in a distribution of values.

The *mean, median,* and *mode* are examples.

measures of dispersion *descriptive statistics* that measure how far *cases* are dispersed around a *mean.*
Examples include *range, standard deviation,* and *variance.*

media buyer in an *advertising agency,* a person who places advertisements; that is, he or she purchases space or time from mass media organizations.
See *media planner.*

media corporations see *corporate media.*

media dependency theory the notion that people who live in highly industrialized and urbanized societies depend heavily on mass media to achieve their goals, and that people become more dependent on mass media as a society becomes more complex, or *structurally differentiated.*
Media dependency theory was developed in the 1970s by Melvin DeFleur and Sandra Ball-Rokeach, who were trying to explain in part why media affect some people more than others. They argued that the greater the dependence people have on mass media, the greater the media effects.
DeFleur and Ball-Rokeach begin their analysis by identifying three major entities: audiences, media systems, and societal systems, which included the courts, schools, police, and political organizations. They argue that all three entities depend upon each other to achieve their goals, and dependence on media increases as societies become more complex.
An election is a good way to illustrate the theory. Voters (audiences) depend upon newspapers (media systems) to learn about local government happenings, and voters depend upon politicians (societal systems) to make public policy. Newspapers depend upon local politicians for the news, and newspapers depend upon voters to buy the newspaper, which generates subscription and advertising revenues. Politicians depend upon the media to get news of government activities and decisions out to the voters, and they depend upon voters to get elected or re-elected. In short, all three groups depend upon each other to achieve their goals.
The dependencies these three groups have on each other contribute to *social order* and integration. As such, media dependency is also a theory of *social control.* But it also is a theory of *social change,* because it posits that dependencies on media increase as societies become more structurally complex (e.g., industrialized, urbanized). This dependency, in turn, increases the media's power or influence over people and groups.
DeFleur and Ball-Rokeach also argue that dependency is heightened when societies experience a high degree of conflict or are in a state of crisis. For example, when a major storm (hurricane or blizzard) approaches a community, people are much more attentive to the news. They watch because they have a need to make preparations to protect their families and property. More formally, the researchers argue that "ambiguity" is stressful, which leads people to mass media for information to reduce the stress.

Media dependency theory is highly compatible with *guard dog theory*. The key difference is that the media dependency model tends to focus more on audience's dependence on media rather than on mass media's dependence on elites.

Many studies support dependency theory. One of its strengths is that it deals with social change: Media dependency increases as societies become more complex. However, like guard dog theory, media dependency theory has been criticized for failing to make judgments about whether social control is good or bad. In response, proponents of the theory can respond, like guard dog theorists, that the question of whether *social control* is good or bad depends on who benefits from it.

See *guard dog theory, social change, social control, social order,* and *status quo*.

Sources: Melvin L. DeFleur and Sandra Ball-Rokeach, *Theories of Mass Communication,* 3rd ed. (New York: Longman, 1975).

media ecology the study of mass media information environments.

There are two branches of media ecology, one positivist and one humanistic. The positive approach has focused mostly on competition between mass media, particularly intermedia competition, or competition between different forms of mass media (e.g., television versus radio or newspapers versus books). The approach is interdependent and holistic, meaning that changes in one form of media (say a decline in the number of newspapers) are expected to have an impact on other forms (e.g, growth).

The humanist approach is often associated with Neil Postman, who defines media ecology as "the ways in which the interaction between media and human beings give a culture its character and ... help a culture to maintain symbolic balance." The goal of this approach is to critique the media from an ethical or moralistic framework, which includes the question of whether media contribute to democratic processes.

Sources: John Dimmick and Eric Rothenbuhler, "The Theory of the Niche: Quantifying Competition Among Media Industries," *Journal of Communication, 34*(1): 103-119 (1984) and Neil Postman, "The Humanism of Media Ecology: Keynote Address Delivered at the Inaugural Media Ecology Association Convention," *Proceedings of the Media Ecology Association, Vol. 1* (2000), [the address was given at Fordham University on June 16-17, 2000].

media effects a field of study which attempts to identify and sometimes quantify the impact or effects that mass media have on individuals, organizations, and society.

The study of mass media effects can be broken down into two major approaches. One focuses upon psychological effects. This involves asking the question: What effect do media have on people's *attitudes, beliefs, values,* and *behaviors*? The second body of the research focuses on sociological effects. What role do media play in maintaining and changing *social order*?

When people think of media effects, they generally think of psychological effects first. That's partly because the psychological approach is more intuitive and less abstract. The psychological approach also generates more research than the sociological approach, partly because it's easier to study individuals than social institutions and processes.

However, the sociological approach has grown in stature since the 1970s, mainly because it has shown that mass media can have powerful effects even when they do not change people's attitudes, beliefs or behaviors. For example, research shows that during a presidential election, almost all of the mass media coverage goes to the two mainstream political candidates (the Republican and Democrat)—alternative candidates get very little coverage. The marginalizing of alternative candidates reinforces the status quo and reduces the potential for radical social change.

See *agenda setting, guard-dog theory, knowledge gap hypothesis, media dependency theory, cultural studies, critical theory, mass media systems theory, media violence, mass communication research, mass communication researcher, scientific inquiry, structural functionalism, theory,* and *media processes.*

Source: Jennings Bryant and Dolf Zillmann (eds.), *Media Effects: Advances in Theory and Research,* 2nd ed. (Hillsdale, NJ: Lawrence Erlbaum, 2002) and Mladenka Tomasevic, *Political Power and Mass Media Coverage of the 2000 Presidential Campaign,* unpublished master's thesis, Washington State University (2003).

media functions see *structural functionalism.*

media imperialism the notion that mass media in Western countries, especially the United States, produce content that imposes Western culture—especially ideas that capitalism is the best economic system—upon less developed countries around the world.

International communications scholar Chin-Chuan Lee defines media imperialism as consisting of four major elements: (1) television program exportation to foreign countries; (2) foreign ownership and control of media outlets; (3) the transfer of the dominant broadcasting norms and media commercialism; and (4) the invasion of capitalist worldviews and infringement upon the indigenous ways of life in the adopting societies. The United States, he points out, is clearly the leading supplier of global television programs.

Many critics believe the ideas and values promoted in global media are destroying indigenous cultures that do not have capitalist economic systems. To the extent this happens, critics believe local customs, traditions, and authority are threatened. Less developed nations in Africa, South America, and Asia are believed to be most vulnerable to Western media "propaganda."

Ironically, although many Third World nations are very critical of Hollywood, they still broadcast a lot of Hollywood programming, partly because it's too expensive to generate original programming. Even Europe, with its own highly developed media systems, feels threatened by American global media.

Since the 1980s, the concept of media imperialism has been criticized for failing to take into account the role of alternative groups and resistance to dominant culture. Instead, many scholars prefer the concept of *hegemony* and the idea that many issues are still on "contested terrain."

See *hegemony*.

Source: Chin-Chuan Lee, *Media Imperialism Reconsidered* (Beverly Hills, CA: Sage, 1980).

media literacy the process of critically analyzing media content.

Scholars who promote media literacy argue that being critical of the mass media is important, but it is not enough. A media-literate person also needs to understand the role of mass media as an agent of *social control* and *social change*.

A tension often exists between media literacy and professional mass communication education, because the latter tends to promote conformity to the status quo. This tension can be reduced to some degree by instructing students on the difference between the ideal and real-world situations and encouraging them to work toward the ideal when they become professionals.

media mail a low-cost postal rate offered through the U.S. Postal Service and available to anyone who mails books, compact disks or other media materials.

The Postal Service charges less to these customers partly to stimulate the flow of information and ideas.

See *periodical postage rate*.

media mix the number and types of mass media in a particular market.

The term "media mix" is usually used in a context where one market is being compared to another. Markets with more people and businesses usually have a more diversified media mix (i.e., more newspapers, magazines, television stations, etc.).

media ownership rules regulations created by the *Federal Communications Commission* (FCC) that put limits on the number of broadcast stations a company can own.

The *Communications Act of 1934* gave the FCC the authority to limit the number of broadcast radio stations—and, eventually, television stations—one entity could own. This action was motivated in part by fears that one company or individual could obtain too much control over the flow of information in society.

Until the early 1980s, the FCC limited one entity to ownership of seven AM radio stations, seven FM radio stations and seven TV stations in different markets. Since then, the ownership rules have been relaxed, which in turn has stimulated mergers and acquisitions and greater concentration of ownership, at least in terms of the number of entities that own media organizations.

In 1983, the FCC upped the limit to 12-12-12. Then, in 1992, the limits for radio stations were upped to 18 AM and 18 FM. The FCC also allowed ownership of two AM and two FM stations in the same market as long as that market had at least 15 competing stations and the new local operation did not account for more than one-fourth of the total listening audience. In 1994, the radio ownership limits were increased to 20 and 20 (television remained at 12).

Ownership limits were again eased in 1996 with the passage of the *Telecommunications Act of 1996*. In large markets with 45 or more stations, one company could now own up to eight stations but no more than five AM or five FM stations in one market. In markets with 30-44 stations, the limits were set at seven stations (up to four AM or FM); in markets with 15-29 stations, six stations (up to four AM or FM); and with fewer than 15 stations, five stations (up to three AM or FM).

In 2003, the FCC proposed relaxing the national television ownership standard to 45 percent from 35 percent, meaning that one entity could own television stations that reached up to 45 percent of the U.S. market. That measure faced stiff opposition from the public and has not yet been implemented.

The relaxation of the ownership rules has led to a tremendous increase in the number of stations owned by chains or groups. Before passage of the Telecommunications Act, about 1,000 stations a year changed hands, and the total value of the transactions ranged from $1 billion to $5 billion. After passage, about 2,000 stations were sold a year, and the value of the transactions ranged from $9 billion to $25 billion.

Large companies are buying up more stations because it is more efficient to operate multiple stations in one market or in multiple markets. The stations can, among other things, share advertising and administrative staffs.

See *concentration of ownership*.
Sources: Mark Fratrik, *State of the Radio Industry: Radio Transactions 2000* (Chantilly, VA: BIA Financial Network, 2001), pp. 6-7, and Mark Fratrik, *State of the Radio Industry: Radio Transactions 2000* (Chantilly, VA: BIA Financial Network, 2001), p. 8.

media planner in an advertising agency, a person who evaluates mass media and puts together a plan for achieving the advertising *campaign*'s goals.

media processes a field of study which attempts to identify and sometimes quantify the origins or development of mass media systems, organizations, and behaviors that create, influence or shape mass media messages or content.

The study of news routines is a good example. Researchers attempt to identify how things like deadline pressures, codes of ethics and the ethic of objectivity influence news content.

See *media effects*.
Source: Leo W. Jeffres, *Mass Media Processes*, 2nd ed. (Prospect Heights, IL: Waveland Press, 1994).

media relations a department in many public relations firms whose responsibility is to maintain good relations with mass media news organizations.

Media relations personnel answer questions that reporters and other media professionals have about the organization and its products or services. Media relations workers also write and distribute press releases to news organizations. Occasionally they also will organize press conferences at which company executives make major announcements.

See *community relations, corporate communications* and *public*.

media research see *mass communication research*.

media specialists advertising or public relations workers who attempt to find the most effective media to promote a product, service or idea.

Sometimes this means placing a message in media that reaches everyone. However, many times a client will want to reach specialized audiences, a task that often involves *market segmentation* and *target marketing* analyses.

media system theory see *mass media system theory*.

media violence depictions or scenes of violence (e.g., robbery, rape, murder) that are contained in mass media content.

Aside from the *social control* consequences of mass media, the single most controversial aspect of media effects is whether media violence makes people violent. This also is by far the most thoroughly researched question in the field of mass communication. At least 5,000 studies have examined the impact of violence.

The findings show that exposure to violent content does stimulate aggressive behavior in children. However, as yet there is no significant body of research linking violent programming to adult criminal behavior.

The history of concern about media violence goes back to at least the 19th century, when many newspapers refrained from publishing information about crimes because they worried such stories would corrupt the morals of young people. The *Payne Fund Studies* also concluded that movies did, indeed, promote delinquency and violence.

During the 1950s, psychiatrist Frederic Wertham claimed that comic books were turning children into juvenile delinquents. More recently, psychologist David Walsh argues that violent movies are responsible for a 264 percent increase in violent crime among 15-year-old boys from 1987 to 1991.

Studies show that television and movies have a lot of violent content. Programs broadcast on weekends during daytime hours, when children frequently are watching, contain even more violence than prime time shows. Cartoons are the most violent.

In 1982, the National Institute of Mental Health released a report that reviewed the findings from more than 3,000 scientific studies of television. The report concluded that both laboratory and field experiments overwhelmingly demonstrate that televised violence increases aggressive behaviors in many children. The so-called Bobo Doll experiments provided support for this proposition.

The classic study assignedr preschool and elementary school children into two groups, one "experimental" and the other "control." The experimental group watched a film showing an adult or child punch, kick or sit on the Bobo Doll, a plastic blow-up toy, while the control group watched the adult or child engage in innocuous, nonviolent behaviors. Later, the children were allowed to play in a room that contained a number of toys, including a Bobo Doll. Trained observers then recorded the children's behavior.

The results: Children who watched the attack on the Bobo doll were far more likely to behave aggressively toward the doll than children who had not seen the attack. In addition, children who had seen the attack also became more aggressive toward adults and other children in the room—sometimes hitting or pushing them.

Mass communication researchers have advanced a number of theories to explain why violent content leads to aggressive behavior in children. Three of the most prominent are:

• Observational Learning. This explanation holds that children learn to behave aggressively in ways similar to how they learn other behaviors: by imitating and modeling parents, teachers, siblings, and friends. Some scientists believe behaviors and verbal statements related to the televised violence are stored in the brain, retrieved, and imitated when the appropriate cues are present. But the exact process through which observational learning occurs is still a mystery and probably will be so for some time.

• Attitude Change. Another explanation for the relationship between viewing and aggression is that television influences children's attitudes, which in turn guide their behavior. Again, the exact mental processes involved are not known, but many studies show that the more televised violence a child watches, the more favorable his or her attitude toward aggressive behavior. Heavy viewers of television also are more likely than light viewers to believe aggressive behavior is normal and to believe people are aggressive.

• Desensitization. The third explanation is that television desensitizes and habituates children to real-life violence and aggressive behavior. Studies find, for instance, that boys who watch a lot of televised violence show less physiological arousal than other boys when viewing violent programming. In other words, the more violence they watch, the more tolerant of violent behavior they become.

Although most scientists agree that violent programming stimulates aggressive behavior in children, linking such aggression to juvenile or adult criminal activity has been much more difficult. One of the problems is that few long-term studies have been conducted. Also, to show that violent programming can lead to violence in adulthood, scientists have yet to advance good theories that explain away the effects of other social institutions (e.g., family, church, schools), that research shows generally have more impact on children's lives than mass media and consistently teach that violence is wrong.

See *media effects, mass communication research, Payne Fund Studies* and *Zamora, Ronny.*

Sources: Willard Grosvenor Bleyer, *Main Currents in the History of Journalism* (New York: Houghton Mifflin, 1927), p. 157; Frederic Wertham, *Seduction of the Innocent* (New York: Rinehart, 1954); Chris Hewitt, "Hollywood Fare Provides Fuel for Violence Debate," *Saint Paul Pioneer Press* (October 22, 1995), p. 14A; David Allen Walsh, *Selling Out America's Children: How America Puts Profits Before Values and What Parents Can Do* (Deaconess Press, 1994); T. M. Williams (ed.), *The Impact of Television: A Natural Experiment in Three Communities* (Orlando, FL: Academic Press, 1986); D. Pearl, L. Bouthilet, and J. Lazar (eds.), *Television and Behavior: Ten Years of Scientific Progress and Implications for the Eighties, Vols. I & II* (Washington, D.C.: U.S. Government Printing office, 1982); Albert Bandura, *Aggression: A Social Learning Analysis* (Englewood Cliffs, N.J.: Prentice-Hall, 1973) and Albert Bandura, *Social Learning Theory* (Englewood Cliffs, N.J.: Prentice-Hall, 1977); V. B. Cline, R. G. Croft and S. Courrier, "Desensitization of Children to Television Violence," *Journal of Personality and Social Psychology* (Vol. 27, 1973), pp. 360-365; and Albert Bandura, "Social Cognitive Theory of Mass Communication," pp. 61-90 in Jennings Bryant and Dolf Zillmann (eds.), *Media Effects: Advances in Theory and Research* (Hillsdale, NJ: Lawrence Erlbaum Associates, 1994).

median the midpoint *value* in a *distribution*, derived by arraying the *values* and finding the one that lies in the middle, or in the case of an even number of values, the *mean* of the two in the middle.

For instance, if the income of four brothers is $12,000, $13,000, $13,000 and $55,000, the median is $13,000. Note that the *mean* is $23,250, a value that is substantially higher than three of the four incomes. The value of the median, unlike the mean, is not affected by extreme cases, or *outliers*, and for this reason is often used as a *measure of central tendency.*

megatheater see *multiplex theater.*

Méliès, Georges (1861-1938) a filmmaker who helped pioneer the idea of using a film to tell a story.

Although early filmmakers experimented with a number of techniques, the notion that motion pictures could be used to tell a story didn't emerge until the late 1800s. French magician Méliès was at the forefront of this notion. He purchased filmmaking equipment and constructed a glass studio on the grounds of his house at Montreuil.

Between 1896 and 1913, Méliès produced, directed, photographed, and acted in more than 500 films, including "Trip to the Moon" (1902). In 1899, he produced "L'Affaire Dreyfus" ("The Dreyfus Affair"), a film that told the story of a French Jewish officer wrongly convicted of treason. (Dreyfus later was exonerated, and the scandal helped propel left-wing politicians into power.)

message see *communication*.

metaphysics a branch of philosophy that seeks to explain the nature of existence or reality (*ontology*) and the origin and existence of the world (cosmology).
See *ontology*.

metric scale a *level of measurement* which is interval or ratio.

Myers, Dee Dee (1961-) the first woman to hold the title of press secretary of the United States.
In 1993, Myers became the first woman and the youngest person, at age 31, to hold the title of press secretary for a U.S. president. She had a sharp mind and was highly respected. Asked how she could tolerate combative journalists, she said, "Never take it personally and never lose your sense of humor."
But she quickly learned that even a liberal administration like Bill Clinton's had its limits. She was given a small office, worked in the shadow of communications director George Stephanopoulos, and had fewer responsibilities than other press secretaries. She was often excluded from important briefings and meetings. She resigned in frustration after nearly two years on the job.
After her stint at the White House, Myers cohosted CNBC's public affairs show "Equal Time" for two years. She offered a view that countered conservative cohosts. She also became a political editor to "Vanity Fair" magazine. In 1999, Myers was appointed to the University of California Board of Regents. She also is a consultant to the television show "West Wing."
Sources: Susan Reimer, "Dee Dee Myers Feels Tug of Press Secretary Role," *The Baltimore Sun* (October 30, 2001), p. 1F; Jenifer Warren, "For Clinton Press Aide, Climb Was Steep, Rapid," *The Los Angeles Times* (October 14, 1992), p. A5; Pamela Burdman, "Davis Continues Trend of Picking Celebrity Southern Californians," *The San Francisco Chronicle* (March 27, 1999), p. A19; and Emily Fuger, "Former White House Rep. Visits Campus," <www.purpleonline.com>.

Milton, John (1608-1674) an Englishman who wrote *Areopagitica*, a classic work in defending freedom of the press. Ironically, Milton would later serve as chief censor for Oliver Cromwell and the Puritans.
See *Areopagitica* and *Star Chamber Court*.

mode the *value* that occurs most frequently in a *distribution*.
If two or more values are "tied" with the most *cases*, the mode takes on the lowest value.

modem a device for converting digital computer signals for transmission on analog telephone lines.
See *digital subscriber line* and *broadband*.

modernism a theory, paradigm or perspective (depending upon the observer) that emphasizes scientific rationality, empiricism, realism, objective truth, and an overall faith in progress of human kind and ability of science to solve social and environmental problems.

Contrast with *postmodernism.*

modernity the condition or state of *modernism.*

monadic ratings a study in which *respondents* evaluate only one product or service.

Moore, Michael (1954-) an independent filmmaker whose humorous jabs at corporate America and conservative politicians have made him America's best-loved left-wing critic.

Moore was born in 1954 in Davison, Michigan. His father and grandfather both worked for General Motors. As a Boy Scout, he won a merit badge for creating a slide show that exposed environmentally unfriendly businesses in Flint. At age 18, he became one of the youngest people in the United States to be elected to political office (school board).

He dropped out of college and began writing for an alternative weekly newspaper, eventually becoming its editor. He worked briefly for "Mother Jones" and the Ralph Nader organization. He used his settlement money from the magazine to produce "Roger and Me" (1989), a humor-laced documentary that skewered General Motors and its chairman, Roger Smith, for laying off 30,000 auto workers in Flint, Michigan. Moore nearly went bankrupt producing the film, which took three years. The film won a number of honors and went on to become one of the most financially successful documentaries ever made.

In the 1990s, Moore produced several television shows, but none lasted long. He wrote another book in 1996, titled "Downsize This!," before writing "Stupid White Men." When Random House considered scrapping publication of "Stupid White Men" because it was too critical of President George W. Bush, Moore revealed the plan to a convention of librarians, who initiated an e-mail campaign that forced the publisher to release the book. The book became a No. 1 best-seller.

In 2002, he produced "Bowling for Columbine," a documentary film that criticized the gun industry and right-wing groups. When Moore won an Academy Award in 2003 for the film, he used his acceptance speech to criticize President Bush. This angered many people on both the left and right, who believe recipients of Oscars should not mix politics with acceptance speeches.

But Moore ignored them. "I don't compromise my values and I don't compromise my work," he says. "That's why I've been kicked from one network to the next. I won't give in."

In 2004, he finished work on "Fahrenheit 9/11," a film that indicts the Bush administration for its close financial ties to Saudi Arabia and relatives of terrorist Osama bin Laden. The film was the first documentary to win the Cannes Film Festival's Palm D'or, the festival's top prize.

When Disney refused to distribute the film, apparently because of concerns over the political fallout, the rights were sold to Miramax heads Bob and Harvey Weinstein, who then were able to secure theatrical release in the United States. In three days, "Fahrenheit 9/11" grossed more money than "Bowling for Columbine" and also became the first documentary in history to be crowned the top money-maker of the weekend.

Moore admitted on Fox Television that he lives in a $1.6 million house in New York City. But he's also given millions of dollars to charitable causes, including to workers in Flint.

Sources: "Biography of Michael Moore," Yahoo.com; "Biography of Michael Moore," The Biography Channel, <www.thebiographychannel.com>

Morse, Samuel (1781-1872) inventor of the *telegraph*.

Morse was raised in Massachusetts and attended Yale College. He wrote and edited geography textbooks and became a portrait painter. In 1832, he came up with the idea of employing electromagnetism in telegraphy. It took five years to perfect his machine.

On May 24, 1844, he sent the first electronic message between Washington, D.C. and Baltimore: "What hath God wrought."

See *telegraph*.

motion picture a form of entertainment, usually about 90 minutes in length and shown at a movie theater or on television, that tells a story through a sequence of images that gives the illusion of continuous movement.

The first motion pictures were shown in the 1890s on a *Kinetoscope*, a large box that allowed only individual viewing in the 1890s. Although crude, the Kinetoscope was very popular. But this technology was soon replaced by the film projector and the *nickelodeon* and *movie palace* environments, where many people could view the motion picture at the same time.

The silent film era (i.e., motion pictures without sound) lasted until the late 1920s. The first movie to include dialogue in addition to a musical score was "The Jazz Singer" (1927). Walt Disney produced the first animated sound cartoon, "Steamboat Willie" (1928), which debuted Mickey Mouse. In less than two years, the entire American film industry converted to talking pictures. By 1930, silent pictures were extinct.

Color was introduced in the 1930s, but it did not become a staple of movie-making until the 1960s because it was expensive.

Many motion picture historians argue that Hollywood studios reached their zenith during the late 1930s and the 1940s. The studios were producing nearly 500 movies a year.

During the late 1940s and 1950s, the motion picture industry began losing money because it (1) lost monopolistic control over film distribution; (2) could not make up for inflationary costs; (3) came under attack from right-wing extremists in Congress (e.g., *House Un-American Activities Committee*); and (4) had difficulty competing with television, which was free.

During the early 1960s, the prevailing wisdom to maximize profits was to produce movies that appealed to the entire family. However, this approach didn't work well, because parents and older people were going to the movies a lot less often. The typical movie-goer was becoming younger and had different tastes than older people.

So, by the late 1960s, the studios violated the traditional formula and began producing movies geared to the interests of younger people. This approach worked with movies like "Bonnie and Clyde" (1967), "2001: A Space Odyssey" (1968), and "The Wild Bunch" (1969).

During the 1970s, a younger generation of directors dubbed the "movie brats" emerged on the scene. Most had learned filmmaking at film school or in college. But the studios weren't complaining. Francis Ford Coppola's "The Godfather" (1972), Martin Scorsese's "Mean Streets" (1973), Steven Spielberg's "Jaws" (1975) and "Close Encounters of the Third Kind" (1977), and George Lucas' "Star Wars" (1977) generated tens of millions of dollars in profits.

During the 1980s, the Reagan administration deregulated the filmmaking industry, allowing the major studios to own theaters.

Because of these changes, the film industry held its own during the 1970s and 1980s. Although attendance rates remained relatively flat, revenues rose partly because of higher admission costs and population growth. In 1950, one could still attend a movie for less than a buck. By 1980, the ticket price had risen to about $3. From 1960 to 1980, population increased by nearly 50 million. The industry was making money again. The seven MPAA studios grossed $1.4 billion in 1970 and $2.7 billion in 1980.

During the 1980s, *video cassette recorders* (VCRs) and cable television began generating new sources of revenues for filmmakers. At first the studios were worried that movies on video cassette tapes would cut into movie attendance. However, videos expanded the film industry's market, in some cases generating more revenues than the first-run showing. Many people, in fact, preferred to watch videos in the comfort of their homes.

The growth of cable television also was a bonus to some of the film studios. Before cable, the studios depended on one of the three major *television network*s for re-broadcasting a movie after its first-run showing. After cable, studios had many more outlets, and some—like Disney and Fox—even set up their own networks.

These new sources for marketing films also helped the independent film industry. In 1985, the independents for the first time released more motion pictures than the major studios.

At the start of the 21st century, the film industry was relatively healthy. Film production has increased to 1950s' levels. Movie attendance also has increased slightly during the last decade (going from 4.5 to 5.1 movies per year per person), even though ticket prices climbed to an average of about $5 in 2000 ($7 for first-run movies).

In 2000, revenues reached $7.7 billion. Officials attribute the increased attendance to higher quality movies, better marketing, and more comfortable theaters.

Today, many motion picture afficionados also distinguish between a "movie" and "film." To them, a movie is a motion picture made for mass audiences and for profit. The story line is usually simple and straightforward. Movies usually are made by Hollywood studios or other commercially oriented mass-market movie production studios.

A film, in contrast, is a motion picture made primarily to express a complex idea or point of view, often one that is controversial. Influencing people is considered more important than making a profit.

Dictionaries do not usually make distinctions between the terms film, motion picture, and movies. But the distinction between a "film" and a "movie" is part of a larger debate between what some mass media scholars call high culture versus low culture or popular culture. High culture is educational, informative, and thought-provoking. "Citizen Kane" would be an example. In contrast, popular culture is said to be trivial, commercialized, and mind-dulling, making people easier to control. "The Lord of the Rings" movies might be examples.

The implication is that "Citizen Kane" is culturally superior. But whether one agrees or disagrees with this notion, the more important point is that most movies—including "Citizen Kane"—contain themes of social control that support dominant values and institutions in a society (e.g., greed is bad). To the extent that "Citizen Kane" is perceived as an attack on the institution of capitalism, then it might also be called an agent of change (see *social change*).

See *motion picture technology*.

motion picture technology a sequence of photographs or drawings projected in such rapid succession that they create the illusion of moving persons and objects

The illusion of motion pictures is based on two optical principles: persistence of vision and the phi phenomenon. Persistence of vision causes the brain to retain images from the eye for a fraction of a second beyond their disappearance. The phi phenomenon creates apparent movement between the images when they rapidly succeed each other. When images are presented at 24 frames per second (or thereabouts), the mind perceives a continuous image.

The concept of a motion picture was recognized long before the development of cameras and film. A rotating drum or disk was used to create the illusion of motion using drawings in the 1830s. After the invention of photography in the 1840s, posed photographs replaced drawings. But a motion picture industry could not emerge until a device was invented that could photograph images in rapid succession. Also needed was a film highly sensitive to light—one that would require a fraction of a second for exposure.

The camera breakthrough came in 1882, when French physiologist Étienne-Jules Marey invented the chronophotographic gun, a rifle-shaped camera that recorded 12 successive photographs per second. The film breakthrough came in the late 1880s, when industrialist George Eastman began mass producing celluloid roll film for still photography at his plant in Rochester, New York. The *Kinetograph*, patented in 1893 by *Thomas Alva Edison*, was an improvement on the chronophotographic gun and produced the first short films. Edison and his assistant also invented the *Kinetophone*, which synchronized sound and pictures. However, it did not function well, and it wasn't until the 1920s that the process was perfected.

The first optical sound-on-film recording system, patented as Phonofilm, was developed by Lee De Forest, an American inventor. His technique involved transcribing sound waves into impulses of light that were photographed on to a strip of film. When the developed film passed between a light source and a photoelectric cell in a motion-picture projector, the images were converted back into electrical voltages that were then transformed into sound through a loudspeaker system. De Forest also developed the Audion tube, a vacuum tube that magnified sound and enabled radio broadcasting. De Forest made more than 1,000 synchronized short films during the 1920s, but he was never able to convince Hollywood studios to use his technology.

Western Electric developed a more sophisticated system called the Vitaphone, which Warner Brothers studio eventually adopted and first used in 1926. That effectively was the beginning of the end for silent pictures. But it wasn't until the mid-1930s that problems in sound-on-film recording were solved. Prior to then, microphones had limited range and often picked up the sound of the cameras, which were noisy. Awkward glass boxes were constructed to encase cameras and crews. By the late 1930s, cameras were devised that were much less noisy, and microphones were much improved.

But the single most important improvement was postsynchronization, or dubbing. This involved printing the image and sound on separate pieces of film so that they could be manipulated and edited independently. This practice continues today.

Source: Raymond Fielding, *A Technological History of Motion Pictures and Television: An Anthology from the Pages of the Journal of the Society of Motion Picture and Television Engineers* (Berkeley: University of California Press, 1983).

Motion Picture Association of America (MPAA) an association that represents the interests of major motion picture studios in Hollywood.

MPAA was founded in 1922 partly to fend off criticism that movies were having harmful effects on young people. Then, as today, movies focused on three major themes: sex, crime, and violence. And then, as today, many moviegoers were minors. Religious organizations and parents were concerned about the effects these movies were having on young people, and there were threats of boycotts and protests.

In March 1922, the studio heads formed MPAA (formerly called the Motion Picture and Producers and Distributors of America), a self-regulatory organization. Although MPAA didn't have the power to censor, the MPAA promoted a "Production Code" that placated critics for a time.

The MPAA continues to function as a "protectorate" and "safety valve" for the U.S. film industry. It represents the seven major producers and distributors: The Walt Disney Company; Sony Pictures Entertainment, Inc., Metro-Goldwyn-Mayer Inc., Paramount Pictures Corporation, Twentieth Century Fox Film Corp., Universal Studios, Inc., and Warner Brothers.

See *motion picture studio* and *Motion Picture Patents Company.*

Motion Picture Patents Company (MPPC) a 20th-century association that represented motion-picture companies.

In 1908, about 20 motion-picture production companies were operating in the United States. The companies were highly competitive and fought over patent rights, but they eventually formed the MPPC to resolve some of their differences and fend off problems from the growing distribution and exhibition industries.

The MPPC pooled 16 patents on motion-picture technology and gave Eastman Kodak Company an exclusive contract to supply raw film stock. The MPPC effectively operated as a trust, controlling who could purchase film and obtain royalties. Two years later the MPPC formed the General Film Company, which combined licensed distributors into a single corporate entity.

These associations increased the efficiency of the industry, but they sparked a counter-reaction from independent filmmakers who formed the National Independent Moving Picture Alliance (earlier called the Independent Film Protective Association). The NIMPA embraced the idea of longer, multi-reel films—a move MPPC had resisted, eventually contributing to its demise.

motion picture studio an organization, usually profit-driven, that produces movies.

Hollywood has seven major motion picture studios. They include Warmer Brothers, The Walt Disney Company, Sony Pictures Entertainment Inc., Universal Studios Inc., Twentieth Century Fox Film Corp., Paramount Pictures Corp., and Metro-Goldwyn-Mayer Inc.

movie see *motion picture.*

movie palace a large theater that eventually replaced *nickelodeons.*

As movie attendance and revenues increased during the early 1900s, exhibitors began building more elaborate movie palaces—theaters that were larger and more comfortable than the nickelodeons. Some also included live orchestral music to accompany the production. Feature films also drew more attendance from the middle classes, who saw them as "legitimate theater" (or "high culture").

By 1916, more than 21,000 movie palaces were operating in the United States, and the nickelodeon was in decline. About 60 percent of film production was based in Hollywood, and the industry employed more than 15,000 workers and invested more than $500 million annually.

See *motion picture* and *nickelodeon.*

MP3 a software that compresses large audio files, allowing efficient downloading of music or other content from the *Internet.*

muckraker an investigative reporter.

The term was coined by President Theodore Roosevelt, who was angered over one magazine article that exposed corruption in the U.S. Senate. He intended to ridicule the reporters. In those days a muckraker was a person who spread or picked up manure and garbage. But the journalists took the insult as a badge of honor and, to this day, the term has had a positive connotation in the field of journalism.

See *muckraking era* and *Tarbell, Ida.*

muckraking era a two-decade time period lasting from about 1895 to 1915 during which investigative reporters helped uncover corruption and abuse of power in business and in government in the United States.

The muckraking era coincided with the progressive social movement, which wanted greater democratic participation for individuals. The movement also believed in science and wanted to check the power of large businesses and restore the power of the individual entrepreneur or craftsman.

Dozens of journalists were investigating unfair business practices, as well as corruption in city and state government, poor sanitation in meat packing plants, fraud in patent medicines, and poor housing, working, and health conditions. These journalists included *Ida Tarbell, David Graham Phillips, Jacob Riss, Lincoln Steffens,* and *Upton Sinclair.*

These and other exposés encouraged legislation to protect children and the environment, give women the right to vote, reform the judicial system, increase anti-trust prosecutions, and improve the safety of food and drugs.

multiple response measure a survey *question* in which the *respondent* may give more than one answer.

multiplex theater a movie theater complex that contains multiple screens, sometimes 30 or more. Megatheaters are multiplexes that have 16 or more screens. A 16-screen theater seats about 5,000.

Multiplex theaters offer exhibitors several advantages. First and most importantly, they reduce costs. Wages and salaries for ushers and projectionists and the cost of insurance are spread out over many screens.

Second, multiplex theaters offer audiences more choice of movies, which enables groups of people to attend and see the movie of their interest.

Third, multiplexes contain theaters of different sizes, which enables the theater owner to minimize seat vacancy rates. As attendance for a movie declines, it can be moved to a screen in a smaller room. Fourth, the newer multiplex theaters have become much more audience friendly. Seats are more comfortable, views are less obstructed, and seats are equipped with moveable arm rests and cup holders.

multivariate analysis research analysis that involves three or more *variables*. *Regression analysis, analysis of variance,* and *discriminant analysis* are some of the statistics used to conduct multivariate analysis.

multivariate statistics statistics that are used in the analysis of three or more *variables*. *Regression analysis, analysis of variance,* and *discriminant analysis* are multivariate statistics.

Murdoch, Rupert (1931-) chief executive officer of The News Corporation, often criticized by mass media scholars and social activists who oppose the growth of large-scale corporate media.

Murdoch was born in Melbourne, Australia, and studied at Oxford University in the United Kingdom. He worked briefly at the "Daily Express" before inheriting two Australia newspapers from his father in 1952. Twelve years later Murdoch launched the first national daily in Australia. Four years after that he purchased "News of the World," a London Sunday paper.

In 1969, Murdoch purchased another London newspaper and turned it into a tabloid that published sensationalized stories and pictures of bare-breasted women. He began purchasing newspapers in the United States during the 1970s, including the "New York Post." Using sensationalism to boost circulation, Murdoch has acquired a world-wide reputation as a *"yellow journalist."* Critics of global media also attack him more than any other media executive.

Some say, however, that Murdoch is not entirely deserving of such criticism. He and his family also own or have investments in what many people consider to be very respectable media, including "The (London) Times," "TV Guide" (and 25 other magazines), Twentieth Century Fox Film Corporation, the Fox Television Network, and HarperCollins Publishers.

News Corporation operates companies on six continents in every major medium except music. It owns more than 100 newspapers, making it one of the top three newspaper companies in world. In 1986, the company launched Fox Broadcasting, the first new U.S. *television network* since 1948.

News Corporation is one of the fastest growing global media companies. In 1998, it was ranked fourth in the world in terms of total revenues. It moved into second position, behind Time Warner, after Vivendi Universal sold most of its media holdings to NBC (see discussion below).

Total revenues for News Corporation exceeded Disney's for the first time in 2003. About a fourth of News Corporation's income is generated from film entertainment, a fourth from newspapers, a fifth from television, and 30 percent from magazines and books. About 75 percent of that income flows in from the United States, but the company expects the growth markets to be in Europe, Asia, and Latin America. News Corporation is investing heavily in satellite television communications systems—a risky but potentially very profitable enterprise.

Murdoch's family owns about 30 percent of News Corporation's stock. Murdoch became a U.S. citizen in 1985, which enabled him to comply with FCC regulations governing ownership of U.S. broadcast media. He intends to move the headquarters from Australia to the United States, partly to increase the company's reach in the United States.

In 2003, News Corporation had profits of $1.6 billion on revenues of $21 billion (7.6%).

Murrow, Edward (Egbert) Roscoe (1908-1965) a radio and television journalist and personality who helped define broadcast journalism and today is probably the most revered man in the history of broadcasting.

Murrow was born in North Carolina and moved in 1913 to Blanchard, Wash., where his father became a logging-locomotive engineer. Murrow excelled in academics, debating, and politics in high school and college. He attended Washington State College (now Washington State University).

After graduating with a bachelor's degree in speech, he was elected president of the National Student Federation and traveled the country giving speeches and arranging student travel and exchanges with foreign schools. He continued doing that kind of work in 1932, when he became assistant director of the Institute of International Education. He met Janet Huntington Brewster at a convention. They married in 1934 and had a son, Charles Casey Murrow.

In 1935, he took a job at CBS radio and was responsible for finding participants for radio discussions. Two years later CBS sent him to London to cover special events. In 1940, he broadcast live reports from London during the "Battle for Britain." Adoph Hitler's air force conducted nightly raids on London and other English cities from June 1940 to April 1941.

For five years Murrow reported the war. He began his broadcasts with the simple declaration: "This is London." He broadcast live from rooftops as the bombs burst around him and ignited numerous fires that did massive damage to London. Thousands of civilians and several hundred British fighter pilots were killed. On December 25, 1940, he reported, "This is not a merry Christmas in London. I heard that phrase only twice in the last three days."

Murrow also flew more than 40 combat missions aboard Allied bombers and paratrooper planes. After the war, he visited a recently liberated concentration camp and reported: "I pray you believe what I have said about

Buchenwald (concentration camp). I reported what I saw and heard, but only part of it. For most of it, I have no words."

Murrow went on to become the most famous and trusted U.S. journalist of the war. His quiet, monotone voice enhanced his credibility.

After the war, Murrow was promoted to vice president and director of public affairs of CBS. In 1951, he took his radio program "Hear It Now" to television and called it "See It Now." His television show made history on March 9, 1954, when he openly criticized Sen. Joseph R. McCarthy for falsely accusing people of being communists. That show was based on four months of research. Fred Friendly, Murrow's colleague and co-producer of "See It Now," put together a mountain of evidence against the Republican senator.

"We will not walk in fear, one of another," Murrow told his 12 million viewers. "We will not be driven by fear into an age of unreason if we dig deep in our history and doctrine and remember that we are not descended from fearful men, not from men who feared to write, to speak, to associate and to defend causes which were for the moment unpopular."

McCarthy's influence diminished substantially after that program and after a nationally televised, 36-day hearing on McCarthy's charges of subversion. In late 1954, the Senate finally condemned him on a vote of 67 to 22 for conduct "contrary to Senate traditions." McCarthy died in 1957, a discredited man.

In 1953, Murrow also hosted a popular interview show called "Person to Person," in which he interviewed movie stars and famous people. That program lasted until 1959.

The "See It Now" program, which first aired in 1951, was popular with everyone except CBS executives, who were concerned about alienating corporate sponsors. CBS Board Chairman William S. Paley pulled the plug on the program in 1958. Many supporters of the program were outraged.

Murrow continued broadcasting his nightly radio news show and appeared on television regularly on "Person to Person" and on "CBS Reports." In 1960, he left CBS to take charge of the U.S. Information Agency. But illness forced him to retire in 1963. Murrow, who was a heavy smoker, died of cancer in 1965 two days before his 57th birthday.

See *Paley, William S.*

Sources: Edward R. Murrow, *This is London* (New York: Simon and Schuster, 1941); Joseph E. Persico, *Edward R. Murrow: An American Original* (New York: Dell, 1988), p. 173; Joseph Wershba, "Edward R. Murrow and the Time of His Time," Eve's Magazine (www.evesmag.com/murrow.htm; Copyright 2000); "Senator Joseph R. McCarthy," *See It Now*, CBS News (March 9, 1954).

music video a music recording accompanied by video, usually of the singer and the band.

The videos are often broadcast on MTV (Music Television) or other music television stations. Recording labels use videos to promote an artist or recording.

N

narcotizing effects (of mass media) the notion that mass media, especially television, "sedates" people and makes them less likely to engage in democratic political activity.

The idea was developed by sociologists Robert K. Merton and *Paul Lazarsfeld*, who wrote: "It is termed dysfunctional rather than functional on the assumption that it is not in the interest of modern complex society to have large masses of the population politically apathetic and inert." Mass media make people apathetic and inert because, according to Lazarsfeld and Merton, it decreases the amount of time "available for organized action." They added:

"The individual reads accounts of issues and problems and may even discuss alternative lines of action. But this rather intellectualized, rather remote connection with organized social action is not activated. ... mass communications may be included among the most respectable and efficient of social narcotics. They may be so fully effective as to keep the addict from recognizing his own malady."

Although Lazarsfeld and Merton were writing before television became a powerful force in society, the narcotizing dysfunction has been associated with television more than any other medium. That's partly because people spend more time with television than with any other mass medium and because many scholars say it is the most powerful medium. The entertainment programming on television is often viewed as "low culture." In fact, during the 1950s and 1960s, many people referred to television as the "boob (slang for 'stupid') tube."

Sources: Paul F. Lazarsfeld and Robert K. Merton, "Mass Communication, Popular Taste, and Organized Social Action," pp. 554-578 in Wilbur Schramm and Donald F. Roberts (eds.), *The Process and Effects of Mass Communication* (Urbana: University of Illinois Press, 1971, revised edition, originally published in 1954), pp. 565-566.

narrative a style of news writing that emphasizes story telling instead of the summary, hard-news, *inverted pyramid* style of writing.

Feature stories often employ a narrative style. The theme is not always in the first paragraph. Instead, the goal is to engage the reader in an interesting story, anecdote or example that ties into the theme.

In the 1980s and 1990s, journalists increasingly turned to the narrative style in an attempt to make newspapers more interesting to readers. However, there is no evidence to suggest that this has had much of an impact on circulation, since newspaper *circulation* has continued to decline since World War II.

narrative criticism a methodology that analyzes persuasive messages as stories and evaluates how effective they were at shaping an audience's perception of reality.

national advertiser a company or business that places advertisements in mass media that reach consumers across the nation.
    See *retail advertiser.*

National Association of Broadcasters, The a trade association that represents the interests of over-the-air radio and television broadcasters.
    Its Web site <www.nab.org> has a wealth of information about the broadcast industry.

National Cable and Telecommunications Association, The the principal trade association of the cable television industry in the United States.
    Its Web site <www.ncta.com> contains news and information about the cable television industry.

National Communication Association a nonprofit education association representing mass communication, speech communication, interpersonal,and organizational communication scholars and students.
    Its Web site <www.natcom.org> contains information about its conferences and jobs.

National Independent Moving Picture Alliance see *Motion Picture Patents Company.*

NBC (National Broadcasting Company) a *television network* owned by General Electric (80%) and NBC Universal (20%).

negative reinforcement an environmental event that uses punishment (e.g., scolding, time out) to increase the probability of a behavior or response.
    See *positive reinforcement.*

neo-Marxism any theoretical approach that draws heavily upon but modifies or amplifies in one way or another the ideas of *Karl Marx.*

Critical theory is one example. In explaining the existence of capitalism as an economic institution, it places more emphasis on *ideology* than Marx did in his original writings.

See *Marx, Karl.*

neo-positivism see *positivism.*

network see *television network.*

new journalism a style of reporting and writing that deviates from or challenges mainstream journalism, especially its heavy reliance on established elites and institutions for the news.

Although the term "new journalism" has been applied to the populist style of journalism practiced at newspapers owned by *Joseph Pulitzer* in the late 1800s, the term is most closely associated with new forms of journalism that challenged the *ethic of objectivity* in the 1960s.

The new journalism movement was highly critical of objectivity and traditional reportorial methods, because they tended to generate a *mainstream bias* that excluded alternative or unorthodox points of view. Instead of objectivity, the new journalists advocated various forms of subjectivity, which they said were more effective at revealing the truth.

Tom Wolfe, Jimmy Breslin, Gay Talese, Norman Mailer, Truman Capote, Nicholas von Hoffman and others wrote articles and books that reported on real-life events but combined elements of a novel, such as people's motivations and feelings and extensive analysis of events and surroundings. Truman Capote's "In Cold Blood,"which told the story of a man who killed a family, epitomizes this genre.

The new journalism movement also got a boost from social movements opposed to the Vietnam War and in favor of more rights for women and minorities. They pointed out that traditional methods of reporting historically had marginalized these groups, or failed to give them a voice. Journalism was too dependent on powerful government and corporate elite sources.

The Watergate scandal in the early 1970s also gave alternative journalism a shot in the arm. Investigative reporting, in particular, was seen as a method that could overcome some of the problems associated with the ethic of objectivity and routine news reporting. What distinguished investigative reporting from routine news reporting was that the burden of proof lay on the journalist, not the sources, per se. The news media (especially the "Washington Post" and "New York Times") were highly praised for helping to uncover corruption in the Nixon administration.

The new journalism movement began to wane in the late 1970s. The end of the Vietnam War and new laws and court decisions providing more rights and protections to women and minorities took much of the steam out of the movement.

See ethic of objectivity, literary journalism, and *Pulitzer, Joseph.*

Sources: Everette E. Dennis, "The New Journalism: How It Came to Be," pp. 115-132 in Michael C. Emery and Ted Curtis Smythe (eds.), *Readings in Mass Communication: Concepts and Issues in the Mass Media,* 2nd ed. (Dubuque, Iowa: Wm. C. Brown Company Publishers, 1974) and Truman Capote, *In Cold Blood: A True Account of a Multiple Murder and Its Consequences* (New York: New American Library, 1965), Douglas Anderson, "How Managing Editors View and Deal With Ethical Issues," *Journalism Quarterly,* 64:341-5 (1987).

news reports of recent happenings or events, or, more specifically, reports that appear in mass media.

News is said to have derived its origins from the four winds, north-east-west-south, and presumably was coined to distinguish between casual dissemination of information and the deliberate attempt to gather it.

Journalists often distinguish between "hard news" and "soft news." The former almost always involves reports of recent happenings or events, while the latter usually involves human interest topic or personality profiles.

Hard news that involves coverage of fast-breaking events is called "spot news." Most hard news stories (e.g., political news and crime news) are written in the *inverted pyramid* style.

news beat a place where news is routinely collected.

Beats are usually structured around institutions or topics. A good example of the former is the police beat. A good example of the latter is the environmental beat.

Beats are not randomly chosen. They are usually anchored in powerful institutions or around controversial issues. In either case, newspapers and other news media rely very heavily on elite sources for supplying the news.

At the national level, this includes the President (or White House beat), Congress (Capital Hill beat), Supreme Court, and Wall Street executives. All major newspapers and many *television networks* have reporters covering these beats.

At the state and local level, beats are structured to cover the governor's office, the legislative houses, city council, county commissions, police agencies, and other governmental agencies and departments. Lifestyle reporters cover prominent people and companies in fashion, design, and the film and television industries.

Of course, not all news stories come from beats. General assignment reporters often cover events or write personality profiles that may or may not involve interviews with prominent or famous people. But there is little question that most news sources are drawn heavily from the ranks of powerful government and corporate officials.

newsgroup (or discussion group or bulletin board) an online "bulletin board" or discussion group, in which *social actors* exchange information and ideas.

news hole the amount of space in magazines or newspapers that is available for news as opposed to advertising or other content.

Most newspapers, for example, reserve about 60 percent of the page space for advertising and fill the rest with news, information, and entertainment content. Early in the day, the advertising department will inform the editorial department about how much space is available. The ads are placed on blank pages. The editorial department then is responsible for filling the news hole.

newsletters a *periodical* that provides news, interpretations, and predictions about highly specialized topics or issues.

Newsletters tend to be shorter than magazines and even more specialized, often focusing on technical, political or business-oriented topics. Many newsletters do not contain photographs or advertising. They generate most of their revenues through subscriptions instead.

news media *mass media* organizations that produce and distribute news to a large number of geographically separated people through a technologically based medium.

Newspapers are most apt to receive this label, because they specialize in the production of public affairs news and information and produce a lot more of it than other forms of media. Television and radio stations and networks also produce news.

See *mass media.*

newspaper a publication regularly printed and distributed, usually daily or weekly, that contains news, opinions, advertisements, pictures, and other content of general interest.

But the term "newspaper" is often applied to other types of publications. Many corporations and nonprofit groups, for example, produce publications that they call "newspapers," even though they may not fit all aspects of the definition presented above. They sometimes only publish monthly or quarterly, and they may not contain advertisements or items of general interest. The content of many in-house newspapers, in fact, can be very specialized.

See *penny press.*

news service a news organization that provides its members or subscribers with news stories, features or other content that they, in turn, place in their publications or broadcasts.

The world's first news service, Havas, was established in France in 1835. It offered subscribers translations of stories from French newspapers. The company still survives today and is part of a large global media corporation.

Morning newspapers in New York City created the *Associated Press* in 1848. Through cooperative agreements with other newspapers around the country, they shared stories via the telegraph. Other news services were formed in Germany (Wolff) in 1849 and Great Britain (Reuters) in 1851.

New York Times, The (1851-) one of the most prominent and respected newspapers in the world.

The "Times" was founded by Henry Raymond and George Jones in 1851. The original name was "New York Daily Times," but the name was changed in 1857. Raymond managed the newsroom and Jones the business office.

The "Times" quickly developed a reputation for accuracy, truthfulness, fairness, and objectivity—despite Raymond's passion for and involvement in politics (he eventually became a state legislator and U.S. Congressman)—and for insightful analyses of foreign news events.

In 1859, the "Times'" reputation was enhanced even more when Raymond went to Italy to cover the French and Italian war with Austria, particularly the Battle of Solferino. The "Times" supported Abraham Lincoln for president in 1860, and Raymond's coverage of the Battle of Bull Run during the Civil War also drew critical acclaim to the newspaper. Lincoln called Raymond "my lieutenant general in politics."

In 1867, Raymond retired from politics to devote his attention to turning the "Times" into a national newspaper. The newspaper began exposing corruption in government and crusaded for tariff reduction and monetary and civil service reforms. But Raymond became despondent when several friends and two of his children died. He died in 1869 from a stroke.

Jones was not a journalist, but he had been in the news business for more than a quarter century when he assumed control of the newsroom. In 1870, he launched an attack on the infamous Tweed Ring, a corrupt network of Democratic politicians and bureaucrats who bilked the New York City government of $200 million. The newspaper and "Harper's Weekly" succeeded in driving the Tweed Ring from power. Jones died in 1891.

The "Times" foundered after Jones' death and was on the brink of bankruptcy until Adolph S. Ochs, the son of Bavarian immigrants, purchased the newspaper in 1896. Ochs was not a very good writer, but he was outstanding as a leader and organizer. After several months of negotiations, he managed to persuade a number of investors, including tycoon J. P. Morgan, to invest in the deal. Ochs put up $75,000 of his own money. On October 25, 1896, the "Times" published its now-famous motto in the masthead: "All The News That's Fit To Print."

To raise circulation and decrease debt, Ochs published a pictorial Sunday magazine and created the "Review of Books," which continues to be a regular feature of the Sunday "Times." In 1898, he reduced the price of the paper to one cent and circulation tripled. But the real strength of the paper lay in the staff and the editorial philosophy. Ochs went to great lengths to hire the best reporters and editors in the field.

Ochs died in 1935, after which his son-in-law, Arthur Hays Sulzberger, became publisher. Sulzberger diversified the company with the purchase of two New York City radio stations in 1944. During the 1950s, the "Times" investigated racism and discrimination in the South. This prompted U.S. Sen. James Eastland (D-Miss.), a segregationist and a supporter of Joseph McCarthy, the right-wing communist witch-hunter, to investigate the "Times" in 1956 for alleged "communist influences." The "Times" said it would not knowingly hire a communist, but former reporter James Aronson did claim that at least three "Times" reporters were fired for taking the Fifth Amendment.

In 1961, Salzberger retired and was replaced by Orvil Dryfoos, Sulzberger's son-in-law. But Dryfoos died two years later and was replaced by Adolph's grandson, Arthur Ochs "Punch" Sulzberger. Declining ad revenue and a strike sent the newspaper into the "red," but Punch responded by building the largest news reporting staff in the world.

In 1969, The New York Times Company, the parent company of the "Times," went public on the New York Stock Exchange. During the 1970s the company purchased magazines, publishing houses, smaller newspapers, television stations, cable television systems, and pulp and paper companies. The company also began co-publishing the "International Herald Tribune," an English-language newspaper widely available in Europe and other areas around the world.

"Times'" coverage of the Vietnam War during the late 1960s helped turn public opinion against the war, and in 1972 the newspaper won a *Pulitzer Prize* for publishing the *"Pentagon Papers,"* which revealed that the U.S. government had been lying to the American public and withholding information about the U.S. policies in Southeast Asia and Vietnam. In the early 1970s, the "Times," along with the Washington Post, also gave prominent coverage to the *Watergate* scandal, which led to President Nixon's resignation.

During the 1980s, the "Times" criticized President Reagan and his administration for illegally selling arms to the Iranians and diverting the funds to U.S.-backed rebel fighters in Nicaragua. During the 1980s and 1990s, The New York Times Company continued to buy and sell properties and has made modest profits. In 1992, Punch's son, Arthur Ochs Sulzberger Jr., took over as "Times" publisher, and in 1997 he was elected chairman of the board of directors. In 1996, the company launched a Web site <www.nytimes.com>, which continues to be one of the most frequently visited sites in the news business.

Today "The New York Times" consistently ranks in polls of journalists as the best newspaper in the United States—and many would say "the world." The newspaper and its staff have earned 79 Pulitzer Prizes, 36 more than any other news organization. The newspaper has more than 1,000 reporters and editors, nine bureaus and 29 international bureaus. "Times'" circulation has also been growing in recent years. The newspaper has the third highest daily circulation in the United States (about 1,095,000) and the highest Sunday circulation (1,650,000).

See *New York Times v. United States*.

Sources: Michael Emery, Edwin Emery and Nancy L. Roberts, *The Press and America: An Interpretive History of the Mass Media* (Boston: Allyn and Bacon, 2000), pp. 107-108, 147-149, 234-240; 457-460; Thomas A. Schwartz, "Raymond, Henry Jarvis," pp. 572-575 in Joseph P. McKerns (ed.), *Biographical Dictionary of American Journalism* (New York: Greenwood Press, 1989); Janet E. Steele, "Jones, George," pp. 370-372 in Joseph P. McKerns (ed.), *Biographical Dictionary of American Journalism;* Kristen Dollase, "Ochs, Adolph S.," pp. 521-523 in Joseph P. McKerns (ed.), *Biographical Dictionary of American Journalism;* James Aronson, *The Press and the Cold War* (New York: Bobbs-Merrill, 1970), p. 146; and *The New York Times* Web site: <www.nytimes.com>.

New York Times v. Sullivan (1964) see *libel*.

New York Times v. United States (1971) a U.S. Supreme Court case which established that the U.S. government has the authority to use *prior restraint* against news media, but the burden of proof is on the government to show how publishing or broadcasting the information would produce grave harm to the nation.

In the late 1960s, Daniel Ellsberg, a senior research associate at the Massachusetts Institute of Technology's Center for International Studies, helped write the "Pentagon Papers," a top-secret 47-volume history of America's involvement in Southeast Asia. Before the project, Ellsberg was an ardent supporter of U.S. military involvement in Indochina. But as he learned more about that involvement, he became an impassioned opponent of the Vietnam War. In fact, he was so outraged, he secretly photocopied most of the 7,000-page report and turned over portions of it to "The New York Times" and "The Washington Post."

On June 13, 1971, the "Times" began publishing a series of articles based on the report. Officially called the "History of the U.S. Decision-Making Process on Viet Nam Policy," the "Pentagon Papers" revealed that the U.S. government frequently lied to the American people about its role in Vietnam. The papers also revealed that the U.S. government deliberately provoked the North Vietnamese to attack a U.S. ship in order to justify more U.S. military involvement.

The news stories embarrassed government officials. Attorney General John Mitchell asked the "Times" to stop publishing the series, but the newspaper refused. Mitchell then went to court and obtained a temporary restraining order to halt publication.

He argued initially that publication of the articles violated federal espionage statutes. When that argument didn't satisfy the lower courts, he argued that President Richard Nixon had the authority to conduct foreign affairs to protect national security. But that argument didn't work either. So, when the case arrived at the U.S. Supreme Court, he argued that publication of the papers might harm national security and its ability to conduct foreign affairs. Nixon was worried that the papers might scare the Chinese from secret negotiations to establish diplomatic relations with the United States.

The newspapers made two arguments. First, they argued that the government's top-secret classification system was a sham, because government officials often declassify documents in order to sway public opinion or influence a story. Second, the newspapers argued that the restraining order prohibiting publication violated the *First Amendment.* The newspapers didn't argue that the government never had a right to stop publication. They conceded that the government could exercise *prior restraint* if publication would seriously threaten national security, but this case didn't justify that.

The U.S. Supreme Court ruled 6-3 in favor of the newspapers. The court said the government could stop publication only if it could prove grave harm to national security. But this "heavy burden" of proof had not been met.

Historians believe publication of the "Pentagon Papers" helped sway public opinion against the Vietnam War. The war ended in 1975 when the United States evacuated its troops and the North Vietnamese defeated the South Vietnamese army.

The federal government indicted Ellsberg for espionage and other crimes. But in 1973, a judge dismissed the charges because a White House team known as the "plumbers" illegally wiretapped his phone and broke into his psychiatrist's office in an effort to obtain information to discredit Ellsberg. The "plumbers" later were arrested for breaking into Democratic National Headquarters—an incident that touched off the *Watergate* scandal.

See *Woodward and Bernstein.*

Sources: *New York Times v. U.S.; U.S. v. Washington Post,* 713 U.S. 403 (1971).

niche as applied to the field of mass communication, the "space" or place that a media organization occupies in the community or market.

A magazine for model railroaders, for example, has its niche in the model railroading community or market.

See *niche marketing.*

niche marketing a *market segmentation* strategy in which a company or organization focuses on serving the needs of one particular group, or niche, of consumers.

An organization whose products or services are well received in the market is said to be "serving its niche well." The term "niche" is derived from ecology, where it refers to the specific space an organism occupies in its environment.

See *marketing segmentation* and *target marketing.*

nickelodeon a small movie theater.

By 1908, about 9,000 nickelodeons (often converted store fronts) were operating in the United States. More than 20 million people were going to the movies. They each paid 5 cents to see about an hour's worth of short films.

See *movie palace* and *motion picture*.

Nielsen Media Research the world's best known TV ratings company.

The company's Web site <www.nielsenmedia.com> provides background and information about the company and its rating systems.

See *rating*.

noise something that interferes with the delivery of a message.

There are three major types of noise.

1. Semantic noise occurs when people attach different meanings to words or phrases, or when a communicator's message is poorly worded or presented.

2. Mechanical noise occurs when a machine or electronic device that aids in the transmission of the message breaks down or fails to deliver the message or any part of it. This includes static in broadcasts, or denying a user access to online information when Internet services "go down."

3. Environmental noise comes from sources external to the communication process. This would include things like interruptions when people are reading a book or watching a television documentary.

nominalism the ontological doctrine that the mind creates *universals* by abstracting from particulars; universals exist only as thoughts in our minds.

See *realism* and *ontology*.

nominal measures see *levels of measurement*.

nonparametric statistics statistics used with nominal or ordinal data.

See *parametric statistics* and *levels of measurement*.

nonprobability sampling a type of sampling method in which the cases selected cannot be generalized to a larger *population*.

Focus groups are usually composed of nonprobability samples, which are often used when it is difficult to obtain a probability sample or when the research is exploratory.

nonrecursive modeling *causal analysis* that involves two-way, or mutual, effects between *variables*.

See *recursive modeling*.

nonsampling error *measurement error* that is not a function of *sampling error*.

For example, a poorly worded survey question can produce nonsampling error.

normative theory a general set of ideals or principles that, if followed, will result in an ideal or desired condition or state.

In the field of *mass communication*, normative theory addresses the following question: What is the ideal mass media system? At the broadest level, the debate focuses on general ideals or principles for guiding mass media institutions and their workers. Scholars call these normative theories, which attempt to construct the ideal media system.

Normative theory focuses on how things should be. It establishes an ideal for structuring and operating a mass media system. If people or institutions work toward that ideal, the result is assumed to be good for society and media workers. Because normative theories deal with what is good or desired, they fall under the purview of *ethics* rather than science. *Scientific theory*, in contrast, is an explanation or interpretation of why things happen or occur; it attempts to explain what is.

Some scholars and professionals argue that normative theories ideally should provide general guidelines for developing specific *codes of ethics*, or specific rules of conduct. In practice, however, the linkage between the two is not always clearly specified.

During the 20th century, scholars and journalists created and proposed a number of normative theories of the press. The best known work was a book produced in 1956 called "Four Theories of the Press." The authors, Frederick Siebert, Theodore Peterson, and Wilbur Schramm, synthesized much of the discussion and debate up to that time into four major normative theories: authoritarian, libertarian, social responsibility, and Soviet or communist. Development and democratic participant theories are two more recent theories.

• Authoritarian theory holds that the press should promote and never challenge the interests of those in power. In addition, those in power have the authority to control and censor the press, if necessary. Media workers who violate these rules can and should be punished.

This theory has been used to describe the early development of the press. Monarchs and rulers in Great Britain and Europe during the 16th and 17th centuries often exercised direct control over the press and severely punished those who violated their rules.

Although authoritarian theory is not held in high regard in Western countries today, it must be remembered that during the Middle Ages many people believed monarchs were divine rulers. In other words, people believed rulers received their power directly from God. If that was the case, it followed that rulers had the right to control the press.

Although this belief is less prevalent today, much of the world's media systems still operate under authoritarian practices. In many countries, especially in those struggling economically and where political conditions are unstable, people can and often are jailed for printing information that offends rulers. Rulers often justify punitive actions by arguing their policies and actions eventually will benefit the public, but they must be able to implement such policies without criticism or protest.

• Libertarian theory is at the other side of the political continuum. It holds that government or the public should have no authority or control over the mass media. The media should be free to do whatever they want, even if that leads to the production of false or misleading content. The libertarian theory is basically classical free-market economic theory (or laissez-faire economics) applied to mass media.

Although at first glance this theory also does not appear to be very attractive, proponents argue or assume truth will emerge in a libertarian-based system, because the marketplace will eliminate falsehood. In other words, people and organizations will not spend money on mass media that produce false or misleading information. They need the "truth" to make good personal and business decisions, so only those media that excel in this regard will thrive and grow.

The origins of the libertarian or "free press" theory are usually traced to the writings of John Milton (*Areopagitica*) and John Stuart Mill (*On Liberty*). Formal application of the theory to real life is sometimes attributed to the U.S. Constitution, which states that "Congress shall make no law ... abridging the freedom of speech or of the press."

However, absolute freedom of speech and press does not exist, even in the relatively press-tolerant United States. Many legal and informal constraints on the distribution of information and ideas (e.g., libel laws) limit the applicability of the libertarian model to U.S. media. In fact, most media theorists argue that the U.S. system comes closer to a social responsibility model.

• Social responsibility theory is said to have its origins in the Commission on Freedom of the Press report issued in 1947. Basically, the commission's recommendation challenged the libertarian model.

More specifically, the commission was concerned that the growth of large-scale news media organizations would hinder diversity in the marketplace of ideas. In other words, big business threatened the free flow of ideas and information. The commission assumed that big business would serve its own interests before those of the public.

Although this assumption has yet to be thoroughly tested, the social responsibility model is widely assumed to be the normative theory that most closely models mass media in the United States today. According to the commission, the press, in order to perform its function, must (1) provide truthful accounts in a context that gives these accounts meaning to people; (2) serve as a public forum for comment and criticism; (3) provide a representative picture of society's various cultures and groups; (4) clarify a society's goals and values; and (5) give people full access to the day's intelligence.

Consistent with the libertarian model, proponents of the social responsibility model argue that, for the most part, mass media, not government, should regulate and police themselves. Media and journalists who are irresponsible should be censured or punished by the profession, not the government, since the latter could threaten the free flow of information.

One exception, however, involves over-the-air broadcast media. Since bandwidth is limited, the government (*Federal Communications Commission*) has the authority to license some broadcast media and demand that they serve the public interest. In this respect, the social responsibility model probably fits broadcast media better than print media.

One can quibble about whether broadcast media are really meeting the public's need for information and entertainment programming. Even major critics of the media agree the media must be responsible to the public in one form or another. But critics disagree on the methods for ensuring responsibility. The democratic theory of the press comes closer to capturing their views (see discussion below).

• Soviet or communist theory holds that the media should be used to advance and further the aims of communism. At the time Siebert and his colleagues were writing, one-third of the world was communist and the Soviet Union was this ideology's unchallenged leader. The breakup of the Soviet Union in the late 1980s has diminished the importance of this theory, but the model may still be applied to China (although that country's media system also is changing), Cuba, North Korea, and other countries.

Ideally, the goal of communism is to create a classless society, one in which everyone is equal not just in political terms (one vote, one person) but also economic terms (equality in income). In a communist country, the people or the working class, in principle, own the mass media. In practice, though, the communist party usually has been the publisher and editor. And points of view critical of the communist party were often censored.

• Development media theory emerged after "Four Theories of the Press" was written and holds that the press should promote economic development and should use restraint when criticizing the government until a nation attains a comfortable level of economic development and wealth. This model, which draws its roots from the authoritarian theory, was said to be suitable for the so-called third-world countries, which were struggling economically and politically.

Many news organizations in third-world countries do cooperate heavily with government officials. They refrain from printing information critical of the government or its leaders. Yet there is little evidence to show the "kid gloves" approach has any beneficial effects. Few of the so-called developing nations have been able to escape poverty and grow economically.

• Democratic-participant media (DPM)theory seeks to create a media system in which everyone has an opportunity to participate in a democratic fashion. This theory has been advanced by many neo-Marxist and cultural theorists who are critical of capitalism as an economic institution. They argue that mass media in Western countries primarily serve corporate elites. They seek a more equitable and fair society and contend that more citizen access to the media is necessary to do that.

Some DPM theorists also argue in favor of discourse ethics, which would give ordinary people, not just media professionals, a say in the development of media ethics. Codes of ethics should not be established in advance. Rather, they should be negotiated through an on-going discourse between professionals and citizens.

DPM theory is a much more liberalized version of social responsibility theory. It seeks greater democratic participation and is appealing because it should help decentralize power in mass media industries.

However, it would be difficult to implement without major economic and structural changes. Mass media organizations themselves are not very open to the idea of outside interference or control. There also is the pragmatic problem of how to give everyone an opportunity for input. Moreover, even if such access were available, elites no doubt would still participate in the discourse at higher rates than ordinary citizens, thus blunting the impact of democratic participation.

Mass communication professor Shelton Gunaratne also argues that the four theories of the press and their offshoots are based on Eurocentric history, theory and practice. He argues that scholars and professionals need to de-Westernize communication theory. Using various strands of systems theory, he advocates a more humanocentric theoretical framework—one that reflects the integration of Eastern *ontology* with Western *epistemology*.

Sources: Frederick Siebert, Theodore Peterson and Wilbur Schramm, *Four Theories of the Press* (Urbana. IL: University of Illinois Press, 1956); John C. Merrill and S. Jack Odell, *Philosophy and Journalism* (New York: Longman, 1983); Dennis McQuail, *Mass Communication Theory: An Introduction*, 3rd ed. (London: Sage Publications, 1994); Theodore L. Glasser and Peggy J. Bowers, "Justifying Change and Control: An Application of Discourse Ethics to the Role of Mass Media," pp. 399-418 in David Demers and K. Viswanath (eds.), *Mass Media, Social Control and Social Change: A Macrosocial Perspective* (Ames: Iowa State University Press, 1999); and Shelton Gunaratne, *The Dao of the Press: A Humanocentric Theory* (Cresskill, NJ: Hampton Press, 2005).

norms rules that guide behavior.

Norms usually reinforce *values*. Norms may be *formal* (written rules or laws) or *informal* (unwritten verbal rules).

null hypothesis a statement or claim that there is a no relationship between two or more variables—that a *state of independence* exists.

See *hypothesis*.

N. W. Ayer & Son a 19th-century advertising agency that created the open contract.

Francis Wayland Ayer was only 21 in 1869 when he founded N. W. Ayer & Son, an advertising agency that borrowed his father name even though he was not involved in the business. Ayer used his father's name to give people the impression that the business was larger and more established than it really was. (He gave his father 50 percent control of the business.) It seemed to work.

At the end of the first year, the firm made $15,000. Within four years, in 1873, the agency earned $79,000. His father died that year and Francis took over full control of the business.

In 1874, the agency published "Ayer & Son's Manual for Advertisers," which listed newspapers with which the agency did business. In 1875, the agency introduced the "open contract," which guaranteed clients the lowest possible advertising rates the agency could negotiate with publications. The clients paid Ayer for buying the space. Previously, advertising agents worked for and were paid directly by the publications.

In 1876, N. W. Ayer & Son began publishing "The Advertiser's Guide," a quarterly magazine for clients and others that contained articles and essays on business, advertising, and other information. In 1877, the company purchased Coe, Wetherhill & Co., which is believed to be the first advertising agency in the United States.

N. W. Ayer & Son began offering its clients production services in 1884. The company wrote its first ad for a tobacco company. It hired a full-time copy writer six years later and an artist eight years later. The company's client list eventually included industry giants R. J. Reynolds, Canada Dry, H. J. Heinz, Cadillac, and American Telephone and Telegraph.

When Ayer died in 1923, his son-in-law, Wilfred W. Fry, took over control of the agency. The company opened offices overseas in 1927 and changed its name to N. W. Ayer ABH International. Later, the company changed its name again to N. W. Ayer & Partners and was purchased by Bcom3, a holding company that employs 18,000 people in 92 countries.

N.W. Ayer was the first advertising agency to develop commercials for radio and for television, and the first to sponsor television shows. In the early 2000s, the company had more than $250 million in billings. Its clients include Continental Airlines, KitchenAid, and General Mills.

In April 2002, Bcom3 announced it would retire the N. W. Ayer name and consolidate the operations with Kaplan Thaler Group, another advertising agency owned by the holding company. To commemorate the retirement of the Ayer name, Bcom3 donated its historical archives dating back 133 years to the National Museum of American History at the Smithsonian Institute in Washington, D.C.

See *advertising*.

Sources: The Center for Interactive Advertising at the University of Texas at Austin, <www.ciadvertising.org>; N. W. Ayer & Partners Web site, <www.nwayer.com>.

objectivity see *ethic of objectivity.*

obscene material pornographic (sexually arousing) content that is not protected by the *First Amendment.*
　　See *obscenity.*

obscenity, law of an area of media law that focuses on whether pornographic content is protected by the *First Amendment.*
　　No area of the law is less settled and more controversial than that associated with obscenity. The courts, police, and pornographers have all struggled to define the term, and no solution is in sight. Almost everyone agrees *pornography* is content intended to be sexually arousing. But not all pornography is obscene, which means it does not have protection under the First Amendment.
　　The U.S. Supreme Court has handed down two major rulings on obscenity. The first, Roth v. U.S. (1957), stated that obscene material is not protected by the First Amendment because it is "utterly without redeeming social importance." However, after that decision it was difficult for prosecutors to convict people who produced and distributed hard-core pornography, because it was hard to prove something had no redeeming social importance.
　　Sixteen years later, the court relaxed the standard and established a three-part test for determining whether sexual materials are obscene. The case (Miller v. California, 1973) involved a California man who was convicted under a state law for mailing a brochure that advertised four books ("An Illustrated History of Pornography," "Intercourse," "Man-Woman, Sex Orgies Illustrated") and a movie ("Marital Intercourse"). The brochure contained graphic pictures of genitalia and sexual activities.
　　The court held that the materials were obscene because they (1) appealed to the "prurient interest" (i.e., they incited unwholesome lust and

desires) of the "average person applying contemporary community standards," (2) were "patently offensive" (i.e., excess of hardcore sexual detail, such as bestiality, sadomasochism), and (3) lacked serious literary, artistic, political or scientific value, when judged as a whole. All three criteria must be met for something to be labeled obscene.

In the Miller case, the court also decentralized the process of determining whether something was obscene. The local community, which might be defined as a city, county or state, could now determine what was obscene. This meant definitions could vary from community to community. Needless to say, this definition created problems for the pornographic industry, whose products were often distributed through national distribution networks and chain stores. A magazine could be judged obscene in one jurisdiction and legal in another.

Despite making it easier to prosecute producers of obscene materials, the Miller case has not put a damper on the production of pornographic material. The industry has grown dramatically since the 1970s. About $15 billion a year is spent on pornographic materials. Easy access to pornography on the Internet has contributed greatly to its expansion since the 1990s.

See *law*.

Sources: *Roth v. United States*, 354 U.S. 476 (1957), p. 484, and *Miller v. California*, 413 U.S. 15 (1973).

observation the act of making or recording a measurement.

ombudsman an experienced journalist who has been given the authority and independence to investigate complaints filed against a newspaper and to criticize that newspaper, if necessary.

According to Organization of News Ombudsmen, which has 75 members worldwide, the job of an ombudsman is to receive and investigate complaints from readers, listeners or viewers. The word "ombudsman" is Scandinavian in origin, and was first applied to a man who was appointed in 1809 to handle complaints against the government. The news ombudsman also is sometimes called reader representative, reader advocate or public editor.

In 1968, the "Louisville Courier-Journal" created the first news ombudsman position in the United States. Since then the number has grown to about 40 and leveled off. Only larger newspapers, like "The Washington Post," can afford to employ an ombudsman.

Although the purpose of the ombudsman is to make the newspaper more accountable to the public, the result has often been less than gratifying to many scholars who study the mass media. Ombudsmen usually rule against readers and in favor of the news organization.

An analysis of 50 such articles listed on the ONO's Web site on December 18, 2001, showed that more than half of the time (27 of the 50 articles) the ombudsmen ruled against the readers and supported the newspaper. Only 20 percent of the time (11 of 50 articles) did the critics criticize the newspaper. The remaining (12 of 50) articles were informational or didn't take a stand one way or the other.

In this respect, the ombudsman plays the role of teacher, helping to educate the public about the job that journalists and news organizations perform.

Media scholars also point out that ombudsmen rarely draw attention to broader issues, such as the *social control* function of mass media. Instead, they often deal with trivial issues, like grammar and factual errors.

Of the 50 articles examined at the ONO Web site, 11 were critical of their newspapers for spelling errors, translation errors, improper use of verbs, inaccuracies, improper use of photographs, failure to call news sources to get their side of the story, and whether it was appropriate to place the World Series on the front page. None dealt with the role and function of mass media or the *mainstream bias.*

As a consequence, critics like James Ettema and Theodore Glasser often argue that ombudsmen are merely public relations spokespersons. Critics see them as a "safety valve" for the newspaper—giving readers, listeners, and viewers the impression that the news organization is responsive to their needs, but failing to provide real insights into why the news generally support the status quo.

Sources: James S. Ettema and Theodore L. Glasser, "Public Accountability or Public Relations? Newspaper Ombudsmen Define Their Role," *Journalism Quarterly,* 64 (1987): 3-12.

off-network programming see *syndicated media service.*

offset printing a process in which the matter to be printed is copied photographically onto a metal plate and then placed on a cylinder in a printing press and inked to make an imprint on the paper.

Offset printing is increasingly being replaced or supplemented by other, more convenient and sometimes less expensive printing methods, including digital printing methods.

Ogilvy, David (1911-1999) an advertising executive who became world famous for his Hathaway shirt advertisements, which featured a man wearing a black eye patch.

Ogilvy was born in England in 1911, the youngest child of a classics scholar and a stock broker. He attended two colleges but never graduated.

During the Depression, he worked at a restaurant and sold stoves. In 1935, he wrote a manual for other stove salesmen, which stated in one part: "The more prospects you talk to, the more sales you expose yourself to, the more orders you will get. But never mistake quantity of calls for quality of salesmanship."

A short time later, one of his brothers, who worked for a British advertising agency, gave him a job. Ogilvy became an account executive and spent a year in the United States, working for George Gallup's Audience

Research Institute. There he learned a great deal about consumer and public opinion.

During World War II, he worked for British Intelligence Service in Washington D.C. and advocated using public opinion polling to gather intelligence. The U.S. government took this advice when implementing policies in Europe after the war.

After the war he farmed briefly among the Amish in Pennsylvania. But he returned to New York in 1948 where, with the financial backing of Mather & Crowther in London, he and a colleague, Anderson Hewitt, founded Hewitt, Ogilvy, Benson & Mather. Although Ogilvy knew little about advertising, he was a superb salesman and had a creative mind.

The Hathaway ad was extremely successful because the man with the eye patch was perceived to be a man of refinement and high social standing, which appealed to consumers. In 1957, Ogilvy also drew praise and recognition for another advertisement: "At sixty miles an hour the loudest noise in this new Rolls-Royce comes from the electric clock."

Ogilvy's firm, which later renamed itself Ogilvy and Mather, serviced English advertisers at first. However, eventually he secured contracts with Lever Brothers, General Foods, Shell, Sears, and American Express.

In 1963, he wrote "Confessions of an Advertising Man," which sold more than one million copies and has been translated into 14 languages. The advice he gave in that book, which also earned him a reputation as the king of advertising aphorisms, included: (1) The consumer is not a moron; (2) We prefer the discipline of knowledge to the anarchy of ignorance; we pursue knowledge the way a pig pursues truffles; and (3) Never run an advertisement you would not want your own family to see.

In 1973, Ogilvy retired and moved to France, where he had purchased an estate. Although not active in day-to-day operations, he continued to advise company executives and came out of retirement briefly in 1980 to oversee an office in India and one in Germany. He also lectured around the world.

In 1989, WPP purchased the Ogilvy Group, a move that made WPP the world's largest marketing communications firm (see text for more information on WPP) at that time.

When he turned 75, Ogilvy was asked if there was anything that eluded him in life. "Knighthood, and a big family—10 children," he said. He had one child in his first marriage. He was married two other times.

Although he didn't achieve knighthood, he was made a commander of the British empire and was elected to the U.S. Advertising Hall of Fame and France's "Order of Arts and Letters." He died in 1999 at the age of 88. A biography on his company's Web site calls him the "quintessential advertising man."

Sources: David Ogilvy, *Confessions of an Advertising Man* (New York: 1963); Ogilvy & Mather Web site, <www.ogilvy.com>.

oligopoly a economic term referring to a market condition where only a few competitors dominate a particular industry or activity.

See *duopoly.*

ontology a branch of philosophy that seeks to explain the nature of existence or reality.

Classical philosophers argued that God must exist because existence is one of the elements of the most perfect being (the ontological argument). Contemporary scientists focus more on trying to ascertain the fundamental physical properties of the universe (atoms, quarks, etc.).

In the social sciences and the field of mass communication, ontology is important because all scholarship and research makes assumptions, explicit or not, about the nature of reality. To the extent those assumptions are inaccurate, so will be the theories or data presented.

In practice, the debate over ontology tends to be an academic one, because there is no way, in the final analysis, to determine the true nature of reality. Part of the problem is that humans know the world mostly through their senses (i.e., they cannot directly perceive reality) and rationalism, as an alternative, cannot be fully divorced from those senses. However, ontological issues are important because they help scholars understand each others' perspectives or theories.

Some of the key debates in ontology center on *free will* vs. *determinism, idealism* vs. *materialism,* and *nominalism* vs. *realism.*

O&O short for own and operate.

See *television network.*

open contract see *N. W. Ayer & Son.*

open-ended measure a question in a survey that does not include a list of *responses.* Instead, respondents are asked to talk freely about their feelings on the subject and responses are coded verbatim.

open-ended question see *open-ended measure.*

open-meetings law (or sunshine law) a law that requires governmental agencies and departments to keep their meetings open to the public.

The federal government and all of the states have passed open-meetings laws, which require public officials to conduct most matters of public policy at public meetings. The public may be excluded, however, when personnel or other private matters are discussed.

operating system a set of programs for organizing the resources and activities of a computer.

During the 1950s, IBM introduced Fortran, which helped scientists solve engineering problems. Today Microsoft Corp. makes operating systems that are used on about 90 percent of the world's computers.

operationalization a *measure* or *indicator* of some concept.
See *operationalize*.

operationalize the process of creating *measures* or *indicators* of *concepts*.
In *survey research*, for instance, the measure or indicator is a question, e.g., "How old are you?" The *question* is the operational definition of age, the measure of age.

oppositional decoding a condition that exists when media consumers read or interpret messages in a manner that differs or is in opposition to the intended, dominant or preferred manner.
See *communication, hegemony, ideology,* and *media imperialism*.

order bias a type of systematic *measurement error* stemming from the order in which a list of *attributes* or products is presented.
In a *telephone survey*, items are often rotated to control for order bias.

ordinal measures see *levels of measurement*.

organizational/group communication communication between two or more *social actors* who are members of a larger organization (or organizations).
The distinction between *interpersonal communication* and *organizational/group communication* is thin, since both may involve the study of *dyad*s. But the latter focuses more on how the communication is shaped by the constraints of a larger organization (or organizations).

original syndication see *syndicated media service*.

outliers extreme *values* in a *distribution* that can distort estimates of some statistics.

over-the-air broadcast signals that are transmitted through the air, as opposed to signals that are transmitted via cable, telephone lines or satellite.
See *Community Antenna Television* and *satellite television*.

ownership rules see *media ownership rules*.

P

packet switched network a procedure for transmitting information from computer to computer by breaking larger files into smaller ones.

Packet switched network was created to make transmission of information more efficient. Large files can tie up a computer for a long periods of time, which in turn could tie up an entire network. Packet switched network breaks down data into small "packets" and transmits them from computer to computer until they reach their final destination.

pagination the process of sequentially arranging pages in a publication.

paired comparison a study in which *respondents* are asked to compare and rate two products or services.

Compare to *monadic ratings*.

Paley, William S. (1901-1990) former owner and chairman of *CBS* radio and television; sometimes called the "godfather of American broadcasting."

Paley purchased CBS radio in 1929 and built the failing company into a profitable nationwide network of hundreds of radio and television station affiliates. He helped launch the careers of many Hollywood stars, including Frank Sinatra, Bing Crosby, and Kate Smith.

In the 1940s, he expanded into television, and by 1950 CBS emerged as the leader in ratings and programming—a position it held for 25 years. CBS television introduced such stars as Lucille Ball and Ed Sullivan and recruited Jack Benny and Jackie Gleason from other networks.

Paley also supported controversial programs such as "All in the Family" and "M*A*S*H" and news programming, including *Edward R. Murrow's* "See It Now" show and "60 Minutes." But he was criticized severely for pulling Edward R. Murrow's "See It Now" program off the air in 1958.

See *Murrow, Edward R.*

Source: "William Paley: 1901-1990," Macleans 45 (Nov. 5, 1990), p. 58.

panel study a *longitudinal study* that includes the same *respondents*.

paper a light-weight thin material usually made in sheets from a pulp prepared from hemp, bark, rags or wood and used for writing or printing.
　　See *papyrus* and *vellum*.

paperback a book whose cover is made of paper-based materials instead of cloth or other harder substances; also called softcover or softbound.
　　Mass paperbacks are found at supermarkets and drug stores and are the most popular. They are small books whose themes focus heavily on romance and mystery. Next most popular are the trade paperbacks, which include nonfiction works for general audiences.
　　See *hardcover* and *trade books*.

papyrus a light-weight paper-like writing material made from a tall reed.
　　The leaves were interlocked like a woven basket and then hammered until they fused together. The final product was a scroll, which was unrolled as it was read. Some scrolls were 30 feet in length. Papyrus made it possible to store and transmit knowledge and information easily over space and through time, which made it easier for elites to rule from distant places.

parameter see *population parameter*.

parametric statistics statistics that can be used with interval or ratio data.
　　Parametric statistics assume that the data are normally distributed.
　　See descriptive statistics, inferential statistics, levels of measurement, and *nonparametric statistics.*

parchment a writing material made from animal skins.
　　See *vellum* for more details.

participant monitoring (or second-party tape-recording) the act of tape recording a conversation between two people, one of whom is unaware that he or she is being recorded and one who is doing the recording.
　　Police often use participant monitoring to catch criminals, and investigative journalists sometimes use it to protect themselves from libel or privacy lawsuits. Ten states ban participant monitoring; the rest allow it.
　　See *libel* and *privacy, invasion of.*

paradigm (a) a typical example or model to be replicated or followed; **(b)** a set of beliefs, values, techniques, and methods shared by members of a given scientific community.
　　The concept of paradigm is often associated with philosopher and historian Thomas Kuhn and his influential book, "The Structure of Scientific Revolutions." In the first edition of the book, he differentiates 21 uses of the

term, but in the postscript to the second edition he distinguishes the two meanings provided above.

Kuhn's book challenges the conventional wisdom about the development of scientific knowledge, which emphasizes the piecemeal accumulation of knowledge through empirical observation. Instead, he argues that science is less rational than most would argue, and its history contains many examples of revolutionary changes, where scientists abandon previous knowledge and epistemologies when a new paradigm challenges conventional theories.

Kuhn's model contains five major stages. The first stage is "immature science," where scientists work to establish some agreement about the problems to be solved. In the next stage, "normal science," there is consensus about the problems to be invested, the theoretical and methodological rules to be followed, and the criteria for judging good research. The third stage is "crisis," where some new theory or paradigm (e.g., Newton's "Principia Mathematica") challenges the traditional paradigm. The fourth stage involves "revolution," where many scientists abandon the older paradigm for the new one. The fifth stage is "resolution," which involves the institutionalization of the new paradigm and the return to normal science.

The key point of Kuhn's model is that there is no strictly logical reason for the change of a paradigm. Science can only be properly understood as a conceptual product that is historically and socially located. Science is socially constructed; it cannot be simply "read-off" nature—it is mediated by history and culturally shaped paradigms.

Kuhn's model has been criticized on a number of fronts. First, critics have accused his model of being too relativistic—of failing to recognize that science has produced knowledge that is meaningful to everyday life (although Kuhn did not think of himself as a relativist). Second, critics point out that science is not as monolithic as Kuhn suggested. This is particularly true in the social sciences, where many scholars argue there are a number of competing paradigms (see mass communication research and positivism). Third, critics argue that his claims that theory-neutral observation is impossible are overstated. Fourth, many critics argue that scientific revolutions are more rational than he depicts them.

However, for all its faults, Kuhn's paradigm does sensitize scientists to the notion that science is not just a collection of obvious facts and theories; rather, it also involves elements of discourse and rhetoric, in which some scientific theories or paradigms garner more support because of unique social and historical circumstances.

Sources: Thomas S. Kuhn, *The Structure of Scientific Revolutions* (Chicago: University of Chicago Press, 1962); Thomas S. Kuhn, *The Structure of Scientific Revolutions*, 2nd ed. (Chicago: University of Chicago Press, 1970); and Roy Bhaskar, *A Realist Theory of Science*, 2nd ed. (Hemel Hempstead: Harvester Press, 1978).

partisan press a time period extending from the end of the Revolutionary War to about the 1830s when newspapers aligned themselves with one or more of the new political parties.

During this time period, newspapers published a great deal of political content supporting or condemning various political parties and leaders. Political parties also provided financial support for newspapers.

More specifically, Alexander Hamilton became the leader of the conservative Federalists. He sponsored and supported the "Gazette of the United States," a paper edited by John Fenno. The federalists argued for a responsible government.

In contrast, *Thomas Jefferson,* who was the leader of the anti-Federalists (or "Republicans," which actually became the Democratic Party in the 19th century) and the third U.S. president, argued for a responsive government—one that meets the needs of the people. The anti-Federalists' views were represented in the "National Gazette," which was edited by Philip Freneau.

These two political parties and their newspapers lashed out against one another in numerous debates, essays and columns. This may not seem all that noteworthy today. But back then the world had never seen anything like it. The United States had become the testing ground for freedom of the press.

But that tolerance only went so far. The content was often inaccurate, scandalous, and libelous. Even Jefferson, who was an adamant supporter of a free press, wrote in 1813 after years of being criticized by Federalist newspapers: "The newspapers of our country by their abandoned spirit of falsehood, have more effectually destroyed the utility of the press than all the shackles devised by Bonaparte."

The partisan press era came into decline after the growth of the *penny papers,* which de-emphasized politics to some degree and placed more emphasis on social and religious events and crime and business news. By the 20th century, newspapers had embraced the *ethic of objectivity* as the guiding principle for generating news stories. Commentary and opinion were placed on the editorial pages.

Source: Saul K. Padover, *Thomas Jefferson on Democracy* (New York: Penguin, 1939), pp. 92-92.

pass-along rate the number of people in addition to the subscribers who read a magazine or a publication.

Most magazines and newspapers are read by more than one person. The pass-along rate tries to account for those people. For example, in the 1970s "Saturday Evening Post" had 6 million subscribers, but a pass-along rate of 14 million readers (20 million readers altogether). Advertising executives use the pass-along rate to convince manufacturers and businesses of the value of *advertising* in their publications.

path analysis a statistical procedure associated with *regression analysis* that enables measuring the strength and direction of influences, including direct and indirect *relationships*, among three or more *variables*.

Payne Fund Studies, The first major scientific study of mass *media effects*.

The project got its name from The Payne Fund, a private foundation which provided financial support. A total of 13 studies were conducted from 1929 to 1932. One set of studies examined the content of the films and another set looked at the effects.

The content studies found that three-fourths of the films had only three major themes: crime, sex, and love. Most also openly portrayed use of tobacco and liquor, even though Prohibition was in effect.

The effects studies found that movies could change attitudes toward racial groups (positive and negative), stimulate emotions (including terror, fright, sorrow), disturb sleep patterns, and generate norms contrary to contemporary values (e.g., promiscuousness). Children who attended more movies exhibited poorer performance in school. And one set of studies concluded that movies contributed to juvenile delinquency. Although the methods used in the latter set of studies were not sophisticated enough to reach such a conclusion, the impact at the time caused a great deal of concern.

In response, the movie industry strengthened its Production Code, which quieted the critics for a while. But the Payne Fund Studies helped fuel the popular belief that mass media could have powerful effects. That belief was reinforced in 1938, when CBS radio broadcast Orson Welles' adaptation of H. G. Wells' classic book, "War of the Worlds." The broadcast was so believable more than a million people panicked.

The Payne Fund Studies and the "War of the Worlds" panic gave rise to what researchers later would refer to as the magic bullet or hypodermic needle theory of media effects. As the metaphors imply, the mass media were viewed as having the power to shoot or inject audiences with various kinds of effects, most of which were viewed as harmful. But this powerful-effects model was relatively short-lived.

See *mass communication research, media effects,* and *War of the Worlds*.

Source: Shearon A. Lowery and Melvin L. DeFleur, *Milestones in Mass Communication Research* (New York: Longman, 1988, 2nd ed.).

payola the practice, which is illegal, of recording companies paying disc jockeys to play their records.

During the 1950s, the *Communications Act of 1934* was amended to ban the practice of payola, which gave an unfair advantage to large recording studios. However, today record companies can still get their records played if the radio station announces who paid for the air time (pay-for-play) or if companies pay for 10-second commercials that run with their songs (pay-for-say).

penny papers see *penny press*.

penny press newspapers that emerged during the 1830s and cost one cent.

On September 3, 1833, the "New York Sun" became the first successful penny newspaper in the United States. Prior to this time, most newspapers cost six cents, an amount that was beyond the means of most ordinary people.

But a 23-year-old Philadelphia printer named Benjamin Day believed he could publish a newspaper that drew most of its revenue not from subscription fees but from advertising. He was right.

An important part of Day's success formula was an emphasis on local and crime news. Day hired George Wisner, a former Bow Street reporter in London, to cover the court beat, and his reports soon took up two full columns in the newspaper. Within six months the newspaper achieved a circulation of 8,000, making it twice as large as the next nearest rival in the city.

Another factor that appears to have contributed to the commercial success of the" Sun" was its moderate editorial stance. Unlike other newspapers, which vigorously supported one of the various political parties and were often funded by them, Day insisted on keeping his newspaper "neutral." He wrote few editorials on controversial subjects. This approach offended fewer readers and advertisers and probably helped boost circulation.

Day sold the paper in the late 1830s, a decision he later regretted. By that time, dozens of other penny papers had been established in New York City, Albany, Boston, Philadelphia, Baltimore and New Orleans. Day's printing and publishing businesses flourished, and he died a very wealthy man in 1889.

The penny press is often thought of as the first mass medium, because it appealed not just to elites but to the masses. The penny press also is given credit for broadening public input into the political system.

Source: Frank M. O'Brien, *The Story of the Sun* (New York: George H. Doran Company, 1918).

Pentagon Papers see *New York Times v. United States*.

percentage a *proportion* multiplied by 100; also called a *relative frequency*.

A proportion is the *ratio* of one group to the total. Thus, if the total sample size is 1,000 and 333 *respondents* are under age 35, the proportion of respondents under age 35 is .333 and the percentage under age 35 is 33.3 (.333 X 100=33.3%).

perceptual map a graphic presentation of the results from *discriminant analysis*, a multivariate statistical technique.

The map shows in visual form how products or services are perceived in relation to each other in terms of price, convenience, service, dependability, etc.

perfect binding a book binding process that involves gluing the pages to the spine of a book cover, which may be paper (softcover) or cloth (hardcover).

Perfect binding came into favor after World War II because it was much cheaper than sewing the pages to the spine. Most books produced today are perfect-bound.

periodical a publication other than a newspaper that appears at regular intervals.

Magazines, newsletters, and *scientific journals* are all periodicals.

periodical postage rate a special, low-cost postage rate offered through the U.S. Postal Service and available only to magazines, periodicals, and other publications (formerly known as second-class mail).

The Postal Service charges less to these customers partly to stimulate the flow of information and ideas.

See *media mail.*

personal interviews interviews that are conducted in person, as opposed to over the phone.

This is generally the most expensive way to collect survey research data, but it offers a greater opportunity to probe issues in more depth.

personalist ethics an action or rule is ethical if the individual makes decisions based on mystical insights, "god," intuition, emotion, conscience or instinct.

See *ethical decision-making.*

Pew Center for Civic Journalism a nonprofit foundation that calls itself "an incubator for civic journalism experiments that enable news organizations to create and refine better ways of reporting the news to re-engage people in public life."

The Pew Charitable Trusts established the Pew Center in 1993. Since then, the Center has sponsored more than 125 civic journalism projects. For more information: Pew Center for Civic Journalism, 7100 Baltimore Avenue, Suite 101, College Park, Maryland 20740 <www.pewcenter.org>.

phenomenology a philosophical approach whose main aim is the analysis and description of everyday life, i.e., the "life-world," and its states of consciousness.

Phenomenology "brackets" (ignores) judgments about the impact of social structure on *social actors.* It argues that people generally take the everyday world for granted, but phenomenological analysis must show how they do that.

Sociologists Peter Berger and T. Luckmann wrote the best-known work of phenomenology, which argues that reality is socially constructed, not an objective entity to be discovered. Phenomenology is critical of positivistic methods of analysis, but phenomenology itself has been criticized for dealing with trivial topics, for failing to employ empirical methods, and for failing to analyze the impact of social structure.

See *humanism, hermeneutics* and *positivism.*

Source: Peter Berger and T. Luckmann, *The Social Construction of Reality* (New York: Doubleday, 1967).

Phillips, David Graham (1867-1911) a newspaper reporter, book author, and freelance writer who exposed graft and corruption in the U.S. Senate in his 10-part series, "The Treason of the Senate," which was published in "Cosmopolitan" magazine.

The series documented how rich businessmen bribed senators.

See *muckraking era.*

phonograph a device for playing back music or sound that has been recorded on a circular disk or a cylinder.

A needle or stylus is used to transmit sound vibrations. In the early days, the recordings were made acoustically as opposed to electronically. A singer would project her or his voice into a horn, which was then transformed into grooves on a cylinder or disk.

See *gramaphone* and *Edison, Thomas A.*

photojournalism the profession or process of producing stories through photographs.

Photojournalism can trace its roots to the late 1800s, with the works of *Jacob Riis* and others. But photojournalism as a profession didn't become a major journalistic force in the United States until the 1920s, when Henry Luce hired Margaret Bourke-White, an accomplished industrial and architectural photographer, to take pictures for "Fortune" magazine. In 1936, Luce then moved her over to "Life" magazine, where she was one of the four original photographers.

The philosophy of "Life" magazine was to create stories from pictures rather than from words. Photographers were encouraged to take a lot of pictures, from which the best would be selected. Text and cutlines were used sparingly and were added after the pictures were laid out. The story was in the pictures, not the words.

Today, newspaper photojournalists have increasingly turned to using digital cameras as opposed to film. Digital photos do not need to be developed—they are simply stored in the camera and downloaded to a computer, where they can be easily manipulated and integrated into newspaper text. However, the technology still is not as sharp as film-based photography, and so it is not yet widely employed in some magazine photography.

Sources: Michael L. Carlebach, *The Origins of Photojournalism in America* (Washington, D.C.: Smithsonian Institution Press, 1992) and Tim N. Gidal, *Modern Photojournalism: Origin and Evolution, 1920-1933* (New York: Macmillan, 1973).

pilot the first episode of a television or radio program.

Television broadcast networks request pilot programs when making a decision about what programs to broadcast in a new season. Most order about 20 pilots but only select about 10 programs for actual broadcast. Pilots may be produced by a network or by independent companies.

When a pilot is selected, the network typically will order more episodes. Thirteen is a full season. However, if a show is viewed as being risky, the network may order as few as two or three episodes. The industry calls this short-ordering.

pirating stealing, either through **(a)** *copyright* infringement or through **(b)** broadcasting without approval of a government.

The first definition deals with duplication and distribution of copyrighted printed material (e.g, books, stories) or CDs or DVDs (e.g., music or movies), usually for a profit (although selling a product is not a necessary condition for copyright infringement).

The second definition refers to "pirate" radio and/or television stations that broadcast on frequencies that have been already licensed by a government to a third party or to the government itself.

Pirating costs mass media industries billions of dollars in lost revenues every year.

See *copyright*.

plaintiff the party that files a *lawsuit* and alleges a wrong or illegal action has occurred.

play time in radio broadcasting, a slang term that usually refers to *audio recordings* that get heard on the air.

political advertising see *advertising*.

political communication (a) news or information about political issues and matters; **(b)** a genre of mass communication research that focuses on the effects of mass media during elections as well as the study of power of power in general.

Political communication is one of the largest fields of research in mass communication, partly because mass media are considered crucial for the existence of a political democracy. Much of the research focuses on the effects of media on voters' opinions and attitudes.

population (or universe) in research, the group to which *generalizations* are made.

In consumer research on women's use of media, for example, the population is often defined as women over age 17.

population parameter the *frequency, percentage* or *mean* obtained on a particular *measure* for an entire *population.*

See *census* and *sample.*

pop-ups a type of online advertisement in which a special box automatically pops up when a Web site or hyperlink is clicked.

See *Internet advertising.*

pornography media content intended to be sexually arousing.

See *obscenity.*

portal a Web site that helps users find their way around the *Internet.*

A portal usually contains advertising banners and links for shopping, news and information, and entertainment. Some portals are also ISPs. AOL is an example. But others, such as Yahoo.com, are not. Anyone can use their Web sites, which also often provide free e-mail accounts and service.

positioning how a product, service or company is perceived in the marketplace.

Marketing research often focuses on how better to position a product, service or company in the marketplace in order to increase sales.

positive reinforcement an environmental event that uses rewards (e.g., praise, gifts) to increase the probability of a behavior or response.

See *negative reinforcement.*

positivism a doctrine or *paradigm* which subscribes to one or more of the following: (1) radical *empiricism,* or the notion that true knowledge is derived only through empirical, inductive observation (i.e., sensory experience); (2) *determinism,* or the idea that forces in nature (organic, psychological, social or cultural) are the true cause of human behavior, thereby necessitating a rejection of free will as a basis for understanding behavior; (3) universal laws of human behavior, or the idea that behavior can be explained by invariant laws similar to physiological forces; (4) a rejection of theology, ethics, and metaphysics, which contain ideas that cannot be empirically verified; (5) a methodology based on the natural sciences, including mathematical explanations for human behavior; and (6) a belief in the strict separation of fact and value, along with the idea that social scientists can objectively observe and measure human activity.

August Comte, who is considered the father of sociology, is given credit for developing in the 19th century the concept of positivism, a term that is often misunderstood and sometimes abused. Comte's purpose was to draw attention to the problem of speculative knowledge, which was embodied in dogmatic religious doctrines and metaphysics. But he did not argue that scientific knowledge was absolute or the only form of knowledge. Rather, his goal was to encourage the use of empirical observation and of methods in the natural sciences to study and understand the world with the purpose of establishing a "religion of humanity." It is ironic that a century later critics would assert that positivism was essentially anti-humanistic.

During the 1920s and 1930s, a group of philosophers who called themselves the Vienna Circle advanced what they called logical positivism, a more extreme form of Comte's conception. Their central doctrine was the Verification Principle, which asserted that the only valid knowledge is that obtained by sensory experience.

The positivist position lost favor in the social sciences during the 1960s and 1970s, partly because of its own failures. Using quantitative research methods and sophisticated statistics, positivists sought to explain the variance in human behavior. But the effort generally produced only mediocre results. Researchers had a difficult time explaining more than 20-30 percent of the variance in any human behavior. Some dismissed the results as poor measurement, but little has changed in the last three decades.

During the 1960s and 1970s, the positivist position also was heavily criticized by the so-called humanists (see *mass communication research*), who emphasized free will as a basis for human action and the idea that reality is socially constructed. They pointed out that the Verification Principle itself could not be empirically verified.

This paradox and other attacks severely damaged the positivist position, but did not destroy it. Today most social scientists continue to study human behavior using empirical and quantitative methods, but they no longer subscribe to the doctrine of determinism or pursue universal laws of human behavior. Instead, their neo-positivist perspective emphasizes a *probabilistic theory of social action*, places primacy on *theory* and deductive knowledge as a guiding principle for research, and acknowledges the role that humans have in creating social reality.

See *probabilistic theory of social action*, *theory*, and *mass communication research*.

Source: August Comte, *August Comte and Positivism: The Essential Writings*, edited and with an introduction by Gertrude Lenzer (New York: Harper & Row, 1975).

postmodernism a theory, paradigm or perspective (depending upon the observer) which asserts that *modernism*—with its emphasis on scientific rationality, empiricism, realism, objective truth, and progress—is hegemonic (see *hegemony)*, is in decline, and is being replaced by a relativistic (see *relativism)* conception of the world, one in which truth and knowledge are subjective and relative, and reality is constructed rather than given by mass media and symbols.

The term postmodern first emerged in architecture and art criticism during the 1950s and 1960s and worked its way into the social sciences in the

1970s, where the initial assault was on scientific rationality and positivism. In 1979, Jean-François Lyotard declared that people in advanced capitalist systems had been living a postmodern world since the early 1960s. Modernism, he argued, had failed to solve many social problems (poverty, war, genocide, etc.), and the underlying reason was simply that knowledge and truth were relative, not absolute (see *absolutism*).

Instead, the postmodern world is one in which imagination, dissensus, and toleration of the incommensurable (i.e., the idea that there is no theory-neutral observation) take center stage. In many conceptions of postmodernism, mass media and popular culture are seen as institutions that create multiple realities as opposed to one that mirrors a so-called objective world.

There are many different conceptions of postmodernism, and adherents themselves often disagree on many points. This divergence has led many scholars to argue that postmodernism is now in decline—paradoxically a victim of its own relativistic conception of the world. In a more worldly critique, Jürgen Habermas sees postmodernism as a dangerous capitulation to a premature assessment of modernity's promise to emancipate people from political and economic oppression. Whatever the failures of modern science and industry, it is clear that many people in Western countries still look to these spheres to solve social problems, and the vast majority still believe in the idea of scientific progress.

Sources: Dominic Strinati, *An Introduction to Theories of Popular Culture* (New York: Routledge, 1995); David Harvey, *The Condition of Postmodernity: An Enquiry into the Origins of Cultural Change* (Cambridge, MA: Blackwell, 1989); Herbert W. Simons and Michael Billig (eds.), *After Postmodernism: Reconstructing Ideology Critique* (Thousand Oaks, CA: Sage, 1994); and Jürgen Habermas, *The Philosophical Discourse of Modernity: 12 Lectures*, trans. by Frederick Lawrence (Cambridge, MA: MIT Press, 1987).

Potter Box see *ethical decision-making.*

power the ability to influence or control the actions of other *social actors.*

The power of the mass media is derived largely from its ability to control the flow of news, information, and entertainment programming to society. However, the ability to define what is newsworthy generally rests with politically and economically elite groups. News media depend heavily on such elites for the news.

Poynter Institute for Media Studies a privately owned school for journalists and journalism teachers that offers more than 50 seminars a year.

The school owns the Times Publishing Company, which in turn owns the "St. Petersburg Times" and "Congressional Quarterly." For more information: The Poynter Institute, 801 3rd Street South, St. Petersburg, FL 33701 <www.poynter.org>.

pragmatic ethics see *ethical decision-making.*

precedent a legal concept which holds that judicial decisions or rulings should be based on previous judicial decisions or rulings.

See *law*.

precision journalism a term that refers to the use of social science research methods, especially quantitative methods, to gather the news.

The two most popular forms of precision journalism have been the *public opinion poll* and quantitative content analysis (see *quantitative research)* of public records. The term was coined by professor Everette M. Dennis and first applied to a book written in 1973 by Phillip Meyer.

Sources: Phillip Meyer, *Precision Journalism: A Reporter's Introduction to Social Science Methods* (Bloomington: Indiana University Press, 1973).

predictor variables same as *independent variables.*

press (a) a news media organization, especially one that produces printed materials; **(b)** a machine that produces printed materials (see *printing press)*.

Strictly speaking, the first definition refers to print news organization, such as newspapers and magazines. However, scholars and practitioners often use the term generically to refer to both print and electronic news media.

In political democracies, the press is expected to produce content that enhances democratic principles and processes. However, there is considerable debate among academics and some professionals about whether a press system that depends heavily on advertising and profits can contribute to that goal.

See *newspaper, mass media,* and *printing press.*

Source: Geneva Overholser and Kathleen Hall Jamieson (eds.), *The Press* (New York: Oxford University Press, 2005).

press council (or news council) a nonprofit organization composed of citizens and media workers who hear complaints against news media and render a verdict that usually has only symbolic authority.

As of this writing, three states had press councils: Hawaii, Minnesota, and Washington state. A potential libel litigant can file a complaint and, in exchange, the parties make a contractual agreement not to sue each other in a formal court of law. The council hears the complaint and renders a verdict.

The councils have been slow to catch on because many journalists and news organizations continue to be defensive about their *First Amendment* rights. A National News Council disbanded in the 1970s after the "New York Times" withdrew its support.

press release a news story written primarily for distribution to news media outlets.

prime-time access rule a rule, adopted in 1971 by the *Federal Communications Commission* but now rescinded, that limited to three hours an evening the amount of commercial *television network* programming in the 50 largest markets.

The rule was intended to encourage local, not just national, programming during the four prime-time hours, and to provide a market for independent producers. However, most local stations turned to syndicated programming, such as game shows and situation comedies. The problem was that local programming was expensive to produce and often could not pay for itself.

See *Fairness Doctrine.*

priming the notion that psychological or sociological phenomena in a *social actor*'s world enhances or increases the probability of a *media effect.*

Researchers have argued, for example, that people who are unemployed are more likely to tune into and pay attention to news about employment and job opportunities. This is an example of social priming. Likewise, a person who uses a medication is more likely to pay attention to advertisements about that drug, which is an example of cognitive priming.

Sources: David Domke, Dhavan V. Shah and Daniel B. Wackman, "Media Priming Effects: Accessibility, Association, and Activation." *The International Journal of Public Opinion Research*, 10(1):51-74 (Spring 1998) and Zhongdang Pan and Gerald M. Kosicki, "Priming and Media Impact on the Evaluations of the President's Performance." *Communication Research*, 24:3-30 (1997).

printing press a machine that puts ink on paper and produces newspapers, magazines and other printed materials.

See *Gutenberg, Johannes,* and *information revolution.*

prior restraint the act of preventing publication in advance.

In the 1760s, one British scholar defined *freedom of the press* as freedom from "previous restraint," or prior restraint. Today, freedom of the press is much more broadly defined. However, *prior restraint* is often considered to be the most insidious kind of government control, because speakers and publishers are stopped even before they can speak or print.

The U.S. Supreme Court decided its first major case on prior restraint in 1931. In Near v. Minnesota (1931), the court ruled that city and county officials could not halt publication of a newspaper even if it printed false information and lies.

The newspaper was the "Saturday Press," a small weekly in Minneapolis. The publishers, Jay M. Near and Howard Guilford, thought of themselves as reformers who were helping to clean up city and county government in Minneapolis. Some historians see them as racists. They charged that Jewish gangsters were in control of gambling, bootlegging, and racketeering in the city and that city government and its law enforcement agencies did not perform their duties energetically.

City and county officials in Minneapolis obtained an injunction to halt publication of the "Saturday Press." They cited a Minnesota statute that empowered a court to declare as "a public nuisance" any defamatory, obscene, malicious or scandalous publication. Violation of the injunction could result in punishment for contempt of court.

The Minnesota Supreme Court upheld the lower court order, saying that the state had broad police power to regulate public nuisances, including defamatory newspapers. The U.S. Supreme Court voted 5-4 to reverse that decision and declared the state statute unconstitutional. The majority opinion said the object of that law was not punishment, but censorship. This constituted prior restraint and, consequently, violated the *First Amendment*. The Court also wrote, however, that censorship is permissible when the publication is obscene or incites people to acts of violence.

The *Near* decision was supported 40 years later by the "Pentagon Papers" case *(New York Times v. United States*, 1971). The "Pentagon Papers" case also made it clear that the government could use prior restraint under some circumstances. Even the newspapers conceded this point. But some media scholars believe this concession was a mistake. The newspapers appeared to be more concerned about winning the immediate case than in establishing a long-lasting constitutional principle.

The fragility of the "Pentagon Papers" decision became apparent in 1979, when the government again tried to block publication of material it claimed could endanger national security (United States v. Progressive, 1979). Freelance writer Howard Morland had prepared an article, titled "The H-Bomb Secret: How We Got It, Why We're Telling It." The article was scheduled for publication in the April edition of the "Progressive" magazine, a liberal publication.

Morland had gathered material for the article from public sources, including libraries. After completing a rough draft, he sought technical criticism from various scholars. Someone sent a copy to federal officials. Since it was no longer a secret, the "Progressive" sent a final draft to the government for pre-publication comments on technical accuracy. The government said the piece was too accurate—someone could use it to build a bomb—and moved to obtain an injunction against publication. The defendants argued that all of the information in the article was publicly available.

But U.S. District Court Judge Robert Warren ruled in favor of the government. He conceded that the article was not a do-it-yourself guide for building a hydrogen bomb. Nevertheless, it could help some nations move faster in developing a hydrogen bomb. Warren concluded that the government had met the heavy burden justifying prior restraint.

The "Progressive" appealed. But in September 1979 a small newspaper in Madison, Wisc., published a story containing much of the same information as was in the Morland article. The Department of Justice withdrew its suit against the "Progressive."

See *libel*, *New York Times v. United States*, *seditious libel*, and *privacy*, *invasion of*.

Sources: *Near v. Minnesota ex rel Olson*, 283 U.S. 697 (1931); *New York Times v. U.S.*; *U.S. v. Washington Post*, 713 U.S. 403 (1971); *United States v. The Progressive*, 467 F.Supp. 990 (W.D.Wis. 1979).

privacy, invasion of an area of media law that focuses on the privacy rights of people.

The U.S. Constitution does not specifically mention any right to privacy. But the courts and state and federal legislatures have accorded some rights to privacy, even though the full scope of those rights is not yet well understood and it is difficult to win a privacy lawsuit.

Boston lawyers Samuel Warren and Louis Brandeis are often credited for originating privacy law in the United States. In 1890, they complained that "instantaneous photographs and newspaper enterprise have invaded the sacred precincts of private and domestic life. Numerous mechanical devices threaten to make good the prediction that what is whispered in the closet shall be proclaimed from the housetops." The individual, they argued, has the right to be left alone.

Laws protecting people's privacy took many years to develop. But today nearly all the states recognize a legal right of privacy. It includes the right to prohibit the unauthorized commercial exploitation of one's name or picture, as well as freedom from unwanted snooping and electronic surveillance. State and federal statutes also give citizens the right to inspect their own medical, tax, and other records.

The U.S. Supreme Court has fashioned a limited right of privacy from the Fourth, Ninth, and Fourteenth Amendments. The *Fourth Amendment* prohibits unreasonable government searches of citizens' homes and papers. The Ninth and Fourteenth Amendments have been used to give people a limited right to sexual privacy and a right to use contraceptives (a private matter), and to give women the right to an abortion.

Four areas of privacy have a direct impact on mass media:

1. Private facts is generally defined as content that (1) would be highly offensive to a reasonable person and (2) is not of legitimate concern to the public. The private-facts plaintiff sues for shame, humiliation, and mental anguish stemming from publication of truthful information. Thus, truth is not a defense in privacy lawsuits.

The media generally win private facts cases. But plaintiffs have been successful from time to time when stories reveal highly personal information about them, such as physical or mental illness, or exposure of intimate parts of the body. For example, some states have allowed parents of mentally handicapped children to sue news organizations when the children's conditions are revealed in stories without parental permission.

The U.S. Supreme Court has ruled the news media can publish just about anything that it legally obtains from official (court, police, and government) records. Privacy laws and judges normally cannot impose a prior restraint on media organizations. However, laws and judges can prohibit government officials from releasing private information about people to the news media.

To defend themselves, news media also try to show that the published information is newsworthy, and that this newsworthiness outweighs any right to privacy. For example, Oliver Sipple, a homosexual who saved President Gerald Ford's life when he deflected Sarah Jane Moore's hand as she aimed a gun at Ford, lost his privacy lawsuit because a lower court said his homosexuality was newsworthy. It was newsworthy because his courageous act cast homosexuals in a positive light.

Consent is also a defense in private facts cases. If a source gives private information to a reporter, consent is implied. However, the source must know he or she is talking to a reporter. That's one reason why it's important for reporters to identify themselves before interviewing people.

2. Intrusion involves a physical or technological invasion of a person's privacy. The Fourth Amendment provides protection from unjustified government searches of homes and offices.

The government also cannot tap phone lines without a court order. Citizens are never allowed to tap phone lines, which is called third-party tape-recording. However, about 40 states allow one party to a conversation to tape-record that conversation without permission of the other party or parties, which is called participant monitoring.

There also is no federal law against participant monitoring (or second-party tape-recording). Some journalists tape telephone conversations to protect themselves from complaints and false allegations. Some attorneys also routinely do so without consent of their clients. However, some journalists believe participant monitoring is unethical.

State and local statutes also provide protection from trespassers. Trespassing is entering private property without the permission of the owner. As a rule, journalists may photograph or observe any activity from public property or from a place in which they have permission to be. However, courts are divided on whether quasi-public places like restaurants are private. In some jurisdictions, journalists may be sued for overzealously following celebrities or for using extreme methods of obtaining pictures of activities on private property (e.g., using a ladder to see over guard walls).

3. False light involves the public portrayal of someone in a distorted or fictionalized way. False light is similar to libel because in both cases someone claims to be a victim of falsehood. However, false light plaintiffs do not sue for damage to their reputations—they sue because someone has distributed embarrassing, private facts about them.

One example of false light occurred when a newspaper story portrayed a widow, whose husband had died in a bridge accident, as embittered and living in abject poverty. The allegations were false, and the Supreme Court ruled in favor of the woman (Cantrell v. Forest City Publishing Co., 1974). Another example involved a biography of a famous baseball player in the 1950s, which falsely portrayed the player as a World War II hero. The New

York Supreme Court ruled in favor of the baseball player and prohibited distribution of the book.

4. Appropriation is the unauthorized exploitation of someone's identity. Most often it involves commercial exploitation, whereby someone uses a celebrity's identity to sell a product without his or her authorization. But noncommercial use of a name or likeness is also prohibited.

One example involved a star football player whose portrait was painted for a sports magazine. Sometime later the portrait appeared in a Coca-Cola advertisement. A court ruled that even though the sports star was a public figure, he still was entitled to control his identity for commercial purposes.

Consent is normally needed to use someone's name or likeness. Photographers, advertisers, and public relations professionals usually prefer to obtain consent in the broadest context possible. They can then use the photographs or images in a variety of ways. But actors and models should be aware that such practices can come back to haunt them.

The courts have also ruled it illegal to copy a person's likeness with the intent of exploiting it. Thus, advertisements cannot use studio singers whose voices sound like famous singers, unless the audience knows the difference.

See *emotional distress, law,* and *libel.*

Sources: Samuel Warren and Louis Brandeis, "The Right of Privacy," 4 *Harvard Law Review* 193 (1890); *Cox Broadcasting Corporation v. Cohn,* 420 U.S. 469 (1975); *Florida Star v. B.J.F.,* 488 U.S. 887 (1988); *Sipple v. Chronicle Publishing Co,* 201 California Reporter 665 (1984); *Cantrell v. Forest City Publishing Co.,* 419 U.S. 245 (1974); *Spahn v. Julian Messner,* 221 N.E.2d 543 (New York 1966); and *Kimbrough v. Coca-Cola/USA,* 521 S.W.2d 719 (Texas 1975).

probabilistic theory of social action a doctrine that rejects extreme versions of both *determinism* and *free will* and argues that humans have the power to make choices between alternative courses of action that are themselves constrained or enabled by physiological, organic, psychological, social or cultural factors or phenomena.

The probabilistic theory of social action, which is often credited to the sociologist Robert K. Merton, attempts to resolve the age-old debate about whether human action is the product of deterministic forces or a free will. It argues that neither the deterministic nor the voluntaristic models alone are sufficient for explaining human action and/or mental processes.

The free-will model imparts too much choice to social actors; it fails to recognize that *social structure* and cultural values, in particular, limit choices and social reality. In many cases, social actors themselves are even unaware of the extent to which their choices are limited (or enabled).

The deterministic perspective, on the other hand, fails to recognize that people are not simply passive recipients of social and political laws, like a ball dropped from a roof. Social actors have the power to choose between alternative courses of action; they have *free will.* But, again, those choices are not limitless; they are constrained or enabled by *social roles, values, norms,* and other phenomena. And the probability of any particular action increases or decreases depending upon the constraints or opportunities of the situation.

An example is the amount of television children watch. Children from poor families watch more television than children from wealthy families, partly because the latter have more financial resources and, thus, more access to alternative recreational activities.

A probabilistic theory of social action implies that human behavior can never be fully explained—there is always an element of uncertainty (or free will) in any situation. However, social action is not entirely capricious or random, and knowledge about the psychological, social, and cultural components of an individual or social system can reduce uncertainty, reveal patterns of behavior, and generate predictions about future action.

See *determinism* and *free will.*

Sources: Jeffrey C. Alexander, "The New Theoretical Movement," pp. 77-102 in Neil J. Smelser (ed.), *Handbook of Sociology* (Newbury Park, CA: Sage, 1988).

probability sampling a variety of methods used to draw samples for studies in which the findings can be generalized to a larger *population.*

A sample will represent a population if each member or unit of that population is given an equal chance of being included in the sample. This is called a *simple random sample* because there is no order or pattern to the selection of its members. With simple random sampling, findings can be generalized to the entire population within a certain margin of error (see sampling error for formula and description).

The logic behind how a sample represents a population can be demonstrated by imagining a huge barrel of marbles, one-third red, one-third blue, and one-third green. If one selects 300 marbles at random, one would expect to have about 100 marbles of each color. Of course, every time one selects 300 marbles one will not get 100 of each color, but the final tally will be close most of the time. The degree to which the percentage of each color varies from its percentage in the actual population represents sampling error, which can be estimated using the law of probability.

See *sampling error.*

probability survey a *quantitative research* method that uses *probability sampling* methods to gather data.

probing obtaining complete responses to *open-ended questions* by following up the original *question* with additional questions, such as "Anything else?"

producer in filmmaking, the person responsible for turning an idea into a finished project.

This involves coming up with the idea or script, obtaining financing, hiring the director and sometimes the stars, and seeing that the project is completed within its budget and on schedule. Bigger projects often have an executive producer, who does all of the preceding except day-to-day management, which is usually delegated to the line producer.

product differentiation the extent to which products or services in a market are different from one another.

In a highly competitive market, producers often attempt to differentiate their product to reduce competition and to capture a profitable segment of the market.

See *segmentation analysis* and *market segmentation.*

product placement in filmmaking, the practice in which advertisers pay film studios or producers a fee to have their products, goods or services "placed" in movies.

For example, private companies paid $70 million in 2002 to have their products placed in the James Bond movie, "Die Another Day."

product placement study a study in which *respondents* test a product for several days or weeks before being interviewed about the product.

production designer see *art director.*

production editor the person responsible for overseeing the production (copy editing, design, and printing) of a manuscript or publication.

programming (a) content produced for radio or television, (b) selecting a day and time for broadcasting a television or radio program.

The first definition refers to the content heard or seen on radio or on television. The second is more specific: It refers to the process of putting a show into a schedule (i.e., selecting a day and time).

Programming a show is an extremely important task. Many shows that were failures in one day- or time-slot became big hits when placed on another day or time.

Audience flow must also be considered. In other words, the networks try to schedule similar programs back-to-back to keep viewers watching. That's why the networks often schedule four to six half-hour comedies together on one night, and then program one-hour dramas on another night. As a rule, comedies also tend to air earlier than dramas.

In scheduling shows, the networks sometimes employ what is called counterprogramming, which involves filling time slots with shows that appeal to an audience that differs from one on a competing network. For example, when sporting events are broadcast on one network, a competing network will often schedule programming geared to the interests of women, who tend to have less interest in sports than men.

In other cases, the networks will engage in challenge programming, which means they pit their strongest shows against each other in the same time slot.

propaganda (a) dissemination or promotion of ideas, practices or doctrines intended to advance a social actor's cause or damage an opponent's cause;

(b) dissemination or promotion of false or deceptive ideas, practices or doctrines intended to advance a social actor's cause or damage an opponent's cause.

The original definition of propaganda matches (a) above and can be traced to the Roman Catholic Church, which sought to spread the word of God through foreign ministries. However, since World War I, propaganda has acquired a more negative connotation, referring not to all ideas, but rather to those that attempt to distort the truth or deceive people. This latter (b) definition is more useful to mass communication researchers, since it distinguishes between coercive and noncoercive persuasive content.

proportion the *ratio* of one group to the total.

For example, if the total number of *respondents* in a *sample* is 1,000 and the those under age 35 number 333, the proportion of those under age 35 is .333.

prosocial effects a type of media effect that is viewed as having "positive" rather than "negative" consequences for individuals, for society or for both.

Research shows that children learn a great deal from movies and television, including how to play sports and interact with others. Although not all of the content of motion pictures results in prosocial effects, movies, like other mass media content, tend to support and reinforce the dominant values and beliefs of a society.

protocols codes that allow one computer to communicate with another.

pseudo event a false event.

The term was coined by historian Daniel Boorstin, who was critical of public relations practitioners (*Edward L. Bernays* in particular) and their penchant for staging news events to promote an idea or cause or to make money. Boorstin says a pseudo-event possesses the following characteristics:

(1) It is not spontaneous, but comes about because someone has planned, planted or incited it.

(2) It is planted primarily (but not always exclusively) for the immediate purpose of being reported or reproduced. The question, "Is it real?" is less important than, "Is it newsworthy?"

(3) Its relation to the underlying reality of the situation is ambiguous. While the news interest in a train wreck is in what happened and in the real consequences, the interest in an interview is always, in a sense, in whether it really happened and in what might have been the motives. Did the statement really mean what it said? Without some of this ambiguity, a pseudo-event cannot be very interesting.

(4) Usually it is intended to be a self-fulfilling prophecy.

Source: Daniel Boorstin, *The Image* (New York: Vintage, 1961).

psychographics the scientific study of the psychological or lifestyle characteristics of a *population*.

Psychographic research attempts to explain *behavior* by examining consumers' *values*, lifestyles, and personality traits. In contrast, demographic research focuses on the social characteristics (age, income, gender, etc.) of consumers or populations.

To identify psychographic groups, market researchers survey people and ask them questions about their hobbies and interests. Then they run the data through the computer to create groups of people with similar interests and behaviors.

The best known psychographic profile is VALS (Values and Life-Styles Program), which was developed at Stanford University in the 1970s. It classifies people into nine different groups. The largest group is the "belongers," which includes nearly 40 percent of the population. They are conformists who tend to hold mainstream values and beliefs. They are religious and watch a lot of television. The "achievers," in contrast, comprise about 20 percent of the population. They are prosperous and inner-directed and don't watch a lot of television.

public in the field of public relations, two or more people who share a common goal that affects others.

The typical public relations practitioner interacts with a number of different groups and organizations, which are roughly divided into two major groups: external publics and internal publics.

External publics usually include all groups and organizations outside of the organization itself. This would include the general public and special interest groups. Internal publics usually include employees (or volunteers in nonprofit organizations), the management, and other subgroups within the organization.

Public Broadcasting Service (PBS) a private, non-profit organization owned and operated by the nation's 349 public television stations; its goal is to provide quality programs and educational services to the American public.

The origins of the PBS can be traced to the 1950s, when *Frieda Hennock*, a member of the *Federal Communications Commission (FCC)*, complained about the lack of educational programming on television. Although she was able to get the FCC to set aside a number of frequencies for educational use, many of the educational stations lacked the resources to produce high quality programming.

This problem was partially solved in 1967, when Congress created the Corporation for Public Broadcasting, which in turn created the Public Broadcasting Service (PBS). PBS doesn't produce original programming. Instead, it serves as a distributor of programming that is produced abroad (English programming) or at major public television stations in the United States. WGBH in Boston, for example, produces about a third of the programming on PBS stations.

Educational shows for children and news and documentary programming have been among the most popular. In the children's genre, "Sesame Street," which first appeared in 1969 and is produced by the Children's Television Workshop at WNET in New York, leads the pack. "The MacNeil/Lehrer NewsHour" (now "The NewsHour with Jim Lehrer") was first broadcast in 1975 and became immensely popular for its in-depth (one-hour) coverage of national and international affairs. One of the most successful documentary programs was "The Civil War," a five-part series that appeared in 1990. "Nature," a documentary program that explores the natural world, also has had an extremely loyal following.

Although public television offered more sophisticated programming to American audiences, it has also faced its share of criticism. Conservatives, in particular, have tried on occasion to cut federal funding to PBS because they believe it has a liberal bias. Those criticisms are not without merit, since education in general and higher education in particular tends to tolerate a greater diversity of ideas and different points of view (conservatives tend to emphasize tradition and often oppose change).

But in recent years, PBS has also been accused of being soft on corporations, which have been contributing an increasingly greater amount of money to public television programming. PBS executives concede they have had to rely more heavily on corporate funding to generate high-quality programming, but deny such dependence biases PBS programming.

The PBS Web site <www.pbs.org> contains a great deal of information about public television programming as well as news and information.

See *Hennock, Frieda.*

public domain creative works of literature, art, music, etc., that are not copyrighted or for which the copyright has expired.
See *copyright.*

public figure a legal term for a prominent nongovernmental person, such as a movie star, who must prove malice to win a libel lawsuit.
See *libel* and *public official.*

public journalism see *civic journalism.*

public official (a) someone who works for the government, **(b)** a legal term for a prominent governmental person who must prove malice to win a libel lawsuit.
See *libel* and *public figure.*

public opinion beliefs and attitudes held by a *public,* which is often defined as the adult population in a community or nation.

public opinion poll a quantitative research method that uses probability sampling methods to measure the beliefs and attitudes of a public, which is usually defined as the adult population in a community or nation.

public relations (PR) **(a)** the process through which an individual or an organization attempts to create a positive image of an individual, an organization, a product, a service or a concept; **(b)** a profession or field of work in which people seek to create positive images of a person, organization, product, service or concept.

    Edward L. Bernays, one PR pioneer, actually called public relations "the engineering of consent."

    Like *advertising*, the goal in public relations is to persuade people about the value of something. Public relations *campaign*s often involve the use of advertising. However, advertising is only one of many marketing and promotional techniques that public relations practitioners can use to achieve their goals. Other tasks or jobs include writing news releases and stories, conducting market research, responding to requests for information, organizing meetings, writing speeches, and establishing and maintaining community contacts.

    Technically, any individual or organization can be a public relations practitioner. One only need promote or advance a particular group or cause. But the term is usually used in a more restricted sense, referring to social actors that intentionally attempt to persuade others as to the worthiness of a group, cause or idea. PR practitioners deal with publics, or groups of people within and outside of the organization.

    Although governments and nonprofit organizations and groups engage in public relations, that function is most frequently associated with private industry. Most large businesses in the United States today and even many small ones employ people who work in a public relations capacity. They don't always use that name. The PR function is often called "community relations," media relations, information services or public outreach. Politicians often hire press agents, or spokespersons, who essentially are public relations people.

    Because public relations involves attempts to persuade, the motivations and self-interest of those engaging in the activity often are called into question—and with some justification. The history of public relations contains many occasions when companies fabricated information and told lies in attempts to win public support.

    But this kind of practice is not condoned today. PR professional groups have enacted *codes of ethics* that strongly condemn lying and other deceptive practices. The origins of public relations as a separate function within an organization arose during the late 19th century, a time when many large businesses generated negative publicity, much of which was deserved. Public relations emerged to combat negative images, and only over time did the field of public relations gain respect.

    See *publics; Lee, Ivy; and Bernays, Edward L.*.

Source: Edward L. Bernays (ed.), *The Engineering of Consent* (Norman: University of Oklahoma Press, 1955).

public relations campaign an activity specifically organized to enhance, improve or promote an individual, organization, concept, service or idea.
See *public relations*.

public relations firm an organization that practices *public relations*.
There are two types of public relations organizations. One is "in-house," meaning the PR function is handled by the company or organization itself. The other type is an "independent agency" or "consulting firm," i.e., a company that offers consulting services to other companies.

Public Relations Society of America (PRSA) a nonprofit organization that represents the interest of public relations practitioners.
PRSA is the world's largest organization for public relations professionals, with nearly 20,000 members in 100 chapters. The organization was chartered in 1947, and its "primary objectives are to advance the standards of the public relations profession and to provide members with professional development opportunities through continuing education programs, information exchange forums and research projects conducted on the national and local levels."
PRSA requires its members to adhere to the society's Member Code of Ethics, which is extremely detailed. The code, which was last modified in 2000, gives not only guidelines or rules, but also examples of violations. The PRSA Board of Directors has the authority to bar from membership individuals who violate the code. However, unlike previous versions of the code, "emphasis on enforcement of the code has been eliminated."
The code begins with a statement of six professional values that "guide our behaviors and decision-making process." They are (1) advocacy (responsible advocacy for clients and the provision of a voice in the marketplace of ideas); (2) honesty (accuracy and truth); (3) expertise (use of specialized knowledge and education); (4) independence ("objectivity" and accountability); (5) loyalty (faithfulness to clients and the public interest); and (6) fairness (respect for free speech rights for all parties).
From these six values derive the specific code provisions themselves. There are six of these as well. They include (1) protecting and advancing the free flow of accurate and truthful information; (2) promoting healthy and fair competition among professionals; (3) fostering open communication; (4) protecting confidential and private information; (5) avoiding real or perceived conflicts of interest; and (6) strengthening the public's trust in the profession of public relations.
A student branch of PRSA, called the Public Relations Student Society of America (PRSSA), is also active on many college campuses. PRSA's Web site <www.prsa.org> also has information about jobs.
See *Public Relations Student Society of America*.

Public Relations Student Society of America (PRSSA) a nonprofit college student version of the *Public Relations Society of America.*

The organization's Web site <www.prssa.org> offers a wealth of information for students, including how to apply for jobs and internships.

public television (or educational television) *television* whose primary goal is to educate rather than entertain.

See *Public Broadcasting Service.*

publisher an individual or organization that owns or controls the rights to produce and distribute printed materials (e.g., *books, magazines* or *newspapers*) for sale or distribution.

There are about 78,000 book publishers, 25,000 magazines and 10,000 daily and weekly newspapers in the United States. At magazines and newspapers, the term "publisher" is usually associated with an individual who holds the top position in the organization. In the book publishing industry, the term often refers to the organization or company publishing the book (i.e., "Random House is my publisher.").

publishing house a company in the publishing business; most often applied to book publishers.

See *publisher.*

Pulitzer, Joseph (1847-1911) a newspaper publisher who helped define the modern newspaper and created the *Pulitzer Prizes,* the most prestigious awards in journalism.

Pulitzer was reared in Budapest and emigrated to the United State in 1864 as a recruit for the Union Army during the Civil War. After the war he became a reporter on a German-language newspaper in St. Louis. He bought a share of the newspaper and resold it at a profit. He was elected to the Missouri state legislature in 1869 and helped to organize the Liberal Republican Party, which in 1872 nominated *Horace Greeley* for president. After the party's demise, Pulitzer became a Democrat.

In 1878 Pulitzer gained control of the "St. Louis Dispatch" and the "Post" and merged them. The "Post-Dispatch" became the city's dominant evening newspaper. On May 10, 1883, he purchased the "New York World," a morning paper, and soon turned it into the leading journalistic voice of the Democratic Party in the United States. Pulitzer also founded the evening counterpart of the "World," the "Evening World," in 1887.

His newspapers contained a unusual mix of high-quality investigative journalism and sensationalism. He was known as the "people's champion," but he often engaged in publicity stunts and blatant self-promotion to attract readership. His newspapers contained a lot of entertainment content, including comics, sports news, women's fashion coverage, and illustrations

The "World" eventually went head-to-head with *William Randolph Hearst's* "New York Morning Journal," and the grandstanding and sensationalistic coverage, especially surrounding the Spanish-American War of 1898, led the coining of the term *yellow journalism*. Poor health forced Pulitzer to abandon the management of his newspapers in the late 1880s, but he continued to exercise a close watch over their editorial policies.

Pulitzer's will endowed the Columbia University School of Journalism in 1912 and established the *Pulitzer Prizes*, which have been awarded annually since 1917.

Sources: W. A. Swanberg, *Pulitzer* (New York: Scribner, 1967) and Julian S. Rammelkamp, *Pulitzer's Post-Dispatch, 1878-1883* (Princeton, NJ: Princeton University Press, 1967).

Pulitzer Prizes the most prestigious awards for writing and reporting in journalism.

The Pulitzer Prizes were created by a $500,000 endowment from Joseph Pulitzer, who died in 1911. He gave the endowment to Columbia University. The awards are made annually based on the recommendation of The Pulitzer Prize Board, which is composed of judges appointed by the university.

The number and kind of prizes have varied since 1917, when they were first awarded. As of this writing, there were 14 prizes in the field of journalism, 6 prizes in letters, 1 prize in music, and 4 fellowships.

The most coveted award is the gold medal for meritorious public service, which is typically given to a newspaper that covers a major story or breaking news event over a period of days, weeks or months. The other awards, such as investigative reporting and reporting on national affairs, come with a $3,000 cash prize for the author or authors.

The awards for letters include distinguished fiction by an American author, distinguished play and distinguished biography or autobiography.

In terms of total awards, *The New York Times* tops the list with 81, far more than any other paper.

Sources: David Shaw, "The *Times* Wins Pulitzer for FDA Investigative Stories and David Willman's Reporting on Deadly Drugs Is Honored; Four Other Papers Are Awarded Two Prizes Each," *Los Angeles Times* (April 17, 2001), p. A1.

purchase intent a consumer's intent to purchase a product or service. Purchase intent is one of the most frequently used *measures* in marketing research studies.

Q

qualitative research research in which the investigator relies upon his or her skills as an empathic interviewer or observer to collect and interpret data.

Focus group and *ethnographic research* are examples.

See *mass communication research* and *mass communication researchers*.

quantitative research research that involves collection and analysis of data that is converted into numbers.

Survey research is an example.

See *mass communication research* and *mass communication researchers*.

question an *operationalization*, or *measure*, of some *concept*.

questionnaire a device or *instrument* for measuring consumer's *attitudes, beliefs, behavioral intentions,* and *behaviors* toward or about products and services.

quota sampling a method of *sampling* in which *respondents* are classified into groups or *cells* on the basis of one or more characteristics.

Quota sampling may or may not involve *probability sampling methods*.

R

radio an aural form of communication in which information or ideas are transmitted electronically from one point to another.

Some of the first radios were used by ships to communicate with each other and with ports of call. However, when most people use the term "radio," they usually think of the device in their cars or homes that receives music, news, and other programming from a distant broadcast radio station. The communication is one-way—from the station to the listener.

Two-way radio communication, in contrast, is used primarily in professional settings, such as for police patrols. Short-wave radio, which enables individuals to communicate with each other or to receive radio broadcasts from around the world, can also be used for two-way communication.

Broadcast radio is a mass medium. Traditional radio involves wireless broadcasts. The sound is converted into electromagnetic waves and then transmitted through the air to a receiver, which converts the waves into sound.

Web radio involves transmission of audio signals through the *Internet*, which is mostly composed of wires or cables. *Satellite radio* involves transmission of signals through a satellite.

See *radio technology, satellite radio,* and *Web radio.*

Radio Act of 1912 and 1927 the first and second national laws, respectively, passed to regular radio transmissions.

The Radio Act of 1912 was passed in the aftermath of the Titanic disaster. The law required ships to leave their radios on 24 hours a day and required federal licensing of all transmitters. All broadcasters were required to identify themselves with call letters (which begin with "W" for stations east of the Mississippi River and "K" for stations west of the river) when they went on the air (stations east of the river that started with "K" were allowed to keep their call letters), but no specific frequencies were assigned, and everyone who applied was given a license. The airwave congestion got so bad in large cities that sales of radios began to decline in 1927.

Congress responded with the Radio Act of 1927, which gave the Federal Radio Commission (FRC) the power to grant and revoke licenses on specific frequencies to those who broadcast in "the public interest, convenience or necessity." The FCC gave licenses to about 600 broadcasters and denied licenses to 150 others. But this resolved the congestion problem.

See *Communications Act of 1934.*

radio advertising advertising aired during radio programming.

There are two major types of radio advertising. Network radio advertisement comes through nationally syndicated radio programs. Local spot radio advertising, in contrast, involves placing advertisements directly with a local radio station. About 80 percent of radio advertising is local spot advertising.

radio station a *mass media* organization that produces content for broadcast on radio.

See *radio* and *radio technology.*

radio technology transmission and reception of audio electromagnetic waves.

When someone speaks to us, we hear sound. Hearing takes place when vibrations of frequencies between about 15 and 20,000 hertz reach the inner ear. The hertz, or Hz, is a unit of frequency that equals one cycle per second. Such vibrations reach the inner ear when they are transmitted through air.

But sound only travels so far through the air. During the 19th century, scientists theorized that sounds could be converted into electromagnetic waves and transmitted over great distances. They were proved right in the late 1800s.

Radio communication involves two major components—a transmitter and a receiver. The transmitter generates electrical oscillations on a radio carrier frequency. The oscillations can be varied in terms of amplitude or frequency. The former is called Amplitude Modulation and the latter Frequency Modulation. Most people just think of them as AM versus FM radio. A receiver, or what most people commonly call a radio, converts the electromagnetic waves back into sound.

AM broadcast radio stations operate between 535 and 1705 kilohertz (53,500 to 1,605,000 hertz) on the radio dial. FM broadcast radio stations operate between 88 and 108 megahertz (88 million hertz to 108 million hertz) on the radio dial. Each has advantages.

AM radio signals can generally travel farther. That's because AM transmissions have longer wavelengths and can bounce off the outer atmosphere. Some signals can travel hundreds or even thousands of miles under the right conditions. A typical FM station, in contrast, covers only 24-105 miles.

But FM generally sounds better than AM. It has higher fidelity. Most AM radio stations cannot faithfully reproduce sounds below 100 hertz or above 5 kilohertz, whereas FM has a range of 50 hertz to 15 kilohertz. Hence, FM is preferred for music radio. FM also is much less susceptible than AM to atmospheric disturbances, such as lightning. AM is popular for talk radio and news formats.

The term short-wave radio is generally reserved for frequencies between 3 and 30 megahertz (3 million to 30 million hertz). Signals in this range can be transmitted over long distances. Amateur, or "ham," radio is often thought of as short-wave radio, but it is allocated frequencies in the medium, very high or ultra high band waves.

The trend in broadcasting is digital. Some radio and *television networks* are transmitting signals digitally, which faithfully reproduces the original sound and/or picture, although distortions may occur depending on the quality of the electronic equipment. Digital transmissions may be sent via satellite, cable or over the air.

relativism the philosophical doctrine that truth is relative, not objective; that it may vary from individual to individual, from group to group, and from time to time.

Opposite of *absolutism*.

random digit dialing a method of drawing a *sample* of telephone numbers which involves randomly selecting the numbers to dial.

Random digit dialing is a *probability sampling* method.

random measurement error see *measurement error*.

random sampling sampling methods that give respondents an equal or known chance of being selected.

Random sampling allows researchers to generalize the findings to larger populations.

See *simple random sampling*.

range the lowest to the highest *values* in a *distribution*.

The range is a *measure of dispersion*.

rate obtained when a *frequency*, such as the number of purchases, is divided by the total population and then multiplied by a *constant* to bring it to a whole number instead of a fraction or *proportion*.

A rate involves a period of time during which the events can accumulate. For example, if consumers in a particular market purchased 50,000 savings certificates over a period of one year, and the population in that market is 1 million, the rate per capita would be 50,000 divided by 1,000,000, or .05 for the one-year period. Because the proportion is cumbersome, it is multiplied by a constant to create a whole number. Using

100,000 as the constant, the savings certificate purchase rate is 5,000 per 100,000 residents.

Rather, Dan (1931-) CBS News anchor from1981 to 2005.

rating the percentage of radio or television households tuned in to a given program.

Market ratings and shares are used to set advertising rates. A rating is the percentage of all households tuned in to a program. A share is the percentage of all households tuned in at that time. The formulas are simple:

Rating =   Number of households tuned in to a given program
                 All households with a television or radio

Share =   Number of households tuned in to a given program
                 All households tuned in to a television or radio show at that time

The United States has about 110 million television households. So if 25 million households are watching a program, the rating is 22.7 (25 million divided by 110 million). If half of all TV households are watching television at that time, the share is 45.4 (25 million divided by 55 million).

The three major television rating companies are A. C. Nielsen, AGB Television Research, and the American Research Bureau. Of the three, Nielsen has the most widely accepted ratings.

To measure viewing of nationally broadcast programs, Nielsen uses a sample of more than 5,000 households. Viewers in these homes complete surveys. Some also have an electronic meter that automatically records what shows are being viewed. The "people meter" also allows individual members of a family to punch in when viewing begins, allowing researchers to associate *demographics* (e.g., age, gender) with viewing patterns.

Nielsen publishes the results in the *Nielsen Television Index* for network broadcasting. The company also publishes the *Nielsen Station Index* for local broadcasters, which measures local viewing. But samples for local viewing are only taken four times a year—in November, February, May, and July. In the ratings industry, these months are known as the "sweeps months." Local stations then use the results from the sweeps months to set advertising rates for the next three months.

To boost ratings, the networks and local stations often schedule their best programs during the sweeps months. Some also are known to increase the amount of programming that contains sex and violence during these months. To lure more viewers, critics also charge that evening newscasts during sweeps months contain more coverage of crimes and murders.

ratio the quantity of one group divided by the quantity of the other.

Ratios are used to compare one group to another. For example, if there are 150 people under 35 and 75 people over 35, the ratio of the first group to the second is 150/75, or 2-to-1 (or 2:1).

ratio measures see *levels of measurement.*

rationalism the notion that knowledge is obtained through pure reason, without aid from the senses, experience or observation.

Opposite of *empiricism.*

Raymond, Henry J. (1820-1869) an influential politician who established and edited the "New York Times" in 1851.

reader-driven marketing the idea that mass media create products and services to meet the interests and needs of individual readers, as opposed to interests of the organization or other factors.

A reader-driven marketing approach assumes that readers have different needs for news and entertainment content. In other words, the one-product-fits-all approach doesn't fit well.

One way newspapers have responded to this need is by producing the "personal newspaper," which can be created through online versions of newspapers. The "New York Times," the "Los Angeles Times," the "Philadelphia Inquirer" and the "San Jose (Calif.) Mercury News," among others, allow their readers to create a "portfolio" of news and information that meets their particular needs. If a reader is interested in sports news and business news, he or she can create a portfolio that allows quick and easy access to these items. More sophisticated programs will eventually allow readers quick access to information on specific people, organizations, events or ideas.

The growth of reader-driven marketing doesn't mean the end of mass marketing. Certain kinds of news and information, such as national politics, will continue to have widespread appeal, even in a highly complex society. But as people and groups becomes more specialized, their needs for information will become more specialized, and mass media that cater to such specialization are expected to have a competitive advantage in the marketplace.

realism the ontological doctrine that universals exist independent of the particulars that instantiate them.

See *nominalism* and *ontology.*

reality television a form of entertainment television programming in which ordinary people or celebrities are placed into real situations, often competing for money or prizes.

Reality television is nothing new. "Candid Camera," a show in which real people were unknowingly placed into usual situations in an effort to obtain a humorous outcome, made its debut on radio in 1947 before successfully making the transition to television. But the genre received new life on May 31, 2000, when CBS aired a television program in which 16 people were sequestered on an isolated island for 39 days and had to work together to survive. One by one they voted each other off the island. The last person standing would win $1 million.

"Survivor" was an instant hit and ushered in a plethora of new programs, including "Who Wants to Marry a Millionaire," "The Mole," "The Osbournes," "The Anna Nicole Show," and "Big Brother 3."

There was no shortage of critics for these shows. However, the TV networks and the viewing public didn't care much what they thought. Reality shows were profitable. They cost an average of $400,000 per episode compared with $2 million for a dramatic series. Audiences liked them partly because the outcomes were not predictable.

research specialist a person in an *advertising, public relations* or *marketing research* firm that conducts research (e.g., surveys, *public opinion polls*, experiments and/or *focus groups*).

Reasoner, Harry (1923-1991) "ABC World News Tonight" co-anchor with *Barbara Walters* from 1970-1978.

reason-why principle the idea that advertising campaigns should employ reasons to persuade people to purchase products and services.
    See *Lasker, Albert*.

recall a concept in market research that refers to the ability of a consumer to remember a brand or advertisement.
    See *aided* and *unaided recall*.

recipient (of a message) the social actor who receives or is the intended receiver of a communicative act.
    See *communication*.

record a sound recording embedded on a disc with grooves and played on a *phonograph*.

recording format the characteristics of audio, video or computer recording media.

    Audio recording formats have changed dramatically over the years. In the 1890s, shellac replaced wax as the material preferred for producing records. In the 1940s, vinyl replaced shellac. In the 1960s, eight-track tape players were introduced and were popular because they could be used in cars. But they were quickly overtaken by the smaller, more reliable audiocassette tape player.

    Each of these changes improved audio technology. But the single most important change in the last 50 years has been digital audio recording. Digitization involves breaking down sounds and notes into a binary system of 0s and 1s (offs and ons) for processing by a computer. The key advantage of digital recording is that the quality of sound does not deteriorate with each reproduction—it remains as good as the original. In contrast, the quality of analogue recordings, such as that found on vinyl records and metal tapes, breaks down the more they are played and when they are recorded from one medium to another.

In the early 1980s, the recording industry began producing music on plastic *compact discs* (or CDs), which contained digitally encoded music read by lasers. The discs can be played over and over again without no loss in quality or sound. CDs quickly replaced vinyl records as the dominant format. By 1990, CDs were generating more revenues than vinyl records and cassette recordings combined. And by 2000, 93 percent of all sales in the recording industry came from CDs. Other formats, such as the digital audio tape (DAT), have appeared on the market but have not been as popular.

Digitization also has filtered into the music video market as well as radio broadcasting. Digital video discs (DVDs) were introduced in 1997 and sales increased seven-fold from 1998 to 2000, to $80 million. Sales increased four-fold from 2000 to 2003. DVDs are more reliable and durable than VHS tapes, hold a lot more data, and have much better quality. In addition, DVDs can be programmed in multiple languages. Users simply select the language they want.

The digitization movement is also spreading to radio. Digital radio has higher quality sound than analogue broadcasts. Digital signals can be transmitted via the Internet or satellite. To date, the Internet has been the major vehicle for digital radio, because it is inexpensive. However, several companies are now transmitting digital signals via satellite to consumers who pay a small fee per month to receive 100 or more highly specialized stations. Consumers must purchase a radio equipped to receive the broadcasts.

See *soundtrack*.

recording industry a collective name for organizations that produce *audio recordings*, especially musical recordings, usually for profit.

Recording Industry Association of America, The (RIAA) a trade group that represents the U.S. recording industry.

Its Web site <www.riaa.org> contains statistics and information about the recording industry, including information about its efforts to stem piracy and illegal downloading.

recording label a company that produces and markets recordings.

In the recording industry, the major companies own a number of different labels, or smaller companies that actually produce and market recordings. EMI, for example, owns Virgin, Capitol, Parlophone, Chrysalis, Priority, Blue Note, and EMI Classic.

Some musicians also produce and market their own music through their own "independent label." Occasionally, when these independent labels have become successful, they are bought out by the larger recording companies. This is especially true when the musical genre is highly specialized and the larger recording company has limited knowledge and expertise about the market for such music.

See *soundtrack*.

record producer the person responsible for coordinating the production and distribution of a recording. Many musicians produce their own work. However, *recording labels* or studios may provide the producer, especially if the musicians have limited experience.

recursive modeling *causal analysis* that involves one-way, or asymmetrical, effects only.

See *cause and effect* and *nonrecursive modeling*.

reductionism explaining a phenomena by means of analysis that simplifies components to a different *level of analysis*.

Water, for instance, can be reduced to H_2O molecules. Although many phenomena in the physical world can be reduced to simpler chemical or physiological properties, social phenomena cannot always be reduced to simpler properties. For example, minority groups will always have a higher proportion of people who marry people of another race than majority groups, not because minority groups have a greater "psychological affinity" for people of different races, but because structurally they have a fewer number of people in them.

In social science research, reductionism is often used in a pejorative way to criticize researchers who attempt to explain complex social or cultural phenomena by identifying psychological, organic or physiological phenomena.

See *level of analysis*.

regression see *regression analysis*.

regression analysis a *multivariate statistical* technique in which the *dependent* and *independent variables* are *continuous measures*.

Regression enables a researcher to hold some variables constant while looking at the effects of one or more independent variables on one dependent variable. It is one of the most widely used and reliable statistical techniques in *quantitative research*.

regression toward the mean an empirical phenomena in which a second measured observation falls closer to the mean than the first observation.

Regression toward the mean occurs in studies where a *repeated measurement* is taken. For example, if a *survey* asks *respondents* to rate the performance of a U.S. president on a 11-point scale and the *mean* value is "6," some of the respondents who gave the president a "1" the first time (an extreme value) have a higher probability of giving a higher value the second time. In other words, their scores will "regress" toward the mean ("6").

Similarly, some of those who gave the president a score of "9" the first time around have a higher probability of giving a lower value the second time around.

As a rule, the more extreme the score, the greater the probability the second measurement will be closer to the mean. Interestingly, however, the overall mean of the two surveys will not change (assuming, of course, that no major event or happening intercedes to affect opinions), because some respondents in the "middle" will have more extreme scores the second time.

relationship a change in one *variable* produces a change in another.

A negative relationship means that as one variable increases in *value*, the other variable decreases. A positive relationship means that as one variable increases in value, the other also increases. *Association* is another term for relationship.

See *cause and effect* and *association*.

relative frequency same as a *percentage*.

reliability the degree to which a *measure*, if repeatedly applied to the same people or in the same situation, yields the same result.

Reliability is one component of *validity*.

remote programming in radio broadcasting, programming that is fed to a local radio station via satellite or cable/telephone lines.

Historically, radio has been a highly local medium. But stations in small markets are increasingly turning to nonlocal programming to fill air time. In some cases, the local stations don't even employ disc jockeys or on-air personalities. They only have an advertising staff, which sells spot air time to local merchants. The rest of the programming and national advertising content is fed from a remote location.

Of course, the big advantage of remote programming to the radio owner is lower costs, since programming can be used on multiple stations. But the trade-off is loss of local programming and autonomy.

Renaissance a historical period, from about the 14th to the 16th centuries, that was characterized by the revival of art, literature, and learning in Europe and that marks the transition from medieval to modern society.

During this time there was increasing emphasis on the worth of the individual and on *humanism*. Art and literature also dealt with subjects other than religion and aristocratic life. The spirit of the Renaissance is reflected in the artistic works of Michelangelo and the literary works of Miguel de Cervantes, who wrote "Don Quixote," which is considered to be one of the world's first major novels.

Other Renaissance thinkers like Francis Bacon and John Locke argued that knowledge came from reason and real-world experience or what scientists call empirical observation. This perspective stood in direct contrast to religious doctrines, which held that the world was mostly unchangeable, with social station understood as predetermined and fixed.

repeated measurement taking a measurement from the same individual or phenomena on more than one occasion.
    See *regression toward the mean*.

replication duplicating the empirical results of a study.

reporter a person who gathers news and writes up stories for publication or broadcast in a news organization.
    Reporters who cover a variety of different stories are usually called general assignment reporters. Those who cover specific institutions or issues are called beat reporters.
    See *news beat*.

Reporters Committee for Freedom of the Press, The a nonprofit organization that serves as a clearinghouse for press freedom and freedom of speech issues and legal cases.
    See the organization's Web site <www.rcfp.org> for more details.

research hypothesis see *hypothesis*.

respondent (a) a person who provides *data* for analysis by responding to a *questionnaire*; **(b)** an *appellee* in a lawsuit.

response category a response made to a *question* in a survey.
    See *attribute* and *value*.

response rate the *ratio* of the total number of completed interviews, or returned *questionnaires*, to the total number of contacts or mailings.
    The number of contacts usually includes—in addition to the number of completed interviews—refusals. These are potential respondents who are not available to answer due to illness, language barriers, hearing impairment or other barriers. Nonworking telephone numbers and noneligible contacts, such as business numbers and households where no eligible respondent is available, are not included.
    Obtaining a high response rate is usually considered important in *survey research*. People who refuse to be interviewed or to respond to a written questionnaire may be different from those who do and, as such, the results may not represent the *population*. No universal standard has been set to define an appropriate response rate, but most social scientists believe 50 percent is acceptable, 60 percent is good, and 70 percent or higher is very good.

retail advertiser a company or business that advertises in local mass media (a local advertiser).

See *national advertiser.*

Reuters a British news service.

See *news service.*

rich media ad a type of Internet advertisement.

See *Internet advertising.*

Riis, Jacob (1849-1914) a New York newspaper reporter who exposed child labor abuses, industrial water pollution, and slum housing conditions.

Riis mastered photography, and his pictures convinced others the problems were real. He wrote and took pictures for several books, including "How the Other Half Lives," "The Children of the Poor," and "The Battle with the Slum."

See *muckraking era.*

Rivington, James (1724-1802) the leading Tory propagandist of the American Revolution.

Rivington edited the "New York Gazette," which initially strived to be open to "all parties." But Patriots attacked his paper and he eventually lost his newspaper and spent four years in debtor's prison.

Rockwell, Norman (1894-1978) an artist whose idealistic paintings of American life graced the covers of "Saturday Evening Post" and endeared him to many Americans.

Rockwell was born in New York City in 1894. At age 14, he enrolled in art classes at the New York School of Art. He left high school at age 16 to study at the National Academy of Design, but transferred to the Art Students League to study with Thomas Fogarty and George Bridgman.

In 1916, at the age of 22, he painted his first cover for the "Saturday Evening Post." Over the next 47 years, he would paint another 321 covers. Although these paintings were almost always too idealistic, too pristine, and too pastoral, nobody seemed to mind. Rockwell and the magazine became the iconic symbol of all that was good in America—all that it could and should be.

The 1930s and 1940s were his most fruitful years. His painting turned more and more toward depicting life in small towns. Inspired by President Franklin Delano Roosevelt's address to Congress in 1943, he painted the "Four Freedoms." They depicted the *freedom of speech*, freedom to worship, freedom from want, and freedom from fear. The exhibit, which went on tour, was highly popular and raised more than $130 million in war bonds. That same year, however, fire destroyed his studio and numerous paintings.

In 1963, Rockwell ended his association with the "Post" and began to work for "Look" magazine. During the next 10 years he painted pictures depicting his concerns about poverty, civil rights, and exploration of space. Rockwell was married three times. He had three sons. In 1977, he received the Presidential Medal of Freedom for his "vivid and affectionate portraits of our country." He died in 1978 at the age of 84.

Although Rockwell paintings are dismissed by many contemporary critics as lacking artistic merit and authentic observation, they still are very popular and worth hundreds of thousands of dollars. "Without thinking too much about it in specific terms," Rockwell once said, "I was showing the America I knew and observed to others who might not have noticed."

Sources: John Tebbel and Mary Ellen Zuckerman, *The Magazine in America: 1741-1990* (New York: Oxford University Press, 1991); James Playsted Wood, *Magazines in the United States: Their Social and Economic Influence* (New York: The Ronald Press Company, 1949), pp. 143-156.

roles social positions with certain rights and obligations.

Roles link individuals to organizations. A "journalist" is a role that links a person to a mass media organization. A major obligation of a journalist is to gather the news and write stories for publication or for broadcast. In exchange, the journalist is compensated.

role specialization a condition that exists when social actors perform a limited number of roles for an organization or a cause.

For example, in the early 1800s, roles at newspapers were not very specialized. The publisher wore many hats, including those of printer, advertising sales manager, director of public relations, and editor. Today the publisher at large newspapers often is involved only in budgeting and public relations. The publisher role has become more specialized. As a rule, roles become more specialized as an organization increases in size.

rotary press a printing press in which plates are attached to a rotating cylinder, upon which a continuous roll of paper, rather than individual sheets, passes.

Newspapers are printed on rotary presses.

royalty a fee paid to authors for obtaining the rights to publish a book.

The royalty usually ranges from 10-15 percent of the net price, or the amount paid by a wholesaler or retail store. The amount of the royalty varies depending on the type of book being published, expected sales, and author's qualifications.

run-of-press advertisements advertising content that is appears within the pages of a magazine or newspaper.

Contrast with *insert advertisements*.

S

sample elements or *cases* from a larger *population*.

sampling the process of selecting *cases* for study.
See *sampling error*.

sampling error the amount of error in measurement obtained when a *sample* instead of a *census* is drawn from a *population* of *cases* or individuals.

Sampling error is one type of random *measurement error*, and it can be estimated if all *respondents* or cases in the population are given an opportunity to be included in the *sample* (i.e., if *probability sampling* methods are used). Estimating sampling error involves calculating the *standard error*.

To understand the principle of sampling error, it is useful to begin first with an example that has no sampling error. Assume for the moment that the population to be studied is all of the students in a classroom or all of the reporters in a newsroom. Since there probably are not too many of them, one could ask everyone, "Do you favor or oppose a ban on violent content on television?" The results are called the *population parameter*, or the percentage of students or reporters who favor or oppose the ban. For illustrative purposes, let's say the results of the survey showed that half are in favor of a ban and the other half say oppose the ban. In this example, there is no sampling error because all of the elements of the population have been sampled—the study is a *census*.

Ideally, mass communication researchers would always like to survey the entire population to eliminate sampling error altogether. However, such a sample isn't practical, especially if the goal is to survey American adults.

To estimate sampling error, one just need give each member of the population an equal chance to be selected. For illustrative purposes, let's say

Sampling Distribution of the Mean

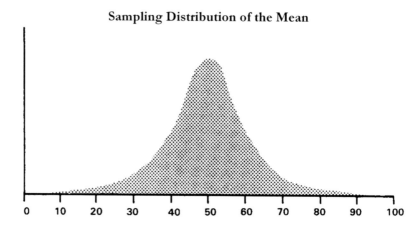

there are 100 students or reporters in the population. To give each person a chance to be selected for the sample, all of the names could be put into a hat and one-fourth could be randomly selected. After tallying the results, one now finds that 56% favor the ban on violent programming and 44% oppose. Note that the poll or sample results do not precisely match those of the population. One has a 6 percentage-point difference (56% - 50%), which represents the sampling error. (Note: In most surveys, researchers do not know the population parameter, but this doesn't prevent them from estimating the population parameter.)

Now let's take another sample of 25 names. This time the result is closer—48% favor and 52% oppose—but it is in the opposite direction of the first sample (few respondents favor). Take another sample. This time the result is 52% and 48%. And another: 44% and 56%. And another: 48% and 52%. And another: 50% and 50%. If one continues to take samples over a long period of time, the average, or mean, of all of the samples would equal the actual population parameter—50% and 50%.

If the results of an infinite number of samples drawn from this same population are plotted, they would look like a bell-shaped curve in the figure at the top of this page. This is known as the *sampling distribution of the mean*. As you can see, most of the sample results are closely grouped around the population parameter of the 50% mark found when everyone was surveyed (the population parameter).

One of the major factors influencing sample error is sample size. The larger the sample, the smaller the sampling error. The bell curve would get taller in the middle and shorter on the ends as the sample size increases.

However, sampling error decreases at a slower rate as the sample size increases, as the figure on the next page shows. Although doubling a sample of 100 results in a large drop in sampling error, doubling a sample of 1,000

Effect of Sample Size on Sampling Error

Sampling Error

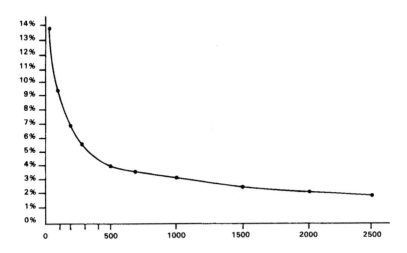

results in a very small decrease in error. For this reason, public opinion polls usually survey no more than 1,500 to 1,600 people. To interview more just increases the cost of the project—it does not appreciably reduce the sampling error.

It should be noted that, as a rule, it does not matter how large the population is. Sampling error is the same whether there are 50,000 or 10 billion in the population. Only when the number sampled represents about 5% or more of the population does the size of the sample begin to have an impact on sampling error. (The error is reduced proportionately, i.e., by 5%.)

Sampling error also is a function of the degree of difference between elements in the population. The error is greatest when two categories are evenly split—50% and 50%—and lowest when there is wide disparity, say 95% and 5%. The greater the homogeneity in the population (i.e., the greater the agreement), the fewer the number of people needed to measure sampling error accurately. In fact, if everyone agrees on an issue (100% agreement), it only takes a sample of one to represent the entire population. (But, of course, there is little agreement on many issues.)

In the social sciences, the sampling error is usually estimated as being nearly twice the *standard error* (or 1.96 to be exact). Here is the formula for estimating sampling error:

$$1.96 \times \sqrt{\frac{\text{Proportion Preferring Ban} \times \text{Proportion Opposing Ban}}{\text{Total Sample Size}}}$$

Thus, if 52% favored the ban and 48% opposed, the standard error is calculated as follows:

$$\text{Standard Error} = 1.96 \times \sqrt{\frac{.52 \times .48}{25}} = .1958, \text{ or } \pm 20 \text{ percentage points}$$

This result means that 95 percent of the time a survey like this is conducted, the true population parameter will lie within plus or minus 20 percentage points of the sample finding. The 95 percent factor refers to the *confidence level* associated with nearly two standard errors. Most researchers and national probability surveys prefer to use two standard errors (or a 95% level of confidence). The more stringent the confidence level, the bigger the confidence interval (the plus or minus factor).

In sum, the survey of students or reporters shows that 95 percent of time a survey of 25 people is taken from a large population, the population parameter will lie within 20 percentage points, plus or minus, of the sample finding. Needless to say, this is a fairly large sampling error and does provide much precision. So researchers almost always sample more than 25 people. A sample of 400, for example, reduces the confidence interval to about plus or minus 5 percentage points, and a sample of 1,500 to 2.5 percentage points.

See *standard error.*

sampling frame a listing of the individuals or *cases* in a *population* from which a *sample* is selected.

Sarnoff, David (1891-1971) a wireless radio operator who rose to become one of the most powerful executives in radio and television.

As a young man, Sarnoff worked as a wireless telegraph operator for a department store. He was on duty when the Titantic was sinking and helped route some wireless messages from nearby ships to families of the victims.

A number of biographers point out that he exaggerated the role he played during the disaster. But Sarnoff played a key role in shaping both the radio and television industries.

He believed radio could become a "household utility" for channeling music into American households. After World War I, Sarnoff emerged as a major executive in the radio industry.

During the 1930s, Sarnoff was president of RCA, which was racing to develop the first viable commercial television system in the United States. He hired Vladimir K. Zworykin, a Russian immigrant who had invented the *iconoscope*, the first electronic camera suitable for a television studio. Zworykin and his team were entrusted with developing a system acceptable for public viewing.

In 1939, they publicly unveiled the system. Sarnoff wanted a lot of publicity, so he selected the New York World's Fair for the debut. The demonstration was a big success. Two years later the *Federal Communications*

Commission adopted what amounted to RCA's standard for black-and-white television.

Sarnoff also played a key role in the development of color television. He eventually rose to the position of chair of the board of directors of RCA. He retired in 1969 and died in 1971.

satellite radio the transmission of radio programming through a satellite.

Satellite radio emerged in the early 2000s as radio's solution to the problem of limited number of frequencies on the broadcast spectrum.

Satellite radio offers consumers more than 100 talk, news, and music channels—many more than conventional radio receivers. The satellite channels also offer commercial-free music in a variety of specialized formats, including bluegrass, rap, classical, rock, swing, and hip-hop.

The main disadvantage of satellite radio is cost. A special receiver, which at this writing cost $100 or more, is necessary, and the satellite companies (e.g., XM and Sirius) charge a monthly fee ($13 to $15).

Satellite radio subscriptions are growing, and the two major companies expect to earn a profit before the end of the decade.

scale (a) categories or *values* for a *measure* that can be rank-ordered; **(b)** an *operationalization* created from two or more *variables*.

scatterplot a graph showing the joint *distributions* of two *continuous variables*.

science a profession or field of study that employs *scientific inquiry* to study the world.

See *scientific inquiry*.

scientific inquiry a method of inquiry that stresses logic and observation, or empirical facts.

Although there is no universal agreement as to what constitutes "scientific," most scholars agree that scientific inquiry differs from common sense and other forms of inquiry in two key ways: First, it strives to be logical, and, second, it strives to be supported by *observations*, or empirical facts.

Quite simply, "logical" means that the inquiry must make sense. For example, if a researcher argued that children become aggressive after watching violent television programming because they imitate the behaviors they see on television and cannot distinguish right from wrong, then most researchers would accept that explanation as logical. On the other hand, if a researcher argued that children become aggressive after watching violent programming because they hate violence, then that explanation would not be very logical. Children who hate violence should be less likely to engage in aggressive behavior.

In addition to being logical, scientific inquiry must also be supported by empirical facts, not hearsay or opinion. *Empiricism* is knowledge gained through observation or experience. One of the simplest approaches is simply to observe people's behavior. Does their behavior change after watching violent television programming? More formally, researchers set up experiments or conduct surveys. These empirical methods add rigor to scientific inquiry.

Many researchers also test formal *hypotheses*, which are statements about relationships between two or more concepts. In this case, the concepts are "TV watching" and "aggressive behavior." Thus, a simple hypothesis would be: The more time children spend watching violent programming, the more aggressive their behavior will be. Conversely, the expectation is that children who spend less time watching violent programming will be less aggressive.

As mentioned above, one possible explanation for this hypothesis is that children imitate what they see and cannot distinguish right from wrong, which is a theory. A *theory* is simply an explanation or interpretation of some behavior or phenomena. People constantly engage in theorizing in every day life, even though they normally don't call it that. A good example is sports. Why did that basketball team lose the game? Because the team members were too slow on the court. This explanation is a *theory*. The only difference is that scientists spend a great deal of time and energy building formal theories of the mind, behavior, and society.

Scientific inquiry is not the only way to understand the world. Common sense, casual observation and trial-and-error inquiry often work quite well. But these informal methods of inquiry are not as rigorous and cannot generate the kind of knowledge necessary to sustain life in a complex society. In short, what separates scientific inquiry from everyday, casual observation is a careful consideration of logic and empirical facts.

Also see *mass communication research*, *mass communication researcher*, and *theory*.

scientific journal a *periodical* geared toward the needs and interests of scientists rather than the general public.

Most journals are published four times a year (quarterly) and are refereed, meaning the submissions are subjected to a rigorous review process be referees before being accepted for publication.

scientific law (or covering law) a sequence of events that occur with unvarying uniformity under the same conditions.

See *mass communication research*.

scientific theory see *theory*.

scores numerical *values* assigned to ratings of products, services, companies or issues.

screener one or more *questions* at the front of a *questionnaire* whose purpose is to select only certain *respondents* for an interview.

screenplay in filmmaking, the script, which includes the story, the dialogue, and the action.

See *screenwriter*.

screenwriter in filmmaking, the person who writes the *screenplay*.

The screenplay may come before or after a project is started. Producers and directors are often screenwriters, but they may hire other individuals to write the screenplay. Most screenplays go through many revisions, with directors and actors playing a role.

scribes people who copied poems, speeches, orations, and *books* by hand.

In Latin, the word "scribe" means "to write." Scribes were usually monks or government officials. In addition to hand-copying books, scribes were often editors and interpreters of the religious as well as governmental laws.

During the Egyptian empire, the government employed thousands of scribes, who became a privileged class. They did not have to do manual labor or pay taxes. In the 5th century B.C., students of the famous philosopher Plato also sold or rented transcripts of his lectures.

The printing press eventually eliminated the occupation of the scribe in most areas around the world.

See *Gutenburg, Johannes,* and *printing press*.

search engine an electronic tool that locates information on the *Internet*.

The first engine was Archie, developed in 1990 at McGill University in Montreal. A year later, the University of Minnesota introduced Gopher.

These early search engines have been eclipsed by commercial (for-profit) engines, which include Google, Alta Vista, Infoseek, Yahoo!, Northern Light, Excite, and MSN Search. Today there are hundreds of search engines.

secondary analysis research that involves analysis of data collected by sources other than the researcher. Analysis of census data is an example.

Secure Digital Music Initiative created in 1998 by major music companies to combat copyright infringement.

The Initiative is developing hardware and software that will make it more difficult to bootleg or *pirate* recordings. It is estimated that illegal recordings every year cost the industry $500 million in the United States and more than $5 billion around the world.

seditious libel the act of writing or publishing material that either stirs up rebellion or criticizes authorities.

Prior to the 19th century, people who committed acts of seditious libel were often jailed or sometimes executed. In the late 1790s, for example, the

U.S. government jailed ten anti-federalist publishers for seditious libel. President *Thomas Jefferson* freed them when he took office in 1800.
See *Alien and Sedition Acts*, *law*, and *libel*.

segmentation analysis analysis whose goal is to identify segments of a market that have different needs when it comes to certain consumption of products or services.
After the segments have been identified, products or services may be modified or created to fit those needs, and researchers often begin the task of searching for the most effective and efficient means of targeting segments.
See *market segmentation*, *product differentiation*, and *target marketing*.

selective attention the notion that media consumers pay attention to some content and ignore other content.
See *limited effects model*.

selective exposure the notion that media consumers expose themselves to some content and ignore other content.
See *limited effects model*.

selective retention the notion that media consumers retain or remember ideas or information from some content and ignore other content.
See *limited effects model*.

September 11, 2001 (media coverage of) see *social control*.

server see *host*.

SES see *socioeconomic status*.

Shannon and Weaver's Mathematical Theory of Communication a model of communication that strongly influenced communication research in the 1950s and 1960s.
The original model was intended to help Bell Telephone company resolve technological problems associated with transmitting electronic messages. But social scientists expropriated the model and applied it to human behavior. The model is summarized on the top of the next page:
In 1970, media sociologist Melvin DeFleur added a feedback effect and noted that social actors may interpret messages differently. The correspondence between the intention of the source and the recipient isn't always a good fit.
See *communication* and *theory*.
Sources: C. Shannon and Warren Weaver, *The Mathematical Theory of Communication* (Urbana: University of Illinois Press, 1949) and Melvin L. DeFleur, *Theories of Mass Communication* (New York: David McKay, 1970).

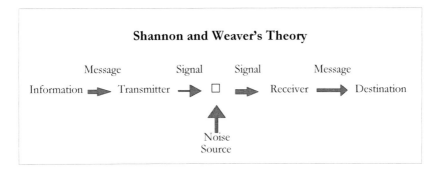

share the percentage of all TV households tuned in to television at that time.
 See *rating*.

shield law a law that prevents the government from requiring journalists to
give up confidential information about sources or stories.
 See *access law*.

shelf life the amount of time a mass media product or service is useful.
Newspapers have a short shelf life (24 hours), whereas magazines are useful
for a week or a month.

short-ordering see *pilot*.

short-wave radio see *radio* and *radio technology*.

sign (a) anything in the environment that is used to represent something
else **(b)** in social construction of reality, an object that is designed to transmit
subjective meaning.
 See *symbol*.

silicon chips (a.k.a. integrated circuits or microchips) the brains of a
computer; each contains millions of microscopic electronic components
which control the computer's overall operation.
 Some chips can perform millions of mathematical operations per
second.

simple mail transfer protocols (SMTP) a technology for transmitting small
files (e.g., *e-mail*) between computers.
 Larger files are sent via *file transfer protocol*.

simple random sampling a method of sampling in which each *respondent* or
case is given an equal chance of being selected.

With simple random sampling, findings can be generalized to the entire *population* of cases within a certain margin of error.

See *sampling error*.

simulcasting broadcasting from two or more electronic media (e.g., radio and television) at the same time.

In recent years, the term has been applied to broadcasting through *radio* and the *Internet*.

Sinclair, Upton (1878-1968) a novelist best remembered for "The Jungle," a book that exposed unsanitary conditions at Chicago meat-packing facilities.

Sinclair was a social activist who hoped his book would motivate people to join the socialist party. There is no evidence to suggest that it had much impact on turning people into socialists. However, the U.S. government responded by invoking legislation that increased safety and health standards at meat-packing facilities.

Sinclair wrote many other books and eventually won a *Pulitzer Prize* in 1942 for "Dragon's Teeth," a book about the rise of Adolph Hitler.

Sources: Upton Sinclair, *The Jungle* (New York: The New American Library, 1960 [1905]).

single copy sales sales of magazines, newspapers or other publications at newsstands or other retail outlets.

Contrast with *subscription sales*.

situational ethics in ethical decision-making, the idea that decisions should be made without rigid adherence to a set of rules.

The facts of a situation should be considered before making a decision. See *ethical decision-making*.

skip pattern arrows or other graphical devices used to direct *interviewers* or *respondents* through a series of *contingency questions*.

skyscraper ad see *Internet advertising*.

slander oral, or spoken, defamation.

See *defamation* and *libel*.

Smothers Brothers the comedy team of Dick and Tom Smothers, whose television show was often censored by CBS executives and eventually canceled because the content was deemed too critical of President Lyndon Baines Johnson and U.S. involvement in the Vietnam War.

"The Smothers Brothers Comedy Hour" aired on CBS from 1967 to 1969. In folk songs and comedy sketches, the brothers and their guests poked fun at the military, the police, middle-class America, President

Johnson, and the government. Actors Steve Martin and Rob Reiner helped write many of the scripts.

Almost everyone thought it was funny except CBS censors. For example, they cut one scene from a Mother's Day special which ended with the words, "Please talk peace" (reference to Vietnam War).

Although the show had high ratings, it was cancelled in 1969. The network justified its decision by making reference to an internal policy that "prohibits appeals for active support of any cause" (even if it was "peace"). However, critics have argued that the real reason was fear of alienating advertisers and losing broadcast licenses.

Ironically, the censors at CBS helped canonize the Smothers Brothers as symbols of the struggle for free speech on television. Dick Smothers continues to lecture on the topic to groups across the country. On Dec. 4, 2002, Bravo aired "Smothered," a documentary special about the Smothers Brothers' censorship struggles.

snapper a value or moral statement broadcast journalists sometimes employ at the end of a news or feature report.

In the field of journalism, print journalists are often admonished for including editorial comments in news stories. However, broadcast journalists have never had the same level of commitment to objectivity. Their news reports often contain snappers, which are editorial comments or value judgments that sum up the moral lesson for the viewer (e.g., "This is great tragedy, Bob. Back to you."). This is particularly true after a tragedy, such as a disaster or major crime story.

Print journalists, on the other hand, are less apt to embellish, reasoning that readers do not need to be told that a disaster is a tragic event.

snowball sample a *nonprobability sampling* method that involves asking each person interviewed to provide the names of other people to interview.

social actor a goal-oriented individual or organization.

social change the difference between current and antecedent conditions in a *culture* or *social structure*.

Culture is the symbolic and learned aspects of human society, which includes language, custom, beliefs, skills, art, norms, and values. *Social structure* is the patterned relationships between individuals and groups. These relationships are guided by role expectations, norms, and values.

The evolution of the newspaper provides a good example of social change.

In the early 1900s, the typical daily newspaper was small (7,500 circulation). It employed a handful of workers and was controlled by a single individual who performed many roles, including that of publisher, advertising manager, editor, and circulation manager. Many newspaper stories also were highly partisan in their content, leaning toward the Democratic or Republican parties.

But now the typical daily is five times larger (40,000 circulation), employs hundreds of workers, has a highly developed management structure, and is controlled and managed by professionals. The owner, who was once involved in nearly every major decision, is now often an absentee stockholder, or a publisher who focuses more on long-term issues than on day-to-day operations. Newspaper stories today also tend to be less partisan; overt opinions are usually reserved for the editorial pages or columns.

Media scholars have spent more time studying *social control* than social change. That's partly because of the influence of *Karl Marx*, who argued that mass media were agents of powerful capitalists and their politicians and produced an *ideology* that helped them rule over ordinary people. Scholars critical of the mass media see them as hindering social change that may benefit less powerful or disadvantaged people or groups.

Still, there are some good examples of mass media as agents of change. Perhaps the best cases are found during the *muckraking era* in the early 1900s. Magazines published many stories focusing on social ills, such as poor housing, unsafe working conditions, and illegal business practices. The government responded with reform legislation, giving more rights to workers and reducing the power of big business.

During the 1950s, the "Nashville Tennessean" and other newspapers published a number of stories drawing attention to the plight of African Americans in the Deep South. Some reporters went undercover, exposing the role of the Ku Klux Klan. Legendary broadcaster *Edward R. Murrow* also helped silence Sen. Joseph R. McCarthy, who was conducting a witch hunt against alleged communists in government and Hollywood. Hollywood film star James Dean also broke barriers for playing characters that challenged authorities and dominant norms and values.

The most celebrated case of the news media as an agent of change is Watergate. The "Washington Post" and other newspapers exposed corruption in President Richard Nixon's administration, which resulted in his resignation and prompted changes to a number of laws governing campaign financing. One of those laws led to the creation of a special federal prosecutor, who investigated alleged scandals in the presidential administrations of Ronald Reagan, George Bush, and Bill Clinton.

Overall, though, research shows that mass media play a relatively minor role in initiating social movements or social change. Instead, media are better viewed as institutions that facilitate and promote social change already initiated by other groups or people. For example, during the 1950s, news stories helped legitimate U.S. Supreme Court decisions that expanded civil rights, but most newspapers did not conduct investigations of civil rights abuses.

See *social control*.

Sources: David Pearce Demers, *The Menace of the Corporate Newspaper: Fact or Fiction?* (Ames: Iowa State University Press, 1996), pp. 3-4; David Demers and K. Viswanath (eds.), *Mass Media, Social Control and Social Change: A Macrosocial Perspective* (Ames: Iowa State University Press, 1999).

social cognitive theory a theory of media effects which posits that people learn through observation, not just though experience.

This perspective is most strongly associated with psychologist Albert Bandura, who became famous for a series of experiments on children that involved a three-foot high plastic, blow-up toy called the Bobo Doll. The experiments showed that children often imitated the violent behaviors they see on television.

See *mass communication research, media violence (effects of)* and *theory*.

Source: Albert Bandura, "Social Cognitive Theory of Mass Communication," pp. 61-90 in Jennings Bryant and Dolf Zillmann (eds.), *Media Effects: Advances in Theory and Research* (Hillsdale, NJ: Lawrence Erlbaum Associates, 1994).

social control attempts, whether intentional or not, by the *state* or by *social institutions*—including *mass media*—to regulate or encourage conformity to a set of *values* or *norms* through *socialization* or through the threat of *coercion*, or both.

Research shows that virtually all news and entertainment content has implications for social control. This is particularly the case when a social system or a community is threatened by war or terrorism. In fact, the greater the perceived threat, the greater the potential for social control.

September 11, 2001, is a good example. This was the day 19 so-called "suicide terrorists" commandeered four U.S. commercial airliners and flew two of them into the twin towers of the World Trade Center in New York City, killing nearly 3,000 people. A third plane was flown into the Pentagon, killing 200 more people. The fourth plane crashed in a Pennsylvania field, killing all 45 on board.

Within two minutes of the downings, Cable News Network (CNN) was broadcasting live near the World Trade Center. Other television and radio networks quickly followed. Initially, there was confusion. Were the crashes intentional? If so, who was behind them? And why would anyone commit such horrendous acts?

To get answers to these questions, the journalists turned primarily to politicians, law enforcement officials, and military leaders (i.e., governmental elites), including President George W. Bush. Journalists depend heavily on such sources for the news. These are the people society entrusts with the authority to explain and interpret such events.

The next day, newspaper headlines reflected outrage and anger: "Acts of Mass Murder" ("Newsday"); "It's War" ("New York Daily News"); "A Day of Infamy" ("Tulsa World"); "Terror Beyond Belief" ("Newark Star Ledger"); "Day of Evil" ("Orange County Register"); "A Day of Horror" ("Reno Gazette-Journal"); "Evil Acts" ("Southeast Missourian"); and "Bring Them to Justice" ("South Bend Tribune").

The authorities eventually placed responsibility for the attacks on Afghanistan-based Osama bin Laden and his al Qaeda terrorist network. For weeks and months afterward, news stories, editorials, commentaries, and letters to the editor condemned the attacks and the "terrorists" and praised the actions of the firefighters, police, and passengers on the hijacked plane. New York Mayor Rudolph Giuliani was elevated to the status of hero for his leadership during the crisis.

In short, news media coverage of 9/11 was not objective in any absolute sense of the word. It defined who was "good" and who was "bad." The content helped mobilize public opinion against terrorism and in favor of a military offensive in Afghanistan—one that led to the ousting the Taliban, who had supported bin Laden, from power. Public opinion polls showed Americans strongly supported the U.S. military intervention in Afghanistan.

After that war, the Bush administration also placed part of the blame for the attacks on Iraqi President Saddam Hussein, even though there was scant evidence of a connection between the terrorists and Hussein. In fact, none of the terrorists were from Iraq, even though public opinion polls showed nearly half of all Americans believed there was a connection.

In early 2003, the Bush administration launched a public relations campaign to drum up support for ousting Hussein from power. The news media played a primary role in convincing Americans and others of the value of attacking Iraq, according to researchers and analysts.

When the U.S. launched a military strike in Iraq in March 2003, the U.S. public was solidly behind the effort. That support began to fade in early 2004, when it became increasingly clear that Hussein did not have weapons of mass destruction or direct links to al Qaeda. But despite these revelations, the American public still supported the President's decision to invade Iraq as late as summer 2004.

As 9/11 illustrates, the social control function of the mass media is most evident during times of war. In fact, historical evidence shows that mainstream mass media produce content that supports the goals of military and political elites and helps maintain morale "back home" in virtually all wars. There is also evidence that news reports often downplay negative outcomes and overplay positive ones.

Mass communication researchers also point out that the social control function is not limited to disasters or wars, or to just the news media.

• News reports and entertainment programming about crime, such as television programs and movies, play an important role in defining the boundaries of appropriate behavior. They also generate sympathy for most victims and outrage for most law-breakers. The overall message is: crime doesn't pay.

• Music videos and radio music play an important role in reinforcing the societal value of romantic love. Young people are drawn to music in part because of this, and the concept of romantic love portrayed in popular music helps reinforce values about the importance of marriage and family.

• Television entertainment programming and movies play an important role in helping people to relax. For some, they provide a means of escape from the mundane aspects of everyday life. To the extent that watching such programming alleviates loneliness or stress, television and movies may be seen as solving psychological problems.

• Advertising encourages people to buy certain products and services, which in turn provides income for businesses. Advertising doesn't always lead to higher sales, but it does work under many conditions. Increased sales maintain the status quo by helping existing companies stay in business.

• Magazines tend to be more specialized in content and function than other forms of media, which means the functions they perform in terms of social control are very specialized. For example, many teenage girls read "Seventeen," "Teen Magazine," "Teen People," and other popular press magazines to learn about relationships and love, to learn how to dress and use make-up, and to learn about how other teens deal with personal problems.

• Business news plays an important role in helping executives and politicians make decisions affecting businesses or economic policy. People who own stock or have investments also often follow business news to keep abreast of changing economic conditions. Helping people achieve their business goals contributes directly to social order.

• Television talk shows, like "Oprah Winfrey" and "Jerry Springer," are often criticized for being too trivial or too sensational. But interviews with movie stars and with ordinary people who have extraordinary problems play an important role in helping define or reinforce the boundaries of acceptable behavior. In fact, when viewed from afar, such programming may be seen as loosely scripted morality plays. Audience applause and boos usually mirror the dominant values in society.

In short, mass media content plays a key role in helping maintain social order in the societies in which they operate. They provide information and entertainment programming that people and groups need or use to achieve their personal and professionals goals.

To many people, the term "social control" often connotes a nefarious force or evil idea. History is, indeed, filled with numerous examples of atrocities committed by various political and religious leaders to maintain control over people or groups.

But it is important to point out that no society or group can exist without some mechanisms for controlling people and subgroups. Indeed, even simple communication is not possible without rules governing language (i.e., grammar)—a form of control that people rarely think about. Thus, the answer to the question of whether social control is good or bad depends at least in part on who benefits from such control.

Sources: Headlines from newspapers obtained from www.September11news.com; Ralph D. Berenger (ed.), *Global Media Go to War: Role of News and Entertainment Media During the 2003 Iraq War* (Spokane, WA: Marquette Books, 2004); American Enterprise Institute, *Public Opinion on the War on Terrorism, the War with Iraq and America's Place in the World* (unpublished report, July 2, 2004), available online at <www.air.org>. Studies and analyses that support the social control function include: J. Herbert Altschull, *Agents of Power* (New York: Longman, 1984); W. Lance Bennett, *News: The Politics of Illusion*, 2nd ed. (New York: Longman, 1988); David Pearce Demers, *Menace of the Corporate Newspaper: Fact or Fiction?*

(Ames: Iowa State University Press, 1996); Stuart Ewin, *Captains of Consciousness: Advertising and the Social Roots of the Consumer Culture* (New York: McGraw Hill, 1976); Mark Fishman, *Manufacturing the News* (Austin: University of Texas Press, 1980); Edward S. Herman and Noam Chomsky, *Manufacturing Consent: The Political Economy of the Mass Media* (New York: Pantheon, 1988); Herbert J. Gans, *Deciding What's News* (New York: Vintage, 1979); Todd Gitlin, *The Whole World Is Watching* (Berkeley: University of California Press, 1980); David L. Paletz and Robert M. Entman, *Media Power Politics* (New York: The Free Press, 1981); and Phillip J. Tichenor, George A. Donohue and Clarice N. Olien, *Community Conflict and the Press* (Beverly Hills, CA: Sage, 1980).

social differentiation the process through which an institutional activity divides and becomes more specialized.

The division of labor is a good example. As a business grows, it tends to create new and more specialized roles and tasks; in other words, the *division of labor* expands.

Social differentiation generally leads to increased *interdependence* among *social actors*. It generally also increases problems of communication and control, which in turn generates increased demands for information and knowledge to solve those problems.

At a macro level, urbanization and industrialization are two measures of social differentiation. In mass media systems theory, mass media are themselves seen as products of increasing social differentiation.

Social differentiation is often used interchangeably with *structural pluralism* and *structural differentiation*.

social distance the closeness a *social actor* feels to other social actors.

Sociologists Robert Park and Robert Burgess coined the metaphor in 1924. In 1926, sociologist Emory Bogardus developed a "social distance scale," which is still commonly used today (with modifications). People are asked to indicate how they would feel to have a member of another (racial, social or national) group: (a) in close kinship marriage; (b) in my club as a personal chum; (c) in my street as a neighbor; (d) as a fellow employee in my occupation; (e) as a fellow citizen in my country; (f) as a visitor only in my country. The last item asked whether they (g) would exclude all members of the other group.

social institution a group or organization composed of people working to achieve goals that are sanctioned by the larger society.

The goals are guided by values, norms and roles. Examples are the police, churches, schools, the family, and mass media, such as the New York Times."

social interaction two or more social actors who act upon each other, often through communication.

socialization the noncoercive process by which people learn to conform to social *norms* and *values*.

Historically, parents and religious leaders played key roles in teaching (or socializing) children into the dominant norms and values in a community or society. As societies modernize, schools, government, and the mass media also play a role.

social learning theory see *social cognitive theory*.

social order a condition of stability or *social control* in a *social system*.

Three major explanations have been offered to account for social order: The utilitarian approach is based on the idea that people agree to give up some freedoms in exchange for social order. The cultural approach contends that social order is primarily a function of shared values and norms. The compulsion approach argues that force or threat of force helps maintain order.

See *social control*.

social responsibility theory see *normative theory*.

social science a branch of science that studies society, people, and relationships.

See *mass communication research*.

social scientist an individual who studies society, people, and/or relationships and who usually has an advanced degree and works for a college, university or other major *social institution*.

See *mass communication researcher*.

social structure the patterned relationships (repetitive behaviors) between individuals and groups. These relationships are guided by role expectations, norms, and values.

See *social change* and *probabilistic theory of social action*.

social system two or more people or organizations who depend upon each other to achieve their goals.

Some researchers also assume that a social system encompasses the *values, rules* (or *norms*), and *laws* that govern those relationships and enables social actors to achieve their goals.

Society of National Association Publications a nonprofit organization that serves as a clearinghouse for ideas and information for publishers of magazines and other media.

The organization's Web site <www.snaponline.org> includes job listings and information that helps publishers to network.

Society of Professional Journalists (SPJ) a nonprofit professional association composed of about 9,000 working journalists, students journalists, and media scholars from around the world.

According to its Web site, SPJ is dedicated to "the perpetuation of a free press as the cornerstone of our nation and our liberty. ... It is the role of journalists to provide this information in an accurate, comprehensive, timely and understandable manner. It is the mission of the Society of Professional Journalists: to promote this flow of information; to maintain constant vigilance in protection of the *First Amendment* guarantees of *freedom of speech* and *freedom of the press*; to stimulate high standards and ethical behavior in the practice of journalism; to foster excellence among journalists; to inspire successive generations of talented individuals to become dedicated journalists; to encourage diversity in journalism; to be the pre-eminent, broad-based membership organization for journalists; and to encourage a climate in which journalism can be practiced freely."

The SPJ *code of ethics* is the most cited code in the field of journalism. The preamble of the SPJ code states that "enlightenment is the forerunner of justice and the foundations of democracy. The duty of the journalist is to further those ends by seeking truth and providing a fair and comprehensive account of events and issues. Conscientious journalists from all media and specialties strive to serve the public with thoroughness and honesty. Professional integrity is the cornerstone of a journalist's credibility."

More specifically, the code admonishes journalists to: (1) "seek truth and report it," which means they should be "honest, fair and courageous in gathering, reporting and interpreting information"; (2) "minimize harm," which means they should "treat sources, subjects and colleagues as human beings deserving of respect"; (3) "act independently," which means they should be "free of obligation to any interest other than the public's right to know"; (4) be "accountable to their readers, listeners, viewers and each other."

The SPJ code does not specifically mention the *ethic of objectivity*. However, the code admonishes journalists to be "fair," to "distinguish between advocacy and news reporting," and to "diligently seek out subjects of news stories to give them the opportunity to respond to allegations of wrongdoing."

The SPJ code is a very strong statement in support of the *social responsibility theory*.

Sources: Society of Professional Journalists <www.spj.org>.

socioeconomic status (SES) a concept or variable used to rank-order people or families in terms of income, education, and occupation.

SES is a good predictor of some media behaviors. For example, higher SES people are much more likely than lower SES people to subscribe to and read a newspaper.

See *knowledge gap hypothesis*.

Soundscan a computerized system that tracks sales of *compact discs* and other recordings in stores.

The system records the bar codes as a disc or tape is purchased at store. Before this technology, sales data were often distorted to promote some songs and albums over others.

soundtrack (a) an area on the edge of a motion-picture film that carries the sound **(b)** a single recording that, when combined with other recordings (or soundtracks), produces a sound from two or more musicians or singers.

Soundtrack as used in the music recording industry usually means that different instruments and vocals are recorded on separate tracks. This gives the producer or the engineer greater flexibility in "mixing" the various tracks to produce the highest quality sound.

There was a time when music was recorded on just a handful of tracks. Today, the number of tracks is limited only by the equipment, and most studios can record 24 or more tracks simultaneously. As the price of recording equipment has decreased, many musicians are now recording in their homes. Digital 8-track home recording systems are available for less than $1,000 and in principle can produce the same quality as a professional studio. The major difference is that professional studios usually have better soundproofing capabilities and a highly trained staff.

At the studio, musicians in a group may record together or separately. The producer and engineers provide feedback and assistance. The master recording then is available for mass production. A recording company may run its own manufacturing facilities or may contract the work out. Factories then produce the discs, tapes, and records for marketing and distribution.

See *recording format.*

Soviet or communist theory see *normative theory.*

spam unsolicited *e-mail* that contains *advertising.*

Spamming involves sending a large number of e-mails in an attempt to sell a product or service to a user. Spam is extremely unpopular with Internet users. But *freedom of speech* (advertising) issues have contained efforts to ban or control it.

specialization see *role specialization.*

Spielberg, Steven (1946-) one of Hollywood's most successful producers and directors.

Spielberg is the son of an electrical engineer (his father) and a concert pianist (his mother). He seems to have acquired the pragmatic craftsmanship of his father and the artistic and creative talent of his mother.

Spielberg's interest in filmmaking emerged when he was a youngster. At age 12 he had completed his first scripted amateur film. At age 13 he won a prize for a 40-minute war movie called "Escape to Nowhere." And at age 16 his 140-minute science-fiction production, "Firelight," generated a $100 profit in a local theater.

Ironically, Spielberg's application to film school in the 1960s was rejected. His grades weren't good enough. As a youth, Spielberg was more interested in watching television and in producing amateur films than in studying. But failure to gain entry to film school didn't deter him.

He enrolled as an English major at California State University in Long Beach, and after scrounging up $15,000 from friends, produced "Amblin'," a 24-minute film about a pair of hitchhikers. "Amblin'" won several film awards and was shown at the Atlanta Film Festival in 1969.

Executives at Universal-MCA were so impressed that they gave him a seven-year contract in the television division. Spielberg, only 20 years of age, made history as the youngest person to obtain a long-term contract from a major production studio.

After signing the contract with Universal, Spielberg directed some television shows and in 1972 the made-for-TV movie "Duel," which starred Dennis Weaver as a salesman menaced by a diesel truck. Spielberg directed his first feature film, "The Sugarland Express," in 1974. The film won a Cannes Film Festival Award for Best Screenplay. He followed that in 1975 with "Jaws," the blockbuster movie about a great white shark. In 1977, he wrote the screenplay for and directed "Close Encounters of the Third Kind," the science fiction adventure that netted him a Best Director Oscar nomination.

Not everything Spielberg has directed has been successful. His first attempt in 1979 at comedy, "1941," was a disaster. But in 1981 he and friend George Lucas followed this up with "Raiders of the Lost Ark," which netted him another Best Director Oscar nomination. A year later he released "E.T.: The Extra Terrestrial," which became the biggest domestic moneymaker at that time.

Responding to critics who said he could not make a serious adult film, he directed in 1985 the screen adaptation of Alice Walker's "The Color Purple," which garnered 11 Oscar nominations, although none for Spielberg. But the Academy atoned by giving him the Irving G. Thalberg Award in 1987. Around the same time he divorced actress Amy Irving and married "Indiana Jones and the Temple of Doom" leading lady Kate Capshaw.

Spielberg produced two blockbusters in 1993: "Jurassic Park" and "Schindler's List." "Jurassic Park" grossed $100 million in just the first nine days and eventually shattered "E.T."'s record. "Schindler's List" earned his first Best Director Oscar. His second came with "Saving Private Ryan," which was released in 1998. "Amistad," a movie about an 1839 shipboard revolt by African slaves, earned him a Golden Globe nomination.

In 1994, Spielberg joined with David Geffen and Jeffrey Katzenberg to form DreamWorks, a studio which released "Amistad," "Saving Private Ryan," and "American Beauty," the latter of which won the Best Picture Oscar for 1999. In 2002, Spielberg directed "Minority Report," which starred Tom Cruise and has been called one of his finest films.

Today Spielberg is consistently rated one of the top producer/directors in the world. He earned Best Director and Best Picture Oscars for "Schindler's List," which details the true-life story of a German factory owner who saved thousands of Jewish citizens during World War II, and a Best Director Oscar for "Saving Private Ryan," which chronicles the efforts of one World War II soldier whose mission is to find and bring home the only surviving son of a family whose three other sons were killed in action.

A "Hollywood Reporter" survey of studio executives in 2000 rated Spielberg the most "bankable director" of more than 800 rated.

Spielberg and Capshaw are raising seven children, two adopted and two from previous marriages. Spielberg is worth about $2 billion and earns more than $2 million a year..

Sources: Joseph McBride, *Steven Spielberg: A Biography* (New York: Simon & Schuster, 1997); and Philip M. Taylor, *Steven Spielberg: The Man, His Movies and Their Meaning* (London: Batsford, 1999).

spin doctor a derogatory term referring to people, especially public relations practitioners, who distort the truth or put a positive spin on a story even if the news is unfavorable.

spiral of cynicism a theory that the mass media's heavy focus on the game rather than the substance of politics makes voters more cynical about politics and government.

See *spiral of silence.*

Sources: Joseph N. Cappella and Kathleen Hall Jamieson, *Spiral of Cynicism: The Press and the Public Good* (New York: Oxford University Press, 1997).

spiral of silence hypothesis a theory that political opinions and ideas viewed as widely held become even more dominant because, in this context, people who hold minority views are afraid to express such values openly.

This theory, which was proposed by German public opinion researcher Elisabeth Noelle-Neumann, has four major assumptions: (1) people fear isolation from other people; (2) society threatens deviant people with isolation; (3) fear of isolation causes people to assess public opinion; and (4) if people think the majority holds a view other than their own, they are less likely to publicly express their own views because of fear of isolation. Over time, a "spiral of silence" develops.

The spiral of silence hypothesis has a lot in common with the notion of the "bandwagon effect." That is, people change their opinions to get on the bandwagon and be a part of the winning rather than the losing side. Research provides a fair amount of support for this model. However, the model doesn't explain why some people remain steadfast in their beliefs, despite being in the minority, and how minority opinions sometimes become majority opinions.

The notion of a spiral of silence also has spurred the development of other concepts, such as the "spiral of cynicism," which accuses the mass media of making people cynical about politics and government.

See *spiral of cynicism.*
Sources: Elisabeth Noelle-Neumann, "The Spiral of Silence: A Theory of Public Opinion," *Journal of Communication*, 24:24-51 (1974).

spot news see *breaking news.*

spuriousness a *relationship* or *association* between two *variables* that is false.
A spurious relationship stems from those variables' joint correlation with another, third variable. *Multivariate analysis* is used to identify spurious relationships.

Stamp Act of 1765 a British law that imposed heavy duties on legal documents and paper used in publishing newspapers.
Many historians argue that the Stamp Act contributed to the start of the Revolutionary War. The Act alienated two important colonial groups: lawyers and journalists. When the British pointed out that the colonists themselves had imposed local stamp taxes in Massachusetts and New York, the colonists responded that it wasn't the tax per se, it was the fact that they didn't have representation in Parliament ("taxation without representation").

standard deviation square root of the average squared distance around the *mean*, or the square root of the *variance.*
The standard deviation is a *measure of dispersion.*

standard error in a *probability survey*, the standard error is usually calculated as the square root of .25 divided by the number of *cases.*
For example, the standard error for a sample size of 600 is about 2 percentage points. This means that 68 percent of time a *survey* like this one is conducted, the actual population figure or parameter will vary no more than plus or minus 2 percentage points of the sample finding. When estimating *sampling error*, most market researchers use about two standard errors (1.96 to be more accurate) as the cutoff for determining whether a finding could have occurred by chance. For a sample size of 600, this means that 95 percent of the time the actual *population parameter* is no more than plus or minus 4 percentage points from the sample finding. The formula for the standard error is:

$$\sqrt{\frac{p \times q}{n}}$$

where

p = Proportion of cases in one category or value
q = Proportion of cases in all other categories
n = Sample size

The standard error is greatest when the proportions are .50 (denominator equals .25), but it declines as the p and q diverge toward 0.00 and 1.00. (Note: p + q = 1.00)

See *sampling error* for another example.

stare decisis see *law*.

star system a marketing approach in filmmaking that involves using famous actors to increase demand for and attendance at motion pictures.

The idea was borrowed from Broadway and theater. Douglas Fairbanks, Sr., Mary Pickford, Buster Keaton, and Charlie Chaplin became big box-office draws.

state a political entity legally permitted to use force within a particular geographical area.

state of independence a condition that exists when two *variables* are unrelated, i.e., when they have no *association*.

Star Chamber Court an English regulatory body that imposed severe penalties on printers, publishers, and others who criticized British authorities.

In 1584, William Carter was hanged for printing pamphlets favorable to the Catholic cause. This act infuriated the Puritans, who in the mid-1600s overthrew the monarchy and ruled Great Britain for a short time. Led by Oliver Cromwell, the Puritans abolished the Star Chamber in 1641.

See *Areopagitica, Milton, John,* and *Stationers Company.*

Stationers Company an English regulatory entity created by Queen Mary in 1557 to regulate printed material.

The term "stationer," applied to people who published or distributed books, distinguished them from printers. The Stationers Company conducted weekly searches of London printing houses, confiscating unauthorized works and sometimes punishing publishers. The Stationers Company eventually was abandoned in part because rapid growth in the number of books and printed material made it difficult to review all the material.

See *Star Chamber Court.*

statistical significance when the difference between two or more *percentages* or *means* in a study is not likely to be a function of chance or *sampling error*

In essence, this means that there is a high probability that a difference exists in the *population.*

See *sampling error* and *standard error.*

statistics a branch of applied mathematics that focuses on the collection and interpretation of quantitative data, including data for estimating *population parameters*.

See *descriptive statistics, inferential statistics, sampling error,* and *standard error.*

status quo the existing state of affairs, or current conditions.

Steffens, Lincoln (1866-1936), a former newspaper reporter and managing editor of "McClure's" magazine who investigated corruption in government in numerous cities (Chicago, Cincinnati, Cleveland, Minneapolis, New York, and Pittsburgh) and in state government (Illinois, Missouri, New Jersey, Ohio, Rhode Island, and Wisconsin).

His 1904 book on corruption in city government, "The Shame of the Cities," was a best-seller.

Steinem, Gloria (1934-) a journalist and a leader in the feminist movement.

Steinem was an ambitious journalist who, among other things, took a job as a "bunny waitress" in 1963 to expose sexual discrimination and harassment at New York's Playboy Club. The article failed to advance her hope for a career as a serious political journalist, but it furthered her interest in the women's movement.

In 1971, she founded and edited "Ms." magazine, the first national magazine edited and run by women. The magazine promoted the belief that when women are liberated, men will be too.

"Ms." magazine reached a circulation of 500,000 by 1983, but eventually went out of business. It was later revived as an adless monthly. Steinem continues to write and speak about feminist issues.

Stern, Howard (1954-) a controversial radio host and self-proclaimed *First Amendment* advocate whose program often focuses on issues of sex and sexual experiences.

In April 2003, Stern, the so-called "shock jock," and his radio cohorts discussed on air their sexual experiences and the use of a personal hygiene product called "sphincterine." One listener complained to the *Federal Communications Commission,* which fined Clear Channel $495,000. Clear Channel then responded by dropping Stern's program from the six radio stations that carried the program. Stern then responded with charges of censorship against both the FCC and Clear Channel.

Stern's basic complaint is over the definition of indecency. His Web site <www.howardstern.com> points out that many television and radio programs (such as Oprah Winfrey's) have broadcast "indecent language," but they were not fined.

Clear Channel says it dropped Stern's program simply because it was getting expensive. Since 1990, Stern's program has generated $2.5 million in fines against radio stations across the country. In 2004, Stern announced that he was taking his program to satellite radio, which the FCC does not regulate.

Sources: John Dunbar, "Indecency on the the the Air: Shock-Radio Jock Howard Stern Remains 'King of All Fines," The Center for Public Integrity (July 28, 2004), <www.publicintegrity.org>.

Stowe, Harriet Beecher (1811-1896) a social activist and writer whose book "Uncle Tom's Cabin" helped mobilize public opinion against slavery before the Civil War.

Stowe was the daughter of a liberal clergyman. She learned Latin before age 10 and was teaching it at age 12. She helped her sister open a school and wrote a geography textbook before moving to Ohio at age 25. Stowe was very religious and promoted feminist causes as well. Many of the female characters in her writings are presented as equals to men.

Her husband, a teacher, was also an ardent opponent of slavery. To supplement his income, Stowe began writing short stories dealing with domestic life. The royalties enabled her to hire household help to assist with raising their seven children. In Cincinnati, which was separated only by the Ohio River from a slave-holding community, Stowe met many fugitive slaves and listened to their stories. She also visited Southern states. "Uncle Tom's Cabin" (or Life Among the Lowly)" was published serially in the "National Era" in 1851. The book was published the following year and sold more than a half million copies in the United States within five years and was translated into more than 20 foreign languages. It was the first book to include a Black character as a hero. Historians and scholars widely agree it has been one of the most influential books in American history.

Sources: John R. Adams, *Harriet Beecher Stowe* (New York: Twayne Publishers, 1963); Harriet Beecher Stowe, *Uncle Tom's Cabin* (New York: Macmillan Publishing Company, 1994 [1852]); and Noel Bertram Gerson, *Harriet Beecher Stowe: A Biography* (New York: Praeger Publishers, 1976).

stratified random sampling a probability method of sampling in which the *population* is divided into two or more subgroups and a separate *sample* is extracted from each.

For example, the United States could be divided into 20 regions. The number of interviews in each region would be in *proportion* to that region's percentage contribution to the total population. This is called proportionate stratified random sampling. Sampling could also be done disproportionately, in which case the data could be weighted to ensure proper representation from each region.

Stratification can be done on a number of *variables*, as long as the *population parameters* are known. The primary advantage of stratified random sampling is that it generally has less, and will never have more, *sampling error* than *simple random sampling*, since there is no sampling error on the stratified variable (i.e., the proportion of cases in each category for that variable matches the proportion of cases for the population parameter).

stratified sampling see *stratified random sampling.*

structural differentiation see *structural pluralism* and *social differentiation.*

structural functionalism a sociological theory that explains a social institution or phenomena by examining the functions it performs for maintaining an organization or a social system.

The structural functionalist approach has roots that go back to the 19th century, but the most important advocate was sociologist Talcott Parsons, who focused on how solidarity, trust, meaning, and power are institutionalized in the construction or production of *social order.* Although all of these dimensions were defined as needs that every social system must cope with in order to survive, cooperation and consensus were given a much more prominent role than power and conflict in the regulation of social activities.

In his quest to explain social order, Parsons spent a great deal of time trying to identify the functional imperatives of social systems — i.e., the needs or requisites that all social systems must solve in order to survive. Parsons developed the "four-function paradigm," which proposed that all systems face four major problems — adaptation, goal attainment, integration, and pattern maintenance (later renamed latent pattern maintenance-tension management). To solve these problems, he argued that social systems have developed four major subsystems or institutions: the economy to satisfy the adaptation need (i.e., the acquisition of resources from the environment); the polity to solve the goal attainment need; culture (or public associations), such as religious and mass media institutions, to meet the integration need; and the family and educational institutions to satisfy the need for pattern maintenance. A social system that resolves each of these four system needs successfully was, according to Parsons, in a state of equilibrium, or a state of balance.

The equilibrium assumption led many of the functional theorists to take for granted the creation and emergence of values, norms, and institutions. As a consequence, any behavior that deviated from the dominant system of values and rules was considered deviant and undesirable. The goal of social science research under such an approach was to eliminate or control such behaviors. Needless to say, the equilibrium assumption became a lightning rod for criticisms that systems theory was conservative and helped support an oppressive, inqualitarian status quo. Parsons, in particular, was frequently criticized for allegedly advancing a theory that appeared to be ideologically conservative, a label he dismissed but was never able to shake.

Although structural functionalist theorists placed a great deal of emphasis on how institutions maintain social order, they did not ignore *social change*, a point that is sometimes overlooked by critics. Many adopted a neo-evolutionary model of social change, in which structural differentiation and functional specialization were the primary agents. They acknowledged that revolutionary change was possible; however, they could not account for such change because they viewed it as too complex to explain, given the current state of knowledge.

One of the substantive areas particularly influenced by structural functionalism was comparative research on modernization in the 1950s and 1960s. These studies sought to explain differences between traditional and modern societies, arguing that traditional societies were perceived as being restrictive and limited, whereas modern societies were seen as being much more adaptable to a wide range of internal and external problems, especially social and technological change. These theories assumed that the organizational dynamics of economic, political, and industrial institutions provide the dynamic force of structure in any complex society. *Mass media* were seen as playing an important role in breaking down traditional authority and ways of life and ushering in modern values and norms. Furthermore, as the world becomes more urbanized and industrialized, societies become more similar. This view was highly consistent with classical evolutionary theory, which stressed that most societies passed through relatively similar stages toward a common end-stage of modernity.

Following this line of thought, many mass communication researchers before and after World War II attempted to define the major functions that media perform for society. In the 1940s, Lasswell wrote about three major functions: (1) surveillance of the environment; (2) correlation of the parts of society in responding to the environment; and (3) transmission of the social heritage from one generation to the next. Wright added a fourth: entertainment. And Lazarsfeld and Merton added two more: status conferral and the enforcement of social norms (ethicizing).

Following Merton, many theorists recognized that media and other institutions may have dysfunctional consequences for *social systems* or *social actors*. DeFleur argued, for example, that the function of low-taste content in mass media was "to maintain the financial equilibrium of a deeply institutionalized social system which is tightly integrated with the whole of the American economic institution." Nevertheless, the underlying theme in such research was that media coverage, as a whole, contributed to social order.

The social control function continues to be a major element in contemporary theories of functionalism (see *mass media system theory*). Neo- or post-functional approaches also acknowledge that media content often has detrimental consequences for disadvantaged groups and those not in power. In these respects, modern functional approaches share a lot of common ground with *critical theory* and with *cultural theory*. However, contemporary functional approaches also see media systems as having the ability to produce content that on occasion benefits disadvantaged groups and those not in power. As such, they see mass media as an agent of evolutionary change—change that in turn helps explain many of the social changes that took place during the 20th century (e.g., expansion of civil rights, women rights, environment controls, labor rights).

See *theory, mass media system theory*.

Sources: Talcott Parsons, *The Social System* (New York: The Free Press, 1951); Robert K. Merton, *Social Theory and Social Structure*, 3rd ed. (New York: The Free Press, 1968 [1949]); Ralf Dahrendorf, *Class and Class Conflict in Industrial Society* (Stanford, Calif.: Stanford University Press, 1959 [1957 German version]); Daniel Lerner, *The Passing of Traditional Society* (New York: Macmillan, 1958); Harold D. Lasswell, "The Structure and Function of Communication in Society," pp. 84-99 in Wilbur Schramm and Donald F. Roberts (eds.), *The Process and Effects of Mass Communication* (Urbana, Ill.: University of Illinois Press, 1971); Charles R. Wright, *Mass Communication: A Sociological Perspective* (New York: Random House, 1959); Paul Lazarsfeld and Robert Merton, "Mass Communication, Popular Taste and Organized Social Action," pp. 95-118 in L. Bryson (ed.), *The Communication of Ideas* (New York: Harper and Brothers, 1948); and Melvin L. DeFleur, "Mass Media as Social Systems," pp. 63-83 in Wilbur Schramm and Donald F. Roberts, *The Process of Effects of Mass Communication* (Urbana, Ill.: University of Illinois Press, 1971), p. 83.

structural pluralism the number and variety of groups and organizations in a social system.

Structural pluralism or, as some researchers prefer, social differentiation (or structural differentiation), is a key concept in many sociological analyses of media systems. *Mass media systems theory*, for example, posits that as societies and organizations grow and become more complex, the demand for news, information, and entertainment increases. Mass media have emerged largely in response to those needs for information. They produce content that helps people achieve their goals in a socially complex world.

student expression an area of mass media law that applies to publications and broadcast content created by high school students and sometimes college students.

The courts have generally ruled that students have *First Amendment* rights like others, but high school administrators and in some cases college administrators can control the content of student publications if the publication is part of a curriculum at an institution. Most high school newspapers are produced through the curriculum. But many college newspapers are independent and, thus, enjoy the same, or nearly the same, protections as the commercial press.

During the 1970s and early 1980s, most courts followed the U.S. Supreme Court's ruling in Tinker v. Des Moines Independent School District (1969). In that case, the Court upheld the rights of students to wear black arm bands as a protest against the war in Viet Nam. The First Amendment protected expression by high school students as long as this action was not disruptive or obscene or did not violate the rights of other students.

However, in 1988 the Court upheld a high school principal's decision to censor stories about teen pregnancy and divorce in the student newspaper. The Court ruled that the student newspaper was not a public forum because it was produced in a journalism class. The school has the right to regulate expression the public might associate with it, the court ruled.

College student newspapers that are not produced through a journalism class enjoy the same protection as commercial newspapers, even though they may receive funding from the university and student fees. This freedom may be circumscribed, however, if administrators or teachers have a history of control over the content. Some states limit by statute the censorship power of high school and college administrators.

See *prior restraint, libel, Student Press Law Center,* and *symbolic speech.*

Sources: *Tinker v. Des Moines Independent School District,* 393 U.S. 503 (1969) and *Hazelwood School District v. Kuhlmeier,* 484 U.S. 260 (1988).

Student Press Law Center a nonprofit organization that serves as an advocate for student press rights and a source of free legal services for students.

The organization's Web site <www.splc.org> has a lot of background information on the law and resources for students and teachers.

subliminal advertising, theory of the idea that consumers can be manipulated into buying products or services after viewing brief (too short to be perceived) images or messages embedded within a program or an advertisement.

The concept of subliminal advertising is often traced to 1956, when a New York market researcher, James Vicary, claimed to have embedded the messages, "Drink Coca-Cola" and "Eat Popcorn," in a drive-in theater in New Jersey. Vicary claimed to have flashed the messages for 1/3000 of a second every five seconds—a time too short to be perceived by the viewers (most people have difficulty perceiving messages less than 1/100 of a second).

But Vicary reported sales of Coke increased 58 percent and popcorn 18 percent at the concession stand. He held press conferences, and advertising agencies paid him $4.5 million in retainer fees. But he skipped town with the money and left no forwarding address.

Despite the hoax, the subliminal advertising stunt sparked a nationwide controversy over the effects of advertising. The fires also were fueled by a best-selling 1957 book, "The Hidden Persuaders." The author, Vance Packard, argued that advertising worked on the subconscious mind. Could people be easily manipulated by such methods? Was this ethical?

The theory was that messages viewed just below the threshold of conscious perception were imprinted in the subconscious, which then could motivate behavior. But the controversy subsided when other researchers were unable to replicate the results of the study.

The debate over subliminal advertising emerged again in 1972 with the publication of William Bryan Key's "Subliminal Seduction," which claimed advertisers embedded sexual symbols and words in their ads. But a great deal of research since then also fails to support the subliminal theory. The upshot is that people can't respond to messages they cannot perceive.

Although there is no evidence to support the subliminal advertising theory, advertising associations have taken the position that it is unethical to secretly embed messages in movies or programming.

Sources: William Bryan Key, *Subliminal Seduction: Ad Media's Manipulation of a Not so Innocent America* (Englewood Cliffs, NJ: Prentice-Hall, 1973); Timothy E. Moore, "Subliminal Advertising: What You See Is What You Get," *Journal of Marketing*, 46:38-47 (Spring 1982); Vance Packard, *The Hidden Persuaders* (New York: D. McKay Co., 1957); and Anthony R. Pratkanis, "The Cargo-Cult Science of Subliminal Persuasion," <www.csicop.org/si/9204/subliminal-persuasion.html>.

sublimation see *cathartic effect* and *media violence*.

subscription sales sales of magazines, newspapers or other publications obtained through a subscription, often prepaid and usually for a one-year period.

sunshine law same as *open-meetings law*.

survey see *survey research*.

survey research a method of gathering data that involves interviewing people or having them fill out *questionnaires*.

sweeps months see *rating*.

symbol something that stands for or represents another object or thing.

A skull and crossbones, for example, has come to symbolize poison, danger, or pirates, depending upon the context. Language and words are also symbols representing objects or ideas.

symbolic speech speech that invokes symbols to make a political statement.

The U.S. Supreme Court has given broad protection to symbolic speech. The most notable case is Texas v. Johnson (1989), in which a man burned an American flag in front of Dallas City Hall during the 1984 Republication National Convention to protest policies of the Reagan administration. Protestors chanted, "America, the red, white and blue, we spit on you," while the flag burned. No one was injured or threatened. The court said the *First Amendment* protects flag-burning.

After that decision, Congress passed the Flag Protection Act of 1989, which made it illegal to knowingly destroy or mutilate a U.S. flag. However, the Supreme Court nullified that law a year later, declaring it unconstitutional.

See *commercial speech* and *corporate speech*.

Sources: *Texas v. Johnson*, 491 U.S. 997 (1989) and *United States v. Eichman*, 496 U.S. 310 (1990).

syndicated media service an organization or company that sells entertainment programming, news stories, commentaries, crossword puzzles, games, advice columns, cartoons or other content to broadcast media, newspapers, and magazines.

Syndicated news services usually try to sell columns or commentaries from well-known journalists or commentators, such as David Broder, Ellen Goodman, William Raspberry, William Safire, and Art Buchwald. King Syndicate is one of the better known syndicator companies.

Other syndicators sell pre-recorded broadcast programs or news content to radio and television media. The content includes taped concerts and popular talk shows such as "Oprah," "Howard Stern," "Rush Limbaugh," "Dr. Laura."

Syndicated programming is usually less expensive to produce than locally produced or network programming.

A syndicator may be a television station or a network, but many are independent companies or film companies. Some sell only one type of program, such as a talk show that they produce. Others carry a more extensive line of entertainment programming, such as re-runs from popular shows in the 1960s, 1970s or 1980s.

Independent television stations and some cable networks (such as Nickelodeon, TNT or Lifetime) rely heavily on syndicated programming to fill their programming schedule. They usually pay a fee for the right to broadcast the program for a limited amount of time. The station or network sells advertising to pay the costs and to turn a profit.

Syndicating popular television series, such as "Cheers," "Friends" and "Seinfeld," can be very profitable. These are called "off-network programs," because they were shown earlier on one of the networks. "Original syndication" or "first-run syndication" refers to syndication of original programs like "Oprah" and "Wheel of Fortune," which are shown for the first time on television.

A major broadcast network canceled "Baywatch," a television series about lifeguards on a California beach, after one season. But the program went into syndication and became one of the most successful original syndicated television shows in the world. The show, which owes much of its audience loyalty to its actors' bathing suits, has been translated into 15 languages.

system see *social system*.

system theory see *mass media systems theory, guard dog theory,* and *theory*.

system operator a cable or satellite company that transmits radio or television signals to a consumer.

systematic measurement error see *measurement error*.

systematic random sampling a probability method of selecting a *sample* in which all of the *cases* in a *population* are arrayed and every Nth case is selected.

For example, to interview 100 people from a population of 1,000, every tenth name beginning within a random start is selected.

T

tabloid a newspaper that is about 11 x 14 inches, or half the size of a broadsheet newspaper.

Most tabloids, or "tabs," are found in large cities because subway riders can read them with less annoyance to their fellow passenger.

See *broadside*.

talk radio a slang term for radio programs in which a host analyzes issues and events and usually interviews guests and takes listeners' calls.

Talk radio hosts almost always have a point of view, and some are very controversial. Talk radio in the United States is dominated by conservative hosts (e.g., Rush Limbaugh and Dr. Laura Schlessinger), but in recent years more liberal-leaning hosts (e.g., Al Franken and Katherine Lanpher) have taken to the airwaves.

talk shows a television format in which a host interviews most guests in front of a live audience.

The talk show was pioneered by Phil Donohue, but *Oprah Winfrey* created the most popular show in history. Although critics generally have positive comments about Oprah's show, many strongly criticize other shows, such as Jerry Springer's, which emphasize low-brow themes and have been accused of encouraging guests to get into fistfights on the show.

Springer's show titles seem to support these criticisms: "I Am Pregnant by a Transsexual," "I Want Your Man," "Paternity Test: I Slept With Two Brothers," and "Prostitutes vs. Pimps!" The "Los Angeles Times" said Springer's show "deifies dysfunction, exploits unsophisticated guests and gives a promotional forum to the sexually confused and promiscuous, porn stars, adulterers, criminals, Ku Klux Klan members and various other ne'er-do-wells."

But sociologists point out that it would be inaccurate to argue that Springer's show or other talk show programs like it are destroying morality.

In fact, they actually reinforce dominant values. Even Springer recognizes this.

"Our audience always boos the bad guy and cheers the good guy," he told the "Los Angeles Times." "Our show becomes a little morality play. ... if you are concerned about what lessons come out of our show, we make it clear that violence is no good. We make it clear that infidelity, promiscuity, drugs and prostitution are bad."

This doesn't appease many critics. But all talk shows and "real-life" courtroom dramas such as "People's Court" and "Judge Judy" reaffirm dominant values about right and wrong.

See *Winfrey, Oprah.*

Sources: Greg Braxton, "Them's Fightin' Words," *The Los Angeles Times* (April 5, 1998), p. 4 (Calendar); Jeff Daniel, "Springer Fights His Way to the Top of the Trash Heap," *Everyday Magazine* (February 1, 1998), p. D3; *Michael Cameron,* "Springer TV Show Murder Charge," *The Sunday Telegraph* (July 30, 2002), p. 3; Paul Gallagher, "Springer Sued Over 'Murderous' Show," *The Scotsman* (July 12, 2002), p. 5.

Tarbell, Ida (1857-1944) a *muckraker* (journalist) who wrote a 19-part magazine series that led to the breakup of John D. Rockefeller's monopolistic Standard Oil Company into a number of smaller companies.

In 1897, Standard Oil controlled 90 percent of the oil production in the United States. The company had run many competitors out of business, including Tarbell's father.

Tarbell, who was college-educated and independent, worked for S. S. McClure, publisher of "McClure's" magazine. For five years she investigated Standard Oil, digging into files of previous lawsuits and interviewing scores of current and former business partners and clients.

The end result was one of the greatest and most powerful investigative stories of all time—a 19-part series that set into motion a series of events that led to the break-up of the world's greatest oil trust. Tarbell's first story appeared in "McClure's" in November 1902. She profiled Rockefeller, who was conniving, deceitful, greedy, and dishonest.

More importantly, Tarbell's articles revealed that Rockefeller made secret deals with railroad companies to have his company's oil shipped at discount. This was illegal, because the railroads were monopolies and required by law to charge the same rates to everyone.

Nearly two dozen anti-trust lawsuits were filed against Standard Oil from 1904 to 1906. The U.S. Bureau of Corporations launched an investigation and in 1906 handed a report to President Theodore Roosevelt that confirmed Tarbell's findings.

In 1911, the U.S. Supreme Court issued a decree ordering the breakup of Standard Oil because the court determined that the company's goal had been "to drive others from the field and exclude them from their right to trade."

Tarbell wrote a successful biography of President Abraham Lincoln and gave many lectures. She never married because she wanted to preserve her independence and freedom. She died in 1944 at the age of 87.

See *muckraker.*

Sources: Fred J. Cook, *The Muckrakers: Crusading Journalists Who Changed America* (Garden City, NY: Doubleday & Company, 1972), see Chapter V; Michael Emery, Edwin Emery and Nancy L. Roberts, *The Press and America: An Interpretive History of the Mass Media,* 9th ed. (Boston: Allyn and Bacon, 2000), pp. 223-226; and Ida M. Tarbell, *The History of the Standard Oil Company* (New York: McClure, Phillips & Co. 1904). Also see Ida M. Tarbell, *All in the Day's Work: An Autobiography* (New York: Macmillan, 1939) and Kathleen Brady, *Ida Tarbell: Portrait of a Muckraker* (New York: Seaview/Putnam, 1984).

target marketing the process of marketing or selling goods and services to consumers or market segments that represent the best prospects for them.

Target marketing is usually employed after *market segmentation.* The latter involves identifying consumers or segments with similar needs or interests. Target marketing then involves the process of reaching those consumers or segments. This often entails placing advertisements in mass media to target those prospects or developing public relations campaigns, which may involve both mass media and direct contact with community groups and organizations.

See *market segmentation* and *direct marketing.*

targeting the process of *target marketing.*

Tching-pao weekly news reports published by the Chinese around A.D. 1000.

Telecommunications Act of 1996 a law passed for the purpose of increasing competition among broadcasters and cable, telephone, and satellite companies.

The law attempted to do this by easing restrictions on the number of broadcast stations one company could own and by allowing long-distance and regional phone and cable companies to offer any service provided by the others.

Proponents of the bill argued it would lower prices and increase service. However, this hasn't occurred for the most part. Instead, the law stimulated many mergers in the telecommunications field.

telegraph an electronic device for transmitting messages through a wire or through radio waves.

Samuel Morse invented the telegraph in 1837. His device could transmit electric impulses into a series of dots and dashes on paper. The dots and dashes represented letters and numbers in Morse Code.

By the 1890s, telegraph lines were transmitting messages between thousands of places around the world. But the telegraph, which relied on wires and lines, was expensive to install and maintain. Also, the telegraph never became a mass medium, because it was impractical for people to learn Morse Code.

The first practical wireless telegraph was developed in 1895. Guglielmo Marconi, an Italian, couldn't interest the Italian government in his wireless device. But the British gave him a patent. Marconi eventually won the Nobel Peace Prize and became rich from his invention.

In 1899, the first wireless message was sent across the English Channel. The first transatlantic wireless telegraph message was sent in 1901 from England to Newfoundland.

One of the first popular applications for the telegraph radio was in shipping. Boats, including the Titanic, were equipped with them for safety and navigational reasons. Additional advancements in technology during the early 1900s, such as the vacuum tube and the electronic-tube oscillator, helped boost signal strength.

The telephone and wireless radio eventually replaced the telegraph for personal and commercial uses.

See *Fessenden, Reginald.*

telephone survey a method of collecting *data* that involves interviewing people over the telephone.

teleological ethics a rule or action is moral if it produces good results, especially for society.

See *ethical decision-making.*

television a device in homes or other places that receives news and entertainment programming from a distant television station or network.

More specifically, there are five major ways to transmit television:

1. Broadcast television involves wireless transmission of signals through the air. A station's signal is picked up by an antenna on a television receiver. The major advantage of broadcast television is that it is free to the consumer. The major disadvantage is that a limited number of air waves is available in a community. Also, reception is adversely affected by physical objects, such as mountains and buildings, and the signal weakens with distance.

2. Cable television involves transmission of signals through coaxial or fiber-optic cables. Coaxial cables are high-frequency lines or cables in which a conductor is surrounded by an insulating compound. Fiber-optic cables transmit high-frequency signals through beams of light contained in a plastic or glass wire. Better reception and more channels are the major advantages of cable television. The major disadvantage is the cost of installing cables into a community or neighborhood, which must be strung on telephone poles or buried under ground. Subscribers must pay for these costs in their monthly fees.

3. Satellite television, like broadcast television, involves wireless transmission, but the source is a satellite positioned in the earth's atmosphere rather than a ground-based transmission tower. Satellite television offers more channels than coaxial cable television systems, and the reception is often better. However, satellite television can be interrupted by atmospheric

disturbances. Also, in most markets satellite television still is unable to carry local television stations. A separate receiver must be purchased for that.

4. Internet television involves transmission through the *Internet,* which may involve both wired and wireless systems. The technology for viewing Internet television is still not widely available to consumers, but Internet television is expected to grow in years to come.

5. Closed-circuit television involves transmission, usually through a wire-based system to a limited number of viewers. The main consumers of closed-circuit television are corporations and universities, which use it for instruction or meetings.

See *television network* and *television technology.*

television intoxication see *Zamora, Ronny.*

television network a company that provides programming to a *television* station, which is called an affiliate, or to a cable or satellite system operator.

The United States has more than 210 *television networks,* most of which operate for profit. Some, such as PBS and C-Span, are nonprofit.

Some networks also own and operate their own television stations, which are called O&Os. These are usually located in large *designated market areas* and, consequently, often are the most profitable part of the network. All of the major networks own and operate broadcast television stations.

Affiliates usually are compensated for carrying a network program. But networks are paying less today than in the past because of increased competition. Affiliates are relying more on local advertising. The networks allow them to insert a limited number of locally sold commercials in one of their programs. About half of the revenue generated by an affiliate comes from the networks.

Eight of the 210-plus networks (ABC, NBC, CBS, FOX, PAX, PBS, UPN, WB) are broadcast (*over-the-air*) networks. The rest are cable or satellite and are available only to those who pay a fee.

See *television* and *television technology.*

television technology an electronic system that transmits still or moving pictures and sound to a receiver (TV set) that recreates the images and sound for viewing.

Like motion pictures, the technology of television is possible because of the principles of persistence of vision and the phi phenomena (see *motion picture technology*).

The principles of how television works are very similar to a film projector. The process begins with the television camera, which converts an image and sound into an electronic code. The electronic code can be transmitted live or recorded on tape or disc. To transmit the code, it is first converted into high-frequency radio waves.

The FCC has allocated three bands of frequencies to television: 54 to 88 MHz for channels 2 to 6; 174 to 216 MHz for channels 7 through 13; and

470 to 890 MHz for ultra high frequency channels 14 through 83. Once transmitted, the radio waves are then picked up by an antenna, which draws them into the television receiver.

Inside the receiver (or television set) the sound and video signals are separated and amplified, then sent into the picture tube, which is also known as a cathode ray tube (CRT). The tube uses a narrow beam of electrons to recreate the original image. The electrons hit the back of a fluorescent screen in a scanning motion, which causes a coating on the screen to light up to the designed brightness for each area of the image.

In the United States, televisions have more than 500 lines per picture and about 400 "dots," or about 512 X 400 pixels. These lines and the dots are scanned 30 times each second. The end result looks like a continuous moving picture, but, like film, the television screen actually involves a series of quickly moving still images. The difference is that television uses lines of light instead of picture frames.

The CRT is gradually being replaced with LCDs and plasma displays, which are thin. The conventional analog television is also being replaced by digital television, or high definition television (HDTV). The main problem with analog television is resolution, or the crispness of the picture. Digital TV and HDTV provide much better resolution.

Digital television converts images into a series of numbers and produces a picture equivalent to 704 x 480 pixels, sent at 60 frames per second. HDTV is even higher quality, producing pictures equivalent to 1280 x 720 pixels or 1920 x 1080 pixels. The result is a very crisp picture. The aspect ratio of HDTV is also similar to what one sees at a movie theater—the picture is twice as wide as it is high.

After years of wrangling and debate, HDTV is finally being adopted across the country. Many television stations are broadcasting in digital, and prices for high definition television sets continue to drop. All stations are supposed to be transmitting in digital by year 2006.

text-linked advertisement see *Internet advertising.*

theory an explanation or interpretation of why something occurs or is.

Beyond that relatively simple definition, researchers often disagree about what constitutes a theory and how to classify or evaluate theories. Some scholars even dislike the term, even though they often employ explanations, interpretations or reasons to understand or interpret the world.

Despite these problems, many scholars acknowledge two major forms of theory: one predicated upon a social science model and the other predicated upon a humanist model (see *mass communication research, mass communication researcher,* and *scientific inquiry*). Basically, the social science camp sees theory as explanation, and its followers search for social, economic, political, and/or psychological factors to explain human behavior. In contrast, the humanist camp sees theory as interpretation, and its followers search for reasons why *social actors* do what they do.

Historical explanations or theories about the origins and growth of books, newspapers, and magazines traditionally have focused heavily on the humanist perspective, which involves analyzing the decisions and actions of individuals. Some scholars call these "great person theories," which basically hold that people rather than social "forces" are the prime mover of history.

Journalism historian Sidney Kobre provides a good example. Kobre says that *Benjamin Harris*, who published the first printed newspaper in the American colonies, probably got the idea for his newspaper from broadsides published in London in the late 1680s. "There were strong indications of the growing interest in printed news and the discussion of current events," Kobre writes.

However, Kobre also adds that a complete and adequate explanation of the appearance of this newspaper as well as others must take into account factors other than the individual actions of the publisher. He writes that "the first American newspapers grew out of the peculiar conditions in the colonial environment, out of the desire for political and commercial news, foreign and domestic, and the need for an advertising medium."

The focus on social, political and economic factors, enablements or "causes" introduces the social science or explanatory approach to theorizing. The main idea is that decisions and behaviors are not made in a vacuum but are strongly shaped or affected by technology, culture, and social institutions.

See *probability theory of social action, hypothesis, mass communication research, media violence (effects of), limited effects theory, knowledge-gap theory, critical theory, cultural studies, media dependency theory, mass media systems theory, agenda-setting hypothesis,* and *scientific inquiry.*

Source: Sidney Kobre, "The First American Newspaper: A Product of Environment," *Journalism Quarterly*, 17:335-45 (1940).

third-person effect a mass *media effect* in which a subject believes mass media content has no effect on him or her but has an effect on others.

Thomas, Isaiah (1749-1831) the most important Patriot editor during the American Revolutionary war.

Thomas took a moderate stance before the war. Under the name plate of his "Massachusetts Spy" were the words, "A Weekly Political and Commercial Paper—Open to All Parties, but Influenced by None."

But he, like other colonists, became increasingly disenchanted. This disenchantment reached an apex in 1776, when Thomas Paine wrote "Common Sense," a pamphlet which argued that the colonies received no advantage from being governed by Great Britain. It also argued for the establishment of an independent government.

"Common Sense" sold an incredible 120,000 copies six months before the signing of the Declaration of Independence. Historians argue that it played a key role in mobilizing the colonists against the British. In a matter of weeks, almost every colonist was familiar with this pamphlet.

tie-in in filmmaking, a promotional device that involves selling or giving away some products that are associated with a movie.

The idea is to stimulate more demand for the movie. The Walt Disney Company often employs tie-ins, creating toys, clothes, music, or games based on a characters in a movie. The tie-in products often can be purchased for a nominal fee at a fast-food chain restaurant such as McDonalds.

Top 40 a radio format that involves frequent repetition of songs from a constantly updated list of best-selling singles.

topline preliminary results from a study.

tort see *law*.

total advertising awareness *unaided* plus *aided advertising awareness*.

total awareness *unaided* plus *aided awareness*.

total recall *unaided* plus *aided recall*.

tracking study same as *longitudinal study*.

trade books includes general fiction and nonfiction books intended for wide segments of the population and usually found in book stores.

Trade books often are advertised and reviewed in the mass media. They, along with the mass *paperback* books, are the ones that make the best-seller lists.

See *hardcover* and *paperback*.

trailer a two- to three-minute promotion (or advertisement) for a forthcoming movie, shown during "Coming Attractions" at movie theaters.

Promotional clips for movies in the early 20th century used to be shown after the feature presentation. That's why they are called "trailers." Trailers are distributed to theaters sometimes up to a year before the movie is released.

transistor radio a 1948 invention that helped radio broadcasting survive the impact of television.

The transistor radio was much smaller and lighter than the vacuum tube radio and could be carried anywhere, such as to the beach or park. The transistor radio, which was being sold in stores and installed in automobiles in 1954, was also much less expensive.

The transistor radio helped radio survive competition from television, which siphoned off most of radio's dramatic and comedic programming.

See *functional substitute, radio,* and *radio technology*.

transnational media company a mass media organization with operations in more than one country; often used synonymously with *global media* company.

trend study a *longitudinal survey* of the same *population* but different *respondents*.

t-test an *inferential statistic* in which the *independent variable* has only two categories or groups and the *dependent variable* is a *continuous measure*.

Turner, Ted (1938-) founder of Turner Broadcasting System and CNN and one of the world's greatest philanthropists.

Turner was born Robert Edward Turner III on Nov. 19, 1938, in Cincinnati, Ohio. At age 9, he moved with his family to Savannah, Georgia, where his father, Ed, operated a billboard advertising company. Turner graduated from a military-high school in Chattanooga Tennessee and studied classics and economics at Brown University.

After a short stint in the Coast Guard, he began working for his father's business. In 1963, his father, an alcoholic, committed suicide. Turner inherited the business, which prospered under his control.

In 1970, Turner purchased a financially troubled independent UHF television station in Atlanta and created the Turner Broadcasting System (TBS). In 1976, he arranged to have the signal from WTBS broadcast via satellite to cable television systems around the country. WTBS (or TBS for short) became known as the nation's "superstation," which broadcast Atlanta Braves and Atlanta Hawks games. In 1978, he purchased both ball clubs, guaranteeing TBS access to all the home games.

In 1980, Turner launched two more cable network systems: Cable News Network (CNN) and Turner Network Television (TNT). The former was the nation's first 24-hour all-news network, and the latter broadcast old movies, old television programs, and sports events. CNN Headline News was created in 1982.

In the mid-1980s, Turner started and funded the Goodwill Games, a sporting event designed to ease Cold War tensions between the Soviet Union and the United States. He spent $40 million of his own money on the project. By 1985, more than three-fourths of the cable homes in America could tune in to Turner's *television network*s.

In 1986, Turner purchased MGM/UA Entertainment Company for $1.6 billion, which gave him access to more than 4,000 films. He was criticized for "colorizing" many classic black and white films, including Frank Capra's 1946 Christmas Classic "It's a Wonderful Life." Turner eventually had to sell MGM to maintain control of TBS.

In the late 1980s, many critics also ridiculed CNN for amateurish news coverage. But the critics were silenced in 1991 when CNN scooped all the competitors with its 24-hour coverage of the Gulf War. CNN was the only American media organization allowed to report the news from Iraq. Ratings of the network shot up. "Time" magazine named Turner "Man of the Year."

In 1995, Turner sold TBS to Time Warner for $7.5 billion. He became a vice chairman of the company and its biggest stockholder. In 1997, he donated $1 billion—half of his fortune at that time—to the United Nations to solve global problems after the United States failed to pay its dues. In 2000, America Online purchased Time Warner, creating the world's largest media corporation. Turner retained his title as vice chairman of the new company.

Turner has been criticized for being too liberal and for being too conservative. The reality is that he primarily stands in the middle of the road, or perhaps slightly left of center. He is an ardent environmentalist. He supports equal rights for women and minorities. He is also concerned about the proliferation of nuclear weapons. Under his tutelage CNN has produced a number of documentaries in support of these causes.

Turner is America's biggest philanthropist. He has donated more money to charity than anyone in history. Turner has purchased more than 1.3 million acres of forest and wetlands in the United States to protect them from development and pollution. He is America's largest private landholder.

In 2000, Turner created the Nuclear Threat Initiative, whose goal is to curb the proliferation of weapons of mass destruction. He has pledged $250 million to the organization over the next five years.

Since 2002, Turner has concentrated his efforts on philanthropy. "Once I wanted to conquer the world," he told students and faculty at Washington State University in April 2000. "Now I want to help save it."

Sources: Robert Goldberg and Gerald Jay Goldberg, *Citizen Turner: The Wild Rise of an American Tycoon* (New York: Harcourt Brace, 1995); Michael Pellecchia, "Citizen Turner: The Wild Rise of an American Tycoon" (book review), <www.moneyblows.com>; David Demers, "Commentary: Ted Turner, Global Journalism and Objectivity," pp. 183-186 in David Demers (ed.), *Global Media News Reader* (Spokane, WA: Marquette Books, 2002).

TV short for *televison.*

TV Parental Guidelines a rating system developed in 1996 by *The National Association of Broadcasters*, the *National Cable Television Association*, and the *Motion Picture Association of America* to help parents make decisions about which television shows their children can watch.

The ratings are as follows:

TV-Y   Appropriate for all children.
TV-Y7   Appropriate for children age 7 and above.
TV-G   Suitable for all ages, not specifically children.
TV-PG   Unsuitable for younger children; parental guidance suggested.
TV-14   Unsuitable for children under 14 years of age.
TV-MA   Unsuitable for children under 17. This program contains one
        or more of the following: graphic violence (V), explicit sexual
        activity (S), or crude and indecent language (L).

On televisions equipped with a *V-chip*, parents can block access to all programming in one or more of these categories.

two-step flow of communication see *Lazarsfeld, Paul.*

tydings (tidings) an early name for news published in the 16th and 17th centuries.

u

UHF ultra-high frequency: radio waves between 300 and 3000 megahertz, which includes channels 14 and higher on a television.

UHF channels generally have weaker signals than VHF and, thus, can reach fewer households.

See *VHF*.

unaided advertising awareness a measure of respondent awareness (without prompting) of advertising for a product, service or company.

Measures of unaided advertising awareness are used frequently in *advertising tracking studies*.

See *aided advertising awareness* and *total advertising awareness*.

unaided awareness a measure of respondent awareness of a product, service or company without prompting.

See *aided awareness* and *total awareness*.

unaided recall the characteristics or features of a product, service or company that are recalled without prompting from an interviewer.

See *aided recall* and *total recall*.

underground newspaper a newspaper that publishes content highly critical of the status quo and privileged groups.

The term "underground newspaper" is most strongly associated with newspapers that in the 1960s and 1970s published content that opposed the war in Vietnam in and powerful multinational corporations. After the war, many went out of business, and those surviving few focused less on politics and more on promoting arts, literature, and culture.

See *alternative media*.

Uniform Resource Locator (URL) the Internet address for a particular document or resource on the Internet.

The URL is more specific than a *domain name*. For example, the domain name for the publisher of this book is <www.marquettebooks.org>. The URL for the page that provides information about this book is <www.marquettebooks.org/pages/17/index.htm>.

See *domain name, Internet, Internet Protocol, World Wide Web,* and *zone.*

unit of analysis who or what is studied.

The unit of analysis is the population to which *generalizations* are made. With *survey research*, the unit of analysis is most often the individual. Groups or organizations may also be the unit of analysis.

See *unit of observation.*

unit of observation who or what provides the information that is studied.

Often the unit of observation is identical to the *unit of analysis*, such as when consumers are interviewed about their perceptions of various products. However, in some cases people provide the information, but the unit of analysis is a company, or organization. Such people are referred to as informants.

unit production manager in filmmaking, the person responsible for scheduling the production crew, purchasing goods and services, and making arrangements for shooting at locations outside the studio.

United States Government Printing Office the largest publisher in the world.

The Government Printing Office produces more titles than even the largest private publishers in the world. It has nearly 30,000 titles in print, including "Your Federal Income Tax." The GPO publishes books and pamphlets from numerous agencies, such as the Environmental Protection Agency and Office of the Surgeon General.

univariate analysis research analysis that involves one *variable* only. *Means, percentages,* and *frequencies* are some of the statistics used in univariate analysis.

universals the general types of things. For example, this book is an example of a larger category we call "books," and could also be classified as "rectangular" or a "physical object."

universe the group or entity to which generalizations are made from a sample.

Same as *population.*

Univision Communications Inc. the leading Spanish-language media company in the United States.

It's holdings include: (1) Univision Network, which reaches 97 percent of U.S. Hispanic households; (2) TeleFutura Network, a 24-hour general-interest Spanish-language broadcast *television network* reaching 72 percent of U.S. Hispanic households; (3) Univision Television Group, which operates 22 television stations; (4) TeleFutura Television Group, which operates 28 television stations; (5) Galavision, the country's leading Spanish-language cable network; and (6) Univision Music Group, which includes the Univision Music and other labels.

usage the extent to which a product or service is consumed or used.

Measures of usage are frequently employed in market research surveys. See *awareness, attitude, and usage study.*

uses and gratifications a general theoretical perspective which contends that people use mass media because it satisfies psychological and social needs for information.

This approach seems rather self-evident, but the theory, which gained momentum in the 1960s and 1970s, shifted attention away from the question of "what do media do to people" to the question of "what do people do with media." Thus, people are seen as active rather than passive in selecting and consuming mass media. They use media to satisfy (or gratify) their needs for information and entertainment.

Uses and gratifications researchers have focused mostly on the psychological or cognitive reasons that people give for consuming media. They have found, for instance, that people watch television entertainment programming primarily to relax and reduce stress.

See *theory* and *probabilistic theory of social action.*

Source: J. G. Blumler and E. Katz (eds.), *The Uses of Mass Communication* (Beverly Hills, CA: Sage.).

usage study a study that measures usage of products, services or media.

USA Today the largest daily newspaper in the United States, with an average daily circulation of 2.25 million.

The ascendency of "USA Today" into the No. 1 position is one of the most remarkable institutional achievements in the field of mass communication. Gannett Company Inc., one of the nation's largest newspaper chains, founded the newspaper in 1982. Within a year, it had circulation of 1.3 million.

At the time, USA Today was widely ridiculed for its short, punchy stories. But "McPaper," as the critics called it, not only survived, it became a model for other newspapers, who copied its colorful graphics and in some cases its editorial style. Today almost all major newspapers print at least some of their pages in full color.

No newspaper in modern times has had a greater direct impact on design in the newspaper industry.

USENET the first civilian *Internet.*

In 1979, Steve Ballovin, a graduate student at the University of North Carolina, created USENET, the first civilian Internet. It could do everything *ARPANET* (the government version of the Internet) could do, but it also supported discussion groups, which could communicate in real time, and bulletin boards, which are now called newsgroups.

About the same time, the IBM corporation created BITNET, another software system that allowed computer networking, especially for commercial applications.

Within a few years USENET and BITNET joined ARPANET and other university, governmental, and commercial networks to form what is now essentially the Internet.

See *ARPANET* and *Internet.*

V

validity the extent to which a *measure* or *indicator* actually measures what it is intended to measure.

See *external* and *internal validity*.

values (a) for statistical uses, the categories of a *variable* are given a number, or a value, so that the *data* can be read by a computer; **(b)** for sociological analyses, an abstract idea that people in a society or group consider desirable, good or bad.

With respect to the second definition, a *dominant value* is one that most people consider desirable.

In most cultures around the world, the sanctity of human life is a dominant value, as is devotion to family, friends, and work. Events like the Titanic disaster and the September 11, 2001, attacks are almost always viewed as tragic events, and to the extent that mass media transmit information about such events, they help reinforce values about the sanctity of human life.

But values sometimes differ across societies and groups, and complete agreement on any set of values is rarely possible. For example, for many people, the Titanic disaster has come to symbolize all that is wrong with modern society, particularly an overemphasis on technology and materialism. In contrast, others argue that there is nothing wrong with these values; instead, the real problem was simply a captain who failed to use due caution.

In addition to the sanctity of human life, most societies place a high value on *social order*, respect for authority, and religion. Western societies also place a high value on romantic love, education, representative democracy, and a free-market (capitalist) economic system.

vanity press printers or publishers who will edit and print a manuscript for a fixed fee but normally do not distribute or market a book.

variable a *concept* that has two or more categories, or *values*.
Gender is a variable that has two categories, male and female.

variance average squared distance around the *mean*; a *measure of dispersion*.
See *standard deviation*.

v-chip a device that allows parents to block offensive programming on television sets.
All televisions 13 inches and larger are now equipped with the technology, which blocks undesired programs using a rating system developed in 1996 by the *National Association of Broadcasters*, the *National Cable Television Association*, and the *Motion Picture Association of America*.
See *TV Parental Guidelines* and *Voluntary Movie Rating System*.

vellum (or parchment) a writing material made from the skins of goats, sheep or calves. In ancient Greece and medieval Europe, many books were made from "pages" of vellum bound together and protected by a pair of wooden boards. At this time, the Chinese were also were creating books from strips of bamboo and were printing on silk.
Although papyrus, parchment, and silk were light and portable, they were expensive to produce and often difficult to obtain. The Chinese solved this problem in about A.D. 105 with the invention of paper, which was made from a mixture of bark and hemp.

vertical integration a condition that exists when companies control the production, distribution, and selling of a good or service.
During the 1920s, a number of mergers and acquisitions took place in the motion picture industry. By the early 1930s, eight major companies controlled 95 percent of the film production market.
The film industry was very vertically integrated, meaning studios controlled not only the production but also the distribution network for films and the theaters that showed them. Interestingly, most investment went not to film production, which only consumed about 5 percent of corporate assets, but to distribution and exhibition. The film companies, in other words, were basically theater chains and produced films to fill those houses.
Anti-trust legislation was eventually used to break up the production and distribution aspects of filmmaking.

VHF very-high frequency: radio waves between 30 and 300 megahertz, which includes channels 2 through 13 on a television.
VHF channels generally have stronger signals than UHF channels and, thus, can reach more households.
See *UHF*.

VHS a format for recording videos.
See *video cassette recorder*.

video cassette recorder (VCR) a device for recording and playing back audio-video images, either from a camera or a television.

In 1969, Sony Corporation introduced the first low-cost videocassette recorder. But Betamax was never very successful in the United States. Instead, consumers in the 1980s turned to VHS, a format developed by Matsushita Corporation.

In 1980, only about 1 percent of households in the United States had a video cassette recorder. But five years later a fifth of all homes had a VCR, and by 1990 two-thirds (69 percent) had one. The figure is now more than 85 percent. The growth of VCRs spurred a new industry in the 1980s: home movie rentals.

video news release (VNR) a video version of a *press release*.

VNRs may be short (30 seconds to several minutes) or full-length documentaries (30 minutes to several hours). They are usually used to promote an organization or a cause, and the goal is usually to get positive press coverage.

virus see *computer virus*.

Voice of America (VOA), The an organization created by the U.S. government in 1942 for the purpose of broadcasting news and information to support U.S. policies in Europe.

Today VOA reaches 96 million people around the world through radio, satellite television, and the *Internet*. Under law, it is prohibited from broadcasting in the United States, but its Web site <www.voa.gov> can be viewed.

Voltaire (1694-1778) a French philosopher and writer ("Father of the French Revolution") who was a source of inspiration for many American revolutionaries and journalists.

François Marie Arouet, who is better known today by his pen name, Voltaire, was born in 1694 to a middle-class Parisian family. His mother died when he was 7, but he was never close to his father. Rather, he became attached to his godfather, a freethinker and epicurean, or one who enjoys the pleasures of life in moderation.

Voltaire

Voltaire acquired a love for literature, the theater, and social life while attending a Jesuit college. But he was skeptical of religious instruction, and became even more critical of institutionalized religion after Louis XIV tried to purge Catholic France of its Protestant subjects.

After college, Voltaire worked as a secretary for the French embassy in The Hague (Netherlands), and after the death of Louis XIV in 1715 Voltaire became well-known in Parisian society for his witty epigrams. His wit, though, was also a curse. In 1717 he was imprisoned for a year in the infamous Bastille for mocking a nobleman. After release, he wrote "Oedipe," the first of his theatrical tragedies, which immediately made him the leading playwright of his time.

Voltaire became increasingly critical of despotic authority and the Catholic church. He believed in the primacy of reason over dogma and superstition. After a dispute with a leading French family in 1726, he was beaten up and given a choice between exile or prison. He chose the former, and spent two years in London, where he learned English and studied the writings of political philosopher John Locke and the scientist Isaac Newton.

What he most admired, though, was the greater level of tolerance the English had for *freedom of speech* and the press. Although radicals were still punished for treason and *seditious libel*, England by this time was no longer licensing publishers or engaging in *prior restraint*. Voltaire made many friends in high literary circles.

When Voltaire returned to France, he sought to spread the ideas he learned. In 1734 he wrote "Lettres Philosophiques," which was designed to illustrate the benign effects of religious toleration. The book extolled the virtues of science, reason, and empiricism over religion, arm-chair theorizing, and religious dogma. He also argued that the purpose of life is not to reach heaven through penitence but to assure happiness to all humans through progress in the sciences and arts. The book defined the essence of the Enlightenment and the modern mind.

But the French authorities were not amused. A warrant was issued for his arrest in 1734. He escaped and began living with a young woman, Mme. du Châtelet, who shared his intellectual interests and was imbued with a yearning for knowledge. He wrote a number of other successful works, but was often on the move to avoid being arrested.

Voltaire wrote a number of other historical and theatrical works after 1749, but his masterpiece was "Candide," a book written in 1758 that has been compared to the slapstick humor on a modern "Saturday Night Live" skit. The book attacked religious fanaticism and the injustices of class status and war. Voltaire settled in Ferney, France, in 1758 and lived there until 1778, when he died in Paris at the age of 83.

Sources: Wayne Andrews, *Voltaire* (New York: New Directions, 1981); Mary Margaret Harrison Barr, *A Century of Voltaire Study: A Bibliography of Writings on Voltaire, 1825-1925* (New York: B. Franklin, 1972); and Voltaire, François Marie Arouet de, *The Portable Voltaire* (New York: Penguin, 1977).

voluntarism see *free will.*

voluntary movie rating system a system for rating the content of movies.

The history of the Voluntary Movie Rating System goes back to 1966, when Warner Brothers was set to release "Who's Afraid of Virginia Woolf?" The Production Code Administration in California had denied the movie a seal of approval, because it contained nudity, the word "screw," and the phrase "hump the hostess."

Although that content seems pretty tame by today's standards, in 1966 no major Hollywood film studio had released a film that contained nudity or sexually explicit language. Up to that time, the studios had voluntarily complied with the Production Code, which they, as members of the *Motion Picture Association of America,* had created during the 1930s.

But times had changed. The Vietnam War and social unrest were influencing a new wave of films that were more realistic and gritty. "Who's Afraid of Virginia Woolf?," which portrayed a dysfunctional couple who verbally abuse a teacher and his wife, was one of the first in this genre. To get around the Production Code, the film was distributed through a subsidiary company. It went on to earn 13 Academy Award nominations, including Best Picture.

In April 1968, the U.S. Supreme Court ruled that governments could create laws to protect children from materials that contained nudity or sexually explicit content. Jack Valenti, who had recently taken over as president of the MPAA in 1966, recognized that the industry must take action or face the prospects of government control. However, he also believed that filmmakers should have as much freedom as possible in producing films.

So, on Nov. 1, 1968, the MPAA discarded the Production Code and announced a new rating system—one that, instead of regulating content, offered parents advance information about movie content so they could decide what they wanted their children to watch.

The original rating system consisted of four categories: **G** for "general audiences"—all ages admitted; **M** for "mature audiences"—parental guidance suggested, but all ages admitted; **R** for "restricted"—children under 16 would not be admitted without an accompanying parent or adult guardian; and **X**—"no one under 17 admitted."

Since then, the rating system has been modified several times. The **M** rating was abolished and replaced with **PG** and **PG-13** because parents thought **M** was more restrictive than **R**. The **X** rating also was replaced by **NC-17** because **X** had taken on a smutty meaning after being appropriated by the *pornography* industry during the 1970s and 1980s. As of this writing, the movie rating system is as follows:

G	General Audiences—All ages permitted
PG	Parental Guidance Suggested—Some material may not be suitable for children.
PG-13	Parents Strongly Cautioned—Some material may be inappropriate for children under 13

R   Restricted—Under 17 requires accompanying parent or
              adult guardian
NC-17   No one 17 and under permitted

Filmmakers are not required to submit their films for rating. However, most do. The ratings are issued by a full-time Rating Board that consists of eight to 13 members. The president of MPAA selects the chair of the Rating Board. The board members must be or have been parents. They do not judge the quality of movie; rather, they look at themes, violence, language, nudity, sensuality, drug abuse, and other elements. A majority vote determines the final rating. The filmmaker then has a right to inquire as to the rating, and then the right to edit or change the film to get a different rating.

About half of the films judged since 1968 have received an **R** rating. Only 3 percent received a **NC-17** rating. Industry executives widely agree that the **NC-17** rating dramatically curbs the profit potential of a film, because it limits attendance. As such, many films that initially receive a **NC-17** rating are edited "down" to qualify for a **R** rating. Eight percent of films received a **G** rating and the rest, about a third, received a **PG** or **PG-13** rating.

Although the rating system has many critics, the public likes the system. A yearly poll consistently finds that about three-fourths of parents with children under 13 found the rating to be "very useful" or "fairly useful" in helping them make decisions.

Source: Jack Valenti, "How It All Began," (Encino, CA: Motion Picture Association of America, December 2000), at <www.mpaa.org>.

Walters, Barbara (1929)) a journalist who became the first woman television news network anchor and later garnered even more fame for her "scoop" interviews with famous people around the world.

Walters became the first woman network anchor in 1976, co-anchoring "ABC World News Tonight" with *Harry Reasoner*. Later, she co-hosted "20/20" with Hugh Downs.

Walter's style closely resembles the "personality journalism" that was a specialty of *Edward R. Murrow*. Walters has interviewed Egypt's President Anwar Sadat, Israel's Prime Minister Menachem Begin, Russia's Boris Yeltsin, China's Jiang Zemin, the UK's Margaret Thatcher, Cuba's Fidel Castro, as well as Indira Gandhi, Moammar Qaddafi, the Shah of Iran, and King Hussein of Jordan.

want ad see *classified advertising.*

warblog a *Weblog* whose content focuses on war, often as it is unfolding.

War of the Worlds a celebrated case of mass *media effects*, in which an estimated 1 million people panicked after hearing Orson Welles' radio adaption of H. G. Wells' classic book about a Martian invasion.

The incident occurred Oct. 30, 1938, on CBS's "Mercury Theater on the Air," which was broadcasting a radio drama adaptation of the book "War of the Worlds" on the evening before Halloween. Many listeners didn't hear the introduction and the intermittent disclaimers. Some had tuned in late, because they didn't like a guest who was being interviewed on another radio program. And what they heard was the realistic-sounding voice of the "Secretary of Interior," who said:

"Citizens of the nation: I shall not try to conceal the gravity of the situation that confronts the country, nor the concern of your Government in protecting the lives and property of its people. ... Fortunately, this formidable enemy is still confined to a comparatively small area, and we may place our faith in the military forces to keep them there. In the meantime, placing our trust in God, we must continue the performance of our duties ... so that we may confront this destructive adversary with a nation united ... ."

The Martians, or so the program contended, had destroyed police and military forces and were now spraying New York with poison gas. A minute later an announcer came on and said, "You are listening to the CBS presentation of Orson Welles and the Mercury Theatre on the Air," but by then many people had stopped listening.

In New York, hundreds of people fled their homes. In Concrete, Washington, the power went out when the Martians were said to be cutting communications lines, which led to mass hysteria. In Birmingham, Alabama, people went to church and prayed. In Boston, the newspaper was deluged with calls from frightened people. In Rhode Island, many people called the electric company and urged them to turn off all lights so the city could protect itself against the Martians.

One million people panicked, according to estimates. One woman broke her arm after falling down some stairs. But there were few injuries and no one was killed.

Lawsuits were filed against CBS, the Mercury Theatre, and *Orson Welles,* who had produced the program and served as a narrator. But none went to trial because there was no precedence for such claims. The *Federal Communications Commission* adopted a resolution banning the use of "on the spot" news stories in dramatic programming. CBS apologized. Mercury Theatre survived and became very popular.

But the incident was not forgotten. For many people, it reinforced the idea that mass media in general and radio in particular was a powerful medium. Shortly after the incident, researcher Hadley Cantril and others studied the broadcast to discover the conditions that led people to panic and believe the drama was real.

They estimated six million adults heard the broadcast and of them about 20 percent, or slightly more than one million, panicked. They also found that those who panicked tended to be less educated, more religious, and more emotionally insecure. Ironically, these findings suggested media effects may be more limited than previous thought.

Sources: Hadley Cantril, *The Invasion from Mars: A Study in the Psychology of Panic* (Princeton, NJ: Princeton University Press, 1940) and Shearon A. Lowery and Melvin L. DeFleur, *Milestones in Mass Communication Research,* 2nd ed. (New York: Longman, 1988), pp. 55-78. A CD of the original broadcast also has been published: *War of the Worlds* (Plymouth, MN: Metacom, 1994).

watchdog model the notion that the news media are adversaries of government and big business and watchdogs for the people, especially the powerless and those who have no organized voice in the system.

Most professional journalists see themselves as defenders of truth and justice. They do not see themselves as advocates of government or big business. They believe they represent the interests of ordinary citizens, not government bureaucrats or corporate elites.

Investigative news reports are often critical of elites who violate laws and norms, but mass media research shows that mainstream journalism provides broad-based support for dominant institutions and values in Western societies. Some even believe journalists act more like *lap dogs* for the rich and powerful than watchdogs for the poor and weak.

The guard dog model is a middle-ground position. It holds that journalism provides support for dominant institutions and values but can produce content critical of elites. This is especially true when elites (e.g., Republicans and Democrats) criticize each other.

See *guard dog theory* and *lap dog theory*.

Watergate scandal see *Woodward and Bernstein.*

Weblog a Web site where individuals or organizations post information or content on a regular basis, often daily.

The 2003 Iraq War elevated the term Weblogs into everyday conversation. Salam Pax, a resident of Baghdad, became famous worldwide for an online journal he kept of the events happening during before and after U.S. troops converged on his city.

His Weblog, called "Where is Raed?" <http://dear_raed.blogspot.com>, offered first-hand, clandestine observations of the bombing of Baghdad. It attracted more than 100,000 visitors a day. His site was so popular that his Internet provider upgraded his account without charge so he could continue posting messages and photographs.

Supporters of Weblogs (or *Warblogs,* which are Weblogs that chronicle war-related events) argue that they provided some of the most thoughtful and insightful analyses of the war. Indeed, many mainstream journalists visited the Warblogs to get additional information. Bloggers also played a role in exposing fake documents which claimed that President George W. Bush had failed to perform his duties as a National Guard pilot during the Vietnam War. (Note: Although the documents were false, their content was true, according to people who had worked with Bush.)

Critics, however, argue that bloggers (the people who write Weblogs) are often politically biased and the quality of their writing is often poor because it usually is not formally edited.

Irrespective of whether one likes or dislikes Weblogs, it is clear they are having a major impact on the dissemination of news and information. Some surveys show that some segments of the population, often on the extreme right or left of the political spectrum, rely on Weblogs more than traditional media and find them to be more credible.

From a broader perspective, Weblogs can be interpreted as having two major effects: (1) They can lessen dependence on traditional media for news and information, and (2) They can produce content that challenges traditional, mainstream journalism and mainstream views of the world. Weblogs, like the *Internet* in general, may represent a threat to the power that traditional *mainstream media* have had over people.

Sources: Barbara K. Kaye and Thomas J. Johnson, "Weblogs as a Source of Information about the 2003 Iraq War," pp. 291-301 in Ralph D. Berenger (ed.), *Global Media Go to War: Role of News and Entertainment Media During the 2003 Iraq War* (Spokane: Marquette Books, 2004) and Stephen Cooper, *Watching the Watchdogs: Weblogs as the Fifth Estate* (Spokane, Marquette Books, in press).

Web radio (or webcasting) radio programming broadcast through the *Internet*.

Web radio has been one of the hottest trends in the radio industry. In 2000, more than 9,000 radio stations were streaming audio through the Internet. A study by *Arbitron* Company in 2000 found that one-third of Internet users (14 percent of the U.S. population) had listened to online radio at least once.

However, the number of Internet radio stations declined substantially after 2002, because higher royalties were imposed on radio webcasters. Most independent stations, especially college stations, could no longer afford to pay the fees.

Nevertheless, Web radio will survive because it is inexpensive to set up and operate. Anyone with a computer and a little training can do it. Another advantage is that Web radio is not regulated by the *Federal Communications Commission*. That's because there's no limit to the number of stations or channels that can be set up.

Despite these advantages, Web radio is not likely to replace traditional terrestrial broadcasting any time soon. There still are problems to be worked out. One is that the computer isn't very mobile (yet), and the sound systems on computers tend to be lower quality than on household and car stereo systems. Some of the software programs for accessing Web radio also are difficult to use and not very reliable.

A second problem is that many traditional broadcast stations are also simultaneously broadcasting on the Internet. People tend to be loyal to traditional media, and this loyalty gives traditional radio stations an advantage over those stations that only broadcast on the Web.

See *radio*.

Source: Bradley Foss, "Radio Wave of the Future," Spokane *Spokesman-Review* (January 24, 2000), p. A9.

weighting a statistical procedure used to balance a *sample* when a *category* is over- or under-represented.

Welles, George Orson (1915-1985) a writer, director, producer, and actor who achieved great acclaim for his movie, "Citizen Kane."

Welles was only 24 when he signed a contract with RKO Radio Pictures in the summer of 1939 to produce his first movie. He had already become famous in the New York theater community for his creative and offbeat productions of classic plays. He also became nationally known after his October 1938 Mystery Theater radio production of "War of the Worlds," which was so realistic that nearly a million people across the country panicked, believing the earth was being invaded by Martians.

Yet Hollywood didn't exactly greet Welles with open arms. Welles was called an "upstart" because he had no film-making experience. But he ignored the insults and hired respected screenwriter Herman J. Mankiewicz to help him develop the idea for his motion picture. Mankiewicz and Welles went through seven re-writes. But the hard work paid off. The American Film Institute and film critics around the world today overwhelmingly hail "Citizen Kane" as the greatest motion picture of all time.

The film tells the story of Charles Foster Kane, an aging newspaper tycoon whose arrogance alienates him from everyone who loved him. The movie was loosely based on the life of *William Randolph Hearst,* who had built a newspaper empire in the late 19th and early 20th centuries. On his deathbed in his Gothic mansion in Florida, Kane utters his last word, "Rosebud."

What is "Rosebud?" Through the use of flashbacks, a magazine reporter covering the life of Kane searches doggedly to discover the meaning of the word and the man behind it.

"Rosebud" has become the most famous prop in Hollywood. It was sold to producer/director Steven Spielberg in 1977 for $60,500. Interestingly, Mankiewicz appears to have gotten the idea from Hearst's real-life mistress, Marion Davies, who told Mankiewicz that "Rosebud" was the nickname Hearst had given to an intimate part of her body. (For the record, though, the prop in the movie is quite different.)

For two years Welles hid the fact that the movie was based on the life of Hearst. He was worried in part about what Hearst would do. And this was no exaggerated fear.

When word leaked out just before completion of the film in 1941, Hearst newspapers, wire services, and radio stations banned all mention of "Citizen Kane" as well as all other films produced by RKO and refused to accept advertising for the movie. A group of Hollywood executives, fearing the wrath of Hearst on their operations as well, even offered RKO a cash settlement to destroy the film.

But it was too late. Welles had sneak-previewed the film to so many prominent people that it was impossible to expunge it. The film opened in theaters in 1941, received good reviews, and did well in large cities. But the Hearst boycott and Hollywood control of theater bookings hurt the debut. RKO eventually reported a loss of $150,000.

The film was re-released in the mid-1950s, and in the early 1960s an international panel of leading film critics selected "Citizen Kane" as the No. 1 film of all time. The film is acclaimed not only for its script and acting (Welles played Kane), but for its wondrous use of light and photography. The angles, shadows, and perspectives in this black-and-white movie are still widely copied by cinematographers today.

Welles continued to produce, direct, act, and write, but he was never again able to match the acclaim he achieved with "Citizen Kane." Welles also came to symbolize the successful Hollywood outsider—the man who placed art above profits and commercial success. Welles died in 1985. RKO Radio Pictures struggled financially for most of its 25-year existence. The company ceased production in 1953 and was sold to Desilu Productions in 1957.

Sources: Orson Welles and Peter Bogdanovich, *This Is Orson Welles* (New York: Da Capo Press, 1998) and David Thomson, *Rosebud: The Story of Orson Welles* (New York: Alfred A. Knopf, 1996).

Wheeler-Lea Amendments a set of laws passed by Congress in 1938 that made false advertising a violation of the Federal Trade Commission Act.

The *Federal Trade Commission* used the law to issue an injunction against Fleischmann's Yeast, which claimed it cured crooked teeth, poor skin, constipation, and bad breath.

See *Federal Trade Commission*.

wholesaler an individual or organization that orders books from publishers after receiving orders from libraries and bookstores. A wholesaler usually does not stock books, unlike a *distributor*.

About 900 distributors and wholesalers operate in the United States. Two-thirds are general distributors and wholesalers, and a third deal mainly in *paperback* books. Bookstores and school libraries are their biggest customers.

See *distributor*.

Winfrey, Oprah (1954-) a talk-show host and the most successful female and black woman entertainer in television history.

"Oprah" was the daughter of Vernita Lee and Vernon Winfrey, who were not married. At age 4, she began her public speaking career. She toured churches in Nashville, reciting sermons of James Weldon Johnson while other children sang.

Vernita and Vernon separated, and Oprah lived on a pig farm in Mississippi with her maternal grandmother until age 6, when she went to Milwaukee to live with her mother. Oprah was forced to sleep on the porch. She had little supervision and got into trouble. A cousin also sexually molested her.

When she went to live with her father in Nashville, she was pregnant. She lost the child.

But her father, who was a barber and city council member, laid down some rules. Oprah became a good student. At age 17, she was crowned "Miss Fire Prevention" in Nashville. While visiting a radio station one day, she was invited to read copy. The station hired her to read news on the air.

At 19, Oprah, who was now a sophomore at Tennessee State University, was crowned Miss Black Tennessee. In the same year she was hired as Nashville's first female and first black TV news anchor. After graduation she took an anchor position in Baltimore, but she wasn't well suited for the job. Sometimes she would cry when reading sad news. The station moved her into their morning talk show program. She found her niche.

In 1984 she became host of A.M. Chicago, a morning talk show. The name eventually was changed to "The Oprah Winfrey Show," and in 1986 the program was syndicated. Soon thereafter her program surpassed Phil Donahue as the nation's top rated talk show. Oprah was only 32.

Oprah went on to star in many prime-time TV specials, home videos and movies, including "The Color Purple," "Beloved," "The Women of Brewster Place," "There Are No Children Here," and "Before Women Had Wings." She also set up her own television, film, video, and print production companies (all of which have "Harpo"—Oprah spelled backwards—in the name). In 1996, Oprah set up a book club that catapulted virtually every selection to the top of the best-selling list. She has won scores of awards and contributes 10 percent of her fortune to charitable causes.

In 2000, Oprah launched a magazine, titled "O: The Oprah Magazine." The first issue sold more 1.6 million copies, a half-million more than the publisher (Hearst) had expected. In the same year, she co-founded Oxygen, a U.S. cable television station targeted to women. In September 2002, she debuted in "Oprah After the Show," a prime-time weeknight program on Oxygen.

But the foundation of her empire has been "The Oprah Winfrey Show," which is seen by more than 30 million viewers in 160 countries. More than 1 million people also visit her Website, Oprah.com, every day.

"She's certainly the most influential person on television," said Dick Kurlander, vice president of Petry Television, a company that offers consulting services to TV stations. "She's extremely credible."

So credible, in fact, that when she said she stopped eating hamburger because of concerns about mad cow disease, cattle ranchers sued her. Of course, they lost. Oprah is entitled to *"freedom of speech,"* according to the U.S. constitution.

Many people have analyzed Oprah's success, which now includes a fortune of more than $1 billion. "Time" magazine, which selected her as one of the 100 most influential people of the 20th century, wrote: "Women, especially, listen to Winfrey because they feel as if she's a friend. Although Phil Donahue pioneered the format she uses (mike-holding host moves among an audience whose members question guests), his show was mostly ... 'report-talk' ... . The overt focus is on information. Winfrey transformed the format into ... 'rapport-talk,' the back-and-forth conversation that is the basis of female friendship, with its emphasis on self-revealing intimacies. She turned the focus from experts to ordinary people talking about personal issues."

Oprah says she will broadcast her last talk show in 2006. However, her library of old shows will continue to appear on television. Oprah is single but has been dating Stedman Graham, an author, educator, and former pro-basketball player, for more than a decade.

wire services news organizations that provide other news organizations with non-local news, photographs, and/or audio or video clips.

The *Associated Press* is the best known wire service in the United States. News organizations that subscribe to its service get access to thousands of news stories and photographs associated with events around the world. Some wire services gather their own news and sell it to subscribers. Others obtain news stories from their members and redistribute them to other members. AP does both.

See *news service* and *syndicated news services*.

Wolff a German-based *news service*.

woodcuts illustrations carved into wood used in printing before the invention of the half-tone and photographic printing.

"Harper's Weekly," which was founded in 1857, made extensive use of woodcuts, especially during the Civil War, when its highly skilled artisans would recreate war scenes.

Woodward and Bernstein two "Washington Post" reporters who played the lead key role in exposing the Watergate scandal in President Richard Nixon's administration.

Bob Woodward and Carl Bernstein—or "Woodstein" as the team was sometimes called—weren't the only reporters covering the Watergate scandal during the early 1970s. But they played the lead role. Their tenacious reporting skills, coupled with the off-the-record comments of a secret source called "*Deep Throat*" (who turned out to be W. Mark Felt, who was second in charge at the FBI), eventually led to the downfall and resignation of President Richard Nixon in 1974 and to a *Pulitzer Prize* for Meritorious Public Service.

Nixon and his administration were implicated in a botched burglary of the Democratic National Committee at the Watergate complex in Washington D.C. in 1972. The reporters also found that Nixon's administration had been spying illegally on U.S. citizens, harassing political opponents, and forging campaign literature.

Woodward and Bernstein converted their efforts into a popular book, "All the President's Men," which also became the title for a blockbuster movie starring Robert Redford and Dustin Hoffman.

See *Deep Throat*.

Sources: Ben Bradlee, *A Good Life: Newspapering and Other Adventures* (Touchstone Books, 1996); Leonard Downie Jr., *The New Muckrakers* (New York: Mentor, 1976), and Marianne Szegedy-Maszak, "Since Watergate: An Update on Woodward and Bernstein," *Biography* (January 1997).

World Wide Web (WWW or W3) a software system that allows computer users to access and retrieve information over the *Internet*.

The Web includes software for transferring documents and data, for creating Web sites, and for identifying and accessing Web sites.

More specifically, the software for transferring documents, pages, and data was called HTTP, or HyperText Transfer Protocol. HTTP standardized communication between computer servers and clients. In other words, computers with different types of files and operating systems could now communicate with each other.

The software for creating Web sites was called HTML, or HyperText Markup Language. Basically, it works like any word processing software, but it converts letters and numbers for display on the Web or the Internet.

The software for identifying and accessing Web sites was called URL, or Uniform Resource Locator. That's the "http://www ... " address that one types in on a browser to access a Web site. A *browser* is software that enables one to link to the Internet and the Web and see or hear the images and text.

See *Berners-Lee, Tim, Internet, Internet Protocol,* and *zone.*

X the independent variable in *quantitative analysis*.
 X is used in formulas and in *scatterplots*.
 See *Y*.

xerography a photocopy reproduction process in which powdered ink is applied to paper via an electrostatic process.

x-height the standard height of lowercase letters in a particular font, measured by the letter "x."

X-rated a category once used to rate films unsuitable for viewing by persons under age 17.
 See *Voluntary Movie Rating System*.

Y the *dependent variable* in quantitative analysis.
    Y is used in *formulas* and *scatterplots.*
    See *X.*

yearbook an annual publication that reviews activities and events during the previous year.

yellow journalism news or feature stories that distort facts, sensationalize or overemphasize trivial matters in an effort sell more newspapers.
    See *Hearst, William Randolph; Pulitzer, Joseph;* and *Yellow Kid.*

yellow journalist a journalist who practices *yellow journalism.*

Yellow Kid one of the first comic book characters to appear in newspapers.
    The "Yellow Kid" was a comic strip character created in the late 1800s by artist Richard F. Outcault, who worked for Joseph Pulitzer's "New York World." His comic "Hogan's Alley" focused on life in the tenement slums. Outcault gave the "Yellow Kid" vaguely Asian features to lampoon the hysteria that erupted after the Sino-Japanese war. The "Yellow Kid" was often depicted in the midst of funny, chaotic scenes, or was himself getting into trouble.
    But the "Yellow Kid" also came to symbolize the sensationalism that pervaded New York daily newspaper journalism at that time. This was especially true after competitor William Randolph Hearst and his newspaper, the "Morning Journal," hired away some of Pulitzer's top journalists, including Outcault. The competition that ensued gave rise to the term *"yellow journalism."*

Z

Zamora, Ronny (1962-) a convicted killer who made national news when he claimed that television was responsible for his behavior.

In spring 1977, 15-year-old Zamora and a friend confessed to police that they had shot to death Elinor Haggart, 82, a Miami Beach widow, after she discovered them burglarizing her home.

Ronny was tried as an adult and pleaded not guilty by reason of insanity. Television, his attorney Ellis Rubin argued before a Florida jury, had "brainwashed" Ronny. Rubin said Ronny "was suffering from and acted under the influence of prolonged, intense, involuntary, subliminal television intoxication. Through the excessive and long-continued use of this intoxicant, a mental condition of insanity was produced."

Ronny's psychiatrists also testified that he was living in a "television fantasy world" and that "he didn't know the consequence and nature of the act when he pulled the trigger."

The jury disagreed. In October 1977, Ronny was convicted of murder and sentenced to life in prison. In June 2004, the Florida Parole Commission released him. He was deported to his native Costa Rica, where he now lives.

Since 1977, a handful of other criminal defendants have used the "television intoxication" argument as a defense for their crimes. Relatives of victims injured or killed in some shootings also have sued the mass media from time to time. As this book went to press, none had convinced a jury the mass media are culpable.

See *mass communication research* and *theory*.

zapping the use of a remote control to change television stations, often to avoid viewing commercials.

zipping the practice of fast forwarding through a video playback to avoid viewing commercials.

Zenger, John Peter (the trial of) the most prominent legal case involving freedom of the press in the 1700s.

In 1734, a group of wealthy New York merchants and landowners who wanted more control of colonial affairs asked John Peter Zenger, who had just opened up his own printing shop, if he would publish a paper supporting their views. He agreed.

The first issue of Zenger's "New York Weekly Journal" appeared on November 5, 1733. A month later, the newspaper criticized Colonial Governor Sir William Cosby for allegedly permitting French warships to spy on lower bay defenses. The newspaper also published a commentary that accused the British colonial bureaucracy of incompetence for its role in a dispute between Cosby and some colonists.

The colonists were amused, but not the governor. On November 17, 1734, Cosby charged Zenger with *seditious libel*, a crime that normally allowed authorities to punish people who criticized the government even if the criticism were true.

Andrew Hamilton, a famous 80-year-old Philadelphia lawyer, represented Zenger when the trial began on August 4, 1735. To the surprise of almost everyone, Hamilton immediately conceded that Zenger had published the stories critical of the governor. The prosecutor was very pleased with this admission, because normally this would have meant a conviction. Truth was not recognized as a defense for seditious libel.

But Hamilton insisted that the words must be false for a conviction to stand. "The falsehood makes the scandal, and both the libel," he said, adding that he will "prove these very papers that are called libel to be true."

During closing arguments, Hamilton asked the jurors to follow their own consciences without fear of official reprisals. He added: "[T]he question before the court and you gentlemen of the jury, is not of small nor private concern. ... It is the best cause. It is the cause of liberty."

The jury found Zenger innocent of the charges. Zenger and Hamilton became instant heroes to the colonists. Interestingly, though, the Zenger case had no immediate impact on libel law. In fact, after the Revolutionary War a number of American newspaper editors were jailed for seditious libel.

But the major principle of the Zenger case—that truth is a defense for libel—was eventually codified into law. Today, a *libel* plaintiff must prove that the material was false. Cases like Zenger also helped legitimize the press as a *Fourth Estate*—that is, as an institution that has the right to draw attention to abuses of power in the various branches of government.

Sources: Michael Emery and Edwin Emery, *The Press in America: An Interpretive History of the Mass Media,* 6th ed. (Englewood Cliffs, NJ: Prentice Hall, 1988), pp. 38-44.

zines (pronounced "zeens") low-cost magazines that focus on alternative cultures and offbeat subjects.

Zones for Web Addresses

.com	commercial organization (publicly available)
.edu	educational institution (restricted for educational institutions)
.gov	government body or department (restricted for government use)
.int	international organization (restricted mostly for NATO)
.mil	military site (restricted for government use)
.net	networking organization (publicly available)
.org	designed for nonprofit organizations and associations but can be used for any purpose (publicly available)
.info	information and resource sites (publicly available)
.biz	small businesses (publicly available)
.bz	small businesses (publicly available)
.tv	multi-media sites (publicly available)
.cc	(publicly available)

---

zone (a) an area or region to which a zoned edition of a newspaper or other publication is distributed; **(b)** the suffix of a Web address, or *Uniform Resource Locator*.

The suffix of a Web address is called a zone and provides general information about the type of host or *Internet* user. For example, ".edu" identifies an "educational institution." The ".edu" suffix is restricted for use by academic institutions. Other suffixes are available to governments, private businesses, and the public (see table above).

The first seven suffixes in the list above were created in the 1980s. The others are more recent and were added to accommodate growth in the number of Web sites around the world. Suffixes also are available for countries (.us for United States, .mx for Mexico, .uk for United Kingdom, etc.) and can be used after the generic domain suffix (e.g., <www.unimelb.edu.au> for the University of Melbourne in Australia. As of 2005, more than 260 suffixes were in use worldwide.

See *Internet Corporation for Assigned Names and Numbers*.

zoom lens a lens on a movie camera or still camera that can be adjusted to focus more closely on a faraway object.

z-test A group of *inferential statistics* used to detect differences between *proportions* or *means*.

Index

(The List of Terms Defined in this Dictionary)

Association of American Publishers, 26
attitude, 27, 28, 32, 38, 93, 167, 194, 317
attributes, 27, 62, 228
audience, 9, 10, 15, 16, 24, 27, 53, 63, 111,
    118, 132, 133, 192, 204, 225, 246, 248,
    285, 301, 303, 304, 331
audience flow, 27, 248
audio recording, 27, 264
audio recording technology, 27
Audit Bureau of Circulation, 28
autonomy, 28, 267
average, 28
awareness, 17-19, 28, 38, 310, 315, 317
awareness, attitude and usage study, 28
Ayer, Francis Wayland, 28, 220, 221

B

Baird, John Logie, 29
bandwagon effect, 29, 291
bandwidth, 29, 218
banner, 29, 144, 145
banner ad, 29, 144
Barnum, Phineas Taylor, 30
barriers, 30, 268, 282
base, 30, 187
BBC, 30, 39
behavior, 10, 15, 30, 47, 52, 55, 63, 69, 70,
    82-84, 86, 95-97, 100, 103, 105, 118,
    122, 131, 134, 137, 139, 163, 168, 174,
    180, 183, 193-195, 208, 220, 238, 239,
    247, 250, 275, 276, 278, 284, 285, 288,
    296, 299, 308, 339
behavior modification, 30
behavioral intention, 30
behavioral repertoire, 30
behaviorism, 30
belief, 30, 38, 83, 115, 168, 178, 217, 233,
    238, 283, 294
Berle, Milton, 31
Bernays, Edward L., 31, 112, 161, 252
Berners-Lee, Tim, 33, 333
Bernstein, Carl, 33, 82, 124, 215, 327, 332
Betamax, 34, 321
bias of communication, 34
Bill of Rights, 34, 111
binomial, 23, 34
bipolar scale, 34
bivariate analysis, 34
Blair, Jayson, 34, 67, 103
block booking, 34, 35
block printing, 35, 126
blog (see Weblog)

Bly, Nellie, 35
book, 9, 10, 15, 22, 26, 32-37, 41, 44-46,
    54-56, 68, 86, 87, 91, 101, 112, 115,
    116, 120, 122, 126, 128, 131, 144, 149,
    150, 167, 170, 178, 185, 186, 197, 216,
    217, 226, 230-233, 235, 236, 241, 246,
    254, 270, 280, 294, 295, 299, 310, 312,
    316, 319, 322, 325, 331, 332, 337, 339
book club, 36, 331
book prospectus, 36
bookseller, 37
boomerang response, 37
Bourke-White, Margaret, 37
Bradford, William, 37
Brady, Mathew B., 38
brainwashing, 38
brand, 30, 32, 38, 39, 145, 264
brand awareness, 38
brand loyalty, 39
branding, 38, 39
breach of confidentiality, 39
breaking news, 39, 255, 292
Brinkley, David, 39
British Broadcasting Corporation, 20, 29, 30,
    39
British cultural studies, 39
broadband, 39, 85, 196
Broadcast Data Systems, 40
broadside, 40, 303
Brown, Charles Brocken, 40
Brown, Helen Gurley, 40
browser, 41, 145, 333
bulletin board, 41, 213
bureaucracy, 25, 41, 69, 70, 340
business manager, 41
buying intent, 41
B-film, 34
B-picture, 37
B-rated film, 37, 39

C

Cable News Network, 20, 43, 177, 283, 311
cable television, 43, 58, 129, 141, 177, 199,
    208, 211, 306, 311, 312, 320, 331
callback, 43
Cambridge Press, 44
camcorder, 43
camera, 37, 43, 50, 92, 94, 113, 137, 153,
    201, 236, 263, 274, 307, 321, 341
cameras in the courtroom, 43, 44
campaign, 16-18, 31, 32, 37, 44, 53, 73, 160,
    190, 197, 253, 282, 284, 332

D

G

H

I

O

P

Z